Windows Phone 8 Recipes

A Problem-Solution Approach

Lori Lalonde
David R. Totzke

Apress·

Windows Phone 8 Recipes: A Problem-Solution Approach

ISBN-13 (pbk): 978-1-4302-5902-2

ISBN-13 (electronic): 978-1-4302-5903-9

President and Publisher: Paul Manning
Lead Editor: Gwenan Spearing
Development Editor: James Markham
Technical Reviewer: Tom Walker
Editorial Board: Steve Anglin, Ewan Buckingham, Gary Cornell, Louise Corrigan, Morgan Ertel,
    Jonathan Gennick, Jonathan Hassell, Robert Hutchinson, Michelle Lowman, James Markham,
    Matthew Moodie, Jeff Olson, Jeffrey Pepper, Douglas Pundick, Ben Renow-Clarke, Dominic Shakeshaft,
    Gwenan Spearing, Matt Wade, Tom Welsh
Coordinating Editor: Kevin Shea
Copy Editors: Angie Wood, Kim Wimpsett
Compositor: SPi Global
Indexer: SPi Global
Artist: SPi Global
Cover Designer: Anna Ishchenko

Distributed to the book trade worldwide by Springer Science+Business Media New York, 233 Spring Street, 6th Floor, New York, NY 10013. Phone 1-800-SPRINGER, fax (201) 348-4505, e-mail orders-ny@springer-sbm.com, or visit www.springeronline.com.

For information on translations, please e-mail rights@apress.com, or visit www.apress.com.

Apress and friends of ED books may be purchased in bulk for academic, corporate, or promotional use. eBook versions and licenses are also available for most titles. For more information, reference our Special Bulk Sales–eBook Licensing web page at www.apress.com/bulk-sales.

Any source code or other supplementary materials referenced by the author in this text is available to readers at www.apress.com. For detailed information about how to locate your book's source code, go to www.apress.com/source-code.

To my daughter, Taylor, who is the light of my life and my inspiration to strive for better, to persevere in the face of adversity, and who has taught me that self-improvement is a never-ending journey.

To my best friend, Denise, who has been my cheerleader in all aspects of my life, offering support and encouragement when I needed it the most. You are a friend who has lifted me up at times when others have tried to hold me down. Thank you for being there and being the light at the end of the tunnel when I needed it the most.

To my love, Mike Ferguson, who challenges me to try new things and pushes me beyond the bounds of my comfort zone

And to my son, Michael, although you are an adult, you will always be my baby boy. No matter where your journey in life leads, our family bond can never be erased, and your mother's love can never be replaced.

—Lori Lalonde

To my wife, Hong Zheng, for your patience and support throughout the process, for the delicious meals brought to my chair, and for the long summer walks.

To my parents, Richard and Annette, without whom, both literally and figuratively, I would not be here today.

—David R. Totzke

Contents at a Glance

Contents

About the Authors

Lori Lalonde is a consultant, blogger, technical presenter, and avid Windows Phone developer residing in Kitchener, Ontario. She began her career in software in 1997 developing Visual Basic 6 and SQL Server 6.5 client-server desktop applications. Her experience spans numerous industries and a variety of technologies, with the past ten years focused on the Microsoft .NET platform. She recently joined the talented team at ObjectSharp Corp, located in Toronto, Ontario.

Lori is actively involved in the local community; she serves as the president of Canada's Technology Triangle .NET User Group and participates in local Women in Technology groups. Whether mentoring junior colleagues or writing about her experiences in the IT industry on her blog, she is always happy to share her knowledge with the greater community. You can follow Lori on Twitter, @loriblalonde, or read her blog at `www.geekswithblogs.com/lorilalonde`.

David R. Totzke was born, raised, and currently resides in Kitchener, Ontario, Canada. David is a consultant, architect, mentor, and developer focused on Microsoft technologies and has been involved with .NET since the beta releases. He founded Canada's Technology Triangle .NET User Group in 2002 and built a community of nearly 1,000 members. He is a past chair of the Marketing and Sponsorship Committee for the International .NET Association as well as a five-time Microsoft C# Developer MVP.

Recently, David started Dark Wizard Software Inc., a company focused on Windows 8 and Windows Phone 8 Store applications. David serves as Dark Wizard's president and CEO, its architect, its only developer, and its custodial engineer. Somewhat ironically, however, he does not do windows.

About the Technical Reviewer

Tom Walker is a senior software developer with more than 11 years of experience in the .NET stack. In those 11 years he has worked in the auto, medical, and fitness industries. He specializes in building software that enhances people's lives in their day-to-day activities, be it work or play. His current goal is to combine his passion for art and development into beautiful useful apps for both the Windows Phone 8 and Windows 8 Store platforms.

You can find Tom through Twitter, @Tinytoot, or through his blog at http://orangecrushcode.azurewebsites.net/.

Acknowledgments

Thanks to my family and friends for putting up with me during the writing of this book. Through the bouts of sheer panic, stress, and "what did I get myself into" moments, you all helped me in one way or another by serving as the welcome distraction, the voice of encouragement, and the strength in spirit that pushed me through to the end.

Thanks to David Totzke for agreeing to coauthor this book with me, before he knew what he was getting himself into. This was a bigger project than I had expected, and I appreciate you sharing the load with me and putting up with me during the entire process.

Last but not least, thanks to the entire team at ObjectSharp for welcoming me into your group with open arms. Working with so many bright, talented individuals is truly a humbling experience, and I am honored to be part of the O# team.

—Lori Lalonde

Thanks to Lori Lalonde for inviting me on this journey. It was bigger than expected but not bigger than us. You have been a great partner and an even greater friend.

Becoming a published author is a significant milestone in my life. There are far too many family members, friends, and colleagues who have contributed to my success than can be listed here. You know who you are, and you know what you did. Thank you.

—David R. Totzke

Introduction

The .NET Compact Framework 1.0 and `GUID.NewGuid()`... that's where it all began... or rather didn't, as I was discouraged from really getting started at that point. The problem was that the static `NewGuid` method returned an empty string. Many trade-offs were made in the PocketPC operating system and the initial version of the Compact Framework in order to strike a balance between performance, footprint, and time to market. Several of the Windows API functions upon which `NewGuid` relied were not included in PocketPC, and the Compact Framework didn't implement an alternative, so you just ended up with not so much as a `NotImplementedException` for your troubles. Just an empty string. The prescribed workaround took you on a journey into the depths of the Crypto-API, COM Interop, and P/Invoke. I just didn't want to know that much about it. This is probably why at the time I had never met a single happy mobile developer.

The next problem faced by PocketPC developers was that there was no hardware standardization. You couldn't count on anything being the same from one device model to the next even within the same manufacturer. Some devices had hardware-based buttons for certain actions while others did not. Writing an application that would work on any device running the PocketPC operating system was an opportunity for personal growth, to put it somewhat euphemistically. Android developers right now will know exactly what I'm talking about. An even greater challenge awaits them in that not only do they face hardware differences but they also have to cope with the fragmentation of the Android operating system. No thank you.

My dear friend and coauthor, Lori Lalonde, relates a similar experience when developing for BlackBerry. The sheer amount of ceremonial code that needed to be written to accomplish certain seemingly simple tasks was discouraging.

With the introduction of Windows Phone 7 there dawned a new age. Manufacturers that wanted to produce Windows Phone devices were required to support a rigid design specification. Certain hardware elements were required to be present, and certain device interactions were tied to the hardware. The Back button, Windows button, and Search button were the main examples.

The Windows Phone OS as well could now provide a consistent API for interaction with the device. Many of the functions that you used to have to code yourself are now provided as native services or exposed via Launchers and Choosers. You'll see examples of Launchers and Choosers in Chapter 6 on appointments and contacts as well as Chapter 8 on maps and navigation. Chapter 7 on the camera, photos, and media introduces you to the Background Audio Service that you can use. There's no need for DirectX knowledge here.

This is one of the main design goals of Windows Phone. Providing these services through a common operating system–provided API enables developers to focus on providing greater value in their applications rather than having to reinvent the wheel. This also helps protect the user of the device. For example, as shown in Chapter 6, there is no way to flood the contact store with contacts or to even add a single contact without the user's consent. Also, because you must interact with the built-in contact management UI, there is no way to subvert the process

Who This Book Is For

Windows Phone 8 Recipes is for the developer who has a .NET background, with familiarity in either WPF, Silverlight, or C#, and is ready to tap into a new and exciting market in mobile app development. The Windows Phone 8 SDK provides a platform that makes it easy for developers to create and publish quality Windows Phone apps in record time. The book provides the necessary information for developers to get their development environment up and running, build engaging apps that leverage the capabilities and features available in the Windows Phone 8 SDK, and walk through the steps needed to publish those apps to the Windows Phone Store.

How This Book Is Structured

This book is structured so that it does not have to be read from cover to cover. Each chapter is focused on a specific area of functionality and attempts to cover common problems you may encounter. As much as possible, each recipe has been written as a stand-alone solution to a single problem statement.

Some chapters, such as Chapter 12 on Windows Azure Mobile Services, for example, can be read in order from start to finish as the information in each recipe builds upon concepts introduced in the previous one. Having said that, each recipe can still stand on its own. Recipes that may build upon concepts that have been discussed in other recipes or even other chapters will contain references to these dependencies so that you can find them quickly.

Conventions

The style of text in the book follows the standard Apress format, so many of you will already be familiar with it. This introduction follows the same standard. For example, when code is presented inline with body text, it will LookLikeThis. This style is used to call out ClassNames, Types, variableNames, and just about any other text that would normally appear in your code. When code is presented in a block, it will be captioned, referred to in the body text by number, and have a consistent code style applied to it. See Listing 1 for an example.

Listing 1. Device Resolution Enumeration

```
public enum Resolution
{
    WVGA,
    WXGA,
    HD720p
}
```

Text that appears in **bold** is generally reserved for something you need to type into the interface.

Downloading the Code

The code for the examples shown in this book is available on the Apress web site, www.apress.com. A link can be found on the book's information page on the Source Code/Downloads tab. This tab is located underneath the "Related Titles" section of the page.

The sources for this book may change over time to provide new implementations that incorporate the most up-to-date features in Windows Phone 8 or to correct errata that is identified postpublication. As we go to press, we are also working to refine some of the samples into full applications and deploy them to the Windows Phone Store. You can contact Lori or Dave via the book's email address at wp8recipesbook@outlook.com should you have trouble running any of the samples or if you want to inquire about the progress of the sample application publishing process.

Contacting the Authors

Should you have any questions or comments—or even spot a mistake you think we should know about—you can contact both Lori and Dave at wp8recipesbook@outlook.com.

■ ■ ■

CHAPTER 1

Introduction to the Windows Phone SDK

Welcome to this new and exciting journey toward Windows Phone 8 development! In this chapter, we will cover the essential information you will need to hit the ground running in mobile application development for the Windows Phone OS 8.0 platform. If you have developed Windows Phone 7 applications, don't skip over this chapter just yet! We also have a recipe for upgrading your Windows Phone 7.x apps to Windows Phone 8.

For your first taste of Windows Phone 8 development, we will provide you with the following recipes:

- 1-1. Install the Development Tools
- 1-2. Create Your First Windows Phone 8 Application
- 1-3. Launch an App in the Windows Phone Emulator
- 1-4. Launch an App on a Windows Phone Device
- 1-5. Upgrade a Windows Phone 7.x app to Windows Phone 8
- 1-6. Become Acquainted With the Capabilities and Requirements in the Windows Phone Application Manifest

1-1. Install the Development Tools

Problem

Recently, you've been hearing the latest buzz around the newly released Windows Phone 8 devices. You want to capitalize on this by developing mobile apps for this platform while the market is hot. The problem is you don't have a lot of time to spare to figure it out on your own. You want to know what you need to do to get your development environment up and running today.

Solution

Install the Windows Phone SDK 8.0.

How It Works

Just as a great artist needs a specific set of tools to create her masterpiece, a skillful mobile application developer needs the right tools to create quality applications. To develop Windows Phone 8 applications, you will need to download and install the necessary development tools from the Microsoft site. To obtain access to Windows Phone SDK downloads, documentation, developer forums, and more, go to http://dev.windowsphone.com. This web site is one which you will use often as you progress on your development journey, so you may want to bookmark it now.

On the main landing page, click the link "Get SDK," which will take you to the download page. You will notice within the download page there are links to download previous and current versions of the Windows Phone SDK.

Before attempting to download and install the SDK, you should verify that your system meets the minimum requirements. You can check this by clicking the link "Get additional details and languages," or for a quick summary refer to Table 1-1.

Table 1-1. *Minimum Requirements for Windows Phone SDK 8.0 and Windows Phone Emulator*

Windows Phone SDK 8.0	Windows Phone Emulator
Windows 8 or Windows 8 Pro operating system	Windows 8 Pro edition or higher
Windows 8 64-bit (x64) client versions	Same as SDK
6.5 GB of available hard disk space	Same as SDK
4 GB RAM	Same as SDK
64-bit (x64) CPU	Same as SDK
--	Requires processor that supports Second Level Address Translation (SLAT)

As you can see in Table 1-1, the Windows Phone Emulator that is included in the SDK setup has slightly different requirements than the SDK. Most notably, Windows 8 Pro or higher must be installed on your system, as Hyper-V is required to run the Emulator. Additionally, your system must support Second Level Address Translation. If you are not sure whether your system supports Hyper-V or Second Level Address Translation, download and run the Coreinfo command-line utility from http://technet.microsoft.com/en-us/sysinternals/cc835722 (Figure 1-1). If Hypervisor and EPT both depict an asterisk (*), then your system will be able to run the Windows Phone Emulator.

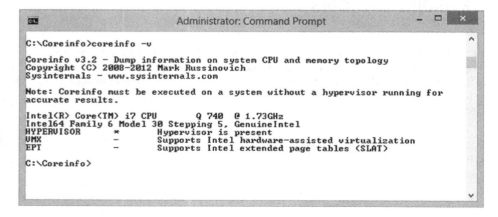

Figure 1-1. *Coreinfo command-line utility results*

If the minimum requirements for the SDK are met, but the minimum requirements are not met for the Emulator, the SDK setup will still run and install the assemblies required for Windows Phone development; however, the Windows Phone Emulator will not be installed, and you will not be able to test your apps in the Emulator. In this case, you will need to test your app on a device, which we will discuss in Recipe 1-4. To install the latest SDK, you will need to perform the following steps:

1. Click the "Download" button for the SDK 8.0. You will be prompted to save or run the installation, WPexpress_full.exe

2. Launch the setup once it has finished downloading.

3. The installation will check to ensure your system meets the minimum requirements for Windows Phone SDK 8.0. If it does not meet the minimum requirements, an error will display and you will not be able to proceed with the installation.

4. Once the installation completes successfully, you may be required to restart your machine. Along with the required assemblies, and the Windows Phone emulator, the setup will install Visual Studio Express 2012 for Windows Phone on your system unless you have Visual Studio 2012 installed prior to running the SDK setup.

5. If you already have Visual Studio 2012 installed (i.e., Professional, Premium or Ultimate edition), then an add-in for your Visual Studio IDE will be installed to enable Windows Phone development. It doesn't matter which version of Visual Studio 2012 that you use, you will still have the same templates available for building Windows Phone applications.

■ **Note**   Windows Phone SDK 8.0 contains the necessary tools to develop apps for both Windows Phone 7.5 and Windows Phone 8 platforms. However, for the remainder of this book, we will focus on Windows Phone 8 application development.

1-2. Create Your First Windows Phone 8 Application

Problem

Now that you have the right development tools at hand, you want to develop your first app but you are not sure where to begin.

Solution

Use Visual Studio 2012 to create a new Windows Phone project.

How It Works

Launch Visual Studio 2012. Select File ➤ New Project . . . You will notice that a dialog displays with a list of built-in templates.

At first, the choice can be overwhelming or confusing. For now, we will keep it simple and select the "Windows Phone App" template under Templates ➤ Visual C#. Be sure to highlight this template as shown in Figure 1-2. The next step is to name this new application. Let's call it "MyFirstWPApp".

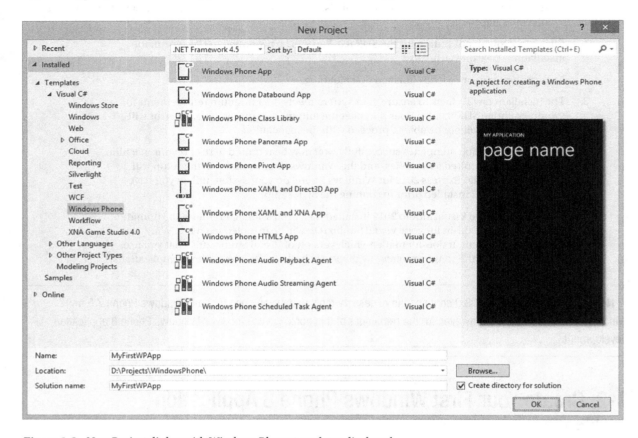

Figure 1-2. *New Project dialog with Windows Phone templates displayed*

Now, you have the choice to select the directory where you will store this project. The default directory provided in the Location field points to your user profile's documents location, under a Visual Studio 2012 Projects subdirectory. I prefer to specify my own location that I reserve for Windows Phone projects, but the choice is up to you.

Also, notice the checkbox labeled "Create directory for solution". Leaving this box checked will ensure that a subdirectory with the name of your project is created, and all project files will be saved within this subdirectory. If you uncheck this option, then your project files will be stored within the directory specified in the Location field. Again, the choice is up to you, but if you plan on creating multiple projects within the same directory, you want to ensure they are stored within subdirectories to avoid confusion and the possibility of files overwriting each other.

Once you have the name and directory specified, click the OK button.

A second dialog will display that will allow you to specify which Windows Phone OS version you want target (Figure 1-3). Click the dropdown arrow to view the different versions available.

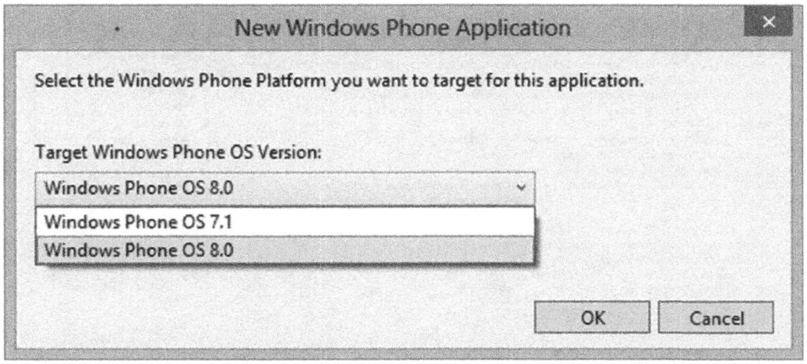

Figure 1-3. *Select the Windows Phone Platform that your application will target*

If you select Windows Phone OS 7.1, it means that this is the minimum OS version on which the application will run. You can create a Windows Phone OS 7.1 application and it will run on Windows Phone 7.x and Windows Phone 8 devices.

The focus of this book is intended to discuss Windows Phone 8 development, so we will create applications that target Windows Phone OS 8.0. Since this is the default selection, all you need to do in this dialog is click the OK button.

A progress bar will appear on screen, and it will take a few seconds or so for the development environment to create the default files and layout for your Windows Phone application.

Once the Visual Studio development environment loads, you will see a visual representation of the default phone page in the left pane. This is a good way to see what the page will look like on the device as you are designing your page. A sample of the Visual Studio IDE view on the initial load of a Windows Phone project is depicted in Figure 1-4.

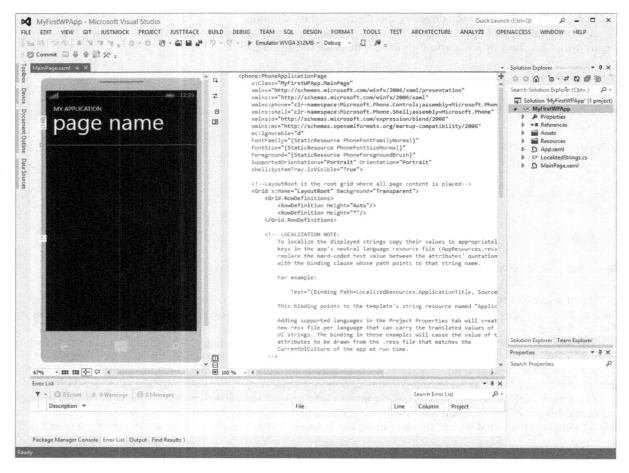

Figure 1-4. *View of Windows Phone project on first load in the Visual Studio 2012 development environment*

Every Windows Phone page will have markup that must remain intact for the page to work. Let's examine the markup of MainPage.xaml.

```
<phone:PhoneApplicationPage
    x:Class="MyFirstWPApp.MainPage"
    xmlns="http://schemas.microsoft.com/winfx/2006/xaml/presentation"
    xmlns:x="http://schemas.microsoft.com/winfx/2006/xaml"
    xmlns:phone="clr-namespace:Microsoft.Phone.Controls;assembly=Microsoft.Phone"
    xmlns:shell="clr-namespace:Microsoft.Phone.Shell;assembly=Microsoft.Phone"
    xmlns:d="http://schemas.microsoft.com/expression/blend/2008"
    xmlns:mc="http://schemas.openxmlformats.org/markup-compatibility/2006"
    mc:Ignorable="d"
    FontFamily="{StaticResource PhoneFontFamilyNormal}"
    FontSize="{StaticResource PhoneFontSizeNormal}"
    Foreground="{StaticResource PhoneForegroundBrush}"
    SupportedOrientations="Portrait" Orientation="Portrait"
    shell:SystemTray.IsVisible="True">
```

Any markup that you add to the page will be contained within the root element of the page, phone:PhoneApplicationPage. Note that the root element is prefixed with the namespace phone. If you look within the element attributes, you will notice the phone namespace is declared, which references the Microsoft.Phone.Controls namespace in the Microsoft.Phone assembly. This is the assembly that contains the definition of a PhoneApplicationPage.

Next, the class reference for the current page is defined, x:Class="MyFirstWPApp.MainPage". This is what is used to associate the proper code behind file which contains any additional code that needs to be executed.

FontFamily, FontSize, and Foreground specify the page defaults for font type, font size, and font color, respectively. These can be changed, but note that they will affect all text on the page that does not have a style defined for font family, size, and/or foreground color. Those page elements that do not have a style defined will inherit their immediate parent's style, or page style, if a parent does not have a style defined.

SupportedOrientations element indicates which orientation the application supports. You can specify Portrait, Landscape, or PortraitOrLandscape. Portrait means that the application page will only display horizontally, even if the phone is rotated by the user. Landscape means the application page will only display vertically, meaning the user needs to rotate the phone to use the application. PortraitOrLandscape means the page will change with the physical rotation of the phone. This is the desired behavior by users, and if you can tailor your application with rotational support, then do so. In Windows Phone development, this is a simple as setting the SupportedOrientations property to PortraitorLandscape.

Orientation element is the default orientation that is displayed when the page is first loaded. For this you have multiple options: Landscape, LandscapeLeft, LandscapeRight, None, Portrait—this is the default option, PortraitDown and PortaitUp.

The final element, shell:SystemTrayIsVisible element, determines whether or not the Windows Phone system tray will be displayed while your application is loaded. The default value is set to True, which means it will continue to display even while your application is loaded. The System Tray on a Windows Phone, also known as the Status Bar, is the area at the top of the screen that displays the device's signal strength, connection status, battery life indicator, and current time. The current time is always displayed, and the remaining indicators are displayed when the user taps on the system tray. For standard apps, it is best to ensure that the system tray remains available from within your application, unless there is a good reason to hide it (e.g., if you're developing a game).

Notice that contained within the phone:PhoneApplicationPage element, there is a child element which is a Grid, named LayoutRoot. This Grid is automatically generated by the Windows Phone App template.

Within the LayoutRoot grid is a StackPanel, which by default is labeled TitlePanel, and a Grid, which by default is labeled ContentPanel.

The TitlePanel contains two textboxes to display the application name and the page name, respectively. The ContentPanel is an empty grid. This is the grid where you will add your page controls. These two panels are not set in stone, and you can essentially remove them and add other elements (i.e., Grid, StackPanel, Text Box, Label, etc.), as you see fit for your application's purpose.

When designing your page, be aware that there can only be one direct child element, either a Grid, StackPanel, or Canvas, within the phone:PhoneApplicationPage element. It must be an element that can serve as a host to other controls. If you attempt to add more than one child element within the phone:PhoneApplicationPage element, outside of the main grid, you will receive an "Invalid Markup" error in the Visual Studio designer.

Now that you have the basics down, let's continue on to developing your first Windows Phone 8 application! This is a birds-eye view of what we are going to do within the main page:

1. Change the application title

2. Change the page name

3. Add some controls

4. Write some code to make it do something

To change the application title, scroll down the MainPage.xaml file, and change the Text property of the first Textbox from "MY APPLICATION" to "MY FIRST WP APP".

To change the page name, change the Text property in the second textbox from "page name" to "welcome".

```xml
<Grid x:Name="LayoutRoot" Background="Transparent">
    <Grid.RowDefinitions>
        <RowDefinition Height="Auto"/>
        <RowDefinition Height="*"/>
    </Grid.RowDefinitions>

    <StackPanel x:Name="TitlePanel" Grid.Row="0" Margin="12,17,0,28">
        <TextBlock Text="MY FIRST WP APP"
        Style="{StaticResource PhoneTextNormalStyle}" Margin="12,0"/>
        <TextBlock Text="welcome" Margin="9,-7,0,0"
        Style="{StaticResource PhoneTextTitle1Style}"/>
    </StackPanel>

    <Grid x:Name="ContentPanel" Grid.Row="1" Margin="12,0,12,0">
        ...
    </Grid>
</Grid>
```

Now, we will add some control elements to the page to really spice things up. You can either drag a control from the Visual Studio toolbox to the page or manually enter the XAML markup for the control you want to add.

The easiest way to add controls to your page is to select a control from the Toolbox and, while holding the left mouse button down, drag it onto your page, then release the left mouse button. This action will create the XAML markup in your page automatically once you drop the control onto the page in the designer. At this point, you can modify your control by modifying the control properties in the XAML markup or by modifying the properties through the designer.

Add a textbox, a button, and two textblocks to the page by dragging those controls from the Toolbox to the page.

Once they are on the page we need to format them and ensure are in the ContentPanel grid. Notice how the main grid, named LayoutRoot, defined rows using the Grid.RowDefinitions elements. We will do the same for ContentPanel, so that we can ensure a nice clean layout, without needing to define spacing or margins to ensure the controls do not overlap.

Add the following markup to the ContentPanel grid:

```xml
<Grid x:Name="ContentPanel" Grid.Row="1" Margin="12,0,12,0">
    <Grid.RowDefinitions>
        <RowDefinition Height="Auto"/>
        <RowDefinition Height="Auto"/>
        <RowDefinition Height="Auto"/>
        <RowDefinition Height="Auto"/>
    </Grid.RowDefinitions>
</Grid>
```

Next, we will enhance the default controls markup to place them in separate rows so that in the UI they look like they are nicely stacked. To do this, we need to specify the row number each control will be contained within. This is achieved by setting the Grid.Row property within each control element.

In the steps that follow, we will provide a name for each control so that we can access it in code. Next, we will set the default text properties for the TextBox and TextBlock controls and change the text of the button by setting its Content property. Finally, we will add an event handler for the button's Tap event. The final markup is depicted in Listing 1-1.

Listing 1-1. The ContentPanel grid within MainPage.xaml

```xml
<Grid x:Name="ContentPanel" Grid.Row="1" Margin="12,0,12,0">
        <Grid.RowDefinitions>
            <RowDefinition Height="Auto"/>
            <RowDefinition Height="Auto"/>
            <RowDefinition Height="Auto"/>
            <RowDefinition Height="Auto"/>
        </Grid.RowDefinitions>
        <TextBlock Name="nameLabel"
                Grid.Row="0"
                Text="what's your name?" />
        <TextBox Name="nameText"
            Grid.Row="1" />
        <Button Name="greetMeButton"
            Grid.Row="2"
            Content="Greet Me"
            Tap="greetMeButton_Tap_1" />
        <TextBlock Name="greetingText"
                Grid.Row="3" />

    </Grid>
```

■ **Note** The Tap event is equivalent to the Click event, which is the event that most .NET developers are accustomed to using. You can create a Click event handler, which will be triggered when the user taps the button via the touch screen on the device. However, for Windows Phone development, it is ideal to get used to handling the Tap event in lieu of the Click event, when available.

Your MainPage.xaml page should now appear in the Visual Studio designer as shown in Figure 1-5.

Figure 1-5. Designer view of the application's main page

At this point, we need to add code to the button's Tap event handler so that it does something when the user taps it. To do this, we have to switch to the page's code behind file. In the Visual Studio Solution Explorer, in the right pane, click the arrow next to MainPage.xaml. You will notice a second file below the MainPage.xaml file, with the same name, but with a file extension of .cs. This denotes that the code behind file is using the programming language C#. Double-click on this file in the Solution Explorer to launch it in the Visual Studio's designer pane.

The first thing you will notice is that the code behind file does not provide the same page designer view that the XAML file does. This is because the XAML defines the way the UI appears, but the code behind the file contains the actions that will be performed. It is not necessary to add code to this file to compile and run your Windows Phone application, but then again, it wouldn't be very useful to the user, would it?

Let's add code to the button's Tap event handler, so that when tapped, it will check the TextBox to determine if a name was entered. If so, then we will display a greeting in the greetingText TextBlock. Otherwise, we will display a message prompting for a valid name.

```
private void greetMeButton_Tap_1(object sender, System.Windows.Input.GestureEventArgs e)
{
    if (nameText.Text.Length == 0)
    {
        greetingText.Text = "Enter your name to receive a proper greeting";
    }
    else
    {
        greetingText.Text = String.Format("It's a pleasure to meet you, {0}", nameText.Text);
    }
}
```

Now, you can build your project, which will compile your code and generate the application's XAP file. The XAP file is simply an archive containing all of the compiled code and related assemblies that are needed to successfully run your app. This is a valid Windows Phone application that you can now run in the Windows Phone emulator or deploy to a device.

Congratulations, you just created your first Windows Phone 8 app!

1-3. Launch an App in the Windows Phone Emulator

Problem

You want to test out the application you just created, but you don't have a Windows Phone handy to run it on.

Solution

Run your app from the Visual Studio IDE, using the Windows Phone Emulator.

How It Works

If your machine met the requirements to run the Windows Phone Emulator, it would have been installed on your system during the SDK installation, which we completed in Recipe 1-1. If it was installed successfully, you should see the Emulator menu next to the "Start Debugging" button in your Visual Studio 2012 toolbar, as shown in Figure 1-6.

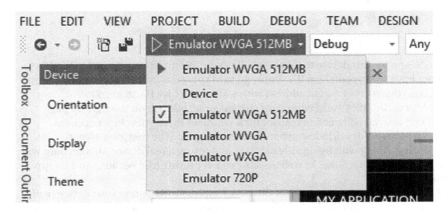

Figure 1-6. *Windows Phone Emulator menu*

Let's use the application that we developed in Recipe 1-2 as the application we will test in this exercise.

To test your newly developed application in the Windows Phone 8 emulator, click on the green arrow button to the left of the emulator menu in the Visual Studio tool bar. Clicking the Debug button will force a build of the project, if it hasn't been compiled yet with the latest code changes and will launch the Windows Phone emulator. Note that the first launch of the emulator will be slow and will take a minute or two to initialize.

Once the emulator has loaded, your application will launch and the main page of your application will display.

You can use your mouse to click on the textbox to set focus in this field, so that we can enter a value. Notice when you set focus to the textbox, that the emulator will display a digital keyboard. This is known as the Soft Input Panel and is the type of keyboard that a Windows Phone device will display when an entry field has focus. You can use your mouse to click on the letters you want to select to enter a value in the textbox. Alternatively, when debugging on a machine, users find it more convenient to use their physical keyboards for data entry in the emulator. To enable physical keyboard entry while running an app within the emulator, press the Page Down key. This will hide the Soft Input Panel and now you will be able to use your physical keyboard for text entry fields. To return back to the Soft Input Panel, simply press the Page Up key.

Now, enter a value in the text field, then click the Greet Me button. Notice that the emulator recognized the mouse click action as a Tap event, and executed the code we had added to the button's Tap event handler, and your custom greeting displayed in the TextBlock below the button.

Clear the value in the textbox, and click the Greet Me button again. As expected, the greeting label prompts for a valid entry in the textbox.

That's all there is to it! We've demonstrated launching your first Windows Phone app in the emulator and tested both cases to ensure we received the desired greeting message when a value was entered and when there was no value in the textbox.

1-4. Launch an App on a Windows Phone Device
Problem

You finally have your hands on a new Windows Phone and you want to take your newly developed app for a test run on the device.

Solution

Sign up for a developer account and then unlock your phone for testing.

How It Works

Before you can deploy a Windows Phone app to your device to test, you will need a Microsoft Live ID and a Windows Phone developer account. If you do not have a Microsoft Live ID, simply go to http://www.outlook.com and sign up for a free account. If you wish to associate your current e-mail address with a Microsoft Live ID, then go to http://go.microsoft.com/fwlink/p/?LinkID=238657 and enter your current email address on the sign-up page.

Once you have a Microsoft Live ID set up, you will need to register for a Windows Phone developer account. To register for a developer account, go to https://dev.windowsphone.com/en-us/join. The cost for a 1-year subscription is $99 at the time of this writing. Along with being able to test your apps on a real device, this account will also allow you to publish apps to the Windows Phone Store, as well as allow you to provide trial versions and in-app purchases within your apps, if you so choose.

Now that you have the required accounts set up and active, you can now continue with getting your device ready for testing. Connect your device to your computer with the USB cable that came with your Windows Phone. If this is the first time you have connected your phone to your computer, you will notice that it takes a few minutes to install some necessary files and you will see a dialog similar to the one shown in Figure 1-7.

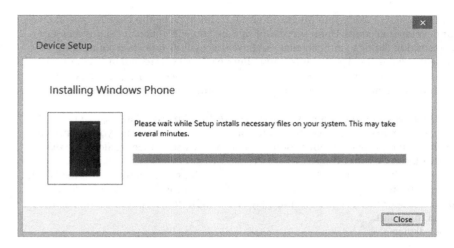

Figure 1-7. *Dialog displayed when connecting your Windows Phone to a computer for the first time*

Once the install has completed, you are ready to proceed with unlocking your device for testing. The first thing you need to do is ensure your device is not at the lock screen. If it is, swipe from bottom up to unlock your device.

On your computer, hit the Windows key to switch to the All Apps view in Windows 8. Start typing the word "Developer" to filter your apps list view. You should see Windows Phone Developer Registration in the list. Click it to launch the Developer Phone Registration dialog as shown in Figure 1-8. Click the Register button within this dialog.

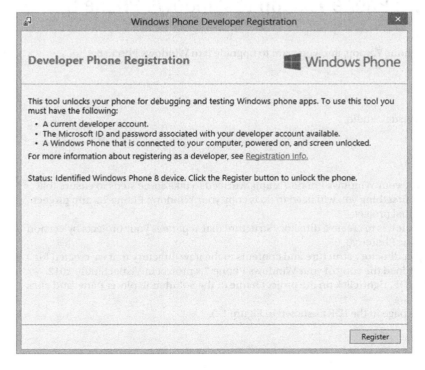

Figure 1-8. *Developer Phone Registration tool is used to unlock a Windows Phone device for testing*

At this point, you will be prompted to sign in using your Microsoft Live ID. This must be the same Microsoft Live ID under which you registered your developer account. Upon successful sign-in, you will notice the Status message changes in the Developer Phone Registration dialog to indicate that you have successfully unlocked your phone.

Now, you can go ahead and close the dialog, then load the Windows Phone project we created in Recipe 1-2 in the Visual Studio 2012 IDE. Be sure to keep your device connected to your computer. Once the project loads, expand the menu options for the Windows Phone Emulator, to change your debugging option from the Windows Phone Emulator to Device.

Hit the F5 key, or click the Start Debugging button to launch your app for testing. You will now see that the emulator does not launch at all. Instead, your app is deployed directly to your device. The difference you will notice when debugging an app on your device is that the performance counters that you are used to seeing along the right side of the emulator screen are also displayed on your device.

Hit Shift + F5, or click Debug ➤ Stop Debugging in the Visual Studio IDE. One thing you should be aware of is that even though you are no longer debugging your app, the app remains on your device. If you launch the app directly from your device, notice that the performance counters no longer display on the right side of your device's screen, because you are not in Debug mode at this point.

To remove this test app from your device:

- Swipe from right to left on your device to reveal your installed apps list

- Locate the test app in the list or use the Search textbox to filter the list

- Tap and hold your test app's name in the list until a context menu appears

- Tap the "uninstall" option from the context menu list

1-5. Upgrade a Windows Phone 7.x app to Windows Phone 8
Problem

You have already developed a Windows Phone 7.x app, and you want to upgrade it to Windows Phone 8.

Solution

Upgrade the application's project within Visual Studio.

How It Works

Before we get into the details on upgrading your Windows Phone 7.x app, we need to take some steps to ensure that your live source code base is not lost. The first thing you will need to do is copy your Windows Phone 7.x app project to a new directory, separate from the original project.

Within Windows Explorer, my suggestion is to create a directory structure that separates your projects by version number. For example: D:\Projects\WindowsPhone\v8_0.

Copy your Windows Phone 7.x project directory structure and contents to the new directory that we created for Windows Phone OS 8.0 projects. Now let's load the copy of your Windows Phone 7.x project in Visual Studio 2012. Once it has loaded into the Visual Studio IDE, right-click on the project name in the Solution Explorer pane, and click Properties from the popup menu.

This will load the project's properties page in the IDE as shown in Figure 1-9.

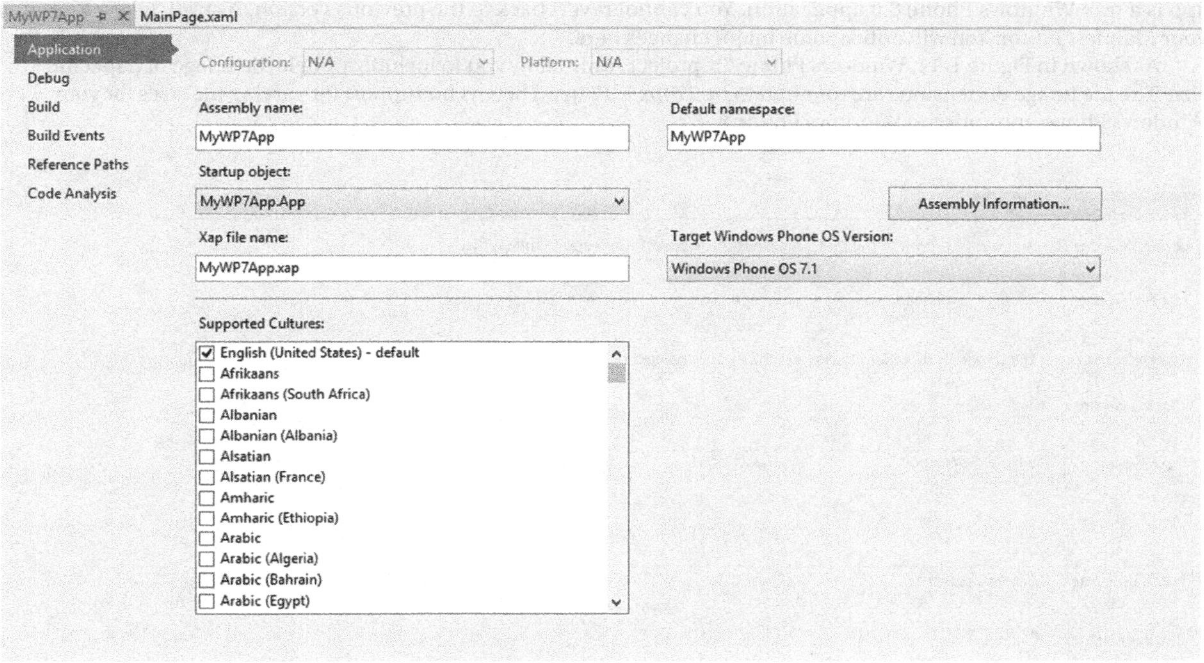

Figure 1-9. *Windows Phone Project Properties Page in Visual Studio 2012*

Notice that for Windows Phone project, there is a special dropdown labeled, "Target Windows Phone OS Version". Expand this dropdown list, and select the option "Windows Phone OS 8.0". This action will cause the confirmation message to display, as shown in Figure 1-10.

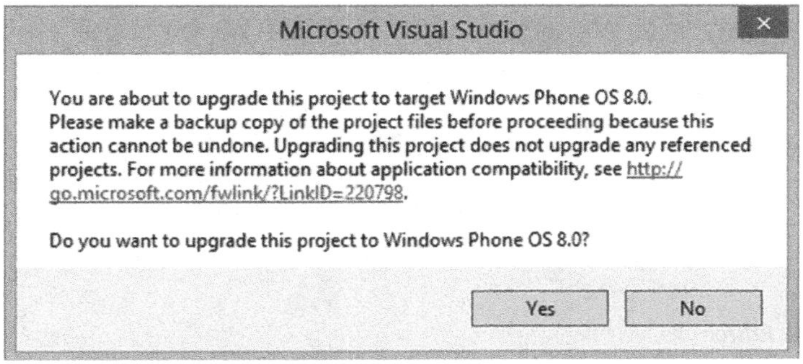

Figure 1-10. *Confirmation dialog when upgrading to project to Windows Phone OS 8.0*

Click "Yes" in this dialog to continue, since we have already performed our due diligence by making a backup copy ahead of time.

You are probably thinking to yourself, "Now what?"

Well, there are changes that have been made to your project quietly behind the scenes, even though it didn't appear as though anything was really changed. For instance, expand the dropdown list for the Target Windows Phone OS Version once again. You should now see only the Windows Phone OS 8.0 option in the list. At this point, your upgraded

15

app is a true Windows Phone 8.0 application. You cannot revert back to the previous version. As well, take a look at your Manifest Editor. You will notice some major changes here.

As shown in Figure 1-11, Windows Phone 7.x projects only allow you to include a single tile image of a specific size. The tile image dimensions are required to be 173px X 173px. There is no support for varying tile sizes for your Windows Phone apps prior to Windows Phone 8.

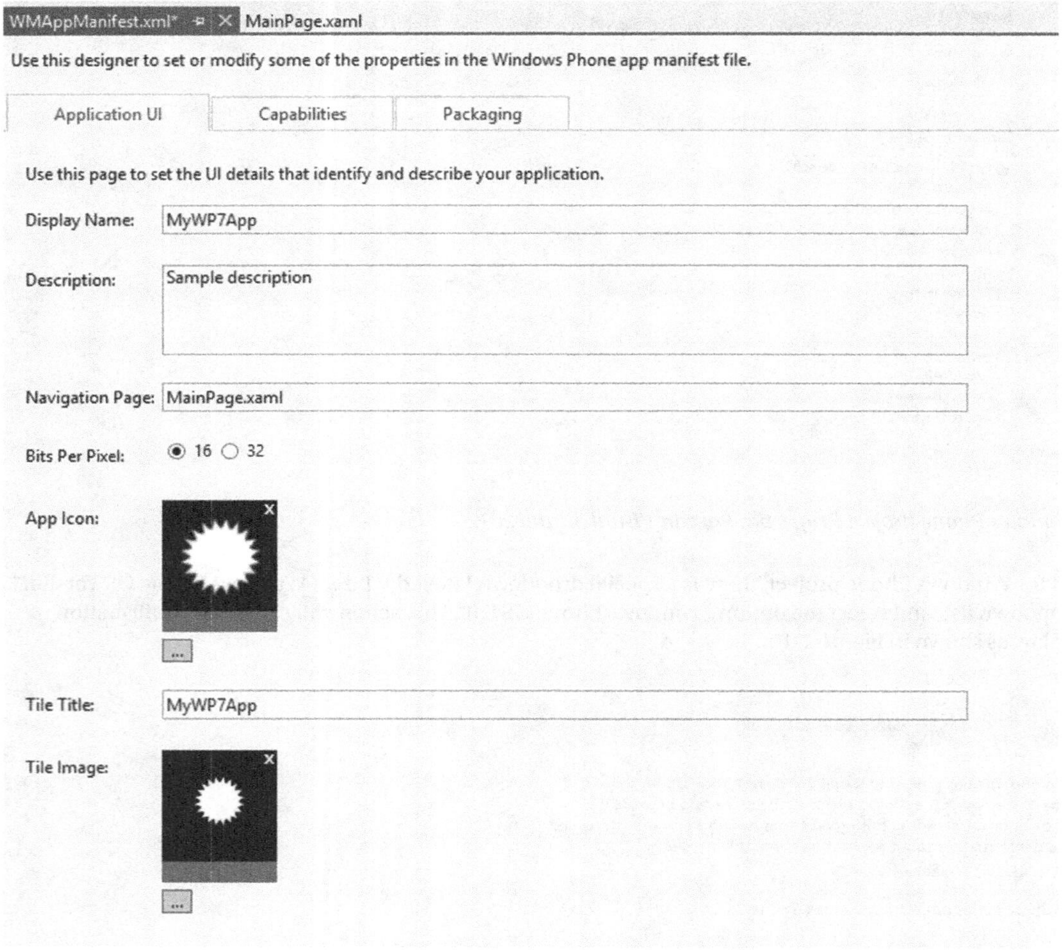

***Figure 1-11.** Windows Phone 7.1 project—Manifest Editor*

In looking at the upgraded project's Manifest Editor, you will notice that you are able to select one of three predefined tile templates, and you must provide tile images for small, medium, and large tiles (Figure 1-12). As well, you can specify which resolutions your app will support (i.e., WVGA, WXGA, and/or 720p). We will get into the details of these topics later in the book. For now, it is enough to know that they are there and need to be configured properly prior to submitting your upgraded app to the Windows Phone store.

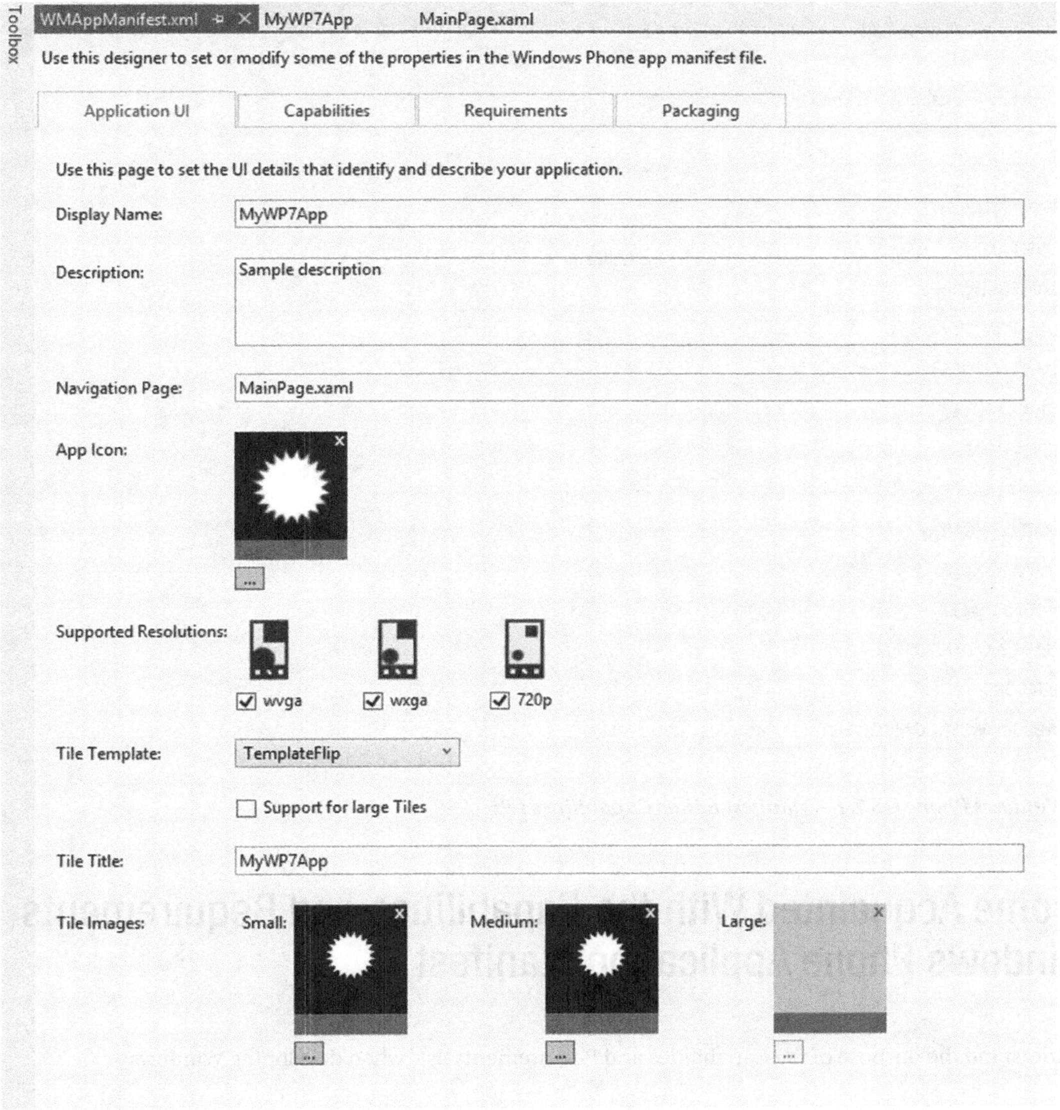

Toolbox

| WMAppManifest.xml | ⊕ | ✕ | MyWP7App | MainPage.xaml |

Use this designer to set or modify some of the properties in the Windows Phone app manifest file.

| Application UI | Capabilities | Requirements | Packaging |

Use this page to set the UI details that identify and describe your application.

Display Name: MyWP7App

Description: Sample description

Navigation Page: MainPage.xaml

App Icon:

Supported Resolutions: ☑ wvga   ☑ wxga   ☑ 720p

Tile Template: TemplateFlip

☐ Support for large Tiles

Tile Title: MyWP7App

Tile Images: Small: Medium: Large:

Figure 1-12. *Windows Phone 8 project—Manifest Editor*

The next thing you will notice is that the Capabilities list for Windows Phone 8 is far more extensive, including capabilities for the new features available in the new SDK, such as speech recognition, near field communications, and wallet. We will be discussing Capabilities in Recipe 1-6. For comparison purposes, Figure 1-13 depicts a screen capture of the Windows Phone OS 7.1 Capabilities list.

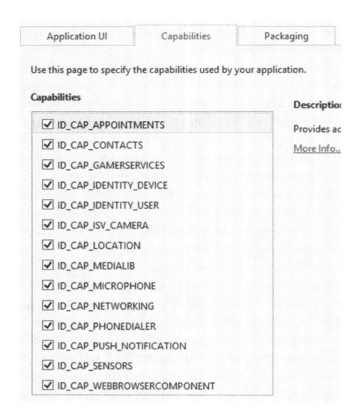

Figure 1-13. Windows Phone OS 7.1—Manifest Editor Capabilities tab

1-6. Become Acquainted With the Capabilities and Requirements in the Windows Phone Application Manifest

Problem

You want to understand the purpose of the Capabilities and Requirements lists when developing Windows Phone apps.

Solution

Checkmark the Capabilities and Requirements needed by your app within the Application Manifest.

How It Works

The Application Manifest file, WMAppManifest.xml, contains information that serves as the metadata for your Windows Phone application. It can be found within the Properties folder in your project, as shown in Figure 1-14.

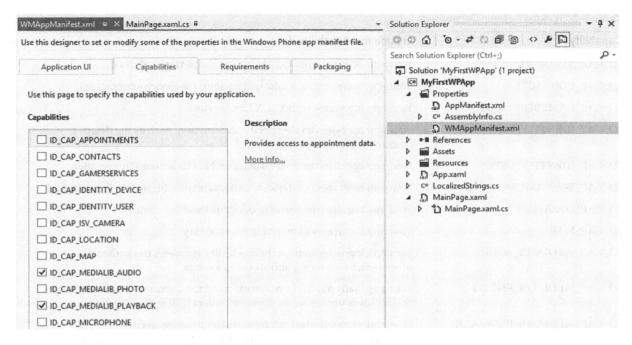

Figure 1-14. *Capabilities list in the Windows Phone Application Manifest*

Capabilities are used to inform the user which device features your application will be using when installed. For this reason, it is important to ensure you check the capabilities that your app leverages before submitting your app to the Windows Phone Store.

Both Windows Phone OS 7.0 and 7.1 provided tools that you could use to verify the capabilities your application utilized. In addition to that, when submitting a 7.x app to the Windows Phone Store, your app capabilities were analyzed and the app manifest file would be corrected and regenerated if there were entries missing.

Unfortunately, this is not the case with apps developed on Windows Phone OS 8.0. The SDK does not contain a tool to detect the capabilities your Windows Phone 8 app requires. When you submit your Windows Phone 8 app to the Store, it does not analyze or correct your app manifest file. In turn, if you submit your app to the Store without including the proper capabilities in your app, your app may not function properly on a device.

When you create a Windows Phone project in Visual Studio, you will notice that some capabilities are checked by default. To view the Application Manifest, expand the Properties folder within your project in the Solution Explorer, and then double-click on the WMAppManifest.xml file to load it in the main Visual Studio pane.

When the Application Manifest is loaded, you will see the following tabs: Application UI, Capabilities, Requirements and Packaging. Click on the Capabilities tab to view the list of available capabilities. Table 1-2 lists the set of capabilities for Windows Phone OS 8.0, with a brief description on when you should include each capability.

Table 1-2. *Windows Phone Capabilities*

Capability	Include this capability if..
ID_CAP_APPOINTMENTS	Your app accesses appointments from the device's calendar.
ID_CAP_CONTACTS	Your app access contact information from the device's contact list.
ID_CAP_GAMERSERVICES	Your app integrates with XBOX Live services.
ID_CAP_IDENTITY_DEVICE	Your app accesses device-specific information, such as the device's unique ID, phone number, etc.
ID_CAP_IDENTITY_USER	Your app accesses the user's Microsoft Live ID account information.
ID_CAP_ISV_CAMERA	Your app leverages the device's camera (rear-facing and/or front-facing).
ID_CAP_LOCATION	Your app requires the use of geographic location services.
ID_CAP_MAP	Your app incorporates mapping functionality.
ID_CAP_MEDIALIB_AUDIO	Your app loads audio from the media library, views the audio item properties, saves songs, and/or deletes songs.
ID_CAP_MEDIALIB_PHOTO	Your app loads photos from the media library, accesses photo properties, and/or saves photos to the device's Camera Roll or Saved Pictures.
ID_CAP_MEDIALIB_PLAYBACK	Your app supports playback from IsolatedStorage, accesses media items that are playing, and/or adds media items to History, Favorites, and New collections.
ID_CAP_MICROPHONE	Your app uses the device's microphone to record sounds.
ID_CAP_NETWORKING	Your app requires a data connection.
ID_CAP_PHONEDIALER	Your app allows the user to make phone calls.
ID_CAP_PROXIMITY	Your app includes Near-Field-Communications services.
ID_CAP_PUSH_NOTIFICATION	Your app receives data updates through push notification services.
ID_CAP_REMOVABLE_STORAGE	Your app saves to, or loads from, a media card.
ID_CAP_SENSORS	Your app leverages the device sensors, such as the accelerometer.
ID_CAP_WEBBROWSERCOMPONENT	Your app loads a web browser.
ID_CAP_SPEECH_RECOGNITION	Your app includes speech recognition or text-to-speech (TTS) services.
ID_CAP_VOIP	Your app allows the user to make Voice Over IP calls.
ID_CAP_WALLET	Your app leverages the Wallet feature for managing memberships, deals, and payment options.
ID_CAP_WALLET_ PAYMENTINSTRUMENTS	Your app requires access to the Wallet payment options, such as debit or credit.
ID_CAP_WALLET_SECUREELEMENT	Your app requires access to the Wallet secure element for NFC transactions.

In many cases, it is obvious which capabilities you will need. For example, if you want to search the device's calendar data for appointments, you would ensure that the capability, ID_CAP_APPOINTMENTS, is checked.

In other cases, it may not be obvious which capabilities are needed. One good example is the Microsoft Ad SDK, which requires multiple capabilities. This is something we will touch on in Chapter 10, when discussing how to implement advertisements into your app. For now, it's enough to know that you will need to come here to enable capabilities within your application.

Similarly, you will notice the Requirements tab allows you to specify the device hardware leveraged within your app (Figure 1-15). In this way, devices that do not meet the requirements will not be able to install your app. For example, if your app depends on Near Field Communications to function, then including the requirement ID_REQ_NFC will prevent devices that do not have an NFC chip from installing your app, since the app will not work properly on those devices anyway. Table 1-3 lists the hardware requirements available for Windows Phone 8.0, with a brief description on when to include each requirement.

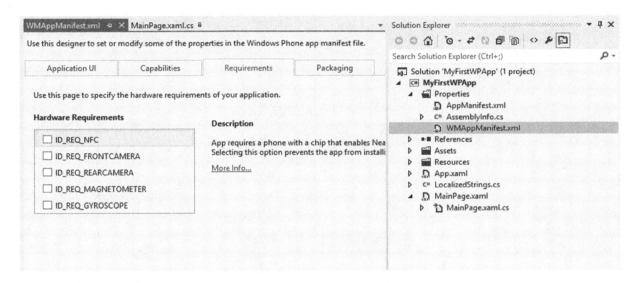

Figure 1-15. *Hardware Requirements list in the Windows Phone App Manifest*

Table 1-3. *Windows Phone Hardware Requirements*

Requirement	Include this requirement if..
ID_REQ_NFC	Your app requires the use of the device's NFC chip.
ID_REQ_FRONTCAMERA	Your app requires the use of the device's front-facing camera.
ID_REQ_REARCAMERA	Your app requires the use of the device's rear-facing camera.
ID_REQ_MAGNETOMETER	Your app requires the use of the device's compass.
ID_REQ_GYROSCOPE	Your app requires the use of the device's gyroscope.

CHAPTER 2

■ ■ ■

Multi-Resolution Support and Basic User Interface Components

Windows Phone 7.x only had support for WVGA resolution. Windows Phone 8 expands that to include WXGA and HD720p. It's important to understand how to tailor your application to these different resolutions.

Therefore, the following recipes are included in this chapter:

- 2-1. Managing Resolution Dependent Assets
- 2-2. Dynamic Layout
- 2-3. Adding buttons and menus to the Application Bar
- 2-4. Page Navigation
- 2-5. The LongListSelector control
- 2-6. Enhancing the UI with the Silverlight Toolkit

Table 2-1 lists the different resolutions and how they relate to each other.

Table 2-1. Windows Phone 8 Supported Resolutions, Aspect Ratios, and Scaling Factors

Resolution	Pixels	Aspect Ratio	Scale Factor	Scaled Resolution
WVGA	480 x 800	15 : 9	1.0	480 x 800
WXGA	768 x 1280	15 : 9	1.6	480 x 800
HD720p	720 x 1280	16 : 9	1.5	480 x 853

The different number of pixels on the x- and y-axis of each resolution is to be expected, but you'll notice that HD720p is unique in that it has a different aspect ratio. The HD720p resolution has its origin in high-definition television and is exactly twice the width and one and one half the height of 4:3 VGA. VGA's aspect ratio and line count is virtually the same as DV-NTSC video. Figure 2-1 shows these resolutions relative to each other.

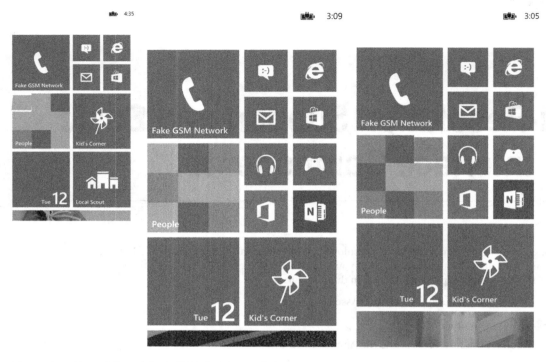

Figure 2-1. *From left to right: WVGA, WXGA, and HD720p*

In general you don't really need to be concerned with these ratios, as everything is worked out for you by the rendering subsystem. There are a few cases, however, where these factors come into play: providing dynamic user interface layout, managing resolution-dependent assets, and working with Direct3D using the `Direct3DInterop` and `DrawingSurface` classes.

`FrameworkElement`-derived classes report their `ActualWidth` and `ActualHeight` values in Device Independent Pixels. You'll notice in Table 2-1 that the scale factor for WVGA is 1.0, which means there is a one-to-one ratio between device independent and native pixels. The `D3DInterop` properties `NativeResolution` and `RenderResolution` need to be set in native pixels and the scale factor helps you work this out.

Direct3D programming is beyond the scope of this book[1] but we are still left with the problem of resolution-dependent assets and dynamic layout. A recipe is included for each of these scenarios.

With proper scaling taken care of, we move on to the basic user interface components that are integral to Windows Phone application development. The chapter wraps up with an example using the LongListSelector control, which is new to Windows Phone 8, as well as a look at using the Silverlight Toolkit to enhance your mobile application's user interface.

2-1. Managing Resolution Dependent Assets
Problem

Sometimes you have no choice but to use a bitmapped image. The problem with bitmaps is that there is always some amount of visual compromise when the image is scaled to a different size and changes to the aspect ratio almost never results in a satisfactory result.

---

[1] Look Mom, my first cliché in print!

Solution

The visual assets you include in your application should, as much as possible, be vector-based. Vector-based graphics have the distinct advantage of being infinitely scalable. You can stretch them as much as you like and they will always look good and not display the pixilation that is common with bitmapped images.

For your application's splash screen you can do one of two things:

1. Add a single 720 x 1280 image named SplashScreenImage.jpg to the root folder of your project and set its **Build Action** to **Content** or...

2. Add three images named SplashScreenImage.screen-WVGA.jpg, SplashScreenImage.screen-WXGA.jpg and SplashScreenImage.screen-720p.jpg each with its corresponding resolution to the root folder of your application. Again, set the **Build Action** of each file to **Content**

■ **Note**   Sample splash screen images can be found in the Chapter02\BasicMultiResolution root folder and sample resolution dependent images can be found in the Chapter02\BasicMultiResolution\Assets folder.

For all other assets you must include a separate image file for each of the supported resolutions and then, based on the resolution of the device, load the appropriate file.

How It Works

For the splash screen, it just works. The phone will automatically scale your image to the proper size if you chose to have a single image or it will automatically select the right image if you provided three correctly named images. Automatic selection of the right image only works for the splash screen. All other resolution-dependent assets require you to write code that selects the right asset.

The Application.Host.Content.ScaleFactor property will give us a value that we can use to determine which asset to load. The ScaleFactor property returns an integer value representing the amount by which the content area scales its contents. By referring to Table 2-1, you can determine the resolution of the device. Let's create a helper class that we can use in our code.

Create a new Windows Phone App by following the directions in Chapter 1 and name your project MultiResolution. First we'll create an enumeration for the supported resolutions. Add a new class to the project and name it Resolution. Delete the default Class1 declaration and add in the following code:

```
public enum Resolution
{
    WVGA,
    WXGA,
    HD720p
}
```

Add a second class to the project and name it DeviceHelper. Again, delete the default Class1 declaration and add the following code:

```
public static class DeviceHelper
{
    private static int scaleFactor = Application.Current.Host.Content.ScaleFactor;
    private static Resolution resolution;
```

```
        static DeviceHelper()
        {
            switch(scaleFactor)
            {
                case 100:
                    resolution = Resolution.WVGA;
                    break;
                case 160:
                    resolution = Resolution.WXGA;
                    break;
                case 150:
                    resolution = Resolution.HD720p;
                    break;
                default:
                    throw new InvalidOperationException(
                     string.Format("The scale factor {0} is not supported", scaleFactor));
                    break;
            }
        }
    }
}
```

The scaleFactor field will be initialized to the ScaleFactor of the current host's Content the first time our DeviceHelper class is used. Next, the static constructor will run and allow us to examine the scaleFactor field's value and set the resolution field's value to the correct enumeration value. The only thing left is to provide a public static property to return the enumeration. Add the Resolution property to your class.

```
public static Resolution Resolution
{
    get
    {
        return resolution;
    }
}
```

Since we've only just met I won't expect you to just take my word for it that this will work. Let's modify the MainPage.xaml so we can see our helper in action. Open the MainPage.xaml file in the Visual Studio designer and look in the XAML. You should see a section marked with the following comment and an empty Grid:

```
<!--ContentPanel - place additional content here-->
<Grid x:Name="ContentPanel" Grid.Row="1">

</Grid>
```

Remove the Margin attribute and add the following XAML inside the Grid:

```
<StackPanel>
    <TextBlock
        Style="{StaticResource PhoneTextNormalStyle}"
        Text="Device Resolution: "/>
```

```
<TextBlock
    Style="{StaticResource PhoneTextNormalStyle}"
    x:Name="resolution"/>
    <Image x:Name="resolutionImage"/>
</StackPanel>
```

Open the MainPage.xaml.cs code-behind file and add the following line of code just after the call to InitializeComponent(). Add the MainPageLoaded method after the constructor.

```
public MainPage()
{
    InitializeComponent();
    this.Loaded += MainPageLoaded;
    // Sample code to localize the ApplicationBar
    //BuildLocalizedApplicationBar();
}

void MainPageLoaded(object sender, RoutedEventArgs e)
{
    resolution.Text = DeviceHelper.Resolution.ToString();
    string uriString = string.Format("Assets/{0}-Asset.jpg", DeviceHelper.Resolution);
    resolutionImage.Source = new BitmapImage(new Uri(uriString, UriKind.Relative));
}
```

Select an emulator from the drop-down list and then run the application. You should see the splash screen for the resolution of the emulator you chose to run. When the main page of the application displays you should see not only the proper text but also the corresponding image. Figure 2-2 shows the screen when running in the WVGA emulator.

Figure 2-2. *WVGA emulator sample screen shot*

2-2. Dynamic Layout

Problem

There was only one supported resolution for phones running Windows Phone OS 7.1: WVGA. You always knew the exact dimensions of the screen on which your application would be displayed. Windows Phone 8 introduces two additional resolutions, and one of them (HD720p) has a 16:9 aspect ratio whereas the others are 15:9. Your application needs to be able to adapt its layout accordingly.

Solution

The WPF and Silverlight developers in the audience will have no doubt already guessed the answer: Don't hard-code the width, height or position of the controls in your application. Use controls such as the Grid and StackPanel and let the layout subsystem do the work for you.

How It Works

Some controls will grow to fill the space allotted to them by their parents while others will expand to accommodate their children. Two of the most commonly used layout controls are the StackPanel and the Grid. A key difference between the two is the way that controls inside them behave.

For example, a Button or TextBlock in a StackPanel with the Orientation set to the default of Vertical will expand to fill the width of the StackPanel but not the height since the height is really the sum of the height of all the child controls inside it. Changing the Orientation to Horizontal causes the children to expand to fill the height of the stack panel but not the width since the width is really the combined width of the children.

A Button or TextBlock in a cell of a Grid control will expand to fill all of the available space. You can achieve a fairly fine degree of control over the layout of your application by using a Grid with properly set row and column definitions and still have it be flexible. There are three common methods of setting the Height of a row and the Width of a column. You can have them automatically adjust to the size of their content, divide themselves evenly across the available space, or divide proportionately according to a ratio you define (called "star" sizing). We'll use row definitions in our example but the rules apply equally to column definitions.

■ **Note**   You can also set a hard-coded Width or Height value but then you lose the flexible layout that we are trying to achieve. For the best results, avoid hard-coded layout property values.

The default behavior of rows and columns in a Grid is to divide themselves evenly across the available space. You don't need to set a value at all if this is the desired result. For example:

```
<Grid.RowDefinitions>
        <RowDefinition/>
        <RowDefinition/>
        <RowDefinition/>
<Grid.RowDefinitions>
```

This is the same as:

```
<Grid.RowDefinitions>
        <RowDefinition Height="*"/>
        <RowDefinition Height="*"/>
        <RowDefinition Height="*"/>
<Grid.RowDefinitions>
```

More often than not, you probably want the space divided up in a more specific manner. You would want a heading row to only take up enough room to display its contents. The "Auto" setting will allow you to achieve this. The following will give you a first row sized to its content and the other two rows dividing the remaining height between them.

```
<Grid.RowDefinitions>
        <RowDefinition Height="Auto"/>
        <RowDefinition Height="*"/>
        <RowDefinition Height="*"/>
<Grid.RowDefinitions>
```

Now that you have the heading row taking up only the space that it needs, you may want to divide up the space for the remaining two rows by a proportion other than 50-50. When you set the Height or Width to "*" this is actually the same as setting it to "1*." If you total up the numbers for each row you can then take an individual row's value and calculate the ratio. In our simple example, 1 + 1 = 2 so each row gets 1 / 2 = 0.5 or 50%. Let's look at another example with some different numbers.

```
<Grid.RowDefinitions>
        <RowDefinition Height="3*"/>
        <RowDefinition Height="6*"/>
        <RowDefinition Height="9*"/>
<Grid.RowDefinitions>
```

How much space does each row get in this example? Again, we simply add up all of the ratios and use that total as the denominator when dividing for each row.

```
Total = 9 + 6 + 3 = 18
Row 1 = 3/18 = 1/6
Row 2 = 6/18 = 1/3
Row 3 = 9/18 = 1/2
```

The numbers themselves are not important. It's the ratio between them that is key. We could achieve the exact same result with this:

```
<Grid.RowDefinitions>
        <RowDefinition Height="2*"/>
        <RowDefinition Height="4*"/>
        <RowDefinition Height="6*"/>
<Grid.RowDefinitions>
```

```
Total = 6 + 4 + 2 = 12
Row 1 = 2/12 = 1/6
Row 2 = 4/12 = 1/3
Row 3 = 6/12 = 1/2
```

Some people go wrong when using star sizing because they don't understand how the calculations are being carried out. Usually these are the same people that are hard-coding the parent control's size as well so it looks good right up to the point when it doesn't. If the sum of your star ratios is the same as, or a multiple of, the fixed size then it's going to look alright. Things are going to go weird if not and it will be hard to figure out what's going on.

Let's apply what we've learned to our sample application. We'll move the image to the bottom of the screen and add a column so that we can put the screen resolution label and the reported value side by side. We'll configure the rows so that the middle row fills any space not used by the heading and the image.

Start by changing the StackPanel to a Grid. Next add in the column and row definition elements. We'll want two columns and three rows. Set the height of the first and last row to "Auto." Don't set a height for the middle row. You also don't need to set a width for the columns because the default split of 50-50 is fine for our purposes. Set the Grid.Row and Grid.Column attached properties to position the label TextBlock in row zero, column zero, the resolution TextBlock in row zero, column one, and the Image in row two, column zero. You'll also need to set the Grid.ColumnSpan attached property on the Image control because we want it to take up the full width of the screen. Your XAML should now look like this:

```
<Grid x:Name="ContentPanel" Grid.Row="1">
    <Grid.ColumnDefinitions>
        <ColumnDefinition/>
        <ColumnDefinition/>
    </Grid.ColumnDefinitions>
    <Grid.RowDefinitions>
        <RowDefinition Height="Auto"/>
        <RowDefinition/>
        <RowDefinition Height="Auto"/>
    </Grid.RowDefinitions>
    <TextBlock
        Grid.Row="0"
        Grid.Column="0"
        Style="{StaticResource PhoneTextNormalStyle}"
        Text="Device Resolution: "/>
    <TextBlock
        Grid.Row="0"
        Grid.Column="1"
        Style="{StaticResource PhoneTextNormalStyle}"
        x:Name="resolution"/>
    <Image
        Grid.Row="2"
        Grid.Column="0"
        Grid.ColumnSpan="2"
        x:Name="resolutionImage"/>
</Grid>
```

■ **Note** The Row and Column attached properties of the Grid default to zero so you don't technically need to set them in XAML if zero is what you need.

Run your application and make sure you see the desired results. Try it in the different emulators to see how the layout is the same at all resolutions and aspect ratios. Finally, let's fill up the middle row with something useful. Add the following XAML between the second TextBlock and the Image:

```
<Grid Grid.ColumnSpan="2" Grid.Row="1">
    <Grid.RowDefinitions>
        <RowDefinition Height="*" />
        <RowDefinition Height="*" />
        <RowDefinition Height="*" />
        <RowDefinition Height="*" />
    </Grid.RowDefinitions>
    <Grid.ColumnDefinitions>
        <ColumnDefinition Width="*" />
        <ColumnDefinition Width="*" />
        <ColumnDefinition Width="*" />
    </Grid.ColumnDefinitions>
    <Button Grid.Row="0" Margin="0" Grid.Column="0" Content="1" />
    <Button Grid.Row="0" Grid.Column="1" Content="2" />
    <Button Grid.Row="0" Grid.Column="2" Content="3" />
    <Button Grid.Row="1" Grid.Column="0" Content="4" />
    <Button Grid.Row="1" Grid.Column="1" Content="5" />
    <Button Grid.Row="1" Grid.Column="2" Content="6" />
    <Button Grid.Row="2" Grid.Column="0" Content="7" />
    <Button Grid.Row="2" Grid.Column="1" Content="8" />
    <Button Grid.Row="2" Grid.Column="2" Content="9" />
    <Button Grid.Row="3" Grid.Column="0" Content="#" />
    <Button Grid.Row="3" Grid.Column="1" Content="0" />
    <Button Grid.Row="3" Grid.Column="2" Content="*" />
</Grid>
```

Run the application again in the different emulators and observe how the layout remains consistent in the different resolutions. It should resemble the screenshot in Figure 2-3.

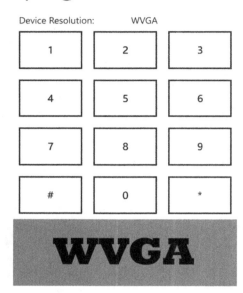

Figure 2-3. *Final sample application screen shot*

2-3. Working with the Application Bar

Problem

The `ApplicationBar`, `ApplicationBarIconButton`, and `ApplicationBarMenuItem` classes do not derive from `DependencyObject` and therefore do not support data binding. The lack of data binding means we can't just wire up our buttons and menu items to a view model and be done.

Solution

We can achieve a happy medium that still gives us a loosely coupled user interface by using a combination of code-behind, custom dependency properties, and delegation.

> *"The MVVM police will not take your family away if you use code behind."*

— Glen Block

How It Works

Most developers that are familiar with Silverlight and Windows Presentation Foundation developement will no doubt be acquainted with the Model-View-ViewModel pattern. This development pattern provides for a very clean separation of concerns between the user interface and the business logic of the application. One of the greatest features of this pattern is the ability to connect the `Command` property of a `Button` to an implementation of the `ICommand` interface exposed via the ViewModel. This allows you to encapsulate any code that would normally be handled in code-behind to be contained in the ViewModel.

There is a problem when it comes to the `ApplicationBar` and its menu items and buttons. They are not derived from `FrameworkElement` and don't implement a `Command` ability. This recipe is an exploration of some techniques for working around this limitation. There's a lot of ground to cover here, so let's get started.

The Basics

The `ApplicationBar`, `ApplicationBarIconButton`, and `ApplicationBarMenuItem` classes are actually system components with which our application is interoperating. `ApplicationBarIconButton` and `ApplicationBarMenuItem` also don't support the `ICommand`. Normally you would just use an attached behavior on the `Click` event to execute a command but since the button and menu item doesn't inherit from `FrameworkElement` behaviors aren't going to work either.

The `ApplicationBar` is exposed as a property of the `PhoneApplicationPage` and the creation and population of it is easily accomplished in either XAML or code. The `ApplicationBar` exposes several properties that we may want to configure at runtime. Table 2-2 lists the properties of the `ApplicationBar`.

Table 2-2. *Properties of the ApplicationBar*

Property	Description
Mode	The Mode property controls the initial appearance of the ApplicationBar as well as the mode to which it returns after the user expands it using the ellipsis. Use the mini setting to maximize available screen space for your page.
	In landscape orientation, the ApplicationBar's setting will be ignored and it will remain in default mode to improve usability. Switching from portrait to landscape will also cause the ApplicationBar to display in default mode.
Opacity	This value can range from 0.0 (complete transparency) to 1.0 (fully opaque). You can set this property to any valid System.Double value. For best results it is highly recommended to limit the choice to three values: 0.0, 0.5, and 1.0.
	• 0.0 - The host page is not resized, the ApplicationBar is completely transparent and is laid over the page contents
	• 0.5 - The host page is not resized and the ApplicationBar is partially transparent and is laid over the page contents
	• 1.0 - The host page is resized to accommodate the ApplicationBar, which is completely opaque. This value must be greater than or equal to one for the transition to be triggered
BackgroundColor	This is the color of the background of the ApplicationBar and can be any valid System.Windows.Media.Color value. This will also be the background color of the buttons if you are using transparent images.
ForegroundColor	This is the color of the foreground of the ApplicationBar and can be any valid System.Windows.Media.Color value. This color will be used for the menu item text as well as the button labels. It will also be the color of the buttons if you are using transparent images.
	It is strongly recommended that you use the default theme colors for your ApplicationBar and its menu items and buttons. Custom colors can have an effect on the display quality of the icon buttons and lead to strange visual artifacts in menu animations.
IsMenuEnabled	A System.Boolean that controls the visibility of the menu items when the user expands the ApplicationBar.
IsVisible	A System.Boolean that controls the visibility of the entire ApplicationBar.

Create a new Windows Phone 8 application and call it ApplicationBarButtonMenu. Open the MainPage.xaml.cs file and add the code from Listing 2-1.

Listing 2-1. Defining an ApplicationBar in Code

```
// add this line right after the call to InitializeComponet()
// in the MainPage constructor
BuildApplicationBar();

private void BuildApplicationBar()
{
    ApplicationBar = new ApplicationBar();

    ApplicationBarIconButton appBarButton =
            new ApplicationBarIconButton(new Uri("/Assets/like.png", UriKind.Relative));

    appBarButton.Text = "like";
    ApplicationBar.Buttons.Add(appBarButton);

    appBarButton = new ApplicationBarIconButton(new Uri("/Assets/save.png", UriKind.Relative));
    appBarButton.Text = "save";
    ApplicationBar.Buttons.Add(appBarButton);

    // Create a new menu item with the localized string from AppResources.
    ApplicationBarMenuItem appBarMenuItem = new ApplicationBarMenuItem("advanced options");
    ApplicationBar.MenuItems.Add(appBarMenuItem);

}

void AdvancedOptionsClick(object sender, EventArgs e)
{
    MessageBox.Show("Advanced Options Clicked");
}
```

Comment out the call to BuildApplicationBar() in the MainPage constructor. Open MainPage.xaml in the editor and then add the XAML in Listing 2-2 to the area just above the layout grid.

Listing 2-2. Defining an ApplicationBar in XAML

```
<phone:PhoneApplicationPage.ApplicationBar>
        <shell:ApplicationBar IsVisible="True" IsMenuEnabled="True">
            <shell:ApplicationBar.MenuItems>
                <shell:ApplicationBarMenuItem Click="AdvancedOptionsClick" Text="advanced options"/>
            </shell:ApplicationBar.MenuItems>
            <shell:ApplicationBarIconButton IconUri="/Assets/like.png " Text="like"/>
            <shell:ApplicationBarIconButton IconUri="/Assets/save.png" Text="save"/>
        </shell:ApplicationBar>
</phone:PhoneApplicationPage.ApplicationBar>

<!--LayoutRoot is the root grid where all page content is placed-->
    <Grid x:Name="LayoutRoot" Background="Transparent">
    ...
```

■ **Note** Images for the ApplicationBarIconButton can be found in the SDK in C:\Program Files (x86)\Microsoft SDKs\ Windows Phone\v8.0\Icons\Dark. You only need to include the Dark versions and Windows Phone will switch them to work with the Light Theme as well.

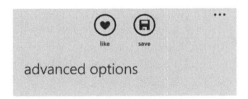

Figure 2-4. *The results are the same whether defining the ApplicationBar in XAML or code*

View Model and Data-Binding Support

Ideally that logic that manages these property values would be encapsulated in a view model. Fortunately, the PhoneApplicationPage ultimately inherits from DependencyObject, which means we can create our own dependency properties. We can then bind these properties to properties of our view model, and in the PropertyChanged event we can update the corresponding property of our ApplicationBar.

We'll work through adding functionality to enable us to control the IsMenuEnabled property from the view model. You can then copy the pattern to extend it to the other properties. You could also extend this technique to control properties of the buttons and menu items. I will leave it as an exercise for the reader.[2]

---

[2]That's cliché number two for those of you that are keeping score at home.

The first thing we need to do is create a view model for our page. Add a new folder to your project and name it ViewModels.

Add a new class to the ViewModels folder and name the class MainPageViewModel. Your view model class will need to implement support for property change notification. This is probably best defined in a base class that can be reused for all ViewModels. Add an IsApplicationBarVisible property to the view model. See Listing 2-3.

Listing 2-3. The MainPageViewModel Class

```
internal class MainPageViewModel : ViewModel
{

    // we'll use this to flip the visibility
    // one per second for demo purposes
    private DispatcherTimer timer;

    public MainPageViewModel()
    {
        timer = new DispatcherTimer();
        timer.Interval = new TimeSpan(0, 0, 1); // one second
        timer.Tick += (s, e) =>
        {
            IsApplicationBarVisible = !IsApplicationBarVisible;
        };

        timer.Start();
    }

    // default to visible...
    private bool isApplicationBarVisible = true;
    public bool IsApplicationBarVisible
    {
        get
        {
            return isApplicationBarVisible;
        }
        set
        {
            isApplicationBarVisible = value;
            RaisePropertyChanged();
        }
    }
}

}
```

Open up the MainPage.xaml.cs file and add the code is Listing 2-4 to setup a Model property that will delegate to the DataContext of the page. This allows us to access the view model in a strongly typed manner without having to cast it every time we need it.

Listing 2-4. Adding a Model Property to Our Page

```
// add this line in the constructor after the call
// to InitializeComponent()
Model = new MainPageViewModel;
```

```
private MainPageViewModel Model
{
    get
    {
        return (MainPageViewModel)DataContext;
    }
    set
    {
        DataContext = value;
    }
}
```

Now that we have a view model with a property of interest to our page, we need to implement a way to have the view respond to changes in that property without the view model "knowing" anything about the view. This is where dependency properties come in.

Add a DependencyProperty of type System.Boolean to the MainPage. Open the MainPage.xaml.cs file and add the code from Listing 2-5 to the code-behind.

Listing 2-5. Declaring a DependencyProperty

```
public static readonly DependencyProperty IsApplicationBarMenuEnabledProperty =
        DependencyProperty.Register("IsApplicationBarMenuEnabled",
                typeof(bool),
                typeof(MainPage),
                new PropertyMetadata(true, OnIsApplicationBarEnabledChanged));

private static void OnIsApplicationBarEnabledChanged(DependencyObject d,
        DependencyPropertyChangedEventArgs e)
{
    ((MainPage)(d)).OnIsApplicationBarEnabledChanged((bool)e.OldValue, (bool)e.NewValue);
}

private void OnIsApplicationBarEnabledChanged(bool oldValue, bool newValue)
{
    ApplicationBar.IsMenuEnabled = newValue;
}

public bool IsApplicationBarMenuEnabled
{
    // IMPORTANT: To maintain parity between setting a property in XAML
    // and procedural code, do not touch the getter and setter inside this dependency property!
    get
    {
        return (bool)GetValue(IsApplicationBarMenuEnabledProperty);
    }
    set
    {
        SetValue(IsApplicationBarMenuEnabledProperty, value);
    }
}
```

Make note of the static `OnIsApplicationBarEnabledChanged` method. Whenever a dependency property's value changes, the property changed callback method that was declared with the `PropertyMetaData` is invoked, and the instance of the object whose property has changed is passed in as the first parameter. We simply cast the object to the correct type and then invoke the instance `OnIsApplicationBarEnabledChanged` method, passing it the old and new values extracted from the `DependencyPropertyChangedEventArgs` parameter. It is in this instance method that we can now simply set the `IsMenuEnabled` property of the `ApplicationBar`.

The only thing left for us to do now is to bind our new dependency property to the corresponding property of the view model. The code in Listing 2-6 demonstrates the creation of a data binding in code. Add it to the constructor of the MainPage.xaml.cs file.

Listing 2-6. Creating a Data Binding in Code

```
// Add this code right after the previous code
Binding menuEnabledBinding = new Binding("IsMenuEnabled");
SetBinding(IsApplicationBarMenuEnabledProperty, menuEnabledBinding);
```

Run the application and you should see that the visibility of the `ApplicationBar` changes at 1-second intervals.

Using Commands

Normally when working with buttons you would bind the `Command` property of the button to the `ICommand` exposed on your view model. Since `ApplicationBarIconButton` and `ApplicationBarMenuItem` do not expose a `Command` property that option isn't available to us. The next option would be to use a Blend Attached Behavior to hook the `Click` event of the control but again we are blocked because `ApplicationBarIconButton` and `ApplicationBarMenuItem` don't inherit from `FrameworkElement`. We're going to have to use some code-behind but only just enough to get the job done.

The first thing we'll need is an implementation of the `ICommand` interface to work with. Listing 2-7 shows a sample implementation of the interface.

Listing 2-7. A Sample Implementation of the ICommand Interface

```
public class RelayCommand : ICommand
{
    readonly Action<object> execute;
    readonly Predicate<object> canExecute;

    public RelayCommand(Action<object> execute) : this(execute, null)
    {
    }
    public RelayCommand(Action<object> execute, Predicate<object> canExecute)
    {
        if (execute == null)
            throw new ArgumentNullException("execute");
        this.execute = execute;
        this.canExecute = canExecute;
    }
    [DebuggerStepThrough]
    public bool CanExecute(object parameter)
    {
        return canExecute == null ? true : canExecute(parameter);
    }
```

```
public void Execute(object parameter)
{
    execute(parameter);
}

public event EventHandler CanExecuteChanged = delegate
{
};

public void RaiseCanExecuteChanged()
{
    CanExecuteChanged(this, EventArgs.Empty);

}
}
```

We'll create a command that executes when someone taps on the advanced options menu item. Add the code in Listing 2-8 to setup a command and the supporting methods in the MainPageViewModel.

Listing 2-8. Code for the Advanced Options Menu Item Command

```
// add the following line to the end of the MainPageViewModel
// constructor to initialize the command
AdvancedOptionsCommand =
        new RelayCommand(AdvancedOptionsCommandExecute,
                AdvancedOptionsCommandCanExecute);

private RelayCommand advancedOptionsCommand;
public RelayCommand AdvancedOptionsCommand
{
    get
    {
        return advancedOptionsCommand;
    }
    set
    {
        advancedOptionsCommand = value;
        RaisePropertyChanged();
    }
}

private bool AdvancedOptionsCommandCanExecute(object parameter)
{
    return true;

}
```

```
private void AdvancedOptionsCommandExecute(object parameter)
{
    // of course, in real life, you would never use
    // a MessageBox in your view model but it's ok
    // for our purposes here...
    MessageBox.Show("Advanced Options selected.");

}
```

The last thing to do is modify the Click event handler we added to the code-behind of the MainPage in Listing 2-1 so that it calls the CanExecute and Execute methods on the AdvancedOptionsCommand property of the Model. Listing 2-9 shows the new Click handler code. Oh, and you'll also want to comment out the timer code in the MainPageViewModel constructor or you won't be able to see the menu item long enough to be able to click on it.

Listing 2-9. Executing the Command from Code-Behind

```
void AdvancedOptionsClick(object sender, EventArgs e)
{
    if(Model.AdvancedOptionsCommand.CanExecute(null)
    {
        Model.AdvancedOptionsCommand.Execute(null);
    }
}
```

By using this approach we still have code that is easy to test, and our view and view model are still loosely coupled.

2-4. Navigation
Problem

You need to provide the ability in your application to navigate to a separate page. For example, you may have a main opening page that acts as a menu and allows the user to navigate to additional pages of functionality.

Solution

Use the Navigate method of the NavigationService to launch the page from a Tap or Click event handler.

How It Works
Basic Navigation

Open Visual Studio and create a new Windows Phone App and name it BasicNavigation. Open MainPage.xaml in the editor and locate the ContentPanel grid and add a StackPanel to it. Add a Button to the StackPanel and set its Content property to "Settings." Add a second button and set its Content property to "About." Double-click the "Settings" button in the designer to add an event handler to the button's Click event. Do the same for the "About" button. Your ContentPanel for MainPage.xaml should look like Listing 2-10.

Listing 2-10. XAML for the ContentPanel in MainPage.xaml

```
<Grid x:Name="ContentPanel" Grid.Row="1" Margin="12,0,12,0">
    <StackPanel>
        <Button Content="Settings" Click="Button_Click_1"/>
        <Button Content="About" Click="Button_Click_2"/>
    </StackPanel>
</Grid>
```

Right-click on the BasicNavigation project and add a new Windows Phone Portrait Page and name it "About." Add a second page and name this one "Settings." Find the TextBlock elements in the TitlePanel section and give each page an appropriate name so you can distinguish between them when testing.

Listing 2-11. Example TitlePanel XAML for the Settings and About Pages

```
<StackPanel Grid.Row="0" Margin="12,17,0,28">
    <TextBlock Text="Widnows Phone 8 Recipes" Style="{StaticResource PhoneTextNormalStyle}"/>
    <TextBlock Text="about" Margin="9,-7,0,0" Style="{StaticResource PhoneTextTitle1Style}"/>
</StackPanel>

<StackPanel Grid.Row="0" Margin="12,17,0,28">
    <TextBlock Text="Widnows Phone 8 Recipes" Style="{StaticResource PhoneTextNormalStyle}"/>
    <TextBlock Text="settings" Margin="9,-7,0,0" Style="{StaticResource PhoneTextTitle1Style}"/>
</StackPanel>
```

The PhoneApplicationPage class exposes a read-only NavigationService property that is populated by the system with the NavigationService used to navigate to the current page. You pass a Uri to the Navigate method and the NavigationService takes care of instantiating and displaying an instance of the target page. Navigation is only supported to relative URIs that are fragments, or begin with '/', or which contain ";component/." Listing 2-12 shows the code for the Settings button Click event handler. Use this example to add code for the About button that will navigate you to the About.xaml page.

Listing 2-12. Using the NavigationService to navigate to the Settings page

```
NavigationService.Navigate(new Uri("/Settings.xaml", UriKind.Relative));
```

Navigation Events

There are three main events in the lifecycle of a page navigation. You can access these events by overriding their corresponding virtual methods listed in Table 2-3. These events together allow you to do things such as load or save data, cancel the navigation, or preconfigure the UI.

Table 2-3. *Navigation Lifecyle Events*

Method	Description
OnNavigatingTo	This method is called when the page becomes the active page in the frame. Typically you would load your data in this method.
OnNavigatingFrom	This method is called just before the page will no longer be the active page in the frame. You can use this method to cancel the navigation.
OnNavigatedFrom	This method is called just after the page is no longer the active page in the frame. You can use this method to save your data.
OnFragmentNavigation	This method is called when navigating to a fragment in the current content or to a fragment in the content of a new navigation.

Let's add some code to our project that will exercise each of these methods. Open the AboutPage.xaml file in the editor and add a StackPanel containing a TextBlock and a CheckBox to the ContentPanel. Set the properties of the controls as shown in Listing 2-13.

Listing 2-13. CheckBox in the ContentPanel of AboutPage.xaml

```
<Grid x:Name="ContentPanel" Grid.Row="1" Margin="12,0,12,0">
    <StackPanel>
        <TextBlock
            HorizontalAlignment="Left"
            TextWrapping="Wrap"
            VerticalAlignment="Top"
            x:Name="instructionTextBlock"/>
        <CheckBox
            Content="I agree"
            HorizontalAlignment="Left"
            Margin="10,10,0,0"
            VerticalAlignment="Top"
            x:Name="confirmationCheckBox"/>
    </StackPanel>
</Grid>
```

Now we'll override the OnNavigatedTo and OnNavigatingFrom methods. We'll set the Text of the instructionsTextBlock in when we navigate to the page. When we are navigating away from the page, we'll check to be sure that the user has checked the confirmationCheckBox and cancel the navigation if they haven't. Before cancelling navigation, however, we need to ascertain whether or not the system will ignore the Cancel property of the NavigatingCancelEventArgs Add the code in Listing 2-14 to the code-behind in About.xaml.cs.

Listing 2-14. Code for OnNavigatedTo and OnNavigatingFrom

```
protected override void OnNavigatedTo(NavigationEventArgs e)
{
    instructionTextBlock.Text = "Please check below to indicate you have seen this screen.";
}

protected override void OnNavigatingFrom(NavigatingCancelEventArgs e)
{
    if (!confirmationCheckBox.IsChecked ?? false)
```

```
    {
        if(e.IsCancelable)
        {
            MessageBox.Show("You must check the confirmation check box to proceed");
            e.Cancel = true;
        }
    }
}
```

The IsCancelable property will return false whenever the navigation destination is an external location. This includes other applications, launchers, and choosers. It will also return false if this is a backward navigation that is going to exit the application. You can always cancel backwards navigation no matter what by overriding the OnBackKeyPress method of the PhoneApplicationPage. This method is called when the hardware back button is pressed.

Passing Information

There are two main methods of passing information between pages during navigation. You can add one or more query parameters to the Uri that you pass to the NavigationService.Navigate method. You could pass an item identifier to a details page, for instance. The other option is to add a fragment to the Uri. The fragment is simply any text value added after the resource name and prefixed with a hash tag. Fragments are commonly used to indicate how the destination page should be displayed. Let's modify our basic navigation application to demonstrate these techniques.

Fragments

To demonstrate a common use of a fragment we modify the About page to contain a Pivot control and use the fragment to control which PivotItem is displayed when we navigate to the page.

Open About.xaml in the editor and replace the entire contents of the LayoutRoot Grid with the XAML in Listing 2-15. Add an override of the OnFragmentNavigation method using the code from Listing 2-16. You'll also want to modify the code in MainPage.xaml.cs and add "#contact" to the end of the Uri as shown in Listing 2-17.

Listing 2-15. XAML for the Modified About Page

```
<!--Pivot Control-->
<phone:Pivot x:Name="aboutPivot" Title="WINDOWS PHONE 8 RECIPES">
    <!--Pivot item one-->
    <phone:PivotItem Header="privacy">
        <Grid/>
    </phone:PivotItem>

    <!--Pivot item two-->
    <phone:PivotItem Header="contact">
        <Grid/>
    </phone:PivotItem>
</phone:Pivot>
```

Listing 2-16. OnFragmentNavigation Override for About.xaml.cs

```
protected override void OnFragmentNavigation(FragmentNavigationEventArgs e)
{
    string frag = e.Fragment;

    switch (frag)
    {
        case "privacy":

            break;
        case "contact":
            aboutPivot.SelectedIndex = 1;
            break;

    }
}
```

Listing 2-17. Using the NavigationService to navigate to the About page

```
NavigationService.Navigate(new Uri("/About.xaml#contact", UriKind.Relative));
```

You'll notice that the fragment has been conveniently parsed for us and is contained in the Fragment property of the FragmentNavigationEventArgs instance that is passed into the method. We just need to examine the fragment value and take the appropriate action. In this example, I've used it to automatically set the selected item of the Pivot control to the contact PivotItem.

QueryString Parameters

It is quite common to have a page with a list of items on it and be able to tap an item and navigate to an item details page. We need some method to tell the destination page which item we want to display. QueryString parameters are just the thing we need to accomplish this. Open up Visual Studio and create a new Windows Phone Databound App and name it MasterDetailNavigation. This template project is a good example of a master-detail navigation and also comes with sample data so this will save us a bunch of typing and let us get right into the details. This will also introduce you to the concept of an "Anchor" view model, which is a common pattern in Windows Phone 8 applications.

Take a look at the code in App.xaml.cs and notice that the App class exposes a static property of type MainViewModel that serves as the "Anchor." The fact that the lifetime of this anchor view model is tied to the application's lifetime and not to that of any particular page greatly simplifies our code. Data persistence, for example, can be handled centrally. A Windows Phone 8 application behaves more like a web application than a traditional, stateful desktop application. The lifetime of each PhoneApplicationPage is uncertain at best, and even the order in which pages are created can change depending on how they are navigated and whether the application is coming back from being tombstoned or not.

Open the MainPage.xaml.cs file and locate the MainLongListSelector_SelectionChanged method or look at Listing 2-18.

Listing 2-18. The MainLongListSelector_SelectionChanged Event Handler Method

```
private void MainLongListSelector_SelectionChanged(object sender, SelectionChangedEventArgs e)
{
    // If selected item is null (no selection) do nothing
    if (MainLongListSelector.SelectedItem == null)
        return;
```

```
// Navigate to the new page
NavigationService.Navigate(new Uri("/DetailsPage.xaml?selectedItem=" +
                (MainLongListSelector.SelectedItem as ItemViewModel).ID, UriKind.Relative));

// Reset selected item to null (no selection)
MainLongListSelector.SelectedItem = null;
}
```

The `MainLongListSeletor.SelectedItem` is tested to see if there if the user has selected anything. The selected item is cast to an `ItemViewModel` and the ID property is concatenated into the Uri as a query string parameter added to the path to the details page. One advantage of `QueryString` parameters over the use of a fragment is that you can have as many parameters as you need, whereas you are limited to a single fragment.

Listing 2-19 shows the override of the `OnNavigatedTo` method in the DetailsPage.xaml.cs file. The ID of the selected item is retrieved from the `NavigationContext.QueryString`, converted to an integer, and then used to index into the `Items` property of the anchor view model.

Listing 2-19. Override of the OnNavigatedTo Method in DetailsPage.xaml.cs

```
protected override void OnNavigatedTo(NavigationEventArgs e)
{
    if (DataContext == null)
    {
        string selectedIndex = "";
        if (NavigationContext.QueryString.TryGetValue("selectedItem", out selectedIndex))
        {

            int index = int.Parse(selectedIndex);
            DataContext = App.ViewModel.Items[index];
        }
    }
}
```

2-5. LongListSelector

Problem

You have a very long list of items and need an efficient way to display them to the user. Long lists can often consume a lot of resources because they need to create the user interface elements for every item. It should also be easy for the user to jump to parts of the list without having to scroll.

Solution

The `LongListSelector` control has become the recommended control of choice for the display of any list and you should choose it over the ListBox. First available in the Silverlight Toolkit for Windows Phone and now available as a native part of Windows Phone 8, the `LongListSelector` supports full data and UI virtualization. The `LongListSelector` can also display grouped data and has built-in provisions for group headers and footers as well as a list header and footer.

How It Works
Basic Configuration

The LongListSelector is simple to use and you configure it the same as you would a ListBox when displaying a flat list. You simply set the ItemsSource property to any collection of items that implements IList, set the ItemTemplate with a DataTemplate and the rest just works. Listing 2-20 is the LongListSelector definition from the Windows Phone Data Bound App project template:

Listing 2-20. XAML for LongListSelector Basic Configuration

```
<phone:LongListSelector
    x:Name="MainLongListSelector"
    ItemsSource="{Binding Items}"
    <phone:LongListSelector.ItemTemplate>
        <DataTemplate>
          <StackPanel Margin="0,0,0,17">
              <TextBlock
                Text="{Binding LineOne}"
                Style="{StaticResource PhoneTextExtraLargeStyle}"/>
              <TextBlock
                Text="{Binding LineTwo}"
                Margin="12,-6,12,0"
                Style="{StaticResource PhoneTextSubtleStyle}"/>
          </StackPanel>
        </DataTemplate>
    </phone:LongListSelector.ItemTemplate>
</phone:LongListSelector>
```

In fact, the LongListSelector is so similar in basic configuration to a ListBox that you can actually replace the phone:LongListSelector with ListBox and it will just work. Visually, you won't even notice the difference. However, you won't find the ListBox in the Visual Studio ToolBox. This was done to emphasize that the LongListSelector is now the default choice and to encourage its use when displaying lists of data. You can still use the ListBox if you want, but you must type it in directly in you XAML.

As mentioned earlier, you can set the ItemsSource to any collection of data that implements IList. The most common choice is the ObserveableCollection<T> . Since it derives from Collection<T> it has support for IList and adds support for INotifyCollectionChanged which allows any ItemsControl bound to it to automatically detect additions and deletions and update the UI accordingly.

Create a new Windows Phone Data Bound App and then open the MainViewModel.cs file in the editor. Notice how there is a hard-coded list of items being added to the Items property. While this gets the job done, it doesn't scale particularly well. What if you wanted to try out your list with a thousand items? Listing 2-21 shows a neat trick using LINQ to quickly generate as many items as you want in just a couple of statements. The declarative nature of LINQ makes it a very powerful tool when it comes to data manipulation. We'll revisit LINQ when we get to grouping data in a later section.

Listing 2-21. Sample test data using LINQ

```
var testItems = from number in Enumerable.Range(1, 1000)
                select new ItemViewModel
                {
                    ID = number.ToString(),
                    LineOne = "First Line " + number,
```

```
                    LineTwo = "Second Line " + number,
                    LineThree = "Third Line " + number
                };
Items = new ObservableCollection<ItemViewModel>(testItems);
```

For scenarios where you just want to get some data into the list and don't need view models, data binding and collection change notification you can set the ItemsSource to the results of a LINQ statement by simply calling the ToList() extension method as shown in Listing 2-22.

Listing 2-22. Setting the ItemsSource to the Results of a LINQ Statement

```
var testItems = from number in Enumerable.Range(1, 1000)
                select new ItemViewModel
                {
                    ID = number.ToString(),
                    LineOne = "First Line " + number,
                    LineTwo = "Second Line " + number,
                    LineThree = "Third Line " + number
                };
MyLongListSelector.ItemsSource = testItems.ToList();
```

In the next section we'll take a look at creating the various templates that define the look of the LongListSelector control.

Templating

The LongListSelector exposes several properties of type DataTemplate that define the look of the various parts of the control. Table 2-4 lists these properties.

Table 2-4. *Template and Style Properties of the LongListSelector*

Property	Description
ListHeaderTemplate	The DataTemplate that defines the item to be displayed in the header of the LongListSelector. It appears once at the top of the control.
ListFooterTemplate	The DataTemplate that defines the item to be displayed in the footer of the LongListSelector. It appears once at the bottom of the control.
GroupHeaderTemplate	The DataTemplate that defines the item that will appear at the top of a group just before the first item in the group. The group header will appear once at the top of each group of items displayed.
GroupFooterTemplate	The DataTemplate that defines the item that will appear at the bottom of a group after the last item in the group. The group footer will appear once at the bottom of each group of items displayed.
ItemTemplate	The DataTemplate that defines the item that will be displayed for each item in the underlying list of data.
JumpListStyle	The Style used to display the jump list when the user taps on a GroupHeader. You define the DataTemplate for the jump list within the JumpListStyle.

Screen space is always at a premium on mobile devices so you need to be aware of how best to use that space when designing your pages. It will probably be a rare occasion when you need to use the `ListHeader` and `ListFooter`. Most likely your list will be hosted in a `PhoneApplicationPage` or `PivotItem` and the `TitlePanel` content of the page or the `Title` and `Header` information of the `PivotItem` should be enough of a description for your list. Figure 2-5 shows a screen shot from the TheLongListSelector sample project. Any additional information would just be redundant.

Figure 2-5. *Sample LongListSelector hosted in PivotItem*

From the sample screenshot in Figure 2-5 you can also see that the `GroupFooter` would more than likely be redundant and add nothing to the display of information. The end of one group is quite effectively demarcated by the header of the next group.

As always when creating your UI you should follow the Modern UI desing guidelines. Listing 2-23 shows the definition of an `ItemTemplate` taken from the Chapter two sample code.

Listing 2-23. ItemTemplate Sample for LongListSelector

```
<DataTemplate x:Name="AlphaItemTemplate">
    <Grid Margin="0,0,0,17">
        <Grid.ColumnDefinitions>
            <ColumnDefinition Width="128"/>
            <ColumnDefinition />
        </Grid.ColumnDefinitions>
```

```
            <Grid.RowDefinitions>
                <RowDefinition/>
                <RowDefinition/>
            </Grid.RowDefinitions>
            <Image
                Grid.Row="0"
                Grid.RowSpan="2"
                Source="{Binding FlagUri}"/>
            <TextBlock
                VerticalAlignment="Center"
                Grid.Column="1"
                Margin="6,0,0,0"
                Text="{Binding EnglishName}"
                Style="{StaticResource PhoneTextLargeStyle}"/>
            <TextBlock
                VerticalAlignment="Top"
                Grid.Column="1"
                Grid.Row="1"
                Margin="6,0,0,0"
                Text="{Binding LocalName}"
                Style="{StaticResource PhoneTextNormalStyle}"/>
        </Grid>
</DataTemplate>
```

■ **Note** You should use make use of the default styles provided with the SDK as much as possible. Styles are provided for TextBlocks as well as some predefined styles for the LongListSelector control. This will help to ensure that your application provides a consistent visual experience for the user. You can find these styles in C:\Program Files (x86)\Microsoft SDKs\Windows Phone\v8.0\Design.

The JumpListStyle is a little different and deserves some further investigation. The JumpListStyle property is of type Style and targets the LongListSelector control type. The alphabetic jump list is almost certainly the most common. Listing 2-24 shows the style for the alphabetic grouping sample in the sample code project.

Listing 2-24. Alphabetic Jump List Style

```
<Style x:Key="LongListSelectorJumpListGridStyle" TargetType="phone:LongListSelector">
    <Setter Property="GridCellSize"  Value="111,111"/>
    <Setter Property="LayoutMode" Value="Grid" />
    <Setter Property="Margin" Value="18,12,0,0"/>
    <Setter Property="ItemTemplate">
        <Setter.Value>
            <DataTemplate>
                <Border
                    Margin="6"
                    Background="{Binding Converter={StaticResource BackgroundConverter}}">
                    <TextBlock
                        Margin="6,0,0,0"
```

```
                    Text="{Binding Key}"
                    Style="{StaticResource JumpListAlphabetStyle}"/>
                </Border>
            </DataTemplate>
        </Setter.Value>
    </Setter>
</Style>
```

There are a couple of properties of note being set in the style. The first is the LayoutMode property. This property gets it value from the LongListSelectorLayoutMode enumeration and the valid values are Grid and List. The jump list items will be arranged in a WrapPanel when the LayoutMode is set to Grid and you must define a size for the cells in the GridCellSize. The values for the GridCellSize probably strike you as a bit odd. How did we arrive at the value of 111? Running the application shows that there are four letters per row in the alphabetic jump list so we'll base our calculations on that assumption.

Refer back to the values in Table 2-1. You'll recall that when setting the height or width of an element you do so using device independent pixels. The logical width of the screen then is always 480 device independent pixels. You'll notice in the style that we are setting an 18-pixel margin on the left side of the jump list only. Assuming that we want to be left with a corresponding 18 pixel margin that would leave us with 480 - 36 = 444 pixels for our cells. The math from here is left as an exercise for the reader.[3]

Look back at Listing 2-24 and notice the reference to a static resource named "BackgroundConverter" in the binding for the Background of the Border in the ItemTemplate of the style. This resource is declared at the top of the resource section and is an instance of the JumpListItemBackgroundConverter. There is also a JumpListItemForegroundConverter. These are two value converters provided by the framework that will automatically determine the right colors based on the user's preferences and return a SolidColorBrush.

Listing 2-25. Declaration of the Jump List Converters

```
<phone:JumpListItemBackgroundConverter x:Key="BackgroundConverter"/>
<phone:JumpListItemForegroundConverter x:Key="ForegroundConverter"/>
```

Shaping the Data

One of the most useful features of the LongListSelector is its ability to provide quick navigation through the list using grouping and the built-in "jump list." Grouping controls that I've worked with usually have built-in support for grouping and displaying data with no shaping of the data required. They do this by making use of the HierarchicalDataTemplate. This is not the case with the LongListSelector and you need to shape the data yourself.

Each grouping of data needs two things: a property that serves as the group key and an enumerable list of items. While you could create your own type from scratch by implementing IList, IList<T>, IEnumerable<T>, and ICollection<T> along with INotifyCollectionChanged so that the addition and removal of items in the list can be observed by the LongListSelector control, that's a lot of work. Fortunately for us, the framework already provides us with 99% of what we need in the form of the ObservableCollection<T> and we can simply subclass that. Adding a property to serve as the group key and some appropriate constructors finishes the implementation. Listing 2-26 shows the just such a class.

---

[3]That's three. One cliché every 10 pages so far. That's not bad.

Listing 2-26. The ObservableLongListGroup Collection

```
public class ObservableLongListGroup<T> : ObservableCollection<T>
{
    public ObservableLongListGroup(IEnumerable<T> collection, string key)
        : base(collection)
    {
        this.Key = key;
    }

    public ObservableLongListGroup(List<T> list, string key)
        : base(list)
    {
        this.Key = key;
    }

    public string Key { get;  set; }

}
```

We'll also use the ObservableCollection<T> to expose our groups on the view model using our ObservableLongListGroup as the generic type. You could create the groups and populate their items one at a time by iteratating over your main list of items, but there is a far more efficient and elegant way of grouping your data using LINQ. Listing 2-27 shows the properties and methods in the main view model of the sample application that creates two groupings. The first one is grouped by the first letter and the second is grouped by the country's region.

Listing 2-27. Grouping the list of coutries using LINQ

```
public ObservableCollection<ObservableLongListGroup<Country>> CountriesByFirstLetter
{
    get;
    set;
}

public ObservableCollection<ObservableLongListGroup<Country>> CountriesByWorldRegion
{
    get;
    set;
}

private void PopulateGroupsByWorldRegion()
{
    var byWorldRegion = from country in Countries
                        group country by country.WorldRegion into groupedCountries
                        orderby groupedCountries.Key ascending
                        select new ObservableLongListGroup<Country>
                            (
                                    groupedCountries, groupedCountries.Key
                            );
```

```
                    CountriesByWorldRegion = new ObservableCollection<ObservableLongListGroup<Country>>
                            (
                                    byWorldRegion
                            );
}

private void PopulateGroupsByFirstLetter()
{
    var byFirstLetter = from country in Countries
                        group country by country.EnglishName.Substring(0, 1).ToLower()
                        into groupedCountries
                        orderby groupedCountries.Key ascending
                        select new ObservableLongListGroup<Country>
                            (
                                    groupedCountries, groupedCountries.Key
                            );

    CountriesByFirstLetter = new ObservableCollection<ObservableLongListGroup<Country>>
                            (
                                    byFirstLetter
                            );
}
```

Now that we have our data we just need to bind the items to our LongListSelector as its ItemsSource and attach the required templates. In your GroupHeaderTemplate and JumpListStyle you can bind the Key property of the ObservableLongListGroup to a TextBlock to display the group. Listing 2-28 shows the templates from the sample application.

Listing 2-28. GroupHeaderTemplate and JumpListStyle from the Sample Application

```xml
<DataTemplate x:Name="AlphaGroupHeaderTemplate">
    <Border
        BorderThickness="1"
        Background="{Binding Converter={StaticResource BackgroundConverter}}"
        HorizontalAlignment="Left"
        Width="50">
        <TextBlock
            Foreground="{Binding Converter={StaticResource ForegroundConverter}}"
            Text="{Binding Key}"
            Style="{StaticResource LongListSelectorGroupHeaderStyle}"/>
        </Border>
</DataTemplate>

<Style x:Key="LongListSelectorJumpListGridStyle" TargetType="phone:LongListSelector">
    <Setter Property="GridCellSize"  Value="111,111"/>
    <Setter Property="LayoutMode" Value="Grid" />
    <Setter Property="Margin" Value="18,12,0,0"/>
    <Setter Property="ItemTemplate">
        <Setter.Value>
            <DataTemplate>
                <Border
                    Margin="6"
```

```
                    BorderThickness="1"
                    BorderBrush="{Binding Converter={StaticResource BackgroundConverter}}">
                    <TextBlock
                        Margin="6,0,0,0"
                        Text="{Binding Key}"
                        Style="{StaticResource JumpListAlphabetStyle}"/>
                    </Border>
                </DataTemplate>
            </Setter.Value>
        </Setter>
</Style>
```

2-6. Using the Windows Phone Toolkit

Problem

You've created a Windows Phone Application but the SDK doesn't contain certain user interface components that would make it special. Things like an `AutoCompleteBox`, `RatingControl`, and some animation effects would be very useful.

Solution

Install the Windows Phone Toolkit provided by Microsoft on the CodePlex website.

How It Works

The Windows Phone Toolkit provides a collection of controls, extension methods, and page animations. Using the toolkit will allow you to create more visually interesting and consistent Windows Phone user interfaces and make common progamming tasks easier.

Formerly called the Silverlight Toolkit for Windows Phone, the toolkit has been given its own separate home on the CodePlex site at `http://phone.codeplex.com`. With an uncharacteristic flourish of creativity, Microsoft has also rebranded the toolkit and given it a dynamic new name: "Windows Phone Toolkit" or "WPToolkit," for short.[4]

Installation

The WPToolkit was previously provided as an MSI-based installer. The Visual Studio extension NuGet has become increasingly popular and just recently the NuGet Gallery surpassed 50 million downloads. The NuGet package manager is also included with Visual Studio 2012 right out of the box. Given this popularity many third-party toolkits and libraries are choosing NuGet as their installation and distribution channel. The WPToolkit is now hosted in the NuGet Gallery.

■ **Note**   To get started with NuGet when working with Windows Phone 8 projects you need to be sure that you have upgraded your version of NuGet to at least version 2.1. Installation and upgrade information along with instructions for use can be found on the NuGet documentation website at `http://docs.nuget.org`.

---

[4]Sarcastic? Me? Never.

Once you have the most recent version, use the package manager to add the WPToolkit libraries to a new Windows Phone App.

Referencing the Controls

Once you have added the WPToolkit to your project you'll notice a new reference to the `Microsoft.Phone.Controls.Toolkit` assembly. You need to define an XML namespace in your XAML so that you can use the controls in the toolkit. The samples available on `http://phone.codeplex.com` are quite comprehensive so we won't go into any depth here. Listing 2-29 shows the namespace reference and a sample of the `Rating` control.

Listing 2-29. XML Namespace for the WPToolkit in XAML

```
<!-- add to the list of namespace declarations at the top of the XAML-->
xmlns:toolkit="clr-namespace:Microsoft.Phone.Controls;assembly=Microsoft.Phone.Controls.Toolkit"

        <!--ContentPanel - place additional content here-->
        <Grid x:Name="ContentPanel" Grid.Row="1" Margin="12,0,12,0">
            <Grid.RowDefinitions>
                <RowDefinition/>
                <RowDefinition/>
            </Grid.RowDefinitions>
            <toolkit:Rating
                Width="250"
                Height="50"
                x:Name="RatingControl"
                RatingItemCount="5"
                Value="3.5"
                ShowSelectionHelper="True"/>
            <TextBlock
                HorizontalAlignment="Center"
                Grid.Row="1"
                Style="{StaticResource PhoneTextTitle1Style}"
                Text="{Binding ElementName=RatingControl, Path=Value}"/>

        </Grid>
```

CHAPTER 3

■ ■ ■

Gestures

When designing a Windows Phone app, an important design feature to keep in mind is the use of gestures. A user will mainly interact with his Windows Phone through the device's touch screen. Through a series of recipes, this chapter will explore the gesture support provided in the Windows Phone SDK, and will help you to design apps that leverage this functionality, by providing the right formula of gesture support for your app.

In this chapter, we will add the following recipes to your developer palate:

- 3-1. Select the Right Action For Your App

- 3-2. Tap, DoubleTap or (Tap-And-)Hold

- 3-3. Don't Be a Drag, Just Flick It

- 3-4. Pinch to Zoom

- 3-5. Be Generous With Size and Considerate of Space

3-1. Select The Right Action For Your App
Problem

You want to develop an app that allows users to interact with objects on the screen using the touch screen, and you want to know which type of actions the device supports.

Solution

Gain an understanding of the gesture and manipulation support available for Windows Phone.

How It Works

Within a Windows Phone app, you can allow your users to interact with the app through the touch screen in a variety of ways, through single- or multi-touch gestures. Single-touch gestures include tap, double-tap, tap-and-hold, pan, and flick. Multi-touch gestures include pinch to zoom in and out. Table 3-1 lists the gestures available with a brief description and examples of when to use each gesture.

Table 3-1. *Single-Touch Gestures*

Gesture	Description	Usage Examples
Tap	The user touches the device screen with a single finger and releases.	Used to trigger a button click, select an item in a list, set focus to an input field such as a textbox, check/uncheck a checkbox, etc.
Double-Tap	The user touches and releases the device screen two times, in quick succession.	A common use for this action is to magnify content, such as text, images or map locations, on the first double-tap action, then zoom out on the second double-tap action.
Tap-And-Hold	The user touches the device screen, and does not release his finger.	A common use for this action is to display a context menu on the item that is the target of the tap-and-hold gesture.
Drag or Pan	The user touches the device screen and drags his finger across the screen in any direction without releasing his finger.	Drag an object to a new location on the screen.
Flick	The user touches the device screen and drags his finger partially across the screen in any direction and quickly releases his finger.	Make an object disappear off screen, flip a "page", slide to the view the next item (photo slide show), etc.
Pinch	The user touches the device screen with two fingers and moves them either closer together or farther apart.	Zoom in or out of an object on a screen.

It is important to note that Windows Phone supports up to four simultaneous touch input points. However, when including more than two simultaneous touch input points on a page, there may be a performance cost since this will create an additional load on the device's processor. This is important to keep in mind when designing your app.

You can employ gesture-based actions in the following ways:

1. Events provided in the UIElement class, including mouse-based events, single-touch gesture events (i.e., Tap, DoubleTap, Hold), and multi-touch gesture events (i.e., ManipulationStarted, ManipulationDelta, and ManipulationCompleted). We will explore this approach in Recipe 3-2: Tap, DoubleTap, or (Tap-And-)Hold.

2. Touch class, which processes touch input and raises an event, FrameReported. This event returns pertinent information related to the touch action such as the primary touch point and its position, as well as a collection of touch. Each touch point's x- and y-coordinate position can also be obtained, relative to a UIElement or the full content area. This approach is also discussed in Recipe 3-2: Tap, DoubleTap, or (Tap-And-)Hold.

3. Implementing a GestureListener through the GestureService that comes packaged in the Windows Phone Toolkit to attach event listeners to Windows Phone controls, either individually, or at a top-level. We will explore this approach in Recipe 3-3: Flick It.

3-2. Tap, DoubleTap, or (Tap-And-)Hold
Problem

You want to make your app simple, engaging, and interactive for the user by leveraging the touch screen capabilities of the device.

Solution

Include the desired actions on the Windows Phone controls by leveraging the Tap, DoubleTap, and Hold events.

How It Works

In this recipe, we will focus on the tap-specific gestures, since they are the type of gestures that most apps will likely handle at least once. All Windows Phone controls that derive from the UIElement class include the gesture-based events which are listed in Table 3-2. Keep in mind that for this section, we will only be working with the Tap, DoubleTap, and Hold events.

Table 3-2. *System.Window.UIElement Events*

Events	Event Arguments	Triggered when...
Tap	GestureEventArgs	The user touches the area on the screen where a UIElement appears and releases the touch immediately. GestureEventArgs provides information on the position where the gestured occurred, either relative to a UIElement or the overall content area.
DoubleTap	GestureEventArgs	The user taps the area on the screen where the UIElement is displayed two times, in quick succession.
Hold	GestureEventArgs	User touches the area on the screen where a UIElement appears and does not release the touch immediately.
ManipulationStarted	ManipulationStartedEventArgs	The user touches the area on the screen where a UIElement is displayed, with one or more fingers. ManipulationStartedEventArgs provides information on the source object that invoked the event, the point that the manipulation originated from, and the container that defines the coordinates for the manipulation.
ManipulationDelta	ManipulationDeltaEventArgs	The user continues the manipulation by moving his finger(s) across the screen without releasing. This event is triggered more than once during a manipulation. ManipulationDeltaEventArgs provides information on the current manipulation including accumulated changes, the most recent change, the rate of change (or velocities), and if the change occurred during inertia.
ManipulationCompleted	ManipulationCompletedEventArgs	The user releases his finger(s) from the screen to end the manipulation. ManipulationCompletedEventArgs provides information on the total transformation that occurred during manipulation, the total rate of change (or velocities), and if the completed event occurred during inertia.

To explore the tap gesture events that may be triggered, we will create a new Windows Phone app which will perform the following actions:

1. Display a single circle on initial launch.

2. Change background color of circle when it is tapped.

3. Create a copy of the circle when it is double-tapped.

4. Display a context menu when the user taps and holds a single circle.

Although the Windows Phone Toolkit comes packaged with a ContextMenu control, we will create our own custom context menu to demonstrate how to use the Hold event along with how to obtain the current touch input point location that the user's finger pressed. This is a "bonus" feature you will learn in this recipe!

Designing the UI

To start, we will need to create a new Windows Phone project. Launch Visual Studio 2012, and create a new Windows Phone project using the same steps provided in Chapter 1, Recipe 1-2. Name the project "TapIt". We will be using the WrapPanel control that comes packaged in the Windows Phone Toolkit. Follow the instructions provided in Chapter 2, Recipe 2-5, to add the toolkit into this project using NuGet.

The next step we will take is to set up the objects we will be working with in the MainPage's XAML markup. We will add a single circle as the initial display object, and place it within a WrapPanel so that as the user adds new objects to the screen, the shapes will automatically wrap around and fill the screen, instead of going off-screen. As we delete objects, we want the existing objects to automatically re-adjust to remove any empty space between objects, which the WrapPanel will handle for us.

To accomplish this, we will need to add the namespace declaration for the `Microsoft.Phone.Controls.Toolkit` assembly to the PhoneApplicationPage root element in the MainPage.xaml file so that we can add the WrapPanel control to the page:

```
<phone:PhoneApplicationPage x:Class="TapIt.MainPage"
xmlns:toolkit="clr-namespace:Microsoft.Phone.Controls;assembly=Microsoft.Phone.Controls.Toolkit"
```

Next, we want to remove the default StackPanels that are added to the LayoutRoot grid by default. We will replace Grid, named ContentPanel, with a WrapPanel instead. This will be the container to which circles are added. Although we could use any type of layout panel to host the shapes, such as a Grid, Canvas, or StackPanel, we will go with the WrapPanel for this example. The reason for this is that the WrapPanel will automatically arrange the shapes as they are added to or deleted from the container. To add the WrapPanel, add the following XAML within the LayoutRoot grid:

```
<toolkit:WrapPanel Name="ContentPanel" />
```

We also need to include a popup menu that will serve as a context menu when a Hold event is triggered on a circle. This can be accomplished simply by adding a Popup control, a ListBox control, and the relevant List Items we want to serve as options in the context menu. For this example, let's create a context menu that allows the user to change color, add a new circle, or delete the current circle. We will add the XAML for the Popup within the LayoutRoot grid.

```
<Popup Name="menuEllipse">
    <ListBox Name="listMenuItems"
            Background="White"
            Foreground="Black"
            BorderBrush="Gray"
            BorderThickness="5"
```

```
            SelectionChanged="listMenuItems_SelectionChanged"
            Width="150"
            Height="150">
      <ListBoxItem Name="itemColorChange" Content="change color" Padding="10" />
      <ListBoxItem Name="itemNew" Content="add circle" Padding="10" />
      <ListBoxItem Name="itemDelete" Content="delete" Padding="10"/>
   </ListBox>
</Popup>
```

Before we head to the code behind, we need to add an event handler for the PhoneApplicationPage's Loaded event within the phone:PhoneApplicationPage element:

```
Loaded="PhoneApplicationPage_Loaded"
```

Creating Shapes Programmatically

With that, we have our UI in place. Now let's head to the code behind file to make this application fully functional!

To navigate to the code behind, hit the F7 key, or double-click on the MainPage.xaml.cs file. The first thing you will notice is that the Loaded event we attached to the page from the XAML file has already been added in the code behind. The first thing we want the application to handle on the initial load is displaying the first circle. Since we know this same code will be used from multiple locations, we can place it in its own method. In addition to that, there will be other common methods we will need to create, so we can start off on the right foot and create a separate helper class for these methods.

In Visual Studio, right-click on the project, and select Add > Class... from the menu. Within the Add New Item dialog, set the class name to EllipseManager.cs, and click the Add button.

The type of methods we will create here will be used to add new shapes, as well as change colors of the selected shapes. We can make this a static class, since this will be used to contain helper methods, and separate instances of it are not necessary. To accomplish this, simply include the static keyword in the class declaration:

```
static class EllipseManager
```

Next, add the following using directives to the class:

```
using System.Windows;
using System.Windows.Shapes;
using System.Windows.Media;
```

Now that we have a shell of our helper class in place, along with the required namespace declarations, let's create a method that will create a new ellipse, set some defaults on the shape, and return the ellipse to the calling procedure, as shown in Listing 3-1.

Listing 3-1. AddEllipse Method Will Return an Ellipse with a Default Color, Border, and Size

```
public static Ellipse AddEllipse()
{
    Ellipse newEllipse = new Ellipse();
    newEllipse.Stroke = new SolidColorBrush(Colors.Gray);
    newEllipse.StrokeThickness = 5;
    newEllipse.Height = 200;
    newEllipse.Width = 200;
    newEllipse.Margin = new Thickness(10);
```

```
newEllipse.Fill = new SolidColorBrush(Colors.Purple);
newEllipse.HorizontalAlignment = HorizontalAlignment.Left;
newEllipse.VerticalAlignment = VerticalAlignment.Top;

return newEllipse;
}
```

Everytime we create a new ellipse, we are setting the default color to the same color each time. This can be quite boring. Let's spice it up a little and have each new ellipse set to a different fill color. In addition to that, we will also want to change the ellipse's fill color anytime the user taps the shape.

Let's create a new method which will return a random color each time it is called. Name the method, GetNextColor, and set its return value to a SolidColorBrush. We will also leverage .NET's built-in random number generator, System.Random, to generate values for the A, R, G, B properties (i.e., alpha, red, green, and blue channels whose combined values define a color), as shown in Listing 3-2.

Listing 3-2. GetNextColor Will Return a Random Color Each Time it is Called

```
//random number generator used to generate the RGB values for a color
private static Random _random = new Random();
public static SolidColorBrush GetNextColor()
{
    Color newColor = new Color();
    newColor.A = (byte)255;
    newColor.R = (byte)_random.Next(0, 256);
    newColor.G = (byte)_random.Next(0, 256);
    newColor.B = (byte)_random.Next(0, 256);
    return new SolidColorBrush(newColor);
}
```

Registering the Events

Now it's time to revisit the MainPage code-behind to work on wiring up the events that are needed so we can manage the user's gestures accordingly. The events we need to handle on the ellipse are the Tap, DoubleTap, and Hold events. We will create a method, named AttachEventHandlers, that accepts an ellipse as a parameter. We will attach the Tap, DoubleTap, and Hold events to each new ellipse that is created by calling this method, and passing in the shape. For completeness, we should also create a similiar method to detach the event handlers when the ellipse is deleted by the user, as shown in Listing 3-3. Last, but not least, remember to add the using directive for the System.Windows.Shapes namespace to the class, since we will be dealing with the Ellipse object in the code.

Listing 3-3. Register the Gesture-based Event Handlers for Each Ellipse

```
private void AttachEventHandlers(Ellipse targetEllipse)
{
    targetEllipse.Tap +=
new System.EventHandler<System.Windows.Input.GestureEventArgs>( Ellipse_Tapped);
    targetEllipse.DoubleTap +=
new System.EventHandler<System.Windows.Input.GestureEventArgs>( Ellipse_DoubleTapped);
    targetEllipse.Hold +=
new System.EventHandler<System.Windows.Input.GestureEventArgs>( Ellipse_Held);
}
```

```
private void RemoveEventHandlers(Ellipse targetEllipse)
{
    targetEllipse.Tapped -= new System.EventHandler<System.Windows.Input.GestureEventArgs>( Ellipse_Tap);
    targetEllipse.DoubleTapped -= new
System.EventHandler<System.Windows.Input.GestureEventArgs>( Ellipse_DoubleTap);
    targetEllipse.Held -= new
System.EventHandler<System.Windows.Input.GestureEventArgs>(Ellipse_Hold);
}
```

Managing Tap-Specific Gestures

Next, we will need to add code to these events, so that when the ellipse receives the respective gesture, something will happen on screen to reflect that action.

Within the `Ellipse_Tapped` event handler, we will set the Fill property of the tapped ellipse to the newly generated color. We will also check to see if a previous context menu is open from a previous action, and close it accordingly.

Within the `Ellipse_DoubleTapped` event handler, we will create a new circle with default properties set, attach the gesture event handlers so that the object will do something, and add the circle to the main WrapPanel. We will separate out this code into its own method, because it will also be called from the context menu and during the initial load. The resulting code is shown in Listing 3-4.

Listing 3-4. Handling the Tap and DoubleTap Events on the Ellipse

```
private void Ellipse_Tapped(object sender, System.Windows.Input.GestureEventArgs e)
{
    if (menuEllipse.IsOpen)
    {
        //if the context menu is open but the user taps
        //outside of the menu, then close it
        menuEllipse.IsOpen = false;
    }

    Ellipse sourceEllipse = (Ellipse)sender;
    sourceEllipse.Fill = EllipseManager.GetNextColor();
}

private void Ellipse_DoubleTapped(object sender, System.Windows.Input.GestureEventArgs e)
{
        Ellipse newEllipse = EllipseManager.AddEllipse();
        AttachEventHandlers(newEllipse);
        ContentPanel.Children.Add(newEllipse);
}

//since this set of actions will be called from multiple
//events, it is ideal to place it in a separate method for reusability
private void AddNewEllipse()
{
        Ellipse newEllipse = EllipseManager.AddEllipse();
        AttachEventHandlers(newEllipse);
        ContentPanel.Children.Add(newEllipse);
}
```

Finally, we will handle the Ellipse_Held event to display a context menu for the selected object. The desired effect is to have the context menu appear in the area of the selected ellipse. To capture the location of the screen that was touched, we will need to leverage the Touch class in the System.Windows.Input library. The Touch class is a static class that processes touch input that it receives and raises the FrameReported event. We will need to handle this event to obtain the points on the screen the user touched, as shown in Listing 3-5.

Listing 3-5. Use the Touch Class to Capture the Location That Was Touched

```
using System.Windows.Input;

//variable used to store the touch input point
//that was received in the Touch_FrameReported event
Point lastTouchedPoint = new Point(0,0);
public MainPage()
{
    InitializeComponent();

    Touch.FrameReported += Touch_FrameReported;

}

void Touch_FrameReported(object sender, TouchFrameEventArgs e)
{
    TouchPointCollection touchPoints = e.GetTouchPoints(this);

    if (touchPoints.Count > 0)
    {
        //get the first touch point position from the collection
        lastTouchedPoint = touchPoints[0].Position;
    }

    //Note: if you wanted to track multiple touch input point positions,
    //simply iterate through the touchPoints collection using foreach and
    //handle each touch input point position accordingly
}
```

When the FrameReported event is triggered, we can obtain the touch points from the TouchFrameEventArgs parameter, by calling its GetTouchPoints method. This method will return a collection of touch points, each one containing a Point value that in turn includes the coordinate values representing the touched location on the device's screen.

With that in place, we can now include the necessary actions in the Ellipse_Held event handler to display the context menu in a location on-screen relative to the shape the user tapped and held. The resulting code is shown in Listing 3-6.

Listing 3-6. Display the Context Menu When the User Taps and Holds an Ellipse

```
private void Ellipse_Held(object sender, System.Windows.Input.GestureEventArgs e)
{
    Ellipse sourceEllipse = (Ellipse)sender;

    //if the point touched is near the right edge of the screen, adjust the
    //HorizontalOffset for the context menu to ensure that it is displayed
```

```
    //within the bounds of the screen
    if ((lastTouchedPoint.X + listMenuItems.Width) > this.ActualWidth)
        lastTouchedPoint.X = this.ActualWidth - listMenuItems.Width;

    //if the point touched is near the bottom edge of the screen, adjust the
    //VerticalOffset for the context menu to ensure that it is displayed
    //within the bounds of the screen
    if ((lastTouchedPoint.Y + listMenuItems.Height) > this.ActualHeight)
        lastTouchedPoint.Y = this.ActualHeight - listMenuItems.Height;

    menuEllipse.HorizontalOffset = lastTouchedPoint.X;
    menuEllipse.VerticalOffset = lastTouchedPoint.Y;
    menuEllipse.IsOpen = true;

    //set the Tag of the context menu to the selected ellipse
    //so that on menu item selection, the action that is taken
    //against the shape that triggered the event
    menuEllipse.Tag = sourceEllipse;

}
```

On initial launch of the application, we will need to create the first shape and add it to the screen. To accomplish this task, call the AddNewEllipse() method within the PhoneApplicationPage_Loaded event.

Last but not least, we will need to add code within the SelectionChanged event for the ListBox, to ensure it will take the appropriate action based on the menu item that was selected, as shown in Listing 3-7.

Listing 3-7. Take the Required Action Based on the Menu Item That Was Selected

```
private void listMenuItems_SelectionChanged(object sender,
System.Windows.Controls.SelectionChangedEventArgs e)
{
    if (e.AddedItems.Count == 0)
        return;

    Ellipse sourceEllipse = menuEllipse.Tag as Ellipse;
    menuEllipse.Tag = null;
    menuEllipse.IsOpen = false;

    ListBoxItem item = (ListBoxItem)e.AddedItems[0];
    switch (item.Content.ToString())
    {
        case "add circle":
            AddNewEllipse();
            break;
        case "change color":
            sourceEllipse.Fill = EllipseManager.GetNextColor();
            break;
        case "delete":
            RemoveEventHandlers(sourceEllipse);
            ContentPanel.Children.Remove(sourceEllipse);
            break;
    }
```

```
    //reset the state of the listbox so that the selected item
    //no longer appears to be selected on the next display of the menu
    listMenuItems.ClearValue(ListBox.SelectedItemProperty);
}
```

Testing the App

Now we can build and launch our app either in the emulator or on a device, and take it for a test drive! Hit the F5 key, or click the Start Debugging button in Visual Studio, to launch the app. Figure 3-1 depicts the screen on the initial launch of the application.

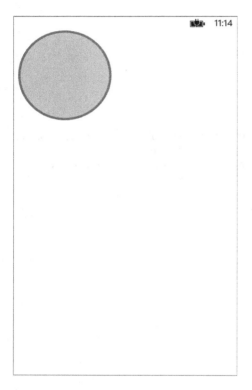

Figure 3-1. TapIt main page on initial launch

Test out the Tap gesture by tapping on the circle, pausing in between taps, to ensure only the Tap event is triggered. Notice that the circle's Fill color changes with each tap.

Next, try double-tapping on the circle. This should create a copy of the circle and display it directly next to the circle. Continue to test this out until you fill the screen with circles. You should see something similar to what is depicted in Figure 3-2, although the colors will vary.

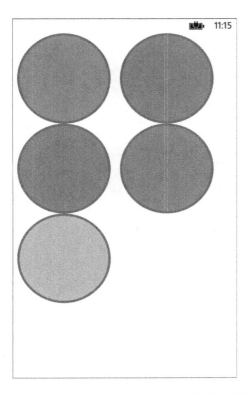

Figure 3-2. *Result after testing out the DoubleTap event*

Finally, let's test the context menu. Tap and hold any of the circles on screen. The context menu should display in the location that you performed the tap and hold action, as shown in Figure 3-3.

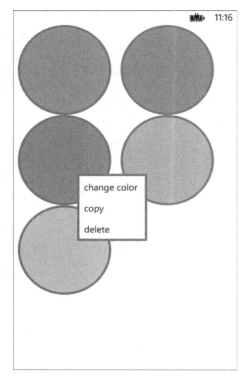

Figure 3-3. *Context menu is displayed for the shape that was tapped and held*

Test out each menu item on the context menu to ensure the actions are working as expected.

To view the full source code for this applicaton, refer to the TapIt project in the \Chapter 3\TapIt directory.

3-3. Don't Be A Drag, Just Flick It

Problem

You really like the app you created in Recipe 3-2, but you want to enhance it by allowing the user to drag objects around and remove them from the screen with a simple flick of the finger.

Solution

Leverage the GestureService that is packaged in the Windows Phone Toolkit to attach a GestureListener to the page, and include handlers for the DragStarted, DragDelta, DragCompleted, and Flick events.

How It Works

The Windows Phone Toolkit's GestureListener simplifies the manner in which you can detect touch gestures in your application. It provides you with the ability to attach a listener to a FrameworkElement, and implement handlers for both single and multi-touch gestures. Table 3-3 lists the events that are available in the GestureListener class.

Table 3-3. *Event Handlers Available in the Windows Phone Toolkit's GestureListener Service*

Events	Event Arguments	Contains information about...
GestureBegin, GestureCompleted, Tap, DoubleTap, Hold	GestureEventArgs	The x- and y-coordinates of the position where the gestured occurred, either relative to a UIElement, or the overall content area.
DragStarted	DragStartedGestureEventArgs	Same as GestureEventArgs, as well as the direction of the drag (i.e., Horizontal or Vertical).
DragDelta	DragDeltaGestureEventArgs	Same as DragStartedGestureEventArgs as well as the distance the gesture has moved horizontally and vertically (HorizontalChange, VerticalChange)
DragCompleted	DragCompletedGestureEventArgs	Same as DragDeltaGestureEventArgs
Flick	FlickGestureEventArgs	Same as GestureEventArgs, as well as the angle, direction, vertical velocity and horizontal velocity of the gesture.
PinchStarted	PinchStartedGestureEventArgs	Same as GestureEventArgs, as well as the angle and direction of the gesture.
PinchDelta	PinchGestureEventArgs	Same as GestureEventArgs, as well as the distance ratio to handle scaling and total angle delta to handle rotation.
PinchCompleted	PinchGestureEventArgs	Same as above.

In this recipe, we will build on the project we created in Recipe 3-2 to implement the GestureListener in place of the UIElement event handlers.

Designing the UI

Create a new Visual Studio 2012 Windows Phone project, named "FlickIt". Delete the default MainPage that was created in the new project. We will be adding a copy of the MainPage from the TapIt project, which was created in Recipe 3-2. Before doing so, we need to add the Windows Phone Toolkit into this project, as we will be using controls and classes contained within the toolkit. Follow the instructions provided in Chapter 2, Recipe 2-5, to add the toolkit into this project using NuGet.

Once the Windows Phone Toolkit has been added, right-click on the project name in the Solution Explorer panel, and select Add ➤ Existing Item... from the menu. In the File Explorer dialog, browse to the TapIt project folder, select the MainPage XAML file, and click the "Add" button. This action will automatically create a copy of the MainPage.xaml file, and its code-behind file, in the current project directory. You can make changes to this file without it affecting the MainPage in the original TapIt project.

This page will serve as our starting point. The first change we will make is to modify the namespace in MainPage XAML and code behind files to match the namespace of our current project. In the XAML file, modify the x:Class attribute from x:Class="TapIt.MainPage" to x:Class="FlickIt.MainPage".In the code behind file, change the class namespace declaration from TapIt to FlickIt. Add the EllipseManager class from the TapIt project as well using the same approach, and update the class namespace to FlickIt.

The next step is to modify the XAML in MainPage to include the GestureListener within the WrapPanel.

```
<toolkit:WrapPanel x:Name="ContentPanel"
                   Grid.Row="1"
                   Grid.ColumnSpan="3">
    <toolkit:GestureService.GestureListener>
        <toolkit:GestureListener
        Tap="GestureListener_Tap"
        DoubleTap="GestureListener_DoubleTap"
        Hold="GestureListener_Hold"
        Flick="GestureListener_Flick"
        DragStarted="GestureListener_DragStarted"
        DragDelta="GestureListener_DragDelta"
        DragCompleted="GestureListener_DragCompleted" />
    </toolkit:GestureService.GestureListener>
</toolkit:WrapPanel>
```

Implementing the GestureListener on the WrapPanel removes the requirement for us to manually attach or detach event handlers to each new ellipse that is created. The listener will now "listen" for events on any UIElement that is added to the WrapPanel. Note that we still can do it in the traditional way, and attach a listener to each ellipse as it is created, but this approach is simple and straightforward. With that being said, we can now delete the AttachEventHandlers and RemoveEventHandlers methods, along with any calls made to those methods in the code behind file.

Managing the GestureListener Events

Next, we need to copy the code from the Ellipse_Tapped, Ellipse_DoubleTapped, and Ellipse_Held methods into the corresponding GestureListener methods: GestureListener_Tap, GestureListener_DoubleTap, and GestureListener_Hold.

Since we have attached the listener to the WrapPanel and not to each individual ellipse, it is a good idea to check that the object that triggered the event is in fact an Ellipse type. At first, you may think that this requires a check against the first parameter named sender. Unfortunately, that will not work, because the sender will not contain the object that triggered the event. The sender will be the object that has the listener attached, which in this case is the WrapPanel.

We need to check the GestureEventArgs class to determine the source object that triggered the event. This class contains a property called OriginalSource, which is an object type and will contain the object that actually triggered the event. So we will need to check OriginalSource to determine whether or not the object is an Ellipse type. If it is, then we can proceed with the desired action in each event. If it isn't, we simply want to do nothing. So, let's strap on some conditional checks to make this happen!

Listing 3-8. The GestureListener Events for Tap, DoubleTap, and Hold

```
private void GestureListener_Tap(object sender, Microsoft.Phone.Controls.GestureEventArgs e)
{
    if (e.OriginalSource.GetType().Equals(typeof(Ellipse)))
    {
        if (menuEllipse.IsOpen)
        {
            //if the context menu is open but the user taps
            //outside of the menu, then close it
            menuEllipse.IsOpen = false;
        }
```

```
        Ellipse sourceEllipse = (Ellipse)sender;
        sourceEllipse.Fill = EllipseManager.GetNextColor();
    }
}

private void GestureListener_DoubleTap(object sender, Microsoft.Phone.Controls.GestureEventArgs e)
{
    if (e.OriginalSource.GetType().Equals(typeof(Ellipse)))
    {
        AddNewEllipse();
    }
}

private void GestureListener_Hold(object sender, Microsoft.Phone.Controls.GestureEventArgs e)
{

    if (!ellipseInDragMode && e.OriginalSource.GetType().Equals(typeof(Ellipse)))
    {
        Ellipse sourceEllipse = (Ellipse)sender;

        //if the point touched is near the right edge of the screen, adjust the
        //HorizontalOffset for the context menu to ensure that it is displayed
        //within the bounds of the screen
        if ((lastTouchedPoint.X + listMenuItems.Width) > this.ActualWidth)
            lastTouchedPoint.X = this.ActualWidth - listMenuItems.Width;

        //if the point touched is near the bottom edge of the screen, adjust the
        //VerticalOffset for the context menu to ensure that it is displayed
        //within the bounds of the screen
        if ((lastTouchedPoint.Y + listMenuItems.Height) > this.ActualHeight)
            lastTouchedPoint.Y = this.ActualHeight - listMenuItems.Height;

        menuEllipse.HorizontalOffset = lastTouchedPoint.X;
        menuEllipse.VerticalOffset = lastTouchedPoint.Y;
        menuEllipse.IsOpen = true;

        //set the Tag of the context menu to the selected ellipse
        //so that on menu item selection, the action that is taken
        //against the shape that triggered the event
        menuEllipse.Tag = sourceEllipse;
    }
}
```

That seems to do the trick, but something is missing. Did you spot the next change that is necessary to ensure our app doesn't crash and burn on the first touch-based gestured?

If you said that we need to change the line of code that casts the sender to an Ellipse, then you're right! If you said that we need to throw in some exception handling, you're also correct!

Change the line in the Tap and Hold events from

```
Ellipse sourceEllipse = (Ellipse)sender;
```

to

```
Ellipse sourceEllipse = (Ellipse)e.OriginalSource;
```

Go ahead and include exception handling in each event, if you're feeling up to it. Since this recipe is about gestures rathar than exception handling, I won't cover it here. If you do not know how to add exception handling in your code, it's time to visit the Microsoft Developer Network site, http://msdn.microsoft.com, and search for articles on exception handling in C#.

Now that we have our modifications done, feel free to compile and run the app to test it and make sure the Tap, DoubleTap, and Hold gestures still behave as expected.

Next we will provide some code to allow the user to drag any ellipse across the screen. When the user starts to drag an ellipse, we want the border color to change to yellow, so that it is obvious which ellipse is selected for the drag operation. As the user drags a finger across the screen, we want the ellipse to follow the same direction. And finally, when the user stops dragging, we want the ellipse's border to return to the default gray color. The resulting code is depicted in Listing 3-9.

Listing 3-9. Handling the Drag Gestured-Based Events

```
private void GestureListener_DragStarted(object sender,
Microsoft.Phone.Controls.DragStartedGestureEventArgs e)
{
    if (e.OriginalSource.GetType().Equals(typeof(Ellipse)))
    {
        ellipseInDragMode = true;

        Ellipse targetEllipse = (Ellipse)e.OriginalSource;

        ContentPanel.Children.ToList().ForEach(c => c.SetValue(Canvas.ZIndexProperty, 0));
        targetEllipse.SetValue(Canvas.ZIndexProperty, 1);

        //change the border of the object that is being dragged
        targetEllipse.Stroke = new SolidColorBrush(Colors.Yellow);
    }
}

private void GestureListener_DragDelta(object sender,
Microsoft.Phone.Controls.DragDeltaGestureEventArgs e)
{
    if (e.OriginalSource.GetType().Equals(typeof(Ellipse)))
    {
        Ellipse targetEllipse = (Ellipse)e.OriginalSource;

        TranslateTransform transform = targetEllipse.RenderTransform as TranslateTransform;
        transform.X += e.HorizontalChange;
        transform.Y += e.VerticalChange;
    }
}
```

```
private void GestureListener_DragCompleted(object sender,
Microsoft.Phone.Controls.DragCompletedGestureEventArgs e)
{
    if (e.OriginalSource.GetType().Equals(typeof(Ellipse)))
    {
        ellipseInDragMode = false;

        Ellipse targetEllipse = (Ellipse)e.OriginalSource;

        //reset the border to the default color
        targetEllipse.Stroke = new SolidColorBrush(Colors.Gray);
    }
}
```

It would also be a nice touch to display the x- and y-coordinates that the user's finger crosses as the ellipse is dragged across the screen. Let's go ahead and add a TextBlock below the WrapPanel in the MainPage XAML file. Since the default behavior when adding more than one UIElement to a Grid is to center them so they all appear on top of each other, we need to define rows to ensure the new TextBlock does not overlap with the WrapPanel. We will use the RowDefinitions collection and RowDefinition element on the Grid to explicitly define two rows.

```
<Grid.RowDefinitions>
    <RowDefinition />
    <RowDefinition Height="Auto" />
</Grid.RowDefinitions>
```

Notice the Height attributes defined on the second row. A value of Auto simply indicates that the second row will only take up as much space as the elements contained within it require. Without this in place, each row will take up equal parts of the screen, thereby reducing the screen real estate for the WrapPanel, which is not the desired result. We want the WrapPanel to continue to take up the majority of the screen, with just enough room at the bottom left over to display the coordinates.

Improving the UI

Now we can add the TextBlock to the Grid, and name it coordinatesText, since we plan on updating it from the code behind file. We also need to specify that the TextBlock is to be displayed in the second row. To accomplish this, we simply set the Grid.Row property on the TextBlock itself. This is called an attached property, because its value is specified on the child element and not the Grid itself.

```
<TextBlock Name="coordinatesText" Grid.Row="1" />
```

The default value is zero, which means those elements that do not specify a value for Grid.Row will be placed in the first row. Grid row and column values are zero-based. We do not have to specify a row value for the WrapPanel, so remove it if one is specified. We will need to specify a row value for the TextBlock, which will end up being Grid.Row="1", to ensure it will be displayed in the second row.

With the TextBlock in place, we can now return to the code behind and add some code to the DragDelta event to display the x- and y-coordinates of the user's finger as it travels across the screen. The DragDeltaGestureEventArgs class contains a method called GetPosition, which returns a Point object. This method allows us to obtain the Point containing the coordinates of the touch action relative to another UIElement. If null is passed into the method, we will receive the screen coordinates. We want to display the screen coordinates, so we will call this method and pass in null. We will then display the result in the TextBlock, as shown in Listing 3-10.

Listing 3-10. GestureListener's DragDelta Event Modified to Include Displaying Coordinates of Last Touch Point in the UI

```
private void GestureListener_DragDelta(object sender,
Microsoft.Phone.Controls.DragDeltaGestureEventArgs e)
{
    if (e.OriginalSource.GetType().Equals(typeof(Ellipse)))
    {
        Ellipse targetEllipse = (Ellipse)e.OriginalSource;

        TranslateTransform transform = targetEllipse.RenderTransform as TranslateTransform;
        transform.X += e.HorizontalChange;
        transform.Y += e.VerticalChange;

        //display the last touched point's coordinates
        //as the user drags a finger across the screen
        Point lastPosition = e.GetPosition(null);
        coordinatesText.Text = string.Format("X:{0}, Y:{1}",
                                        lastPosition.X,
                                        lastPosition.Y);
    }
}
```

As a nice finishing touch, let's add a reset button within the same row as the coordinatesText control:

```
<Button Name="resetButton"
        Content="reset"
        Grid.Row="1"
        Grid.Column="1"
        Width="200"
        Tap="resetButton_Tap" />
```

Include the following code in the MainPage code-behind for the reset button's Tap event:

```
private void resetButton_Tap(object sender, System.Windows.Input.GestureEventArgs e)
{
    ContentPanel.Children.Clear();
    EllipseManager.ResetCounter();
    AddNewEllipse();

    coordinatesText.Text = "X:0, Y:0";
}
```

At this point, you can compile and run it again to see the newly wired events in action. Use the context menu or the double-tap action to add some ellipse shapes to the screen. Now select each one and drag it around the screen. Notice the change in the border color of the ellipse that is being dragged as well as the change in coordinates at the bottom of the screen. Pretty exciting stuff, eh?

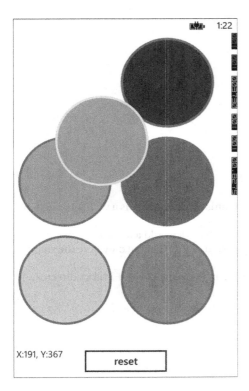

Figure 3-4. *Notice the border color change on drag of an ellipse*

It's Time To Flick It

Let's wrap it up by going back to the code and adding in some logic for the Flick event to make this a complete recipe. After all, the project is called FlickIt. So let's make that happen!

In the GestureListener_Flick event, we are going to include checks to determine the direction of the flick, along with the velocity that the flick occurred. For this example, we will delete the ellipse that is flicked only when the flick occurs in an upward direction and with a velocity that ensures that the action was deliberate. We will choose a velocity constant that we can use to compare against. Since we want to only check for flicks in the upward direction, this means the velocity check needs to be a negative number, so we will use the number -3000. This is just an example, and you can check velocity to any value that you deem to make sense in the context of your app. Once we have determined the flick was a deliberate action, we will perform our desired action, as shown in Listing 3-11. In this case, we will delete the ellipse.

Listing 3-11. Delete the Ellipse When the User Flicks it Upward

```
private void GestureListener_Flick(object sender, Microsoft.Phone.Controls.FlickGestureEventArgs e)
{
    if (e.OriginalSource.GetType().Equals(typeof(Ellipse)) &&
        e.Direction == System.Windows.Controls.Orientation.Vertical &&
        (e.VerticalVelocity < -3000))
```

```
    {
        Ellipse targetEllipse = (Ellipse)e.OriginalSource;
        DeleteEllipse(targetEllipse);
    }
}

private void DeleteEllipse(Ellipse deleteEllipse)
{
    //detach the event handlers and remove the selected shape
    ContentPanel.Children.Remove(deleteEllipse);
    EllipseManager.DecrementCounter();
}
```

As you can see, we are only processing the delete if the flick is in an upwards direction, that is a vertical direction and a negative velocity rate.

Compile the project one more time, and test it either in the emulator or on a device. Add a few ellipse shapes to the screen, then try and "flick" each one off the screen in every possible direction. Verify that the only time the shape is deleted is when the shape is flicked upward.

To view the full source code for this applicaton, refer to the FlickIt project in the \Chapter 3\FlickIt directory.

3-4. Pinch to Zoom

Problem

You want your app to load a photo, and allow the user to use pinch gestures to zoom in and out of the photo.

Solution

Use the GestureService to attach a GestureListener to the Image element in your Visual Studio project, and include handlers for the PinchStarted, PinchDelta, and PinchCompleted events.

How It Works

As we touched on in Recipe 3-3, Table 3-2, the GestureListener provides event handlers for pinch gestures, including PinchStarted, PinchDelta, and PinchCompleted. We will create a new Windows Phone project which will load a photo, attach a listener to its image element, and zoom in/out of the photo when the user uses two fingers to manipulate the photo.

Designing the UI

Create a new Visual Studio 2012 Windows Phone project, and name the project "PinchIt". As was done in the previous recipes, we need to add the Windows Phone Toolkit into this project to leverage the GestureService to attach a GestureListener to our photo. Follow the instructions provided in Chapter 2, Recipe 2-5, to add the toolkit into this project using NuGet.

In the MainPage markup, add an Image element to the LayoutRoot grid, defining the size of the image that will display on initial load of the application. In this example, I've included a photo that I took while on vacation at a cottage in Tobermory. It is packaged in with the source project that is shipped with this book.

We also need to associate a transformation object with the image to simplify the manner in which the image is scaled as the pinch action takes place. For this, we will define a ScaleTransform object to handle the transformation.

```xml
<Grid x:Name="LayoutRoot" Background="Transparent">
    <Grid.RowDefinitions>
        <RowDefinition />
        <RowDefinition Height="Auto" />
    </Grid.RowDefinitions>
    <Image Name="myPhoto"
           Source="Assets\MillerLake.png"
           Height="300" Width="400">
        <Image.RenderTransform>
            <ScaleTransform x:Name="photoTransform" />
        </Image.RenderTransform>
    </Image>
    <TextBlock Name="photoScaleText" Grid.Row="1" />
</Grid>
```

Now, be sure to include a TextBlock in the markup that we will use to display the size of the photo on initial load. We will update the message as the photo is manipulated by the user. In Recipe 3-3, we demonstrated the approach taken to add a GestureListener in XAML.

Creating the GestureListener

For this example, we will add the GestureListener programmatically in the code behind, within the Loaded event of the MainPage. This is achieved by calling the GetGestureListener method on the GestureService class, and passing in the Image element. This method will return the listener that is attached to the object, which is passed in as a parameter during the method call. If a listener has not yet been attached to the object, it will create a new listener, attach it to the object, and return it. With a handle to the listener, we can now wire up the events we want to code actions for. For this recipe, we will only handle the three pinch-based events. Finally, we will set the default text to display the initial size of the photo on load, as shown in Listing 3-12.

Listing 3-12. Registering Event Handlers for the Pinch Events

```
void MainPage_Loaded(object sender, RoutedEventArgs e)
{
    GestureListener listener = GestureService.GetGestureListener(myPhoto);

    listener.PinchStarted += new
EventHandler<PinchStartedGestureEventArgs>(GestureListener_PinchStarted);

    listener.PinchDelta += new EventHandler<PinchGestureEventArgs>(GestureListener_PinchDelta);

    listener.PinchCompleted += new
EventHandler<PinchGestureEventArgs>(GestureListener_PinchCompleted);

    photoScaleText.Text = string.Format("Size: {0}X{1}",
                                myPhoto.Width, myPhoto.Height);

}
```

Managing the GestureListener's Pinch Events

In the PinchStarted event, we will capture the current scale value of the image, obtain the coordinates of the touch points invoked by the user relative to the photo, and perform a simple calculation to set the center axis of the image's scale transformation.

As the user conducts the pinch gesture, we will update the horizontal and vertical scale of the image based on the distance ratio obtained from the PinchGestureEventArgs class within the PinchDelta event. We will also update the TextBlock to indicate that a pinch action is in progress and the current scale value.

Finally, for the PinchCompleted event, we don't really need to do anything except update the TextBlock to reflect that the pinch action has completed and display the current photo scale. The resulting code for these events is shown in Listing 3-13.

Listing 3-13. Using Pinch Events to Scale the Size of an Image

```
private double imageScale = 1;
void GestureListener_PinchStarted(object sender, PinchStartedGestureEventArgs e)
{
    //get the current photo's scale value
    imageScale = photoTransform.ScaleX;

    //get the two touch points
    Point touchPointA = e.GetPosition(myPhoto, 0);
    Point touchPointB = e.GetPosition(myPhoto, 1);

    //set the photo center x and y axis to the center of the
    //corresponding axis between the two touch points
    photoTransform.CenterX = touchPointA.X + (touchPointB.X - touchPointA.X) / 2;
    photoTransform.CenterY = touchPointA.Y + (touchPointB.Y - touchPointA.Y) / 2;
}

void GestureListener_PinchDelta(object sender, PinchGestureEventArgs e)
{
    //scale the photo as the pinch gesture changes
    photoTransform.ScaleX = imageScale * e.DistanceRatio;
    photoTransform.ScaleY = photoTransform.ScaleX;

    photoScaleText.Text = string.Format("Size: {0}X{1}, Scale:{2} - Pinch In Progress",
        myPhoto.Width, myPhoto.Height, Math.Round(photoTransform.ScaleX, 2));

}
void GestureListener_PinchCompleted(object sender, PinchGestureEventArgs e)
{
    photoScaleText.Text = string.Format("Size: {0}X{1}, Scale:{2} - Pinch Completed",
        myPhoto.Width, myPhoto.Height, Math.Round(photoTransform.ScaleX, 2));

}
```

Testing the App

Now we can compile this app and run it in the emulator, but we will not be able to test it. The emulator does not support multi-touch gestures. So the most you can do is view the photo, as shown in Figure 3-5.

Figure 3-5. *Initial view of the PinchIt app on load*

We will need to test this app on an actual device. If you do not know how to unlock your Windows Phone device for testing, revisit Chapter 1, Recipe 1-4, which discusses this topic in detail. Once you have a developer unlocked phone, run and test this app on the device, testing out the gestures to zoom in and out of the photo. Notice that the size of the image remains the same, as indicated in the TextBlock. It is the scale value that changes, in turn causing the photo to zoom in by increasing the image scale or zoom out by decreasing the image scale.

To view the full source code for this applicaton, refer to the PinchIt project in the `\Chapter 3\PinchIt` directory.

3-5. Be Generous With Size and Considerate Of Space
Problem

You developed a Windows Phone app, but users are complaining that every time they try to tap the update button, the cancel button is hit instead and they lose their changes!

Solution

Follow the Microsoft Design Guidelines to ensure you are setting your controls to an appropriate size if they are touch targets and to ensure you are providing adequate spacing between controls in the UI.

How It Works

For first-time app developers that are testing in the emulator, the size of the emulator screen on a laptop or regular PC monitor can be deceiving. Text that appears to be large enough to read on a monitor may be barely legible on a device. Buttons that seem large enough to be hit with the tiny little mouse cursor on your screen, may be difficult for a user to accurately hit on an actual device screen.

The same principal applies to spacing considerations. What may look like sufficient spacing on a larger screen may not be adequate on a device, in turn causing headaches for the user. There's nothing more frustrating than trying to tap one button, but another button receives the event, causing undesirable results.

The main goal when designing an app is to simplify user interaction. Big buttons, larger text, and adequate spacing between controls can make all the difference in your app's usability. For example, any element that is expected to serve as a touch target should be at least 34 pixels in size, according to Microsoft's design guidelines. These guidelines also indicate that a minimum space of 8 pixels should be allocated between controls, but I prefer to give a little more space than that if I can afford it on the screen (i.e., at least 10 pixels).

If a target element is expected to receive heavy user interaction, consider making it larger. If you must set the size of a target element to a smaller value than the standard 34 pixel size, you may be able to get away with including an element that is no smaller than 26 pixels. Designing your target elements to be any smaller may result in the user fussing around, and failing miserably, in attempting to hit the target. If the user becomes aggravated when trying to use your app in the first few minutes, the likelihood is greater that your app will be uninstalled. Think of the size difference between the narrow mouse cursor and a rounded fingertip. The odds are higher that the fingertip will miss the intended target and hit another target if both elements are too close together on the screen, and not a proper size (i.e., too small to accurately hit).

Refer to Microsoft's Design library for Windows Phone which discusses best practices in designing your app, specifically around UI design and interactivity with Windows Phone. These guidelines can be found at the following URL, within the section titled "UI design and touch input": `http://msdn.microsoft.com/en-us/library/windowsphone/develop/jj207076(v=vs.105).aspx`

The best way to determine if your app design is simple and easy to use is to test on a device. Once you are satisfied with the interaction on a device, hand it over to a real user and watch his reaction as he learns how to use the app. If the user is able to get in and understand the app's purpose and is able to use it with ease, then your app is ready to be published to the Windows Phone Store!

CHAPTER 4

■ ■ ■

Tiles and Lock Screen

Tiles are the entry point to a Windows Phone application. Windows Phone 8 provides 3 tile templates that you can use to add flair to their application. Each tile template must define the appearance of a tile for each of the 3 available sizes (small, medium, large), which will be visible when a Windows Phone 8 app is pinned to a user's start screen. You will need to take care to ensure that your live tile represents your application appropriately, while still following the Windows Phone design guidelines, and in a way that captures the user's attention. This chapter will guide you through the basics of adding live tiles to your application for each template. We close off the chapter by stepping through how to enable lock screen customization from within the app, as well as how to handle integration between the lock screen settings page and the application.

- 4-1. Configure the Default Application Tile
- 4-2. Create a flip tile
- 4-3. Create an iconic tile
- 4-4. Create a cycle tile
- 4-5. Create Secondary Tiles
- 4-6. Create lock screen background image
- 4-7. Handle interactivity between lock screen settings and the app

4-1. Configure the Default Application Tile

Problem

You want to configure which tile shows up on the home screen when the user pins your application.

Solution

Configure the Tile Template, Tile Title, and Tile Images properties in the application's manifest file.

How It Works

The default, or primary, tile for your application is defined in the WMAppManifest.xml file located under the Properties folder of your application.

Start Visual Studio, create a new Windows Phone App and name it DefaultTile. Locate the WMAppManifest.xml file in the Properties folder and then double-click on it to open up the editor. Figure 4-1 shows the three properties in which we are interested.

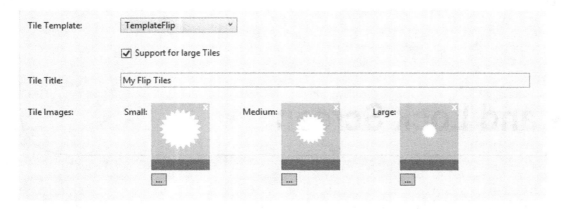

Figure 4-1. *The Tile Template, Tile Title, and Tile Images properties in the application manifest edit*

The Tile Template allows you to choose from three different tile templates: Flip, Iconic, and Cycle. Each of these is examined in greater depth in other recipes but for now Table 4-1 gives you a brief description of each type.

Table 4-1. *Tile Template Descriptions*

Tile Template	Description
TemplateFlip	The flip template gives you two surfaces on which to provide information to the user. Only the front and back of the medium and large tiles sizes display information. The tile flips at random intervals, so it's important to choose the right type of information to display.
TemplateCycle	The cycle template can be configured with one to nine images and cycles through them. The transitions and animations are fixed.
TemplateIconic	The iconic template displays a single image with a place to display a count. It also has predefined areas for the display of information to the user in the large format.

The check box below the Tile Template section allows you to enable or disable support for large Tiles. Large Tile support only applies to the TemplateFlip format and when you check the box an additional selection box is enabled for the Tile Images. The TemplateIconic does not require a large format image, as it reuses the small image when the Tile is set to the large format and content is present. When no content is provided in the large format, the medium image is used.

The Tile Title shows up aligned to the bottom left of the medium and large format Tiles. The small format does not display any text other than the count number. The text is limited to 19 characters for the medium format and to 39 for the large format Tile. The tiles won't wrap any text you supply and will simply truncate it. The Segoe WP font used on the tiles is not a fixed width font so these character lengths are only approximations, and therefore, dare I say it, your mileage may vary.

The final configuraton item then is the Tile Images. You can click on the browse ellipsis below each of the small, medium, and, if required, large icon placeholders to browse for a suitable image. The exact design details of each template tile size will be covered in each of their respective recipes. For now, you can use the default images supplied with the Windows Phone App project template. The placeholders will display your image once selected. Figure 4-2 shows an example of how each of the small, medium, and large tiles display.

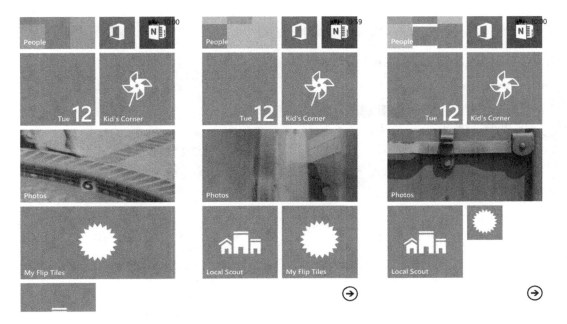

Figure 4-2. *Small, medium, and large Tile examples*

■ **Note**   The Tiles subfolder of the Assets project folder contains default sample images. A small, medium, and large flip tile image is included as well as a small and medium iconic tile image.

Once you have everything configured, run your application in the emulator. Click the Start button on the emulator and then swipe left to get to the application list. Tap (click) and hold the DefaultTile application entry and then select "pin to start" on the popup menu. The system will navigate automatically to the home screen. You see your tile appear there with your title displayed. Tap and hold the Tile to enter the home screen editing mode, and resize your Tile to see the different formats. Set your tile to the large format and then click outside the Tiles to switch the screen back to normal mode.

We used the TemplateFlip Tile template for our applications default Tile but the observant among you might have noticed the the tile is just sitting there mocking you[1] and not flipping at all. There's a far simpler explanation for this behavior than malevolent anthropomorphism. We simply haven't given it anything to show us.

The manifest editor is a convenient but incomplete tool. It didn't provide us with any means to add content to our default tile. Fortunately the tile configuration is stored in the manifest in XML. All we have to do is edit it. Make sure you have closed the manifest editor and then right-click on the WPManifest.xml file and choose Open With. . . In the resulting dialog, choose the XML (Text) Editor and click OK.

---

[1]Ok, maybe it's just me, but look at it sitting there all smug and not flipping. "Oh, I can flip" it mocks, "but I choose not to."

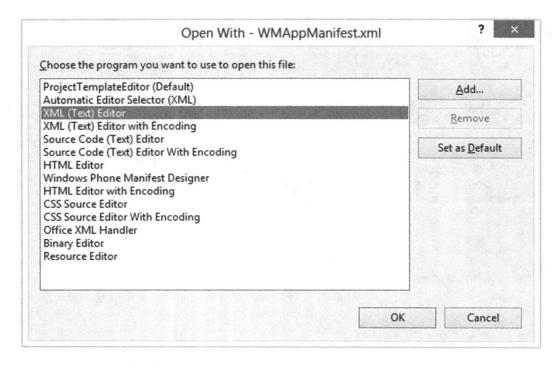

Figure 4-3. *Open With dialog*

Listing 4-1 shows the Tokens section of the application manifest. You'll see the paths to the image files you selected along with the Title text you entered. You'll also see some empty elements in there. This is where we can enter some text for the content of our Tile and set a default count if we want to. Fill in some text for the BackTitle, BackContent, and LargeBackContent and then save and close the file. Run the application in the emulator.

Listing 4-1. Sample Tokens section from the application manifest

```
<Tokens>
  <PrimaryToken TokenID="FlipTilesToken" TaskName="_default">
    <TemplateFlip>
        <SmallImageURI IsRelative="true"
IsResource="false">Assets\Tiles\FlipCycleTileSmall.png</SmallImageURI>
        <Count>0</Count>
        <BackgroundImageURI IsRelative="true"
IsResource="false">Assets\Tiles\FlipCycleTileMedium.png</BackgroundImageURI>
        <Title>My Flip Tiles</Title>
        <BackContent/>
        <BackBackgroundImageURI IsRelative="true" IsResource="false">
        </BackBackgroundImageURI>
        <BackTitle>
        </BackTitle>
        <LargeBackgroundImageURI IsRelative="true"
IsResource="false">Assets\Tiles\FlipCycleTileLarge.png</LargeBackgroundImageURI>
        <LargeBackContent/>
```

```
        <LargeBackBackgroundImageURI IsRelative="true" IsResource="false">
        </LargeBackBackgroundImageURI>
        <DeviceLockImageURI IsRelative="true" IsResource="false">
        </DeviceLockImageURI>
        <HasLarge>True</HasLarge>
      </TemplateFlip>
    </PrimaryToken>
  </Tokens>
```

■ **Note**   You may not see your changes take effect if your application is still pinned to the start screen from a previous deployment. You may have to unpin and repin it for the changes to take effect.

Now that the tile actually has some content to display on the back of the tile, it will start to flip at random intervals. Figure 4-4 shows the front and back of the medium and large Tile formats.

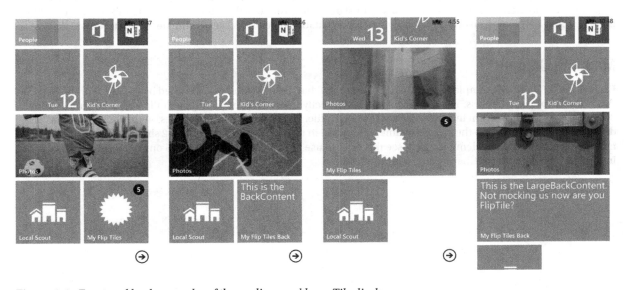

Figure 4-4. *Front and back examples of the medium and large Tile displays*

4-2. Create a Flip Tile

Problem

You want a tile for the main home screen that is capable of showing extra information.

Solution

Use the FlipTile as the default tile for your application.

Recipe 4-1 explored how to configure a particular Tile template as the default for your application but didn't really go into any details regarding the tiles themselves. In this recipe we'll take a detailed look at the Flip Tile and its various properties.

How It Works

The Flip Tile template is best suited for times when you have additional information that the user would be interested in seeing without having to launch your application. A perfect example of this is a weather application. You can show current information on the front of the tile and then more detailed information on the flip-side. Perhaps provide a 5-day forecast.

The key to determining what information to provide on each side is relevance. The interval between flips is random and you don't want the user waiting for informaton. The information on both sides should be as immediately relevant to the user as possible. The 5-day forecast in the example above could still provide the current day as 1 of the 5 days. In this way you aren't keeping the user waiting on your Tile and they will have a more enjoyable experience.

An example of a poor use of the Flip Tile would be a bus schedule that shows the next arrival time on the front but neglects to include that informaton in some form on the reverse side of the Tile. To add variety to your Tile's information you could present the same information in a different format. You could show a map of the current location of the next bus. The user can then infer the time of the next arrival from the position of the bus on the map. In this way the user has the scheduled arrival time on one side and a visual representation that allows her to estimate the actual arrival time.

Mapping Content

Each of the different Tile templates has an associated class that defines the data consumed by the Tile. For the Flip Tile this is the `FlipTileData` class. You don't use this class directly when defining your default tile but rather enter values in the `PrimaryToken` element in the `WPAppManifest.xaml` file. The names of the properties on the `FlipTileData` class don't correspond directly to the element names contained in the PrimaryToken. Table 4-2 shows how each property maps to its corresponding element. You'll see this class in use in the recipes in Recipe 4-5 on creating Secondary Tiles in this chapter as well as in Chapter 5 on Tile notifications.

Table 4-2. *Mapping of FlipTileData Class Properties to the PrimaryToken Element of WPAppManifest.xaml*

Property Name	PrimaryToken Element	Description
BackBackgroundImage	BackBackgroundImageURI	The background image of the back of the Tile. When set to an empty URI, the background image of the back of the Tile will not change during an update.
BackContent	BackContent	The text to display on the back of the Tile, above the title. When set to an empty string, the content on the back of the Tile will not change during an update.
BackgroundImage	BackgroundImageURI	The background image of the front of the Tile. When set to an empty URI, the background image of the front of the Tile will not change during an update.
BackTitle	BackTitle	The title to display at the bottom of the back of the Tile. When set to an empty string, the title on the back of the Tile will not change during an update.
Count	Count	This property is of type Nullable<int> with a valid range that is between 1 and 99. The value will be displayed in the Count field of the Tile. A value of 0 means the Count will not be displayed. When not set, the Count display will not change during an update.
SmallBackgroundImage	SmallImageURI	The front-side background image for the small Tile size.
Title	Title	The text that displays on the front side of the medium and wide tile sizes.
WideBackBackgroundImage	LargeBackBackgroundImageURI	The back-side background image for the wide Tile size.
WideBackContent	LargeBackContent	The text that displays above the title, on the back side of the wide Tile size.
WideBackgroundImage	LargeBackgroundImageURI	The front-side background image for the wide Tile size.
Not Applicable	DeviceLockImageURI	The image to be used on the Lock Screen if your application has been configured to provide Lock Screen information. Recipe 4-6 will cover this element of the PrimaryToken.
Not Applicable	HasLarge	True if your application supports the large Tile format; False if not.

Character Content

Character-based content is limited to predefined areas of the template and therefore limited in length. The Flip Tile template won't wrap text or add an ellipsis to the end of a line and will simply truncate the data if it is too long for display. Table 4-3 shows the number of characters that can be accommodated by each text area in the template. The Segoe WP font that is used to display text on the start screen is not a fixed width font, and therefore the character counts are approximations only.

Table 4-3. *Flip Tile Template Approximate Character Counts*

Tile size	Title	BackTitle	BackContent	WideBackContent
Small	NA	NA	NA	NA
Medium	19	19	3 lines at 13	NA
Wide	39	39	NA	3 lines at 27

Visual Layout

The layout of the Flip Tile is predefined and you have no control over how the content is presented. This is a good thing because it enables you to focus on the content data and not have to worry about providing a consistent visual experience for the user. Figure 4-5 shows a typical Flip Tile with complete content.

Figure 4-5. *A typical Flip Tile*

The content provided by the values you enter for the properties in Table 4-2 gets mapped into the Tile in a predefined way. Figure 4-6 shows how each of these values maps into the Flip Tile template for each of the small, medium, and large Tile formats.

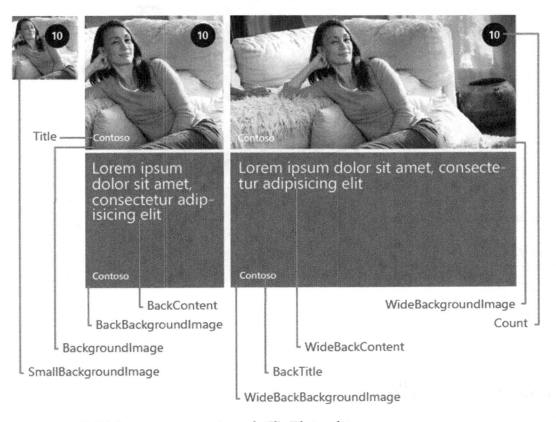

Figure 4-6. *FlipTileData property mapping to the Flip Tile template*

Figure 4-7 illustrates the layout of the various parts of the Tile for each of the sizes. Table 4-4 lists the size of the images used for each size.

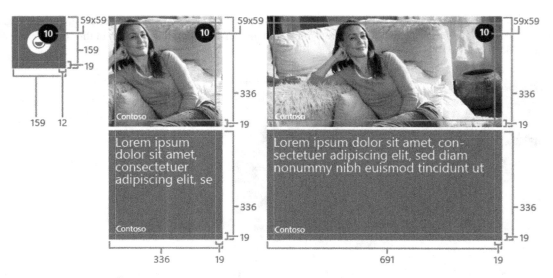

Figure 4-7. *Flip Tile template layout dimensions*

Table 4-4. *Image Dimensions*

Tile Size	Image Dimensions
Small	159 × 159 pixels
Medium	336 × 336 pixels
Wide	691 × 336 pixels

4-3. Create an Iconic Tile

Problem

Your application has information that is count-centric and you want to best method of showing that count to the user.

Solution

Use the Iconic Tile as the default tile for your application.

How It Works

The Iconic Tile template is best suited for times when you have an application for which a current count of items is the most relevant information that the user would be interested in seeing without having to launch your application. A perfect example of this would be an e-mail application. You can show the current number of new e-mails that have arrived since the last time the user launched your application.

The Iconic Tile doesn't support any type of image display beyond a white icon with a transparent background. This makes it unsuitable for applications that rely on images to convey information. The large Tile format does support a few lines of text, but because the user can change the size of the Tile at any time you shouldn't rely on this to communicate the primary information.

An example of a poor use of the Iconic Tile would be a weather application that shows the temperature because the Count property can only display positive integers from 1 to 99. A value of 0 turns the count icon off completely. This might work in the warmer regions of the world but just about anywhere you go the current temperature is likely to exceed the valid range in one direction or another, and in any case you would just be limiting the market for your application.

Mapping Content

Each of the different Tile templates has an associated class that defines the data consumed by the Tile. For the Iconic Tile this is the IconicTileData class. You don't use this class directly when defining your default tile but, rather, enter values in the PrimaryToken element in the WPAppManifest.xaml file. The names of the properties on the IconicTileData class don't correspond directly to the element names contained in the PrimaryToken. Table 4-5 shows how each property maps to its corresponding element. You'll see this class in use in Recipe 4-5 on creating Secondary Tiles in this chapter as well as in Chapter 5 on Tile notifications.

Table 4-5. *Mapping of IconicTileData Class Properties to the PrimaryToken Element of WPAppManifest.xaml*

Property Name	PrimaryToken Element	Description
BackgroundColor	BackgroundColor	The background color of the Tile. Setting this property overrides the default theme color that is set on the phone. See note below for additional usage information.
Count	Count	This property is of type Nullable<int> with a valid range that is between 1 and 99. The value will be displayed in the Count field of the Tile. A value of 0 means the Count will not be displayed. When not set, the Count display will not change during an update.
IconImage	IconImageURI	The icon image for the medium and large Tile sizes.
SmallIconImage	SmallImageURI	The icon image for the small Tile size.
Title	Title	The text that displays on the front side of the medium and wide tile sizes.
WideContent1	LargeContent1	The text that displays on the first row of the wide Tile size. This text is displayed in a larger font than WideContent2 and WideContent3.
WideContent2	LargeContent2	The text that displays on the second row of the wide Tile size.
WideContent3	LargeContent3	The text that displays on the third row of the wide Tile size.
Not Applicable	Message	Do not set a value for the element as it makes a complete mess of things. See note below.

Figure 4-8 shows a typical Iconic Tile with complete content.

Figure 4-8. *A typical Iconic Tile*

■ **Note**   When setting the BackgroundColor element in the WPAppManifest file, be sure that the HEX value you enter DOES NOT include anything for the Alpha channel. Any value at all will result in your custom color being ignored and the default system color will be shown. For example, to set the BackgroundColor to RED you should enter #FF0000 and NOT #FFFF0000.

Character Content

Character-based content is limited to predefined areas of the template and therefore limited in length. The Iconic Tile template won't wrap text or add an ellipsis to the end of a line and will simply truncate the data if it is too long for display. Table 4-6 shows the number of characters that can be accommodated by each text area in the template. The Segoe WP font that is used to display text on the start screen is not a fixed width font, and therefore the character counts are approximations only.

Table 4-6. *Iconic Tile Template Approximate Character Counts*

Tile size	Title	WideContent1	WideContent2	WideContent3
Small	NA	NA	NA	NA
Medium	19	NA	NA	NA
Wide	39	33	33	33

Visual Layout

The layout of the Iconic Tile is predefined and you have no control over how the content is presented. This is a good thing because it enables you to focus on the content data and not have to worry about providing a consistent visual experience for the user.

The content provided by the values you enter for the properties in Table 4-5 gets mapped into the Tile in a predefined way. Figure 4-9 shows how each of these values maps into the Iconic Tile template for each of the small, medium, and large Tile formats. Figure 4-10 shows the dimensions of the various layout areas of the Tile.

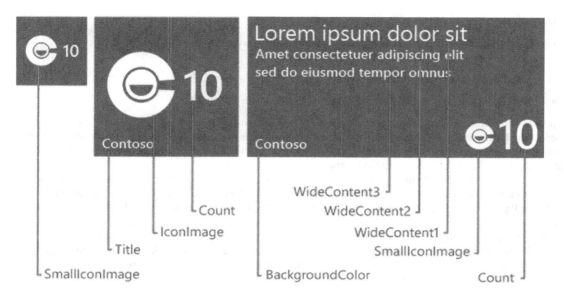

Figure 4-9. *IconicTileData property mapping to the Iconic Tile template*

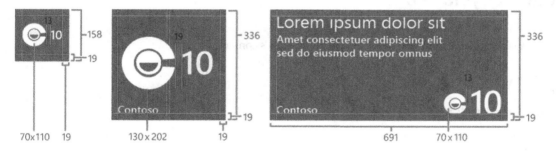

Figure 4-10. *Iconic Tile template layout dimensions*

Icon Design

There are a few things you need to keep in mind when creating your icon to ensure proper scalability across resolutions. You'll need to supply two images: one for SmallIconImage and one for IconImage (SmallIconImageURI and IconImageURI, respectively, in WPAppManifest).

- SmallIconImage

  - Used when the Tile is set to small or when the Tile is set to large and you've provided content in the WideContent properties. See Figure 4-9.

  - The maximum size of this image is 110 pixels by 110 pixels but. . .

  - The recommended "best fit" dimensions are 70 pixels wide by 110 pixels high.

- IconImage

    - Used when the Tile is set to medium or when the Tile is wide and has no content strings on it and may or may not have a count. See Figure 4-9.

    - The maximum size of this image is 202 pixels by 202 pixels, but. . .

    - The recommended "best fit" dimensions are 130 pixels by 202 pixels

For the best results when creating your assets, always pad vertically with a transparent buffer to the full size of the asset you're creating. Let's assume you have an icon where the white pixels in the medium or large image are only 130 pixels high. In this case you would pad the top and bottom of the icon out to 202 pixels high using a transparent buffer area. Remember to always keep the image centered vertically.

Contrary to what is done for the vertical plane, the horizontal plane is always cropped tight to the image. Crop the image to its actual width and don't pad the horizontal plane with a transparent buffer. Adding a transparent horizontal buffer will push the count too far away from the image and it won't look consistent with the icons of other application tiles.

You will achieve the best results if you begin with the layout of your large icon image and, if possible, scale it down for the small icon. For example, if we assume a "best fit" large icon that's 130 pixels wide by 202 pixels tall, set the small aspect ratio to 110 pixels tall and approximately 70 pixels wide. This is virtually the same aspect ratio, so everything should look fine when scaling down.

4-4. Create a Cycle Tile
Problem

You want to display several visual representations of your application's content.

Solution

Use the Cycle Tile as the default Tile for your application.

How It Works

The decision to use the Cycle Tile is fairly straightforward but you should be aware of certain limitations. For example, the Cycle Tile has various animations built into it for the display of the images provided. You have no control over the transitioning, zooming, or cropping of the images as they displayed. This makes the Cycle Tile unsuitable for the conveying of textual information to the user.

An excellent example of an appropriate use of the Cycle Tile is a music application. Pictures or album art can be displayed in rotation for the currently playing artist. The Photos application that ships with Windows Phone 8 is also a perfect example of Cycle Tile use.

The Count property is still available to you, but depending on the application you may or may not find it useful, as it is limited to the range of 1 to 99. Photos in an album could quickly exceed 99 but the number of songs in a current playlist might be acceptable. Having said that, the playlist I am listening to while I write this is currently sitting at 90 songs. If I add a few more into rotation,[2] then the Count becomes irrelevant.

---

[2] I have one playlist I call "Rotation" and just add and remove songs from it. There are enough songs that I don't get bored if it repeats. I also have somewhat ecclectic musical taste so I can mix it up a bit in a single list. I can even "shuffle" up the play order if I'm feeling dangerous. You can't stop me. Don't even try.

Mapping Content

Each of the different Tile templates has an associated class that defines the data consumed by the Tile. For the Cycle Tile this is the CycleTileData class. You don't use this class directly when defining your default tile but rather enter values in the PrimaryToken element in the WPAppManifest.xaml file. The names of the properties on the CycleTileData class don't correspond directly to the element names contained in the PrimaryToken. Table 4-7 shows how each property maps to its corresponding element. You'll see this class in use in the recipes in Recipe 4-5 on creating Secondary Tiles in this chapter as well as in Chapter 5 on Tile notifications.

Table 4-7. *CycleTileData class to PrimaryToken Element Mapping*

Property Name	PrimaryToken Element	Description
Count	Count	This property is of type Nullable<int> with a valid range that is between 1 and 99. The value will be displayed in the Count field of the Tile. A value of 0 means the Count will not be displayed. When not set, the Count display will not change during an update.
SmallIconImage	SmallImageURI	The icon image for the small Tile size.
Title	Title	The text that displays on the front side of the medium and wide tile sizes. See Table 4-8 for character limits.
CycleImages	Photo01ImageURI through Photo09ImageURI	A collection of up to 9 background images for the medium and wide Tile sizes. There should always be at least one URI configured for this property.

Character Content

The only character-based content that can be configured is the Title and has the same limitations as the Title of the other Tile templates. Table 4-8 shows the number of characters that can be accommodated by each text area in the template. The Segoe WP font that is used to display text on the start screen is not a fixed-width font, and therefore the character counts are approximations only.

Table 4-8. *Approximate Character Counts for the Cycle Tile Template*

Tile Size	Title
Small	NA
Medium	19
Wide	39

Visual Layout

The visual layout of the Cycle Tile template is fairly simple. The Count is displayed in the top-right corner of all three sizes of tile and the Title is displayed in the bottom-left corner of the medium and large sizes. No Title is displayed for the small size. Figure 4-11 shows how each property of the CycleTileData class maps into the Tile. Figure 4-12 shows the dimensions of the layout areas.

Figure 4-11. *CycleTileData property mapping to the Cycle Tile template*

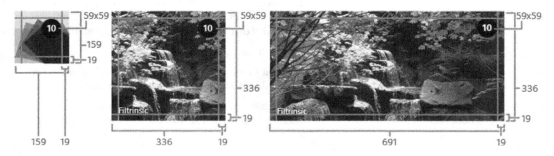

Figure 4-12. *Cycle Tile template layout dimensions*

The images you provide to the Cycle Tile are, you guessed it, cycled through one at a time at random intervals. The image may be cropped or zoomed depending on its size and it is also animated to slide slowly across the tile. Think of someone carrying a large picture past a smaller window. You have no control over any of the manipulations applied to your image and are at the mercy of Windows Phone 8.[3] It's because of these random animations and transitions that text content in the images isn't very practical. Figure 4-13 shows an example, albeit a static one, of this transition.

---

[3]Besides, you've got better things to do—for example, setting up the ultimate "Rotation" playlist of your favorite music.

Figure 4-13. *Images in transition in the Cycle Tile template*

4-5. Create a Secondary Tile

Problem

You want to be able display information from a particular area of your application in a tile on the start screen.

Solution

Use the Tile API to create a secondary Tile on the start screen.

How it Works

In Recipe 4-1 we learned how to configure the default Tile for your application. This is the tile that is used when the user does a tap and hold on your application in the list and chooses pin to start. You can also write code within your app that will allow the user to pin specific content to the start screen.

The choice to expose certain areas of your application on a secondary tile should be made carefully. You can create any of the three Tile template types —Flip, Iconic, and Cycle—and the same guidelines apply whether they are used as the default or secondary. There are a few additional considerations to keep in mind when deciding on a secondary Tile:

- Secondary Tiles can be updated using the same API as the default Tile so the content should be dynamic to attract the user's attention and encourage the use of your application

- The choice to create a secondary Tile is completely up to the user but you must add the capability to suitable areas of your application. Nothing can be pinned by default.

- Use the SDK provided app bar buttons for pin and unpin functionality when you are pinning the current page's content.

- Pinning of an individual item in a list is best accomplished by using a contextual menu.

In addition to these guidelines, there are a couple of Don'ts that you should keep in mind. These are:

- You should not use a secondary Tile as a link to a discrete file or other static content that might disappear.

- Don't use a secondary Tile as a virtual Button to trigger functionality within your application—like a Next Track function in a music player or something similar. Tiles are designed to be a single-click target that launches your application. Subverting that purpose is only going to antagonize the user and make them unistall your application.

Add an App Bar

The first thing you'll need is an application bar for the page that contains the content you want to pin. See Recipe 2-3 in Chapter 2 for the gory details of working with the app bar. We'll keep it simple in this recipe. Listing 4-2 shows the XAML to add to create an app bar with a pin/unpin button.

Listing 4-2. XAML for the App Bar With a Pin/Unpin Button

```
<phone:PhoneApplicationPage.ApplicationBar>
    <shell:ApplicationBar IsVisible="True" IsMenuEnabled="True">
        <shell:ApplicationBarIconButton
            x:Name="btnPinToStart"
            IconUri="/Assets/pin.png"
            IsEnabled="True"
            Text="pin to start"
            Click="PinToStartScreenClick"/>
    </shell:ApplicationBar>
</phone:PhoneApplicationPage.ApplicationBar>
```

Creating the Tile

Unlike the default Tile that you configure in the WPAppManifest.xml file, secondary Tiles can only be created through code at the explicit request of the user. You can refer to the other recipes in this chapter for information on the design of each type of Tile. Here we'll just create a Flip Tile. First, we'll need some content that the user of our application can pin to the start screen. You can follow along in the sample application included with the book's source or you can create a new project using the Windows Phone Databound App project template and work with the Details.xaml page in that.

■ **Note** A sample application SecondaryTiles project can be found in the Chapter04 folder of the sample code.

The next thing we need to do is handle the Click event of the pin button. There are three things we need to do here:

1. If there is already a Tile for the current content, then it was previously pinned and we need to remove it.

2. If a Tile doesn't exist for the current content, then we need to create one.

3. Update the app bar button to reflect the proper state for the current content.

You'll see these tasks reflected in the code from the sample application shown in Listing 4-3. Also included are some helper functions for working with the Tiles. The Source property of the NavigationService will tell us how we got to this page. See Recipe 2-4 in Chapter 2 for more information on the NavigationService. This is the same URI that would have been used to create the secondary tile in the first place. Key to all of these functions is the ShellTile class.

The ShellTile class exposes a static property called ActiveTiles that contains all of the Tiles for your application. ActiveTiles always contains at least one item representing the Application Tile which cannot be deleted. The Application Tile is always the first item in the list. The ActiveTiles list also contains any secondary Tiles that have been created. The CharacterTileExists and DeleteCharacterTile helper methods use the ActiveTiles property to find a specific tile reference.

The ShellTileClass also exposes a static method called CreateTile. The CreateTile method has two implementations. When working with Windows Phone 8, you should always use the overload that requires three parameters. When passed anything other than a StandardTileData object, the other implementation will throw an InvalidOperationException. There's nothing to stop you from using StandardTileData bit it's not part of the official design guidelines and is only there for backwards compatibility with Windows Phone 7.x. It will behave pretty much the same as FlipTileData but has no support for the large size and you can't configure a different image for the small size.

The SetPinBar method is pretty straight forward. It again uses the Source property of the NavigationService to test if a character tile exists and changes the icon and text of the app bar button based on the results.

Listing 4-3. The Click Event Handler for the App Bar Pin Button

```
private void PinToStartScreenClick(object sender, EventArgs e)
{
    string uri = NavigationService.Source.ToString();

    if (CharacterTileExists(uri))
    {
        // If the tile already exists, then we delete it
        DeleteCharacterTile(uri);
    }
```

```
        else
        {
            // Otherwise create it
            SetCharacterTile(uri);
        }

        SetPinBar();

}
private bool CharacterTileExists(string navigationSource)
{
    ShellTile tile = ShellTile.ActiveTiles
        .FirstOrDefault(o => o.NavigationUri.ToString().Contains(navigationSource));
    return tile == null ? false : true;
}

private void DeleteCharacterTile(string navigationSource)
{
    ShellTile tile = ShellTile.ActiveTiles
        .FirstOrDefault(o => o.NavigationUri.ToString().Contains(navigationSource));
    if (tile != null)
    {
        tile.Delete();
    }

}

private void SetCharacterTile(string navigationSource)
{

    FlipTileData tileData = new FlipTileData()
    {
        Title = selectedCharacter.CharacterName,
        SmallBackgroundImage =
            new Uri(selectedCharacter.ImageUri, UriKind.RelativeOrAbsolute),
        BackgroundImage =
            new Uri(selectedCharacter.ImageUri, UriKind.RelativeOrAbsolute),
        BackTitle = selectedCharacter.CharacterName
    };

    ShellTile.Create(new Uri(navigationSource, UriKind.Relative), tileData, true);

}

private void SetPinBar()
{
    var uri = NavigationService.Source.ToString();
    if (CharacterTileExists(uri))
    {
        PinButton.IconUri = new Uri("/Assets/unpin.png", UriKind.Relative);
        PinButton.Text = "Unpin";
    }
```

```
    else
    {
        PinButton.IconUri = new Uri("/Assets/pin.png", UriKind.Relative);
        PinButton.Text = "Pin";
    }
}
```

Handling Navigation

The whole point of a secondary tile is to provide the users of your application with a deep link into your content. If you run the application now with only what we've done so far, you'll find yourself on the right page but the app bar button won't reflect the fact that this content is already pinned. Everything still works fine, but the user is going to be confused. Fortunately, this is easily solved by adding a call to SetPinBar in the OnNavigatedTo method override.

You should already have code in this method to handle setting the DataContext of your page to the right item. Simply add the call to SetPinBar as the last line of code in this method so it can fix up the app bar button. See Listing 4-4 for an example.

Listing 4-4. DataContext management code with SetPinBar function call

```
protected override void OnNavigatedTo(NavigationEventArgs e)
{
    if (DataContext == null)
    {
        string selectedCharacterName = "";
        if (NavigationContext.QueryString
            .TryGetValue("selectedItem", out selectedCharacterName))
        {
            if (!string.IsNullOrEmpty(selectedCharacterName))
            {
                selectedCharacter = (from character in App.ViewModel.Items
                                    where character.CharacterName == selectedCharacterName
                                    select character).FirstOrDefault();
                DataContext = selectedCharacter;
            }
        }
    }

    SetPinBar();
}
```

4-6. Create a Lock Screen Background

Problem

You want to be able to allow the user to use a lock screen image provided by your application.

Solution

Create a lock screen image and register your application as a lock screen background image provider.

How it Works

There are two ways to provide a background image for the lock screen from your applicaton. You can provide a default image that the system can pull from your application or you can set a specific image via code. In this recipe we'll look first at the design guidelines for a lock screen image and then look at how to provide one as a default as well as through a user action from within your application.

Design Guide

There aren't too many restrictions on the background image, but there are a couple of important things to keep in mind. You should keep any text content in your image to a minimum. The image also shouldn't be too "busy". The lock screen is more than just eye candy. It is also interactive in that it provides the user with relevant information at a glance without them having to unlock the phone.

The current time and the next upcoming appointment are two of the default pieces of information that are displayed on the lock screen. Too much text, or a vivid and complex image, is going to interfere with, and distract from, this information as well as annoy the user. Annoyed users ususaly uninstall your application. That's no good for anybody. Figure 4-14 shows a nice example of an appropriate lock screen background image.

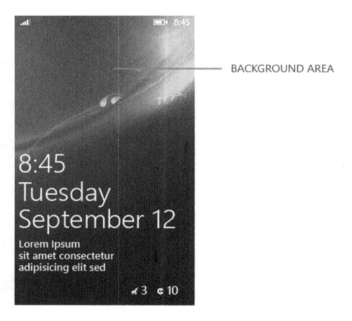

Figure 4-14. A simple and pleasing lock screen image

It's certainly appropriate to include your application's logo and your company name or other brief information on the background, but keep in mind that this information is static. It's possible to replace the lock screen from a background agent to update the information, but this requires swapping out the entire background. The lock screen has a clearly defined area in which you should contain your content. It's always in the top-left region of the screen but differs in dimensions for each screen resolution. Figure 4-15 shows the location and dimensions of the application content section for each of the three device resolutions, and Figure 4-16 shows three excellent examples of the use of this area.

Figure 4-15. *Recommended application specific content area for the lock screen background*

Figure 4-16. *Examples of custom lock screen background image content*

You'll want to keep the text as well as the logo, if you include one, relatively small so that they won't compete with the date, time, and notifications. You might even consider making your logo slightly transparent. The text you include should be directly related to the image you are displaying and not, for example, an advertisement for your application. People have been killed for less.[4] The focus of the lock screen image should be the visual and not the text.

Provide a Default Lock Screen Image

Now that you've designed the most awesome lock screen image anyone will ever need, you must now unleash it upon the world.[5] Providing a default lock screen image couldn't be simpler.

All you need to do is register your application by adding the Lockscreen_Background extension in the WPAppManifest.xml file and provide a default lock screen image in the root of your application named, of all things, DefaultLockScreen.jpg. In the manifest file, immediately after the </Tokens> section, which always exists, you may need to add an <Elements> section to the manifest. Listing 4-5 shows the required XML element. The ConsumerID is just one of those "magic strings" and will never change.

Listing 4-5. Extension Element XML to register as a LockScreen Background provider

```
</Tokens>
<!-- Immediately after Tokens -->
<Extensions>
  <Extension
    ExtensionName="LockScreen_Background"
    ConsumerID="{111DFF24-AA15-4A96-8006-2BFF8122084F}"
    TaskID="_default"/>
</Extensions>
```

Now that you have registered your application to provide a lock screen background you will find that you application now shows up in the Settings on your phone. Deploy your application to your device or emulator and then open the **Settings** on the device. Tap on **lock screen** and you should see the screen in Figure 4-17. Tap on the box below the Background caption and you will be presented with a screen listing all of the applications that can provide a background. Your application should appear in this list. See Figure 4-18.

---

[4]While in all likelihood people haven't *actually* been actually *killed* for less, they have been subjected to merciless and sardonic ridicule.
[5]There is no charge for awesomeness. . . or attractiveness. - Kung Fu Panda

Figure 4-17. *The lock screen settings page*

Figure 4-18. *List of applications that can provide a lock screen background image*

103

Select your application from the list and then lock your device to see your image displayed. If you are using the emulator you can lock the device in one of two ways. You can press F12 when the emulator has focus to turn off the screen and lock the device and then again to wake it up. The other way is to use the Simulation Dashboard in Visual Studio by choosing it from Tools menu. Figure 4-19 shows the Dashboard. Simply toggle the radio button below **Lock Screen** between **Locked** and **Unlocked** to lock the emulator.

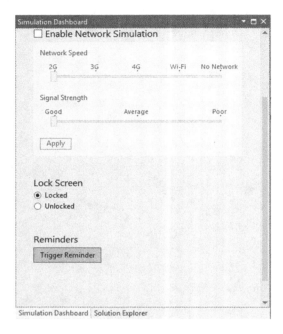

Figure 4-19. *The Simulation Dashboard in Visual Studio*

Let the User Choose a Lock Screen Background

Setting the lock screen image in code is almost as easy as setting up the default. You provide an app bar button for the page that represents the image you want to use and then use the LockScreenManager and LockScreen classes to set the selected image as the background.

Create a method in your code-behind that will be called when the user makes a selection. You can use a contextual menu, an app bar button, or your own button. The method in Listing 4-6 is for the Click event of an app bar button.

■ **Note** By default the Click event handler will be created as a synchronous method. Because we are going to be using await on an asynchronous method call, we need to mark this handler with the async keyword. For more information and async/await, refer to the C# documentation on MSDN.

`http://msdn.microsoft.com/en-us/library/vstudio/hh156513(v=vs.110).aspx`

Listing 4-6. App Bar Button Click Code

```
private async void SetAsLockScreenBackGround(object sender, EventArgs e)
{
    if (!LockScreenManager.IsProvidedByCurrentApplication)
    {
        await LockScreenManager.RequestAccessAsync();
    }

    if (LockScreenManager.IsProvidedByCurrentApplication)
    {
        Uri tempUri = new Uri
            (
            string.Format("ms-appx://{0}", selectedCharacter.ImageUri),
            UriKind.RelativeOrAbsolute
            );

        LockScreen.SetImageUri(tempUri);
    }
}
```

First we check with the LockScreenManager to see if we are currently set as the lock screen background provider, and if not, we request access. Calling The RequestAccessAsync method of the LockScreenManager will pop up a dialog (Figure 4-20) asking the user if they will allow us to set the background. When we return from this call, we again check the IsProvidedByCurrentApplication property and if the user agreed, we go ahead and set the background image. Setting the background image is a simple matter of calling the SetImageUri static method of the LockScreen and passing it a valid Uri pointing to the image you want on the lock screen.

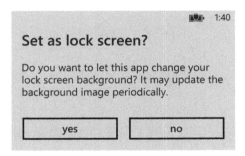

Figure 4-20. *Getting permission from the user to change the lock screen*

4-7. Lock Screen Notification Support

Problem

You want you application to be able to display Live Tile information on the lock screen.

Solution

Configure the required Extensions as well as a lock screen icon in the WPAppManifest.xml file. Optionally, link to the lock screen settings page from within your application.

How it Works

In Windows Phone OS 7.1, only first-party applications could participate in lock screen notifications, but in Windows Phone 8 any third-party can offer notification support. Notification content is pulled directly from your applications default Tile so if you haven't done so, you should check out Recipe 4-1 and get that done now. The Information will only be displayed if the default Tile contains it. If your default Tile isn't showing a Count, for instance, a count will not be displayed on the lock screen. You will also need to configure a lock screen icon in the manifest. Figure 4-21 shows an example of the Lock Screen Notification Area.

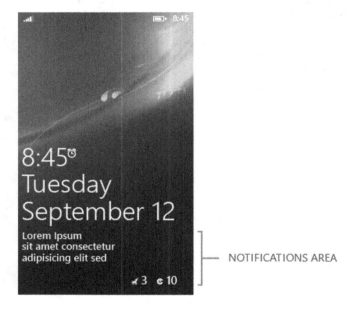

Figure 4-21. *The Lock Screen Notifications Area*

Lock Screen Icon

The lock screen icon must be a PNG file that is 38 x 38 pixels in size. The image must contain only white pixels and have some level of transparency. Once you have the image, edit the WPAppManifest.xml file by right-clicking it and choosing **Open With**. Within the <PrimaryToken> element you will find the <DeviceLockImageURI> element. Set the IsRelative attribute to "true" and the IsResource attribute to "false". Add the full path to your icon inside the element as shown in the following example:

```
<DeviceLockImageURI
  IsRelative="true"
  IsResource="false">Assets\LockIcon.png</DeviceLockImageURI>
```

■ **Note** At the time of this writing there is a bug in the parser related to this particular element. You must ensure that there is NO whitespace around the path to your icon. If your icon isn't showing up on the lock screen, this might be the cause.

Extension Configuration

After configuring the <DeviceLockImageURI> you can add in the extensions while you are editing the manifest. Add the LockScreen_Notification_IconCount and LockScreen_NotificationTextField extensions to the <Extensions> element. You may have to add this element to the manifest, and if so, it should be added immediately after the <Tokens> element. Listing 4-7 shows a properly configured manifest.

Listing 4-7. The <Extensions> Element in WPAppManifest.xml

```
</Tokens>
<!-- Immediately after Tokens -->
<Extensions>
  <Extension
    ExtensionName="LockScreen_Notification_IconCount"
    ConsumerID="{111DFF24-AA15-4A96-8006-2BFF8122084F}"
    TaskID="_default"/>
  <Extension
    ExtensionName="LockScreen_Notification_TextField"
    ConsumerID="{111DFF24-AA15-4A96-8006-2BFF8122084F}"
    TaskID="_default"/>
  <Extension
    ExtensionName="LockScreen_Background"
    ConsumerID="{111DFF24-AA15-4A96-8006-2BFF8122084F}"
    TaskID="_default"/>
</Extensions>
```

Linking to the Lock Screen Settings

The last thing you might want to consider is to add a way for the user to get to the lock screen settings page from within your application. For this example, we'll use an app bar menu item on the main page of the application. Listing 4-8 shows the code and XAML needed. In the Click event handler you simple call the LaunchUriAsync method of the System.Windows.Launcher class passing in the ms-settings-lock: path.

Listing 4-8. App Bar Menu Item and Click Handler for Lock Screen Settings Page Navigation

```
<phone:PhoneApplicationPage.ApplicationBar>
    <shell:ApplicationBar Mode="Minimized">
        <shell:ApplicationBar.MenuItems>
            <shell:ApplicationBarMenuItem
                x:Name="AboutMenuItem"
                IsEnabled="True"
                Text="lock screen settings"
                Click="SettingsMenuItemClick"/>
        </shell:ApplicationBar.MenuItems>
    </shell:ApplicationBar>
</phone:PhoneApplicationPage.ApplicationBar>

private async void SettingsMenuItemClick(object sender, EventArgs e)
{
    // Launch URI for the lock screen settings screen.
    Uri lockSettingsUri = new Uri("ms-settings-lock:");
    await Launcher.LaunchUriAsync(lockSettingsUri);

}
```

■ **Note**　By default the Click event handler will be created as a synchronous method. Because we are going to be using await an asynchronous method call, we need to mark this handler with the async keyword. For more information and async/await, refer to the C# documentation on MSDN.

http://msdn.microsoft.com/en-us/library/vstudio/hh156513(v=vs.110).aspx

CHAPTER 5

■ ■ ■

Background Agents and Local Notifications

Background agents are useful for performing tasks in the background when an application is not running. These tasks can include performing data synchronization, retrieving data from an online source such as an RSS feed or RESTful web service, and displaying notifications to relay information to the user. It is also possible to create local notifications from within the application that will display when the application is not running in the foreground.

Why would a developer want to display notifications when the application is not running? Notifications are a great way to draw a user back into your Windows Phone app! This chapter will cover how to create the different types of background agents available on Windows Phone, as well as how to create different types of local notifications that developers can incorporate into their own applications.

In this chapter, we will beef up your Windows Phone knowledge with the following recipes:

- 5-1. Update the App Tile Using a Background Agent
- 5-2. Engage the User with a Toast (Notification)
- 5-3. Schedule Tile Updates Without a Background Agent
- 5-4. Download Video Using a Background Transfer Service
- 5-5. Schedule Reminders Within Your App

5-1. Update the App Tile Using a Background Agent
Problem

You developed an app to display a list of inspirational quotes. You want to update the app tile so that when pinned to the user's start screen, it displays a different quote at timed intervals.

Solution

Create a Scheduled Task Agent project that registers a periodic task that will update the displayed quote on the application's wide tile.

How It Works

The Windows Phone APIs include a ScheduledTaskAgent class that you will use when creating a background agent that runs on a schedule. The ScheduledTaskAgent class derives from the BackgroundAgent class and contains a method, OnInvoke, which is called when the agent is executed. This is the method you will need to override and provide custom code within to execute the desired actions.

A Scheduled Task Agent can include code for the following tasks:

- *PeriodicTask*: This is used when executing an action that takes little time to process, such as raising a notification, and it runs once approximately every 30 minutes. Note that this time can vary by 10 minutes, and it must complete execution in 25 seconds or less.

- *ResourceIntensiveTask*: This is used when performing tasks that require a long processing time, such as conducting data synchronization with a cloud-based data store. This task will run for 10 minutes and will execute only when all of the following requirements are met:

  - The device screen is locked.

  - The device's battery power is greater than 90 percent.

  - The device is connected to an external power source.

  - The device has a network connection through Wi-Fi or a PC connection.

  - The device is not in the midst of an active phone call.

■ **Note**   Because of the number of requirements needed for a resource-intensive agent to run, it is not guaranteed that it will execute on a user's device.

Agent Limitations

A Windows Phone app can reference only one Scheduled Task Agent project; however, you can register both the periodic and resource-intensive tasks for an application. If your app registers both types of tasks for your background agent, the tasks will run on different schedules and are limited to 11MB of memory usage at any time. If either agent type experiences two unhandled exceptions, it will be removed from the schedule automatically.

Both periodic and resource-intensive tasks have a limited lifetime and are set to expire two weeks from the time they are first registered by the application. So, it is good practice to reregister your agent before the expiration time is met to ensure the agent is not removed from the schedule. There are some cases where an automatic renewal may occur. Most notably, if the app tile is pinned to the phone start screen or is selected to display notifications on the lock screen and the agent makes a call to the Update method on the ShellTile class, which in turn will update the application's tile or lock screen status, then its expiration time will be extended by two weeks.

When designing your app and its associated agent, keep in mind that there are large set of API calls that you simply cannot make from your background agent. Many of these included APIs access components that run in the foreground, such as accessing the camera, the clipboard, and the web browser, to name few. To view the complete list of unsupported API calls from within a scheduled agent, review the article "Unsupported APIs for background agents for Windows Phone" on the MSDN web site at http://msdn.microsoft.com/en-us/library/windowsphone/develop/hh202962(v=vs.105).aspx.

If you've taken a quick peek at that article, you will notice that the list also includes the background audio player as an unsupported API for scheduled agents. You are probably thinking to yourself, "Why wouldn't a background audio player be supported in a background agent? Isn't that the purpose?"

Although that seems like a valid point, this action is not appropriate within a Scheduled Task Agent. The purpose of this agent is to execute an action at timed intervals. Playing audio in the background just doesn't fit in here, since the playback is initiated by the user rather than launched as a timed-based action. There is a separate type of agent you will create so that your app can play audio even while your app is not running in the foreground; however, that is beyond the scope of this chapter. We will discuss this topic in Chapter 7.

Using a Scheduled Task Agent

Now that we have discussed what you can't do within a Scheduled Task Agent, let's go over what you are able to do!

- *HttpWebRequest*: You can make web requests using the `HttpWebRequest` class, which will come in handy if your app needs to use web services to manage data, such as uploading or downloading data.

- *Mutex*: If your background agent needs to access files in isolated storage that are also used by the foreground app, then you will need to use a `Mutex` class to synchronize access to those files. This holds true for any other resources that are shared between the app and the background agent.

- *GeoCoordinateWatcherAPI*: You can use a background agent to retrieve the device's geographic coordinates using the `GeoCoordinateWatcher` API. Note that the location is a cached value, which is updated every 15 minutes, so the user's location may not always be 100 percent accurate. Keep this in mind when designing agents that depend on tracking the user's location.

- *ShellTile* and *ShellToast*: As was hinted at during the introduction to this chapter, you can use a background agent to update your app tiles or raise a toast notification.

Since this recipe alludes to updating tiles from the agent, let's walk through a simple example on how this can be accomplished.

Open the solution named InspireMe, located within the `\Chapter 5\InspireMeStart` directory. This application simply displays a list of quotes when launched. It also provides the user with the ability to pin and unpin a live tile to the device's start screen. For now, when the tile is pinned to the start screen, the wide tile content is set to a random quote. Once this quote is set, it does not change.

■ **Note** The pin/unpin application bar icons featured in the InspireMe app are not included as part of the icon set delivered with the Windows Phone SDK. These icons were downloaded from `http://modernuiicons.com`, which are offered as open source and are also available on GitHub.

We will enhance the application so that the application's wide tile content will update periodically with a random quote from the list when the tile is pinned to the start screen. We will need to create a Scheduled Task Agent project and make use of the `PeriodicTask` to accomplish this goal.

Building a Scheduled Task Agent

Add a new project to the solution. In the Add New Project dialog, select Windows Phone Scheduled Task Agent, as depicted in Figure 5-1. Name the project InspireMe.Agent.

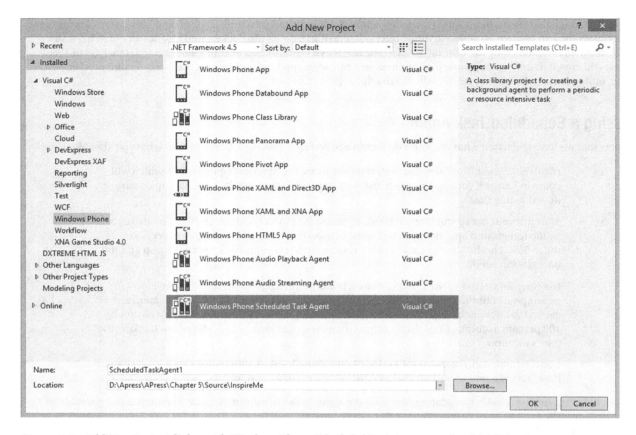

Figure 5-1. *Add New Project dialog with Windows Phone Scheduled Task Agent template highlighted*

When the Scheduled Task Agent project loads, you will notice a single class is included in the file called ScheduledAgent, which derives from the ScheduledTaskAgent class. Open this file and take a look at the generated code that is provided by default. The method that we will be adding code within is the OnInvoke method. However, this will require some modifications to the InspireMe Windows Phone project, which we will get to shortly.

The first thing we will need to do is add a reference within our Scheduled Task Agent to the InspireMe.DataProvider project. The reason we have the Quotes list separated into a data provider class library is so we can access the Quotes list data from both the main app and the background agent. It is extremely important to note that this simplistic approach is being used because we are not modifying the list of quotes at any time.

If the application allowed the user to either add or remove quotes within the foreground app, it would be best to store the Quotes XML file within isolated storage, using the IsolatedStorageFile class. In addition to that, when accessing files from isolated storage from either the foreground app or the background agent, you must use a mutex to secure exclusive access to the file on only one thread. In this way, if one thread acquires a mutex, the second thread is suspended until the first thread releases the mutex. The benefit to this approach is to prevent data corruption in the event the Quotes XML file is being modified by the foreground app at a time when the background agent is also trying to access it. Isolated storage is out of the scope of this chapter, so we will keep our recipe focused on using a background agent with a static collection. We will be discussing IsolatedStorage in more detail in Chapter 11.

Within the InspireMe project, be sure to add a reference to the newly created InspireMe.Agent project. As well, we should ensure that an ExtendedTask element has been added to the application manifest for the background agent, within the Tasks collection. Open the file in Code View, and be sure that the ExtendedTask element is added to the Tasks collection, as shown in Listing 5-1.

Listing 5-1. ExtendedTask Element for the InspireMe.Agent

```
<Tasks>
   <DefaultTask Name="_default" NavigationPage="MainPage.xaml" />
   <ExtendedTask Name="InspireMeTask">
     <BackgroundServiceAgent Specifier="ScheduledTaskAgent" Name="InspireMeTask"
Source="InspireMe.Agent" Type="InspireMe.Agent.ScheduledAgent" />
   </ExtendedTask>
</Tasks>
```

Registering the Agent

It is now time to add the code in the foreground app to register our background agent. We will need to use a couple of classes from the `Microsoft.Phone.Scheduler` namespace to accomplish this action: `PeriodicTask` and `ScheduledActionService`.

In the MainPage code-behind file, add a using directive to include the `Microsoft.Phone.Scheduler` namespace. Next, add a new private method called `RegisterAgent`. In this method, we will do the following:

1) Create a `PeriodicTask` object, setting a name and description for the agent.

2) Check to determine whether the `PeriodicTask` has already been registered with the `ScheduledActionService` by calling the `Find` method on the `ScheduledActionService` class and passing in the task name.

3) If the scheduled action is already registered, we will remove it by calling the `Remove` method on the `ScheduledActionService` class, passing in the task name.

4) We will then register the `PeriodicTask` with the operating system by calling the `Add` method on the `ScheduledActionService` class and passing in the `PeriodicTask` object.

If you are wondering why we are going through the effort to remove the task only to add it back into the schedule, recall the point in the beginning of this section when we talked about how background agents have an expiration date set to two weeks from the date when it was first registered. The action of removing this task and then adding it back in ensures that we push out the expiration date when the user runs the application. You are probably thinking "We update the application's tile. Doesn't that automatically renew the agent?"

It does, but only in the case when the user has pinned the app's tile to the device's start screen. This isn't a guarantee, so the only way we can be sure to extend the life of our agent is to force a new registration of it whenever the user launches the application.

Finally, we will need to call the `RegisterAgent` method when the MainPage is loaded. For completeness, we should include exception handling. For this demonstration, we will simply display errors in a `MessageBox`, as depicted in Listing 5-2. Ideally, if you are publishing your app, you will want to fine-tune your error handling to log errors, notify the user, or provide the user the option to e-mail the exception details to your support e-mail address.

Listing 5-2. RegisterAgent Method in the MainPage Code-Behind

```
private void MainPage_Loaded(object sender, RoutedEventArgs e)
{
    RegisterAgent();
}

private void RegisterAgent()
{
    string taskName = "InspireMeTask";
    try
```

```
        {

            if (ScheduledActionService.Find(taskName) != null)
            {
                //if the agent exists, remove and then add it to ensure
                //the agent's schedule is updated to avoid expiration
                ScheduledActionService.Remove(taskName);
            }

            PeriodicTask periodicTask = new PeriodicTask(taskName);
            periodicTask.Description = "InspireMe task updates the tile with a new quote";
            ScheduledActionService.Add(periodicTask);
        }
        catch (InvalidOperationException exception)
        {
            MessageBox.Show(exception.Message);
        }
        catch (SchedulerServiceException schedulerException)
        {
            MessageBox.Show(schedulerException.Message);
        }
}
```

At this point, you can run the app in the emulator, but for testing purposes, it's not efficient to wait for 30 minutes to see whether your agent runs as expected. For this reason, there is a method available on the ScheduledActionService class, called LaunchForTest, which you can use when debugging your scheduled agent. This is to be used only when in debug mode and should be removed before publishing the app. The LaunchForTest method accepts a task name and a TimeSpan value. The TimeSpan value indicates the amount of time that should pass between task executions. For testing purposes, a 30-second delay time works well; however, you can set it to any value you think suits your testing purposes best. Include the code shown in Listing 5-3, after the scheduled task is registered through the ScheduledActionService, in the RegisterAgent method in the MainPage code-behind.

Listing 5-3. Use the LaunchForTest Method When Debugging Scheduled Agents

```
//only use LaunchForTest when debugging
                //be sure to remove this code section before publishing your app
#if DEBUG
                ScheduledActionService.LaunchForTest(taskName, TimeSpan.FromSeconds(30));
#endif
```

Note that if we wanted to also register a resource-intensive agent, all we would need to do is create a ResourceIntensiveTask object and register the scheduled action with the operating system, in the same manner we created and registered the PeriodicTask.

```
        ResourceIntensiveTask resourceIntensiveTask =
                new ResourceIntensiveTask("InspireMe RI Agent");
        resourceIntensiveTask.Description = "Resource intensive agent for InspireMe";
        ScheduledActionService.Add(resourceIntensiveTask);
```

Since we are simply updating a tile, a resource-intensive agent doesn't make sense in this recipe. Just note that its implementation is similar to the periodic agent.

Updating the Tile

With everything in place in the foreground app, we need to revisit the Scheduled Task Agent project and include the necessary code to actually update the application's tile with a random quote.

Within the ScheduledAgent class, add the using directive for the InspireMe.DataProvider namespace. Now it's time to add code to the OnInvoke method. Notice how there is already a call to the NotifyComplete method. It is important to leave this code intact, because this is what notifies the operating system that the agent has completed the execution of the task's actions on the current run.

Before the call to the NotifyComplete method, we will include a check to determine whether the current task that is being executed is in fact a PeriodicTask, and we will code the desired actions for the task. The scheduled task that is being invoked could be different in the scenario where the foreground app uses both a PeriodicTask and a ResourceIntensiveTask. In this instance, it's not necessary to include this check here because we registered only one scheduled task, but it is something worth mentioning while we're here.

Next, we will want to instantiate a new instance of the QuoteDataProvider class, which will load the quotes from the XML file into the QuoteList collection, making the quotes available within our agent. We will then use the Random class to generate a random number, which will represent the ID of the quote we will then add to the back of the app's wide tile. We will pull the random quote from the collection using the magic of LINQ! This means we must add the using directive for the System.Linq namespace in this class.

Once we obtain the random quote from the collection, we will update the app's tile by creating a new FlipTileData object and setting the WideBackContent property to the new quote. For good measure, we will also update the BackTitle property to display the date and time the tile was last updated. Our code should now look similar to Listing 5-4.

Listing 5-4. Include the Desired Code in the OnInvoke Method in the ScheduledTaskAgent Class

```
protected override void OnInvoke(ScheduledTask task)
{
    if (task is PeriodicTask)
    {
        QuoteDataProvider quoteProvider = new QuoteDataProvider();

        if (quoteProvider.QuoteList.Count() > 0)
        {
            FlipTileData newTileData = new FlipTileData()
            {
                //load a random quote from the quote data provider
                WideBackContent = quoteProvider.GetRandomQuote(),
                BackTitle = string.Format("Last Updated: {0}", DateTime.Now.ToString("MMM dd,
yyyy h:mm tt"))
            };

            ShellTile appTile = ShellTile.ActiveTiles.FirstOrDefault(x =>
x.NavigationUri.ToString().Contains(mainPageUri));
            if (appTile != null)
            {
                appTile.Update(newTileData);
            }
        }
    }

    NotifyComplete();
}
```

We have all the code in place that is required to load quotes into a list in the main application and display random quotes on the backside of the app's wide tile. One thing that is important to note here is that if you are developing an application for which you plan to support wide tiles, you will need to explicitly enable this setting in the application manifest, as shown in Figure 5-2. By default, the "Support for large tiles" option in the manifest is turned off.

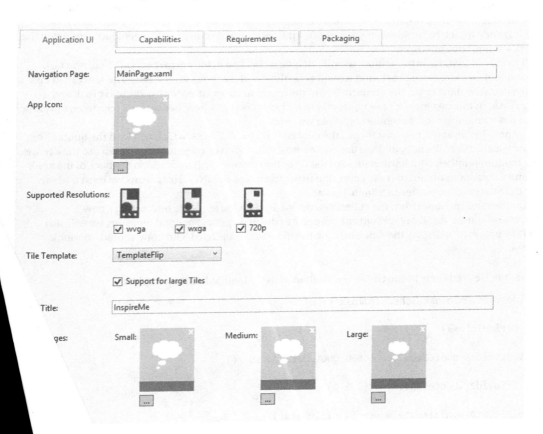

'e support for large tiles in your app

at is worthwhile to mention here is that although the Windows Phone project generates default tiles
of the possible tile templates, it is good practice to get in the habit of creating your own tile images
' the app's purpose. Syncfusion provides a free tool for developers, called MetroStudio, which you
'om tile images. You can download this tool from www.syncfusion.com/downloads/metrostudio.
ate the InspireMe tiles.

he Emulator

ion for a test run. Launch the app in the emulator and notice the Quotes list displayed
application bar icon. If the tile was pinned successfully, you will automatically be
newly pinned tile.
is pinned to the start screen. Tap and hold the InspireMe tile to change sizes.
small tile size. The next size change will expand to the large, wide tile size,

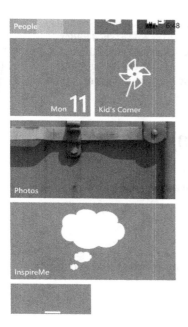

Figure 5-3. *InspireMe wide tile pinned to start screen*

With the app launched and the tile pinned to the start screen, wait for the tile to flip to the backside, as illustrated in Figure 5-4. Notice the random quote that is displayed, along with the last updated date and time. Continue to monitor the start screen to watch the tile as it flips from back to front, and the quotes continue to change on a regular interval.

Figure 5-4. *InspireMe wide tile: back content*

Congratulations on creating your first scheduled agent for Windows Phone 8! We have packaged the complete solution, which includes the scheduled agent for this recipe, within the \Chapter 5\InspireMeFinished folder.

There was a lot of content to digest in this recipe, so take some time to sit back, relax, and enjoy this accomplishment. Although it is simple to create a scheduled agent for your app, there is a lot of thought and consideration that must be given to the design of the app, such as the purpose of the background agent, which background agents you will include, and the limitations of each agent.

5-2. Engage the User with a Toast (Notification)
Problem

You want to develop an app that will provide the user with a notification if there are any weather alerts in the area when the app is not running.

Solution

Create a Scheduled Task Agent project that registers a periodic task that will read from a weather feed and display a toast notification when one or more active weather alerts are discovered.

How It Works

In Recipe 5-1, we discussed in depth what a Scheduled Task Agent is, along with the two types of tasks you can register in an agent. The same concepts apply within this recipe. The only difference is that rather than performing a tile update, we will be creating a toast notification using the ShellToast class.

A toast notification displays in a colored band at the top of the screen for approximately 10 seconds. Its purpose is to notify users of an app-related event and can be used to provide deep linking into your app. This means that when the user taps the notification, it will launch your app and load a specific page, which can be a page other than the main screen. If a deep link is not configured for the toast notification, the app will still launch and load the main page by default. Note that the user may not always tap the notification, so do not rely on this behavior. The user can flick the toast to the right, which dismisses the notification. As well, the user may not see the notification in the short time it is displayed on the device screen. Keep this in mind when designing your app. You may want to queue any notifications that were missed and display them in an alternate way in your app if it makes sense to do so, such as a messaging app that distinguishes between old and new messages.

A toast notification can be triggered locally or through push notifications by a cloud-based service. For the purpose of this recipe, we will be focusing on raising local toast notifications through a background agent.

When creating a toast notification, you are able to configure the notification's title, the message (or content), and a navigation URI to specify the page to load when the user taps the notification. Because of the limited space at the top of the screen for toast notifications, note the following character limitations:

- *Title property*: Approximately 40 characters, if Content is not set

- *Content property*: Approximately 47 characters, if Title is not set

- *Title and Content combined*: Approximately 41 characters

It is important to note the values you set for these properties will be truncated if the values extend beyond the limitations; therefore, it is best to keep your notifications concise. You will notice that the toast also displays a small version of your app icon, which is defined by the icon that is associated with your app and cannot be changed.

If your app is running at a time when a toast notification is to be triggered for your app, the notification will not display. To display any new toast notifications, you must ensure your app is not running in the foreground. This is important to keep in mind when we are testing later.

Let's Make a Toast!

Now that you are familiar with the concepts of a toast notification for Windows Phone, let's develop an agent so we can put it into action. Launch Visual Studio 2012, and open the WeatherAlerts solution in the \Chapter 5\WeatherAlerts folder. Add a new Windows Phone Scheduled Task Agent project to this solution called WeatherAlerts.Agent.

Similar to Recipe 5-1, we will need to add a reference to the application's related data provider, which, in this case, is the WeatherAlerts.DataProvider project. As we discussed earlier, this approach is taken to enable code reuse between the main Windows Phone application and the scheduled agent. Before we make any modifications, open the AlertsDataProvider class to determine the method call that needs to be included in the background agent.

Notice that there is a public method called LoadData, which uses the OpenReadAsync method on the System.Net.WebClient class to retrieve the data from a URL that points to a weather site's XML feed. This is the method that we will need to call from within the agent's OnInvoke method.

Also notice that the OpenReadCompleted event, which receives the result of the data feed, raises another event, AlertsDownloaded. In this way, we can register this event handler within the Scheduled Task Agent so that the agent receives a notification from the data provider when the data has been downloaded from the XML data feed.

Creating the Toast Notification

Within the AlertsDownloaded event, we will create our toast notification by creating an instance of the ShellToast class and setting the Title, Content, and NavigationUri properties. To ensure the notification is displayed, we need to call the ShellToast.Show method. From here, we can also remove the event handler registration. Finally, we will move the NotifyComplete method call from the OnInvoke method to the AlertsDownloaded event. Refer to Listing 5-5 for the code that was added to the ScheduledAgent class.

Listing 5-5. Scheduled Task Agent for the WeatherAlerts App

```
AlertsDataProvider dataProvider = new AlertsDataProvider();
protected override void OnInvoke(ScheduledTask task)
{
    if (task is PeriodicTask)
    {
        dataProvider.LoadData();
    }
}

private void dataProvider_AlertsDownloaded(object sender, System.EventArgs e)
{
    if (dataProvider.WeatherAlerts.Count() > 0)
    {
        ShellToast toast = new ShellToast();
        toast.Title = "Weather Alert";
        toast.Content = dataProvider.WeatherAlerts.Count().ToString() + " active alert(s)";
        toast.NavigationUri = new System.Uri("/MainPage.xaml", System.UriKind.RelativeOrAbsolute);
        toast.Show();
    }

    dataProvider.AlertsDownloaded -= new AlertsDataProvider.EventHandler(dataProvider_AlertsDownloaded);

    NotifyComplete();
}
```

Next, we will need to return to the WeatherAlerts application and add a reference to the InspireMe.Agent project. We will also need to modify the MainPage code-behind file to register the agent when the page loads. Refer to Listing 5-2 in Recipe 5-1 to view an example of how to implement this in your MainPage code-behind.

Last but not least, we need to include the ExtendedTask definition in the application manifest. Refer to Listing 5-1 within Recipe 5-1 as the example to follow. Once that is in place, we can launch our app in the emulator to test it. Note that if there no active weather alerts from the feed provided at the time you run this app, you can alternatively replace it with a weather feed that suits your testing needs or just provide some fake data to force a toast notification to occur. You can make this change within the AlertsDataProvider class in the WeatherAlerts.DataProvider project.

Testing Toast Notifications in the Emulator

In launching the app in the emulator, the first thing you want to do is back out of the app and return to the start screen. At this point, it's just a matter of waiting for the agent to run for the first time. If there are alerts that are active, you should see the toast notification depicted in Figure 5-5.

Figure 5-5. *Toast notification displaying a count of active weather alerts*

When the toast notification displays onscreen, click it with your mouse to launch the WeatherAlerts app and view the full details of any active alerts, as shown in Figure 5-6.

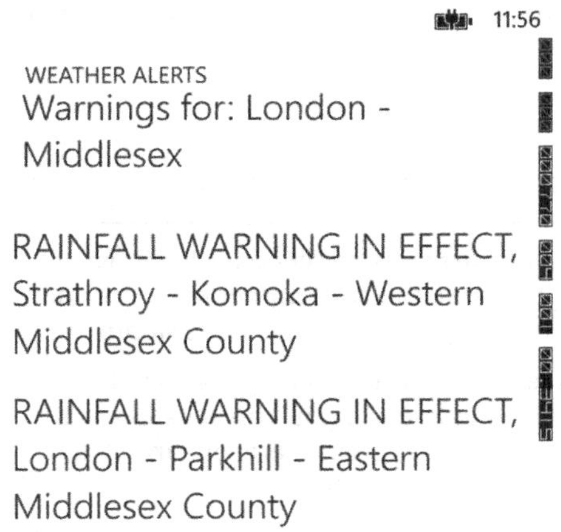

▪▪▪ 11:56

WEATHER ALERTS
Warnings for: London -
Middlesex

RAINFALL WARNING IN EFFECT,
Strathroy - Komoka - Western
Middlesex County

RAINFALL WARNING IN EFFECT,
London - Parkhill - Eastern
Middlesex County

Figure 5-6. *WeatherAlerts main page with alert details*

That is all it takes to create local toast notifications in your app!

To view the source code for the complete solution, load the WeatherAlerts solution located within the `\Chapter 5\WeatherAlertsFinished` folder.

5-3. Schedule Tile Updates Without a Background Agent

Problem

You are creating a traffic app, and you want to update the app tile's image with the most recent image of current traffic conditions at regular intervals. This feature should work even when the app is not running.

Solution

Schedule your tile image updates from within your app using the `ShellTileSchedule` class.

How It Works

The `ShellTileSchedule` class, from the `Microsoft.Phone.Shell` namespace, provides a mechanism to allow you to schedule updates of an app tile's background image from within the application itself, without the need to create a Scheduled Task Agent. The schedule will remain active even when your app is not running. As well, you can choose to update the app tile on a recurring schedule or on a one-time basis. If you choose a recurring schedule, you can optionally configure the schedule to run a specific number of times or indefinitely. Refer to Table 5-1 for a list of these properties and information on how they are used.

Table 5-1. *ShellTileSchedule Properties*

Property	Type	Details
Interval	UpdateInterval (enumerated value)	Use this property when creating a recurring schedule. Set its value to the options defined in the UpdateInterval enumeration. Possible values are EveryHour, EveryDay, EveryWeek, and EveryMonth.
MaxUpdateCount	Integer	Use this property when creating a recurring schedule and to limit the number of times that the schedule will run. This schedule will run indefinitely if a value is not set for this property or if the value is less than 1.
Recurrence	UpdateRecurrence (enumerated value)	Use this property to indicate whether the schedule will be executed only once or on a recurring basis. Set its value to the options defined in the UpdateRecurrence enumeration. Possible values are Onetime and Interval.
RemoteImageUri	Uri	Use this property to set the background of the tile to the image located at the specified URI.
StartTime	DateTime	Use this property to set the start time of the schedule.

In looking at the ShellTileSchedule properties in Table 5-1, you can see that the background image is the only tile property you will be able to update, using the RemoteImageUri property. If you need to update additional tile content, you will need to create a Scheduled Task Agent, as described in Recipe 5-1, or implement push notifications.

Once you have a ShellTileSchedule object instantiated and configured, you can activate it by calling its Start method. To deactivate the schedule and stop the tile background image from updating, simply call the Stop method. Let's walk through an example to see how this works.

At this point, you may be wondering where it is that we can include code to update the RemoteUriImage property on each schedule run. Well, there is no way to do this with a ShellTileSchedule object. If you need more control over your tile updates, you will need to create a Scheduled Task Agent. Now, your next thought may be, "Well, what's the point of this when I can set the property only one time? How do I use this to update the tile to a new image?"

Ideally, the image will be one in which the URI will remain the same but the image is updated on a recurring basis on the web server that it is hosted on. This is useful for apps that want to display the most recent state of an image that changes often, such as weather maps or traffic images.

Now that we know what a ShellTileSchedule is and how to use it, let's put it into practice for our sample traffic app. Launch Visual Studio 2012, and open the TrafficView solution located in the \Chapter 5\TrafficViewStart folder.

The TrafficView app leverages a few of the images from the current traffic views listed within the Traveller's Portal on the Ontario Ministry of Transportation web site. These images are updated on the site every three to five minutes. Although we are able to run the schedule on only an hourly basis as the most frequent interval, we are guaranteed that the selected image will always reflect a new view when the schedule runs.

Run the application in the emulator to get a feel for how it currently works and to note the missing implementation, which we'll be adding during this recipe walk-through.

When launched in the emulator, the main page of the TrafficView app will be displayed, as shown in Figure 5-7. Notice that it contains a selection list, an image depicting the current list selection, and a Pin button in the application bar. The purpose of the application is to select a view from the list and ultimately pin a tile that represents the selected view to the device start screen. The tile will be attached to a ShellTileSchedule object which will update the tile's image on each schedule run. Once a tile has been pinned to the start screen, the app should allow the tile to be unpinned.

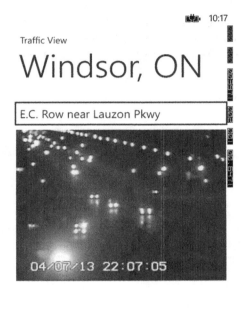

Figure 5-7. Initial launch of TrafficView

Currently, tapping the pin button in the application bar will simply raise a message to indicate that we still have work to do within this app to achieve the desired behavior. The TrafficViewModel class will be where the bulk of the code changes will need to be made.

Within the TrafficViewModel class, we will need to ensure the following actions are handled:

- Pin tile
    - Create a new shell tile that will represent the selected view, using the FlipTileData object.
    - Add, or update, the shell tile within the ShellTile.ActiveTiles collection. This is the action that will pin the tile to the start screen.
    - Create the ShellTileSchedule object to update the tile every hour.
    - Save the current app state to the application settings in isolated storage.

- Unpin tile

    - Stop the ShellTileSchedule for the pinned tile.

    - Remove the tile from the ShellTile.ActiveTiles collection, which in turn will remove the tile from the start screen.

    - Save the current app state to the application settings in isolated storage.

Refer to Listing 5-6 to view the code required to pin a tile to the start screen, which will initiate a ShellTileSchedule. Note that the StartShellTileSchedule method sets the properties listed in Table 5-1 so that the tile will display the image at the specified URI of the selected item and update every hour. A call to the Start method is then made to trigger the schedule start.

Listing 5-6. TrafficViewModel Methods to Pin Tile and Create ShellTileSchedule

```
private const string mainPageUri = "/MainPage.xaml?state=pinned";
private ShellTileSchedule ugTileSchedule;

//current traffic view selected in the list on the Main Page
private TrafficItemViewModel currentTrafficView;
public TrafficItemViewModel CurrentTrafficView
{
    ...
}

//the traffic view that is pinned to the start screen
//returns null if a tile is not pinned
private TrafficItemViewModel pinnedTile;
public TrafficItemViewModel PinnedTile
{
    ...
}

public void PinTile()
{
    //update the pinned tile to the selected item
    //on the Main Page
    this.PinnedTile = this.CurrentTrafficView;

    FlipTileData tileData = new FlipTileData();
    tileData.Title = "";
    tileData.BackTitle = "Windsor Traffic View";

    //set the back tile content to indicate which traffic view is represented on the front tile
    tileData.BackContent = this.PinnedTile.Description;

    //if a traffic view tile has not yet been pinned to the start screen, create a new one
    //otherwise, update the existing tile with the new traffic view selection
    ShellTile scheduledTile = ShellTile.ActiveTiles.FirstOrDefault(x =>
x.NavigationUri.ToString().Contains(mainPageUri));
```

```
    if (scheduledTile == null)
    {
        ShellTile.Create(new Uri(mainPageUri, UriKind.Relative), tileData, false);
        scheduledTile = ShellTile.ActiveTiles.FirstOrDefault(x =>
x.NavigationUri.ToString().Contains(mainPageUri));
    }
    else
    {
        scheduledTile.Update(tileData);
    }

    //with the tile pinned to start, start the shell tile schedule
    StartShellTileSchedule(scheduledTile);

    //SaveAppState is a private method in the ViewModel
    //that saves the current view selection and pinned
    //tile info to IsolatedStorage.ApplicationSettings
    SaveAppState();

}

private void StartShellTileSchedule(ShellTile scheduledTile)
{
    ugTileSchedule = new ShellTileSchedule(scheduledTile);

    //set the schedule to update every hour, indefinitely,
    //or until the user chooses to stop the schedule
    ugTileSchedule.Recurrence = UpdateRecurrence.Interval;
    ugTileSchedule.Interval = UpdateInterval.EveryHour;
    ugTileSchedule.StartTime = DateTime.Now;
    ugTileSchedule.RemoteImageUri = App.ViewModel.CurrentTrafficView.ImageUri;

    //start the schedule
    ugTileSchedule.Start();
}
```

Furthermore, we need to add code to the ApplicationBarPin_Click event within the MainPage so that when the pin button is tapped, the PinTile method in the TrafficViewModel class is called to trigger the expected behavior.

```
private void ApplicationBarPin_Click(object sender, EventArgs e)
{
    App.ViewModel.PinTile();
    UpdateAppBar();
}
```

The UpdateAppBar method within the MainPage code-behind simply handles swapping out the pin/unpin application bar buttons accordingly.

The next thing that needs to be handled is the action of stopping an existing ShellTileSchedule and removing a pinned tile from the start screen, as shown in Listing 5-7.

Listing 5-7. TrafficViewModel Methods to Delete ShellTileSchedule and Unpin Tile

```
public void UnpinTile()
{
    if (this.PinnedTile != null)
    {
        //get the shell tile from the ActiveTiles collection
        ShellTile appTile = ShellTile.ActiveTiles
                .FirstOrDefault(x => x.NavigationUri.ToString().Contains(mainPageUri));

        //stop the shell tile schedule, and then unpin the tile
        StopShellTileSchedule(appTile);

        //remove the pinned tile from the start screen
        appTile.Delete();
    }

    //clear the pinned tile from the view model
    this.PinnedTile = null;

    //save app settings to reflect the change
    SaveAppState();
}

private void StopShellTileSchedule(ShellTile scheduledTile)
{
    if (scheduledTile != null)
    {
        //to stop a running schedule, we must attach to an existing schedule
        //to do that, we will need to recreate the schedule and start it,
        //if the schedule was started during a previous run of the application
        if (ugTileSchedule == null)
        {
            StartShellTileSchedule(scheduledTile);
        }

        ugTileSchedule.Stop();
    }
}
```

Additionally, we need to add code to the ApplicationBarUnpin_Click event within the MainPage so that when the unpin button is tapped, the UnpinTile method in the TrafficViewModel class is called to carry out the desired actions.

```
private void ApplicationBarPin_Click(object sender, EventArgs e)
{
    App.ViewModel.UnpinTile();
    UpdateAppBar();
}
```

The completed solution provided with this chapter source code, in the \Chapter 5\TrafficViewFinished folder, also contains methods to handle saving and loading app state from the IsolatedStorageSettings.ApplicationSettings collection.

Launch the project to view the fully functioning TrafficView application in action. On load, select a view from the list, and tap the pin button in the application bar. If the tile is pinned to the start screen successfully, you will be taken to the start screen automatically to view the pinned tile. The traffic view you selected should be reflected in the app tile, as shown in Figure 5-8.

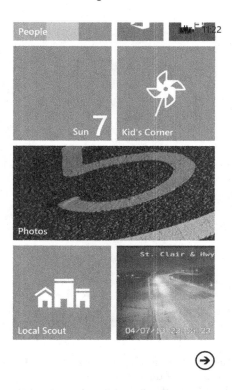

Figure 5-8. *TrafficView tile pinned to the start screen, whose image will update every hour by the ShellTileSchedule*

Click the back button in the emulator to return to the application. Notice that the unpin button now appears, and a message is displayed at the bottom of the screen indicating that the current traffic view is pinned to the start screen. The selection list is also disabled and will become enabled only when the current image view's tile is unpinned from the start screen, as shown in Figure 5-9.

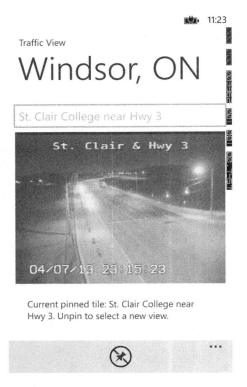

Figure 5-9. *TrafficView main page depicting current pinned tile state*

This recipe demonstrated an approach to update the image on an application tile without using a background agent. However, as we have seen, it is extremely limited in comparison to using a Scheduled Task Agent, in that it allows you to update the tile's image only by pointing to a predefined URI. It is expected that the image you specify in the URI is one that is updated on the web server in which it is hosted. The ShellTileSchedule object simply refreshes the image during each scheduled run.

It is also important to keep in mind that, just as with Scheduled Task Agents, should the ShellTileSchedule cause an exception or failure a number of times, its schedule will be canceled. When using this approach, you may want to consider forcing the start of the schedule each time the application is run, if it makes sense to do so in the context of your application.

5-4. Download Video Using a Background Transfer Service
Problem

You want to develop an app that allows you to download your favorite videos from the Channel9 MSDN site.

Solution

Use the Background Transfer Service to download the video using an HTTP file transfer request.

How It Works

The background transfer APIs, available in the `Microsoft.Phone.BackgroundTransfer` namespace, allows an application to queue up multiple HTTP or HTTPS file transfer requests that will continue to be performed when the app is no longer running in the foreground. Both file download and upload are supported.

The `BackgroundTransferRequest` class will be used to define a file transfer request. It also includes the `TransferStatusChanged` and `TransferProgressChanged` events, which you can register in your application to monitor the status of existing file transfers and current transfer progress state, respectively.

The `BackgroundTransferService` class allows you to add these transfer requests to a queue so that the requests will be executed in the background. The file transfers will continue to execute even when the application is not running in the foreground.

There are a few things to keep in mind when working with background transfers for Windows Phone.

- Background transfers must include a local file path.

- All download requests must specify a download location within the `/shared/transfers` root directory in isolated storage. Once the file has been downloaded, you can move it to another location in isolated storage, if you so choose.

- Maximum size of file transfers are as follows:

    - 20MB when downloading files over a cellular connection

    - 100MB when downloading files over a Wi-Fi connection when the device is not plugged into a power source

    - 5MB when uploading a file

- Up to five transfer requests are allowed for a single application.

- Up to 500 transfer request are allowed across all applications.

- Only two transfer requests may run concurrently at any given time across all applications.

■ **Note**   When a background transfer request has completed, it is not automatically removed from the background transfer service. You must call the service's Remove method, passing in the completed request object, to clear the request from the service queue so that it can accept new transfer requests.

Designing the Background Transfer Service

To understand how background transfer requests work, we will create an application that will allow the user to queue up a list of videos for download. Launch Visual Studio 2012, and create a new Windows Phone Databound App project, named DownloadMe. Since we have chosen a databound app template, we have the basic shell of our ViewModels already created for us, along with some basic data binding already wired up for us in the MainPage. We will be making quite a few modifications, but this is a good starting point.

The purpose of this app is to allow the user to do the following:

- Select videos to download from a static media list of our choosing

- Ensure the download completes even if the user exits the app

- Track the video download progress

- Enable the user to play the video once it is downloaded

The MainPage will be modified slightly to display more information about the media items available for download. As well, we will include a download button and a check box next to each media item to allow the user to selectively download one or more items. Furthermore, when the download completes, we want the user to be able to view any of the video files that downloaded.

In the LongListSelector control, we will modify the DataTemplate to include the check box for each item in the list and some additional TextBlock controls. The TextBlock controls will be used to display the download location of the file and a progress message only while the item is being downloaded. We will also display a button to allow the user to play the file once it has been downloaded. The markup for the LongListSelector should now be similar to the markup in Listing 5-8.

Listing 5-8. LongListSelector Markup Modifications in the MainPage.xaml File

```
<phone:LongListSelector.ItemTemplate>
    <DataTemplate>
        <Grid>
            <Grid.ColumnDefinitions>
                <ColumnDefinition Width="Auto" />
                <ColumnDefinition Width="*" />
            </Grid.ColumnDefinitions>
            <Grid.RowDefinitions>
                <RowDefinition />
                <RowDefinition />
                <RowDefinition />
            </Grid.RowDefinitions>
            <CheckBox IsChecked="{Binding ItemSelected, Mode=TwoWay}"
                    Grid.RowSpan="2" />
            <Button Content="Play"
                    Height="80"
                    Grid.RowSpan="2" />
            <TextBlock Grid.Column="1" Grid.Row="0"
                    Text="{Binding Title}" TextWrapping="Wrap"
                    Style="{StaticResource PhoneTextLargeStyle}"/>
            <TextBlock Grid.Column="1" Grid.Row="1"
                    Text="{Binding Speaker}" TextWrapping="Wrap"
                    Style="{StaticResource PhoneTextSubtleStyle}"/>
            <TextBlock Grid.Column="1" Grid.Row="2"
                    Text="{Binding LocalUri}" TextWrapping="Wrap"
                    Style="{StaticResource PhoneTextSubtleStyle}"/>
            <TextBlock Grid.Column="1" Grid.Row="2"
                    Text="{Binding DownloadProgress}" TextWrapping="Wrap"
                    Style="{StaticResource PhoneTextSubtleStyle}"/>
        </Grid>
    </DataTemplate>
</phone:LongListSelector.ItemTemplate>
</phone:LongListSelector>
```

Enhancing the User Interface

You may have noticed that we have both the check box and button elements in the same grid row and column location. We plan on showing the check box only when a file has not been selected for download yet. Once the file has been downloaded, we will hide this element and display the button instead. To control the visibility of these elements, we need to use a Converter class.

Add a new class to the project, and name it VisibilityConverter. Modify the class to implement the IValueConverter interface. The Converter value that will be passed in will be the ItemDownloaded property for a single media item. If true, the button should be visible, and the check box will be hidden.

```
public object Convert(object value, Type targetType, object parameter, CultureInfo culture)
{
    bool visibility = (bool)value;
    if (parameter.Equals("checkbox"))
    {
        visibility = !visibility;
    }

    return visibility ? Visibility.Visible : Visibility.Collapsed;
}
```

We will need to add the newly created converter as a resource in the MainPage markup.

```
    xmlns:local="clr-namespace:DownloadMe"
....
    <Grid.Resources>
        <local:VisibilityConverter x:Key="buttonVisibilityConverter" />
    </Grid.Resources>
```

With that in place, we can now modify our elements to use the new converter to determine which element is displayed based on whether the media item was downloaded. As well, we will include the DownloadUrl and LocalUri values of the item in the Tag properties of the Checkbox and Button, respectively. We will be using these values later to determine the download location of each selected item and to indicate which file to launch when the play button is tapped. On that note, we should also wire up the Tap event handler for the button, because we will be coding for it shortly.

```
<CheckBox IsChecked="{Binding ItemSelected, Mode=TwoWay}"
        Tag="{Binding DownloadUrl}" Grid.RowSpan="2"
        Visibility="{Binding ItemDownloaded, Converter={StaticResource buttonVisibilityConverter},
ConverterParameter=checkbox}"/>
<Button Content="Play"
        Height="80"
        Tap="PlayButton_Tap_1"
        Tag="{Binding LocalUri}"
        Grid.RowSpan="2"
        Visibility="{Binding ItemDownloaded, Converter={StaticResource buttonVisibilityConverter},
ConverterParameter=button}"/>
```

Finally, we will add a button in the ContentPanel to appear below the LongListSelector, which will be used to launch the download of any selected media items.

```
<Button Content="download selected videos" Grid.Row="1" Tap="Button_Tap_1" />
```

Now, we can move along to the `MainViewModel` class. In the `LoadData` method, we will include a set list of Channel9 videos to download.

```
public void LoadData()
{
    this.Items.Add(new ItemViewModel()
        {
            ID = "1",
            Title = "Building Windows Phone Apps",
            Speaker = "Lori Lalonde",
            DownloadUrl = "http://media.ch9.ms/ch9/a2ec/8673d554-4992-48d4-80e7-b9acdda4a2ec/DEVC3.wmv"
        });

    //add a few more items here
        ...

    this.IsDataLoaded = true;
}
```

The complete list of items that is used for this recipe is available in the `MainViewModel` class within the project that is packaged with this book, in the \Chapter 5\DownloadMe folder.

Handling Background Transfer Requests

The next method that needs to be added to the `MainViewModel` class is important, because this will be the method that creates the background transfer requests based on the media items that are selected by the user. We will create a method called `DownloadSelectedItems`. The method will iterate through the list of selected media items to create a background transfer request for each item and add the request to the Background Transfer Service. We will also register the `TransferProgressChanged` and `TransferStatusChanged` events on each request so that we can display the download progress in the UI and so we can monitor the status of each download request.

There is an additional method called `ReinitTransferRequests` that should be called when the application is reactivated or relaunched after download requests for one or more media files have been started. The purpose of this method is to rewire both transfer events on each active request so that the download progress and status are received by the application when it is relaunched. Refer to Listing 5-9 to see the resulting code.

Listing 5-9. Register Each Download Request and Monitor Its Download Progress and Status

```
public void DownloadSelectedItems()
{
    List<ItemViewModel> selectedItems = this.Items.Where(i => i.ItemSelected).ToList();

    _downloadsInProgress = selectedItems.Count;

    //register a background request for each media item separately
    foreach (ItemViewModel item in selectedItems)
    {
        Uri videoUri = new Uri(item.DownloadUrl, UriKind.Absolute);
        Uri downloadLocationUri = new Uri("shared/transfers/" + videoUri.Segments.Last(),
UriKind.RelativeOrAbsolute);
```

```
        //add the request for the selected item to the service if it has not already been added
        if (BackgroundTransferService.Requests.Where(r => r.RequestUri == videoUri).FirstOrDefault() == null)
        {
            BackgroundTransferRequest request = new
BackgroundTransferRequest(videoUri, downloadLocationUri);
            request.TransferPreferences = TransferPreferences.AllowCellularAndBattery;

            //register the background request with the operating system
            BackgroundTransferService.Add(request);

            item.LocalUri = "";
            item.DownloadProgress = "downloading video...";

            //register events for each request to monitor download progress and status
            request.TransferProgressChanged += new
EventHandler<BackgroundTransferEventArgs>(request_TransferProgressChanged);
            request.TransferStatusChanged += new
EventHandler<BackgroundTransferEventArgs>(request_TransferStatusChanged);
        }
    }

    SaveToIsolatedStorage();
}

void request_TransferProgressChanged(object sender, BackgroundTransferEventArgs e)
{
    //calculate the progress percentage so that we can display it in the UI
    double progress = (e.Request.BytesReceived * 100) / e.Request.TotalBytesToReceive;

    //get the current item from the collection that is being downloaded by this request
    //this can be determined by matching the item's DownloadUrl to the RequestUri
    ItemViewModel currentItem = this.Items.Where(i => i.DownloadUrl ==
e.Request.RequestUri.AbsoluteUri).FirstOrDefault();
    if (currentItem != null)
    {
        //update the DownloadProgress property so that it is reflected in the control that it is
bound to in the UI
        currentItem.DownloadProgress = string.Format("download progress: {0}%", progress.ToString());
    }
}

void request_TransferStatusChanged(object sender, BackgroundTransferEventArgs e)
{
    BackgroundTransferRequest currentRequest = e.Request;
    if (currentRequest.TransferStatus == TransferStatus.Completed)
    {
        TransferCompleted(currentRequest);
    }
}
```

```csharp
private void TransferCompleted(BackgroundTransferRequest currentRequest)
{
    //get the current item from the collection that is being downloaded by this request
    //this can be determined by matching the item's DownloadUrl to the RequestUri
    ItemViewModel currentItem = this.Items.Where(i => i.DownloadUrl ==
currentRequest.RequestUri.AbsoluteUri).FirstOrDefault();

    if (currentItem != null)
    {
        if (currentRequest.TransferError != null)
        {
            //update the DownloadProgress to indicate the download failed and include
            //the error message received in the TransferError object on the request
            currentItem.DownloadProgress = "download failed: " + currentRequest.TransferError.Message;
        }
        else
        {
            currentItem.DownloadProgress = "";
            currentItem.ItemDownloaded = true;

            //format the download location Uri to use forward slashes such that when
            //the user attempts to play the media files in the UI, the file system location is recognized
            string[] downloadUri = currentRequest.DownloadLocation.OriginalString.Split(new char[]
{ '\\' }, StringSplitOptions.RemoveEmptyEntries);
            currentItem.LocalUri = string.Join("/", downloadUri);
            currentItem.ItemSelected = false;
        }
    }

    //unregister the events from the request
    currentRequest.TransferProgressChanged -= request_TransferProgressChanged;
    currentRequest.TransferStatusChanged -= request_TransferStatusChanged;

    //remove the request from the BackgroundTransferService
    BackgroundTransferService.Remove(currentRequest);
    _downloadsInProgress -= 1;

    //if all downloads have completed, updated the current state of the Items collection in
IsolatedStorage
    if (_downloadsInProgress == 0)
    {
        SaveToIsolatedStorage();
    }
}

public void SaveToIsolatedStorage()
{
    if (IsolatedStorageSettings.ApplicationSettings.Contains("Items"))
    {
        IsolatedStorageSettings.ApplicationSettings.Remove("Items");
    }
```

```
        IsolatedStorageSettings.ApplicationSettings.Add("Items", this.Items);
        IsolatedStorageSettings.ApplicationSettings.Save();
}

public void ReinitTransferRequests()
{
    foreach (BackgroundTransferRequest request in BackgroundTransferService.Requests)
    {
        if (request.TransferStatus == TransferStatus.Completed)
        {
            //if a queued up request has completed when the app was not running
            //be sure to reflect the completed state for the item in the collection
            TransferCompleted(request);
        }
        else
        {
            //if we have active requests in the BackgroundTransferService, rewire the events
            request.TransferProgressChanged += new
EventHandler<BackgroundTransferEventArgs>(request_TransferProgressChanged);
            request.TransferStatusChanged += new
EventHandler<BackgroundTransferEventArgs>(request_TransferStatusChanged);
        }

    }
}
```

Adding the Finishing Touches

Last but not least, we need to include the code for the button Tap events for both the download and play buttons. As you can see in Listing 5-10, the code required in the MainPage is minimal.

Listing 5-10. Button Event Handlers to Handle Download and Playback of Media Items

```
private void Button_Tap_1(object sender, System.Windows.Input.GestureEventArgs e)
{
    App.ViewModel.DownloadSelectedItems();
}

private void PlayButton_Tap_1(object sender, System.Windows.Input.GestureEventArgs e)
{
    Button btn = (Button)sender;

    //the file location is stored in the Tag of list item's play button
    if (btn.Tag != null && btn.Tag.ToString() != "")
    {
        string fileLocation = btn.Tag.ToString();
        //use IsolatedStorageFile to check the file location to be sure the file exists
        //before attempting to launch the video
        IsolatedStorageFile isoFile = IsolatedStorageFile.GetUserStoreForApplication();
```

```csharp
            if (isoFile.FileExists(fileLocation))
            {
                Uri videoUri = new Uri(fileLocation, UriKind.RelativeOrAbsolute);

                try
                {
                    MediaPlayerLauncher mediaPlayerLauncher = new MediaPlayerLauncher()
                    {
                        Media = videoUri,
                        Location = MediaLocationType.Data,
                        Orientation =  MediaPlayerOrientation.Landscape,
                        Controls = MediaPlaybackControls.All
                    };

                    mediaPlayerLauncher.Show();
                }
                catch (Exception ex)
                {
                    MessageBox.Show(ex.Message);
                }
            }
        }
    }
```

Finally, modify the LoadData method in the MainViewModel to include a check for any saved data in IsolatedStorage. If the Items collection is found in the ApplicationSettings collection, then load the saved collection. Otherwise, create a new collection using our set media item list.

```csharp
if (IsolatedStorageSettings.ApplicationSettings.Contains("Items"))
{
    this.Items = IsolatedStorageSettings.ApplicationSettings["Items"] as
ObservableCollection<ItemViewModel>;

    ReinitTransferRequests();
}
else
{
    //first time launching the app, so add the default list of media items to the Items collection
        ...
}
```

Testing the Background Transfer Service

Launch the application in the emulator to test. When the application loads, select one or more media items for download and tap the download button. Notice that the download progress message updates as each item is downloaded. Exit from the app before the download completes. Wait a few seconds, relaunch the application, and notice how the current state is reflected in the UI. Also note that the download progress continues to update. This occurs because we rewired the events on the existing requests when the application was reloaded.

Once a media item has successfully been downloaded, select the play button for the downloaded item to launch the video within the Media Player on the device.

5-5. Schedule Reminders Within Your App

Problem

You want to develop an app that allows a user to track their upcoming bill payments, which will raise a reminder one day before the next bill is due.

Solution

Use the `ScheduledActionService` within your app with a scheduled notification that will serve as a reminder of the upcoming bill.

How It Works

Alarms and reminders for Windows Phone are the two types of scheduled notification you can use to create local notifications that will display at a specified time. Scheduled notifications are displayed in a pop-up dialog at the top of the device screen and provide options for the user to dismiss the notification or have the notification launch again at a later time. This is the same dialog that you will see when setting reminders for appointments that are added to the device's calendar or setting an alarm through the Alarms app. A single application may register up to 50 alarms or reminders at any given time.

Alarms and reminders both inherit from the `ScheduledAction` class, so they contain many of the same properties, with the following exceptions:

- Alarms can specify a URI that points to the location of a sound file that will be played when the notification is launched. Reminders do not have this option. If an invalid URI is specified, an exception will be thrown.

- Reminders can include a navigation URI that will provide deep linking to a page in your app so that when the reminder is tapped on an area outside of the snooze and dismiss action buttons, the application will launch and load the specified page. Alarms do not have that option.

To demonstrate the concept of how a scheduled notification is used within an application, we will create a new Windows Phone Databound app in Visual Studio 2012, named RemindMe. We will design the application so that the MainPage displays a list of bills using the LongListSelector control. When a single bill is selected in the list, the details page of the bill will be displayed.

Within the Details page, add controls to the page that will allow the user to enter the bill amount and due date. Also, we will need to add a check box to allow the user to turn on/off reminders for each bill. When a reminder is activated for a bill, we will do the following:

1. Set a title and display message for the reminder by setting the `Title` and `Content` properties, respectively.

2. Configure the date/time on which the reminder's schedule will begin by setting the `BeginTime` property.

3. Configure the reminder to launch one day before the bill's due date by setting the `ExpirationTime` property to that date/time value.

4. Configure the reminder's `NavigationURI` property to the Details page, including the bill's ID in the query string of the URI. This will ensure the details page is loaded with the relevant bill's details.

5. Add the reminder to the `ScheduledActionService`.

Furthermore, when the user chooses to turn off the reminder for a bill, we will remove the existing reminder from the ScheduledActionService.

If you recall the project we developed in Recipe 5-1, we used the ScheduledActionService to register periodic tasks in the background agent for an application. The ScheduledActionService can also be used locally within an application to register scheduled notifications.

The code that contains the work to create our reminder, add the reminder to the service, and remove it from the service will be handled in the application's MainViewModel class and is depicted in Listing 5-11.

Listing 5-11. SetNotification in the MainViewModel Class, Which Handles the Creation, Scheduling, and Unscheduling of the Reminder

```
public void SetNotification(ItemViewModel item)
{
    bool removeFromSchedule = (item.DueDate.Subtract(DateTime.Now).Days < 0);
    string reminderName = item.Description + " reminder";
    string notificationMessage = string.Format("Amount due: ${0}. Due by: {1}", item.AmountDue,
item.DueDate.ToShortDateString());

    if (item.ShowReminder && !removeFromSchedule)
    {
        Reminder reminder = new Reminder(reminderName);
        reminder.Title = reminderName;
        reminder.BeginTime = DateTime.Now;
        reminder.ExpirationTime = item.DueDate;
        reminder.RecurrenceType = RecurrenceInterval.Daily;
        reminder.Content = notificationMessage;
        reminder.NavigationUri = new
Uri(string.Format("/DetailsPage.xaml?selectedItem={0}", item.ID), UriKind.Relative);
        try
        {
            if (ScheduledActionService.Find(reminderName) != null)
            {
                ScheduledActionService.Remove(reminderName);
            }

            ScheduledActionService.Add(reminder);
        }
        catch (InvalidOperationException ex)
        {
            MessageBox.Show(reminderName + " Error: " + ex.Message);
        }
    }
    else
    {
        item.ShowReminder = false;
        ScheduledActionService.Remove(reminderName);
    }
}
```

In the Details page, we will include a Save button in the application bar. When the button is tapped, the SetNotifications method will be called, which will handle the management of the reminder scheduled action. In this way, when a reminder is set for an item, the scheduled notification will be created and added to the ScheduledActionService. Alternatively, if the reminder is unchecked on the item, the scheduled notification will be removed from the ScheduledActionService.

```
private void ApplicationBarIconButton_Click_1(object sender, EventArgs e)
{
    ApplicationBarIconButton btn = sender as ApplicationBarIconButton;
    App.ViewModel.SetNotification((ItemViewModel)DataContext);
    NavigationService.GoBack();
}
```

At this point, we can run the application for testing in the emulator. The sample project for this recipe will display a static list of bills with default data displayed. Selecting a bill in the list will load the Details page, as shown in Figure 5-10.

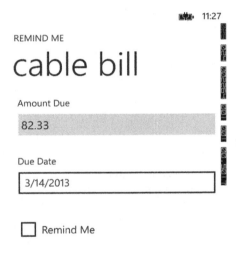

Figure 5-10. *Details page*

Tap the Remind Me check box to schedule a reminder for this bill, set the due date to one day ahead, and tap the Save button. Tap the Back button in the emulator to return to the device start screen. Wait a brief period until the reminder displays, as shown in Figure 5-11.

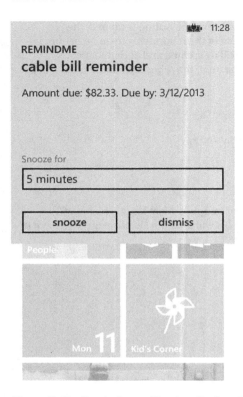

Figure 5-11. *Reminder notification displayed as expected for the selected bill*

As demonstrated in this recipe, managing scheduled notifications for your application is quite easy when leveraging the built-in Alarm and Reminders object and using the ScheduledActionService class to add, or remove, these notifications.

CHAPTER 6

■ ■ ■

Appointments and Contacts

Interaction with the built-in applications in Windows Phone is achieved through the Launcher and Chooser APIs. These APIs are contained in the `Microsoft.Phone.Tasks` namespace and expose their functionality through *tasks* that provide a consistent and seamless experience for your application users.

As the name implies, a Launcher task launches one of the built-in applications such as the e-mail client or web browser to allow the user to complete some task. Composing an e-mail, sharing something on a social network such as Twitter, or opening the browser to a specific web site are common examples of Launcher tasks. A Launcher task doesn't return a result or status to your application, so you need to be aware of that when using them. There is no way to directly determine success or failure of the launched task or even whether the user completed or cancelled the task.

A Chooser task, true to its name, launches one of the built-in applications and allows the user the choose something. Examples of Chooser tasks include selecting a contact's e-mail address, a photo stored on the phone, or some other piece of information. Unlike the Launcher tasks, a chooser returns the information you requested in addition to a `Microsoft.Phone.Tasks.TaskResult` that you can use to determine what happened.

The various Launchers and Choosers provided in the `Microsoft.Phone.Tasks` namespace provide access only to specific functionality. Interaction with the actual stored data after it has been created is done through classes in the `Microsoft.Phone.UserData` namespace. The main classes in this namespace are Contacts, Contact, Appointments, and Appointment. They provide an aggregated view of the user's contact and calendar data across all of the user's accounts.

Before any access to the user's data is allowed, whether through tasks or the UserData classes, these capability requirements must be declared in the application manifest. Recipe 1-6 provides an excellent discussion, but I wanted to call out one important item here. The application capabilities documentation on MSDN[1] states the following:

> *"When you test your app on Windows Phone Emulator during the development process, if your app uses APIs associated with items such as location services or device ID, your app is automatically granted the corresponding capability."*

This is a lie. Your application will compile. It will deploy. It will even run. The ensuing crash of your application when it actually tries to use one of these capabilities will be spectacular.[2] Once again, for the full details surrounding capabilities, see Recipe 1-6.

---

[1]You can find the application capabilities and hardware requirements for Windows Phone at `http://msdn.microsoft.com/en-us/library/windowsphone/develop/jj206936(v=vs.105).aspx#BKMK_Softwarecapabilities`.
[2]In reality, most would consider the demise of your application to be anything but. It is simply shut down, and you are returned from whence you came. I stand by the adjective, as all things of this nature are relative, and I don't get out much since I've been writing this book.

The recipes included in this chapter are as follows:

- 6-1. Save an Appointment
- 6-2. Retrieve an Appointment
- 6-3. Save a Contact
- 6-4. Retrieve a Contact
- 6-5. Create a Custom Contact Store

6-1. Save an Appointment

Problem

You want to be able to allow the user to create and save an appointment in the Calendar application.

Solution

Use the SaveAppointmentTask in the Microsoft.Phone.Tasks namespace.

How It Works

The SaveAppointmentTask falls under the Launcher category of tasks, and its use couldn't be easier. The first thing you need to do, however, is ensure that your application specifies the capabilities needed in the WPAppManifest.xaml file. Double-click the manifest file under the Properties folder in your project and then select the Capabilities tab. Make sure there is a check in the box beside ID_CAP_APPOINTMENTS.

With the capability added, you are now ready to create a new appointment. You might want to get comfortable and put on some coffee because this is going to take a little time to demonstrate. Ready?

```
SaveAppointmentTask newAppointment = new SaveAppointmentTask();
newAppointment.Show();
```

OK, so I might have been exaggerating just a little bit. Those two lines are all you need to launch the new Appointment screen in the Calendar application on the phone. The user can then fill in all of the details and save the new appointment. Or not. You'll remember from the introduction to this chapter that Launchers don't return a value or any kind of result to your application. They are "fire and forget." You won't even be notified if the user cancels the task. More than likely, you are going to have a specific reason in your application for wanting to create a new appointment, so let's expand the example a little bit more. First let's add an app bar button, as shown in Listing 6-1.

Listing 6-1. App Bar Icon Button for Adding an Appointment

```
<phone:PhoneApplicationPage.ApplicationBar>
    <shell:ApplicationBar IsVisible="True" IsMenuEnabled="False">
        <shell:ApplicationBarIconButton
            Click="AddAppointmentClick"
            IconUri="/Assets/AppBar/add.png"
            Text="add"/>
    </shell:ApplicationBar>
</phone:PhoneApplicationPage.ApplicationBar>
```

■ **Note** When creating buttons on the application bar, you should use the icons provided with the Windows Phone 8 SDK. They can be found in `C:\Program Files (x86)\Microsoft SDKs\Windows Phone\v8.0\Icons\Dark`. You need to use the Dark versions only, and the phone will take care of the rest if the user switches to, or is already using, the Light theme.

Listing 6-2 shows the XAML for a UI that allows the user to enter a few details. We'll add a `DatePicker` for the start and end dates of the appointment and provide a `TextBox` for the user to enter a location. Figure 6-1 shows the visual results. Ignore the `LongListSelector` for now. It's just hanging out backstage waiting for its cue coming up in Recipe 6-2.

Listing 6-2. XAML for the New Appointment User Interface

```xaml
<Grid x:Name="ContentPanel" Grid.Row="1" Margin="12,0,12,0">
    <Grid.RowDefinitions>
        <RowDefinition/>
        <RowDefinition Height="Auto"/>
        <RowDefinition Height="Auto"/>
        <RowDefinition Height="Auto"/>
        <RowDefinition Height="Auto"/>
    </Grid.RowDefinitions>
    <Grid.ColumnDefinitions>
        <ColumnDefinition/>
        <ColumnDefinition/>
    </Grid.ColumnDefinitions>
    <phone:LongListSelector
        Grid.Row="0"
        Grid.Column="0"
        ItemsSource="{Binding Appointments}"
        ItemTemplate="{StaticResource SelectorDataTemplate}"
        Grid.ColumnSpan="2"
        VerticalAlignment="Stretch"
        HorizontalAlignment="Stretch"
        x:Name="appointmentList"/>
    <TextBlock
        VerticalAlignment="Center"
        Grid.Row="1"
        Grid.Column="0"
        Text="start"
        Style="{StaticResource PhoneTextNormalStyle}"/>
    <toolkit:DatePicker
        Grid.Column="0"
        Grid.Row="2"
        x:Name="startDatePicker"/>
    <TextBlock
        VerticalAlignment="Center"
        Grid.Column="1"
        Grid.Row="1"
        Text="end"
        Style="{StaticResource PhoneTextNormalStyle}"/>
```

```
<toolkit:DatePicker
    x:Name="endDatePicker"
    Grid.Column="1"
    Grid.Row="2"/>
<TextBox
    Grid.Column="0"
    Grid.Row="3"
    Grid.ColumnSpan="2"
    x:Name="locationTextBox"/>
</Grid>
```

Figure 6-1. *The screen to add an appointment*

With the user interface in place, we'll add some code to the Click event of the app bar icon button that prepopulates some of the new appointment's properties. Listing 6-3 shows the required code.

Listing 6-3. App Bar Icon Button Code for Adding a New Appointment

```
private void AddAppointmentClick(object sender, EventArgs e)
{
    SaveAppointmentTask newAppointment = new SaveAppointmentTask();
    newAppointment.StartTime = startDatePicker.Value;
    newAppointment.EndTime = endDatePicker.Value;
    newAppointment.Location = locationTextBox.Text;
    newAppointment.Subject = "The CODEZ";
    newAppointment.Show();
}
```

We just pick up the values from the controls and set the various properties of the SaveAppointmentTask and then call the Show method. Figure 6-2 shows the result of the call to Show. It's worth repeating that as a Launcher, the SaveAppointmentTask does not return a result or status to the calling code. The only way to know if it succeeded would be to retrieve the appointments and see whether an appointment exists that corresponds to the values you were expecting. Of course, the user may have changed the values that you preset, so your code shouldn't count on anything being the same.[3] Recipe 6-2 will cover searching for an appointment.

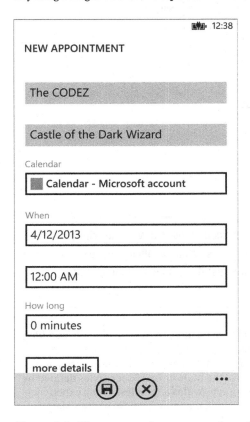

Figure 6-2. *The new appointment page from the Calendar application*

---

[3]No. There is no way to prevent the user from changing the values provided by your application.

6-2. Retrieve an Appointment

Problem

You want to display a list of appointments from the Calendar application within your application.

Solution

Use the SearchAsync method of the Appointments class in the Microsoft.Phone.UserData namespace.

How It Works

As mentioned in the introduction to this chapter, the Microsoft.Phone.UserData namespace contains classes that provide an aggregated view of the user's contacts and appointments across all accounts.

The first thing you need to do, however, is ensure that your application specifies the capabilities needed in the WPAppManifest.xaml file. Double-click the manifest file under the Properties folder in your project and then select the Capabilities tab. Make sure there is a check in the box beside ID_CAP_APPOINTMENTS. With the capability added, you are now ready to provide appointment search functionality in your application.

First let's add an app bar button, as shown in Listing 6-4.

Listing 6-4. App Bar Icon Button for Searching Appointments

```
<phone:PhoneApplicationPage.ApplicationBar>
    <shell:ApplicationBar IsVisible="True" IsMenuEnabled="False">
        <shell:ApplicationBarIconButton
            Click="SearchAppointmentsClick"
            IconUri="/Assets/AppBar/feature.search.png"
            Text="search"/>
    </shell:ApplicationBar>
</phone:PhoneApplicationPage.ApplicationBar>
```

■ **Note** When creating buttons on the application bar, you should use the icons provided with the Windows Phone 8 SDK. They can be found in C:\Program Files (x86)\Microsoft SDKs\Windows Phone\v8.0\Icons\Dark. You need to use the Dark versions only, and the phone will take care of the rest if the user switches to, or is already using, the Light theme.

Listing 6-5 shows the XAML for a UI that allows the user to enter the date range they want to search. We've added a DatePicker for the start date and end date. The DatePicker control can be found in the Windows Phone Toolkit available on CodePlex.[4] We've also added a LongListSelector to display the results of our search. Take special note of the ItemTemplate element defined for the LongListSelector and its use of the built-in TextBlock styles defined by the Windows Phone 8 SDK. Using these styles will ensure that your application provides a seamless visual experience for your users. The display of calendar appointments in your application will look the same as those in the Calendar app. It also respects the user's theme and accent color choices.

---

[4]See the Windows Phone Toolkit at http://phone.codeplex.com.

Listing 6-5. XAML for the Search Appointments User Interface

```xml
<Grid x:Name="ContentPanel" Grid.Row="1" Margin="12,0,12,0">
    <Grid.RowDefinitions>
        <RowDefinition/>
        <RowDefinition Height="Auto"/>
        <RowDefinition Height="Auto"/>
        <RowDefinition Height="Auto"/>
        <RowDefinition Height="Auto"/>
    </Grid.RowDefinitions>
    <Grid.ColumnDefinitions>
        <ColumnDefinition/>
        <ColumnDefinition/>
    </Grid.ColumnDefinitions>
    <phone:LongListSelector
        Grid.Row="0"
        Grid.Column="0"
        ItemsSource="{Binding Appointments}"
        Grid.ColumnSpan="2"
        VerticalAlignment="Stretch"
        HorizontalAlignment="Stretch"
        x:Name="appointmentList">
        <phone:LongListSelector.ItemTemplate>
            <DataTemplate >
                <StackPanel Margin="0,0,0,5">
                    <TextBlock
                        Style="{StaticResource PhoneTextLargeStyle}"
                        Text="{Binding Subject}"/>
                    <TextBlock
                        Style="{StaticResource PhoneTextAccentStyle}"
                        Text="{Binding StartTime}"/>
                    <TextBlock
                        Style="{StaticResource PhoneTextAccentStyle}"
                        Text="{Binding Location}"/>
                </StackPanel>
            </DataTemplate>
        </phone:LongListSelector.ItemTemplate>
    </phone:LongListSelector>
    <TextBlock
        VerticalAlignment="Center"
        Grid.Row="1"
        Grid.Column="0"
        Text="start"
        Style="{StaticResource PhoneTextNormalStyle}"/>
    <toolkit:DatePicker
        Grid.Column="0"
        Grid.Row="2"
        x:Name="startDatePicker"/>
    <TextBlock
        VerticalAlignment="Center"
        Grid.Column="1"
```

```
            Grid.Row="1"
            Text="end"
            Style="{StaticResource PhoneTextNormalStyle}"/>
        <toolkit:DatePicker
            x:Name="endDatePicker"
            Grid.Column="1"
            Grid.Row="2"/>
        <TextBox
            Grid.Column="0"
            Grid.Row="3"
            Grid.ColumnSpan="2"
            x:Name="locationTextBox"/>
</Grid>
```

Next we'll need a property to hold the results of our search that we can bind to the LongListSelector for display. To keep things simple and not distract from our goal, we'll just expose it in a code-behind file and then set the DataContext of the page to itself. MVVM is a fantastic pattern that enables much, but it is not without its overhead. In simple applications, it's just more pragmatic to just use the code-behind. Listing 6-6 shows how to accomplish this.

Listing 6-6. Setting the DataContext and Exposing the Results of the Search

```
public AppointmentsView()
    {
        InitializeComponent();
        DataContext = this;
    }

    private ObservableCollection<Appointment> appointments
        = new ObservableCollection<Appointment>();

    public ObservableCollection<Appointment> Appointments
    {
        get
        {
            return appointments;
        }
        set
        {
            appointments = value;
        }
    }
```

Now that we have everything we need in place, all that's left is the code to retrieve the data based on our date range. The SearchAsync method of the Appointments class takes a start date, an end date, and a parameter of type Object that allows you to pass any state information to the SearchCompleted event handler. The state object is stored in the AppointmentsSearchEventArgs. It also has three overloads that allow you to narrow your search by restricting the number of results or by limiting the search to a single account. See Table 6-1 for a description of each overload. Listing 6-7 shows the code-behind for our example.

Table 6-1. *SearchAsync Overloads of the Appointments Class*

Name	Description
SearchAsync (DateTime, DateTime, Object)	Asynchronously searches for appointments that occur between the specified start date and time and end date and time
SearchAsync (DateTime, DateTime, Account, Object)	Asynchronously searches for appointments in the specified account and returns results between the start date and time and the end date and time
SearchAsync (DateTime, DateTime, Int32, Object)	Asynchronously searches for appointments between the start date and time and the end date and time and returning no more than the specified number of appointments
SearchAsync (DateTime, DateTime, Int32, Account, Object)	Asynchronously searches for appointments in the specified account that occur between the specified start date and time and end date and time and returning no more than the specified number of appointments

Listing 6-7. Code-Behind for a Simple Appointment Date Range Search

```
private void SearchAppointmentsClick(object sender, EventArgs e)
  {
      GetAppointmentsByDateRange(
          startDatePicker.Value ?? DateTime.Today,
          endDatePicker.Value ?? DateTime.Today.AddDays(7));

  }

  private void GetAppointmentsByDateRange(DateTime startOfRange, DateTime endOfRange)
  {
      Appointments apps = new Appointments();

      apps.SearchCompleted += AppointmentsSearchCompleted;

      apps.SearchAsync(startOfRange,
          endOfRange,
          null);
  }

  void AppointmentsSearchCompleted(object sender, AppointmentsSearchEventArgs e)
  {
      Appointments = new ObservableCollection<Appointment>( e.Results);
  }
```

There are a couple of things to note in the code. The Value property of the DatePicker is defined as Nullable<DateTime>, but the SearchAsync method does not accept nulls. The easiest way to work with Nullable<T> types is to use the null-coalescing operator (??) to substitute in an appropriate value should the control not have a value set. For this example, a suitable substitute range might be the next seven days.

■ **Note** The Windows Phone 8 emulator images don't ship with any preconfigured appointments, so you will have to create a few using the code in Recipe 6-7 or the built-in Calendar application. Also, each time you shut down the emulator, it gets reset to its original state, and the data you create will be lost. For this example, I just created a single appointment that recurs every weekday to get a range of appointments that would show up in a search.

The GetAppointmentsByDateRange method takes a start date and an end date, adds a SearchCompleted handler, and then calls the SearchAsync method, passing in null for the state parameter because we have nothing interesting to communicate to the handler. The Results property of the AppointmentsSearchEventArgs parameter is an IEnumberable<Appointment>, which we pass to the constructor of a new ObservableCollection<Appointment> to reset the Appointments property we have bound to the LongListSelector.

Figure 6-3 shows the results of a search.

Figure 6-3. *Search results shown in the sample application*

6-3. Save a Contact

Problem

You want the users of your application to be able to create a new contact in contacts of their Microsoft account.

Solution

Use the SaveContactTask in the Microsoft.Phone.Tasks namespace to configure and launch the new contact page of the built-in People application.

How It Works

The SaveContactTask falls under the Launcher category of tasks, and its use couldn't be easier. The first thing you need to do, however, is ensure that your application specifies the capabilities needed in the WPAppManifest.xaml file. Double-click the manifest file under the Properties folder in your project and then select the Capabilities tab. Make sure there is a check in the box beside ID_CAP_CONTACTS.

LAUNCHERS AND CHOOSERS

Or How I Learned to Stop Worrying and Love Windows Phone 8

The code needed to use the various tasks is startlingly simple; it's so simple in fact that I couldn't figure out how to do it when I first started playing with Windows Phone 8. I wanted to "new up" a contact and add it to something. Where are the contacts stored? Contacts doesn't have a public constructor, so I can't "new up" one, which means there is probably a factory method somewhere. Hey look, Contacts. I'll bet that's where they. . .nope. Only a SearchAsync method. Contacts has an Accounts property. . .surely[5] that's where they. . .only Kind and Name, you say? I abandoned my first foray into Windows Phone 8 development in frustration. Besides, I had more pressing work to do at the time.

Unlike traditional development, where you had to provide every feature, in Windows Phone 8 there is much that is already done for you. The main rationalization for this design is to protect the user and to prevent rogue programs from filling up the user's contacts or appointments with junk. Applications must not only declare their intended capability requirements up front but also interact with those capabilities through the designated APIs. Keep this in mind as you embark on your discovery of the platform, and you'll avoid the frustration that I experienced.

With the capability added, you are now ready to create a new contact. Here is the code required:

```
SaveContactTask newContact = new SaveContactTask();
newContact.Show();
```

Those two lines are all you need to launch the new Contact page in the People application on the phone. The user can then fill in all of the details and save the new contact. Or not. Just as I described in the introduction to this chapter, Launchers don't return a value or any kind of result to your application. They are "fire and forget." You won't even be notified if the user cancels the task.

---

[5]And don't call me Shirley.

Let's expand the example a little bit more and add the ability for your application to pass in some additional details before launching the new Contact page. First, let's add an app bar button, as shown in Listing 6-8.

Listing 6-8. App Bar Icon Button for Adding an Appointment

```
<phone:PhoneApplicationPage.ApplicationBar>
    <shell:ApplicationBar IsVisible="True" IsMenuEnabled="False">
        <shell:ApplicationBarIconButton
            Click="AddContactClick"
            IconUri="/Assets/AppBar/add.png"
            Text="add"/>
    </shell:ApplicationBar>
</phone:PhoneApplicationPage.ApplicationBar>
```

■ **Note** When creating buttons on the application bar, you should use the icons provided with the Windows Phone 8 SDK. They can be found in C:\Program Files (x86)\Microsoft SDKs\Windows Phone\v8.0\Icons\Dark. You need to use the Dark versions only, and the phone will take care of the rest if the user switches to, or is already using, the Light theme.

Next we'll add some controls that let the user enter a first name and a last name that will prepopulate the add contact page. The PhoneTextBox is available in the Windows Phone Toolkit, which you can add to your project using NuGet. The PhoneTextBox provides properties such as the Hint help to simplify the user interface. The Hint is displayed as a watermark placeholder in the text box, so there is no need for a label. See Recipe 2-6 for additional information on working with the Windows Phone Toolkit. Listing 6-9 shows the XAML we need.

Listing 6-9. XAML for the Add Contact Functionality

```
<Grid x:Name="ContentPanel" Grid.Row="1" Margin="12,0,12,0">
    <Grid.RowDefinitions>
        <RowDefinition Height="1*"/>
        <RowDefinition Height="2*"/>
        <RowDefinition Height="Auto"/>
        <RowDefinition Height="Auto"/>
    </Grid.RowDefinitions>
    <Grid.ColumnDefinitions>
        <ColumnDefinition/>
        <ColumnDefinition/>
    </Grid.ColumnDefinitions>
    <StackPanel Grid.Row="0" Grid.ColumnSpan="2">
        <TextBlock
            Text="accounts"/>
        <phone:LongListSelector
            Name="accountSources"
            ItemsSource="{Binding Accounts}"
            Margin="24,0,0,0">
            <phone:LongListSelector.ItemTemplate>
                <DataTemplate>
                    <TextBlock
                        Name="ContactResults"
                        Text="{Binding Path=Name}"/>
```

```
                </DataTemplate>
            </phone:LongListSelector.ItemTemplate>
        </phone:LongListSelector>
    </StackPanel>
    <StackPanel Grid.ColumnSpan="2" Grid.Row="1">
        <TextBlock
            Text="contacts"/>
        <phone:LongListSelector
            ItemTemplate="{StaticResource ContactDataTemplate}"
            ItemsSource="{Binding Contacts}"
            Margin="24,0,0,0"
            x:Name="contactList"/>
    </StackPanel>
    <toolkit:PhoneTextBox
        Grid.Row="3"
        Grid.Column="0"
        x:Name="firstNameTextBox"
        Hint="first name" />
    <toolkit:PhoneTextBox
        Grid.Column="1"
        Grid.Row="3"
        Hint="last name"
        x:Name="lastNameTextBox"/>
</Grid>
```

The only thing left to do now is to add some code to create a SaveContactTask, set the first and last name properties to the values entered in the PhoneTextBox, and start the Show. Listing 6-10 has the required code.

Listing 6-10. The Code Required to Save a New Contact

```
private void NewContactClick(object sender, EventArgs e)
{
    SaveContactTask saveContact = new SaveContactTask();
    saveContact.FirstName = firstNameTextBox.Text;
    saveContact.LastName = lastNameTextBox.Text;
    saveContact.Completed += SaveContactCompleted;
    saveContact.Show();

}

void SaveContactCompleted(object sender, SaveContactResult e)
{
    if (e.TaskResult == TaskResult.OK)
    {
        MessageBox.Show("Contact Added");
    }
    else if (e.TaskResult == TaskResult.Cancel)
    {
        MessageBox.Show("Contact not added. You cancelled it.");
    }
}
```

And that's all there is to it. As I mentioned in the sidebar, interacting with user data and the Launcher and Chooser APIs is incredibly simple and straightforward.

6-4. Retrieve a Contact

Problem

You want to allow the user of your application to search for a specific contact or a piece of information about that contact.

Solution

There are several ways to solve this problem depending on the information you desire to retrieve. You can use the SearchAsync method of the Contacts class in the Microsoft.Phone.UserData namespace to find a contact. There are also several chooser tasks available to find specific pieces of information about a contact. They are as follows:

- AddressChooserTask

- PhoneNumberChooserTask

- EmailAddressChooserTask

How It Works

We'll forego the creation of any type of user interface in this recipe so that we can devote more space to searching using the Contacts class in the Microsoft.Phone.UserData namespace. Using the Chooser tasks is quite straightforward, so we'll focus on using the Contacts class only. As you will see, its implementation is. . .interesting.

The first thing you need to do, however, is ensure that your application specifies the capabilities needed in the WPAppManifest.xaml file. Double-click the manifest file under the Properties folder in your project and then select the Capabilities tab. Make sure there is a check in the box beside ID_CAP_CONTACTS. With the capability added, you are now ready to work with the various elements of this recipe.

Microsoft.Phone.UserData.Contacts

Those of you who have already reviewed Recipe 6-2 on searching using the Appointments class might expect, as I did, that the Contacts class would work in pretty much the same fashion. Unfortunately, it looks like this:

```
Bubble yourBubble = new Bubble();
yourBubble.Burst();
```

Sorry about that. It turns out that searching in Contacts is a little more, or less depending on your perspective, complicated than Appointments. There is only a single implementation of the SearchAsync method that takes three parameters, as described in Table 6-2.

Table 6-2. Parameters of the SearchAsync Method of the Contacts Class

Parameter	Type	Description
Filter	System.String	The filter string to use for search matching.
filterKind	Microsoft.Phone.UserData. FilterKind	The kind of filter to be used when searching.
State	System.Object	This object is stored in the State property of the ContactsSearchEventArgs that is returned to the SearchCompleted delegate.

The behavior of the search is controlled by the `filterKind` parameter. Table 6-3 describes the members of the `FilterKind` enumeration. A sample search for each member is also included.

Table 6-3. The Members of the Microsoft.Phone.UserData.FilterKind Enumeration

Filter kind	Sample search	Description
None	SearchAsync(String.Empty, FilterKind.None, null)	Searches for all contacts
PinnedToStart	SearchAsync(String.Empty, FilterKind.PinnedToStart, null)	Searches for all contacts that are pinned to the start screen
DisplayName	SearchAsync("A", FilterKind.DisplayName, null)	Searches by the display name
EmailAddress	SearchAsync("Chris@example.com", FilterKind.EmailAddress, null)	Searches by e-mail address
PhoneNumber	SearchAsync("555-0004", FilterKind.PhoneNumber, null)	Searches by phone number

In addition to using the built-in filters and the `SearchAsync` method, you can also use LINQ to query for `Contacts`. You would first search for all contacts with an empty string for a filter and using `FilterKind.None` and then use LINQ to query the results any way you want. The built-in search filters, however, are indexed to improve performance, so a LINQ query that filters all contacts in memory is going to be slower. How much slower? Well, assuming you have every person in your home state or province in your contacts, I'm guessing it could run into the tens of nanoseconds at least.[6]

As you can imagine, each of the different filters also has its own set of rules that it uses to determine a match. The following sections examine these rules in turn.

FilterKind.DisplayName

The name filter uses the filter string and tries a prefix-match of the first, middle, and last names of the contacts. It is a `StartsWith` string match as opposed to a `Contains`. Table 6-4 shows the match results of the same filter string against various name combinations.

---

[6]To within experimental error. Number of experiments conducted by author: Zero. Sarcasm Detected: Yes.

Table 6-4. *Match Results of the Same Filter String with Different Data*

Filter String	Name	Match?
Ri	Ricardo Montalbán	Yes
Ri	David Richard Totzke	Yes
Ri	Richie Rich	Yes
Ri	Ed Harris	No
Ri	Lori Lalonde	No

FilterKind.PhoneNumber

The PhoneNumber filter uses a combination of exact and smart matching. You must provide at least the last six digits of the phone number in order for a match to be returned. The documentation on MSDN[7] states that "differences such as dialing codes and international dialing codes are ignored." Unlike earlier claims regarding the veracity of search performance, I did do some experiments to validate these claims, and the results are contained in Table 6-5. The results are . . . interesting.

Table 6-5. *PhoneNumber Search String Test Results*

Test Number	Filter String	Phone Number	Match?
1	5195551212	(519) 555-1212	Yes
2	2065551212	(519) 555-1212	No
3	5551212	(519) 555-1212	Yes
4	551212	(519) 555-1212	Yes
5	425555	(519) 555-1212	No
6	+1551212	(519) 555-1212	Yes
7	+12551212	(519) 555-1212	Yes
8	+123551212	(519) 555-1212	Yes
9	+1234551212	(519) 555-1212	No
10	[a-z]5551212	(519) 555-1212	Explosion*

** OK, so not really an explosion as such. I mean no smoke and fire, but a **hard** crash; see the text.*

Test 1 was not a surprise, whereas test 2 was, in that the difference in area code is clearly not ignored as stated in the documentation. Tests 3 through 5 are consistent with the documentation. Adding a plus sign prefix created some interesting changes. Based on the results of tests 6 through 9, the first three digits immediately following the plus sign are ignored presumably as international dialing codes. Ten was a big surprise.

You crash *hard*. It's the kind of crash that a try/catch can't even save you from. Figure 6-4 shows the exception details when you end up in the UnhandledException handler at the top of the stack. It's not pretty.

---

[7]http://msdn.microsoft.com/en-us/library/windowsphone/develop/hh286417(v=vs.105).aspx

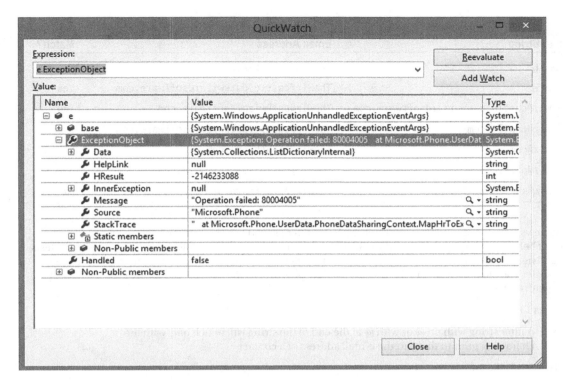

Figure 6-4. *Crash!*

Those of you who have been around a bit will recognize the 80004005 error code. That's our good, ol' friend and generic COM error E_FAIL - Unspecified error. It's rather an odd thing to happen really. At the time of this writing, the only workaround for this is to validate the string you pass as the filter and ensure it conforms to the accepted patterns and doesn't start with anything other than a plus sign, an open bracket, or a number.

I find this odd because the implementation of the event-based asynchronous programming model would require that the SearchAsync method swallow the exception silently and then assign the exception to the Error property of the relevant CompletionEventArgs class for examination in your handler. There isn't even an Error property on the ContactsSearchEventArgs. Oh, the shame of it.

■ **Note**   I have verified with the Windows Phone 8 SDK folks that I have indeed discovered a bug in the SDK. It's been logged with low priority, so. . .you know. You are going to want to be sure to validate the filter string you submit to the SearchAsync method or your app is going to crash. And that's not good for anybody.

FilterKind.EmailAddress

The EmailAddress filter kind uses a combination of exact and smart matching to find contacts. The first part of the e-mail address that precedes the @ symbol must match exactly. Table 6-6 shows some examples of various filter strings and how they match with certain e-mail addresses.

Table 6-6. *Pattern Matching with FilterKind.EmailAddress*

Test	Filter String	Email Address	Match?
1	TheWiz	TheWiz@darkwizardsoftware.com	Yes
2	TheWiz	TheWiz@castle.darkwizardsoftware.com	Yes
3	TheWiz@castle.darkwizardsoftware.com	TheWiz@darkwizardsoftware.com	Yes
4	TheWiz@castle.com	TheWiz@castle.darkwizardsoftware.com	No
5	thewiz@com	TheWiz@[anything].com	Yes
6	thewiz@dark.com	TheWiz@darkwizardsoftware.com	No
7	thewiz@darkwizardsoftware	TheWiz@darkwizardsoftware.com	No

The good news is that I was unable to outright crash this filter as I did with `FilterKind.PhoneNumber`; however, the filter doesn't behave exactly as described on MSDN.[8] We can infer the matching rules from the results of our tests in Table 6-6, and here, to within experimental error, is what I believe the requirements for a positive match to be:

Primary Rule: The characters before the @ symbol in the filter string *must always* match the characters before the @ of the e-mail address of the contact.

- Tests 1 and 2 in Table 6-6

    - A filter string with no @ or with @ at the end of the string will match *only* with the characters prior to the @ in the e-mail address of a contact.

- Test 5 in Table 6-6

    - Primary Rule match and

        - There is no dot separator in the characters *after* the @.

        - The characters after the @ match the top-level domain .

- Test 3 in Table 6-6

    - Primary Rule match and

        - The characters *after* the @ are of the form subdomain.domain.topleveldomain.

        - The topleveldomain portion of the filter string match the top-level domain of the e-mail address of the contact.

        - The domain portion of the filter string match the domain of the e-mail address of the contact.

        - Any and all subdomain portions of the filter string are ignored.

As far as I can tell, any other combination of characters in the filter string will result in there being no matches returned, but, hey, at least you don't crash.

---

[8]http://msdn.microsoft.com/en-us/library/windowsphone/develop/hh286417(v=vs.105).aspx

FilterKind.None and FilterKind.PinnedToStart

These two filters are the easiest to use and behave nearly identical to each other. Both of these filters ignore any filter string that is passed. FilterKind.None returns a list of all of the contacts that is aggregated across all accounts. FilterKind.PinnedToStart returns all of the contacts that have been pinned to the start screen. It couldn't be simpler.

6-5. Create a Custom Contact Store

Problem

You have an application that has a need to create and store its own contacts. You would like it if these contacts were also available to the user in the People hub.

Solution

You can create application-specific contacts that are stored on the phone by using the ContactStore class in the Microsoft.Phone.PersonalInformation namespace.

How It Works

I've been writing these recipes in the order in which they are listed in the book, so I'm coming from a different perspective than you might be if you just jumped right into this recipe. If you've been reading this chapter from the beginning, then you'll understand when I say, "I get to use async/await! Finally!"[9]

Asynchronous programming is generally regarded as a must for Windows Phone 8 development, and almost everything you interact with has an asynchronous implementation. What is somewhat surprising, however, is that the APIs are implemented using the event-based asynchronous pattern. The .NET daddy of multithreading and asynchronous programming, Jeffrey Richter, believes that this model should never have been introduced into the framework,[10] as do many others. There are very few classes in the entire Framework Class Library that implement this pattern. There are 17 to be exact. In any case, rant over. On with the code.

Opening the Store

As with all functionality, you'll need to declare the capabilities required by your application. For this recipe you will need the ID_CAP_CONTACTS capability. Double-click the WPAppManifest.xml file in your project, click the Capabilities tab, and then check the box beside ID_CAP_CONTACTS.

You create application-specific contacts using the CreateOrOpenAsync factory method of the ContactStore class. This method has two overloads, as shown in Table 6-7.

Table 6-7. *CreateOrOpenAsync Method Overloads on the ContactStore Class*

Method	Description
CreateOrOpenAsync()	Opens the app's custom contact store, creating the store with the default options if it does not already exist
CreateOrOpenAsync(ContactStoreSystemAccessMode, ContactStoreApplicationAccessMode)	Opens the app's custom contact store, creating the store with the specified options if it does not already exist

---

[9]Asynchronous Programming with Async and Await (C# and Visual Basic): http://msdn.microsoft.com/en-us/library/vstudio/hh191443.aspx
[10]*CLR via C#* by Jeffrey Richter (Microsoft Press, 2010)

The default values of `ReadOnly` for `ContactStoreSystemAccessMode` and `LimitedReadOnly` for `ContactStoreApplicationAccessMode` are used if you choose to use the parameterless version of the method. Tables 6-8 and 6-9 show the values of the `ContactStoreSystemAccessMode` and `ContactStoreApplicationAccessMode` enumerations, respectively.

Table 6-8. *ContactStoreSystemAccessMode Enumeration*

Member	Value	Description
ReadOnly	0	The operating system can only read from the contact store.
ReadWrite	1	The operating system can modify contacts in the store.

Table 6-9. *ContactStoreApplicationAccessMode Enumeration*

Member	Value	Description
LimitedReadOnly	0	Other applications can only read the description and display picture for contacts in the store.
ReadOnly	1	Other applications can read all properties for contacts in the store.

Stocking the Shelves

The defaults are good enough for our purposes, so we'll just use the parameterless version.

```
ContactStore store = await ContactStore.CreateOrOpenAsync();
```

Now that we have our `ContactStore`, we pass that to the constructor of a new `StoredContact`, set some property values, and then save the new contact to the store.

```
StoredContact contact = new StoredContact(store);
contact.FamilyName = "Totzke";
contact.GivenName = "Dave";
await contact.SaveAsync();
```

The number of properties available to you on the `StoredContact` are limited. Table 6-10 lists the properties available.

Table 6-10. *Properties of the StoredContact Class*

Property	Access type	Description
DisplayName	Read/write	Gets or sets the display name of a stored contact
DisplayPicture	Read-only	Gets the display picture of a stored contact
FamilyName	Read/write	Gets or sets the family name of the stored contact
GivenName	Read/write	Gets or sets the given name of the stored contact
HonorificPrefix	Read/write	Gets or sets the honorific prefix of the stored contact
HonorificSuffix	Read/write	Gets or sets the honorific suffix of the stored contact
Id	Read-only	Gets the local identifier of the stored contact
RemoteId	Read/write	Gets the remote identifier of the stored contact
Store	Read-only	Gets the ContactStore in which the contact is stored

In addition to the basic properties, however, the StoredContact supports additional properties by making a collection of name-value pairs available to you in the form of an IDictionary<string, object>. You can retrieve this list of custom properties by calling the GetExtendedPropertiesAsync method, as shown in the following snippet:

```
IDictionary<string, object> props = await contact.GetExtendedPropertiesAsync();
props.Add("FavoriteColor", "CobaltBlue");
await contact.SaveAsync();
```

You can also use the static class KnownContactProperties, which exposes quite a few static string properties with common contact property names. Using this class will help you remain consistent in the storage and retrieval of custom information, as shown here:

```
props.Add(KnownContactProperties.JobTitle, "Dark Wizard");
```

And that's all there is to it. The custom ContactStore makes it very simple for you to create and store application-specific contacts. Your contacts will show up in the People hub as well as search results.

CHAPTER 7

Camera, Photos, and Media

This chapter will walk you through the methods in which a developer can enhance their application's photo experience by integrating with the built-in extension points provided in the Windows Phone 8 SDK. We will start off the chapter by covering how to access the user's media library, as well as basic and advanced photo capture integration. We will then demonstrate how to extend your Camera app for media-sharing purposes. Finally, we will wrap up the chapter with a recipe that demonstrates how to incorporate background audio into a Windows Phone application.

In this chapter, we will go over the following recipes:

- 7-1. Access Photos from the User's Media Library

- 7-2. Integrate Basic Photo Capture in Your App

- 7-3. Integrate Advanced Photo Capture in Your App

- 7-4. Register Your App as a Media-Sharing App

- 7-5. Play Background Audio from Your App

7-1. Access Photos from the User's Media Library

Problem

You want to develop a photo gallery app that displays all the photos that are saved in albums on the user's device.

Solution

Leverage the MediaLibrary class within your app.

How It Works

The MediaLibrary class is part of the Microsoft.Xna.Framework.Media namespace. It provides read-only access to photos and songs that are in the media library on the user's device and that are made available through a set of enumerable collections. Table 7-1 lists these collections, along with additional properties that can be used to access information about the device's media library.

Table 7-1. *MediaLibrary Properties*

Property	Type	Details
Albums	AlbumCollection	Enumerable collection of all albums in the device's media library. Each album contains a collection of songs, along with information about the album's name, artist, genre, duration, and album art.
Artists	ArtistCollection	Enumerable collection of all artists in the device's media library. Each artist contains a collection of albums and songs that are associated to a specific artist, along with the artist's name.
Genres	GenreCollection	Enumerable collection of all genres in the device's media library. Each genre contains a collection of albums and songs that are associated to a specific genre, along with the genre's name.
MediaSource	MediaSource	The source from which the media is retrieved. On a Windows Phone, the media source is always the local device.
Pictures	PictureCollection	Enumerable collection of all pictures in the device's media library. Each picture contains information about the picture's name, width, height, and date. It also includes an Album property, which is of type PictureAlbum, and refers to the picture album that the picture exists within on the device.
Playlists	PlaylistCollection	Enumerable collection of all playlists in the device's media library. Each playlist contains a collection of songs that are associated to the playlist, along with the playlist's name.
RootPictureAlbum	PictureAlbum	The root picture album for all pictures in the device's media library. The PictureAlbum property contains a collection of PictureAlbums, which return all child albums that are saved within the current album. It also contains a Pictures collection, which returns all pictures within the current album.
SavedPictures	PictureCollection	Similar to the Pictures collection. Enumerable collection of all saved pictures in the device's media library.
Songs	SongsCollection	Enumerable collection of all songs in the device's media library. Each song contains information about the song's name, artist, duration, genre, rating, track number, play count, and whether the song is DRM-protected. It also includes an Album property, which refers to the album that the song appears on.

The MediaLibrary class provides the SavePicture and SavePictureToCameraRoll methods, which allow you to save pictures to the device's Saved Pictures album or Camera Roll, respectively. We will demonstrate the use of the SavePicture method in Recipe 7-3. The MediaLibrary class also provides a GetPictureFromToken method, which allows you to retrieve a picture from the device based on a picture token. This method is useful when the app is exposed as a media-sharing app in the Photos Hub and must load a specific picture when launched, which we will show in Recipe 7-4.

Once we have access to any single picture on a device, we need to be able to load it and display it within the application. The Picture object exposes two methods that simplify this: GetThumbnail and GetImage. Both methods return a stream that contains the image data of the selected picture. As shown in Listing 7-1, the stream can be used to render a BitmapImage object, and then displayed within an Image control.

Listing 7-1. Create a BitmapImage from a Picture's Image Data Stream

```
Microsoft.Xna.Framework.Media.MediaLibrary library =
    new Microsoft.Xna.Framework.Media.MediaLibrary();

//retrieve the first picture in the collection
Microsoft.Xna.Framework.Media.Picture firstPicture = library.Pictures.FirstOrDefault();

//retrieve the stream for the current picture's full-size image
System.IO.Stream pictureStream = firstPicture.GetImage();

//generate a BitmapImage from the current picture's image data stream
System.Windows.Media.Imaging.BitmapImage image =
    new System.Windows.Media.Imaging.BitmapImage();

image.SetSource(pictureStream);
```

Creating a Photo Gallery App

Now, let's create a simple photo gallery app that uses the MediaLibrary class to load pictures that are on the user's device. Launch Visual Studio 2012, and create a new Windows Phone project using the same steps provided in Chapter 1, Recipe 1-2. In this scenario, you will select the Windows Phone Databound Project template, in the New Project dialog. Let's set the name of the new project to MyGalleryApp.

Since the application will be accessing photos on the device, we need to be sure to include the ID_CAP_MEDIALIB_PHOTO capability in the application manifest. If you are unsure how to include this capability, review Recipe 1-6.

Next, modify the MainViewModel class as follows:

1. Include the using directive for the Microsoft.Xna.Framework.Media namespace.

2. Delete the Sample properties that were added by default.

3. Create the following properties:

    a. public ObservableCollection<PictureAlbum> PhotoAlbums - collection of albums on the device

    b. public PictureAlbum CurrentAlbum - the album that the user selected to drill down into

    c. public ObservableCollection<Picture> CurrentAlbumPictures - collection of pictures that are contained within the selected album

    d. public Picture CurrentPicture - the picture the user selected to view

4. Modify the LoadData method in the MainViewModel class to set our PhotoAlbums observable collection to the RootPictureAlbum.Albums collection from the MediaLibrary class.

Refer to Listing 7-2 to view the code changes that are needed within the MainViewModel class.

Listing 7-2. MyGalleryApp Project's Updated MainViewModel

```
using System;
using System.Linq;
using System.Collections.ObjectModel;
```

```
using System.ComponentModel;
using Microsoft.Xna.Framework.Media;

namespace MyGalleryApp.ViewModels
{
    public class MainViewModel : INotifyPropertyChanged
    {
        private ObservableCollection<PictureAlbum> photoAlbums;
        public ObservableCollection<PictureAlbum> PhotoAlbums
        {
            get
            {
                return photoAlbums;
            }
            set
            {
                photoAlbums = value;
                NotifyPropertyChanged("PhotoAlbums");
            }
        }

        private PictureAlbum currentAlbum;
        public PictureAlbum CurrentAlbum
        {
            get
            {
                return currentAlbum;
            }
            set
            {
                if (currentAlbum != value)
                {
                    currentAlbum = value;
                    NotifyPropertyChanged("CurrentAlbum");

                    //when the current album changes, update the CurrentAlbumPictures collection
                    //to reflect the pictures in the newly selected album
                    CurrentAlbumPictures = new
ObservableCollection<Picture>(currentAlbum.Pictures.ToList());
                }
            }
        }

        private ObservableCollection<Picture> currentAlbumPictures;
        public ObservableCollection<Picture> CurrentAlbumPictures
        {
            get
            {
                return currentAlbumPictures;
            }
```

```
            set
            {
                currentAlbumPictures = value;
                NotifyPropertyChanged("CurrentAlbumPictures");
            }
        }

        private Picture currentPicture;
        public Picture CurrentPicture
        {
            get
            {
                return currentPicture;
            }
            set
            {
                currentPicture = value;
                NotifyPropertyChanged("CurrentPicture");
            }
        }

        public void LoadData()
        {
            using (MediaLibrary library = new MediaLibrary())
            {
                this.PhotoAlbums = new
ObservableCollection<PictureAlbum>(library.RootPictureAlbum.Albums.ToList());
            }

            this.IsDataLoaded = true;
        }

        public bool IsDataLoaded
        {
            get;
            private set;
        }

        public event PropertyChangedEventHandler PropertyChanged;
        private void NotifyPropertyChanged(String propertyName)
        {
            PropertyChangedEventHandler handler = PropertyChanged;
            if (null != handler)
            {
                handler(this, new PropertyChangedEventArgs(propertyName));
            }
        }
    }
}
```

Leveraging Data Binding in the App

Next, we will modify the LongListSelector in the MainPage markup to bind to the PhotoAlbums collection in our view model. The LongListSelector's DataTemplate will include a thumbnail image of the first picture in the album, the album's name, and the total number of pictures in the album (Listing 7-3).

Listing 7-3. Main Page's LongListSelector to Display List of Albums with the First Image in Each Album Displayed as the Thumbnail Image

```
<phone:LongListSelector
    Margin="10"
    Grid.Row="1"
    ItemsSource="{Binding PhotoAlbums}">
    <phone:LongListSelector.ItemTemplate>
        <DataTemplate>
            <StackPanel Orientation="Horizontal"
                        Margin="10"
                        Height="105"
                        Width="430">
                <Image Width="99"
                       Height="99"
                       Source="{Binding Pictures[0]}"/>
                <StackPanel Width="300">
                    <TextBlock Text="{Binding Name}"
                               TextWrapping="Wrap"
                               Margin="10,0"
                               Style="{StaticResource PhoneTextExtraLargeStyle}"
                               FontSize="{StaticResource PhoneFontSizeLarge}" />
                    <TextBlock Text="{Binding Pictures.Count, StringFormat='Pictures Count: {0}'}"
                               TextWrapping="Wrap" Margin="10,0"
                               Style="{StaticResource PhoneTextSubtleStyle}" />
                </StackPanel>
            </StackPanel>
        </DataTemplate>
    </phone:LongListSelector.ItemTemplate>
</phone:LongListSelector>
```

Take a minute to review the DataTemplate markup in Listing 7-3. We are binding the first picture in the collection to an Image control, along with the picture name and a count of all pictures in the collection for each album. However, there is still something not quite right in this markup. Did you spot it?

The binding for the Image control will not work the way it is shown. If you recall, the only way we can obtain an image from a Picture object is to call the GetThumbnail or GetImage method on the object. In this case, we will need to create a converter to handle this. For the sample project that ships with this recipe, I simply created a converter, called ThumbnailImageConverter, that leverages the concept we discussed earlier in the recipe to convert a Picture object's thumbnail or full-size image data stream to a BitmapImage.

Using a Converter to Render a Picture Object as a BitmapImage

As shown in Listing 7-4, I've extended the converter by checking for a parameter value. This will provide us with the flexibility to choose which image we would like to convert from the Picture object, either the thumbnail or the full-size image, since we will be using this type of converter to handle both cases in this application. If a parameter of "thumbnail" is passed in, we will return the picture's thumbnail image. Otherwise, we will return the picture's full-size image.

Listing 7-4. ThumbnailImageConverter Class

```
using System;
using System.Windows.Data;
using System.Windows.Media.Imaging;
using Microsoft.Xna.Framework.Media;

namespace MyGalleryApp.Converters
{
    public class ThumbnailImageConverter : IValueConverter
    {
        public object Convert(object value, Type targetType, object parameter,
System.Globalization.CultureInfo culture)
        {
            if (value is Picture)
            {
                Picture pic = value as Picture;
                BitmapImage image = new BitmapImage();

                if (parameter != null && parameter.ToString() == "thumbnail")
                {
                    image.SetSource(pic.GetThumbnail());
                }
                else
                {
                    image.SetSource(pic.GetImage());
                }

                return image;
            }
            return value;

        }

        public object ConvertBack(object value, Type targetType, object parameter,
System.Globalization.CultureInfo culture)
        {
            throw new NotImplementedException();
        }
    }
}
```

We can now modify the MainPage markup to include the converter as a page resource.

```
<phone:PhoneApplicationPage.Resources>
    <conv:ThumbnailImageConverter x:Key="thumbnailImageConverter" />
</phone:PhoneApplicationPage.Resources>
```

Next, we will modify the Image element in the LongListSelector's DataTemplate to leverage the converter in the Source property binding.

```
<Image Width="99" Height="99"
       Source="{Binding Pictures[0],
         Converter={StaticResource thumbnailImageConverter},
         ConverterParameter=thumbnail}"/>
```

Handling User Interaction

Finally, add an event handler for the LongListSelector's SelectionChanged event (Listing 7-5). We will use this event to set the CurrentAlbum property in the view model to the album that was selected by the user. Once the CurrentAlbum is set to the selected item, the application will then navigate to a new page, which will display the current album's pictures in a grid layout.

Listing 7-5. The LongListSelector's SelectionChanged Event in the MainPage Code-Behind

```
private void LongListSelector_SelectionChanged(object sender, SelectionChangedEventArgs e)
{
    if (e.AddedItems.Count > 0)
    {
        App.ViewModel.CurrentAlbum = e.AddedItems[0] as Microsoft.Xna.Framework.Media.PictureAlbum;
        NavigationService.Navigate(new Uri("/AlbumGalleryPage.xaml", UriKind.Relative));
    }
}
```

As we hinted at in the SelectionChanged event handler, we will need to create a new page called AlbumGalleryPage, which will be used to display the collection of pictures from the CurrentAlbum. Every time the CurrentAlbum property is set to a new value, the CurrentAlbumPictures collection is updated with the selected album's pictures collection. So, the only thing we need to do is provide a page to display the pictures.

For this we will again leverage the LongListSelector control, setting its LayoutMode property to Grid and defining a GridCellSize of 140x140. The control's ItemSource will be set to the CurrentAlbumPictures collection. The DataTemplate will include an Image control whose Source property is bound to each picture in the collection. In this case, the binding will be to the source object itself, so we will not include a property name in the binding. We do, however, need to include the ThumbnailImageConverter as we did in the MainPage markup. As a nice touch, we will be sure to include the album's name in the title of the page, as shown in Listing 7-6.

Listing 7-6. AlbumGalleryPage Markup

```
<phone:PhoneApplicationPage.Resources>
    <conv:ThumbnailImageConverter x:Key="thumbnailImageConverter" />
</phone:PhoneApplicationPage.Resources>
<Grid x:Name="LayoutRoot" Background="Transparent">
    <Grid.RowDefinitions>
        <RowDefinition Height="Auto"/>
        <RowDefinition Height="*"/>
    </Grid.RowDefinitions>
    <StackPanel Grid.Row="0" Margin="12,0,0,28">
        <TextBlock Text="MY GALLERY APP" Style="{StaticResource PhoneTextNormalStyle}"/>
        <TextBlock Text="{Binding CurrentAlbum.Name}"
                   Margin="9,-7,0,0"
                   Style="{StaticResource PhoneTextTitle1Style}"/>
    </StackPanel>
```

```xaml
<Grid x:Name="ContentPanel" Grid.Row="1" Margin="12,0,12,0">
    <phone:LongListSelector LayoutMode="Grid"
                            GridCellSize="140,140"
                            ItemsSource="{Binding CurrentAlbumPictures}"
                            SelectionChanged="LongListSelector_SelectionChanged">
        <phone:LongListSelector.ItemTemplate>
            <DataTemplate>
                <Image Width="120"
                       Height="120"
                       Margin="10,5"
                       Source="{Binding
                       Converter={StaticResource thumbnailImageConverter},
                       ConverterParameter=thumbnail}"/>
            </DataTemplate>
        </phone:LongListSelector.ItemTemplate>
    </phone:LongListSelector>
</Grid>
</Grid>
```

As depicted in Listing 7-7, we will modify the AlbumGalleryPage code-behind by setting the DataContext to our view model instance in the page's constructor. We will also wire up the SelectionChanged event in a similar manner that was done for the MainPage, except we will set the CurrentPicture property in the view model to the selected item. As well, we will navigate to a new page that will display the full-size image of the selected picture.

Listing 7-7. AlbumGalleryPage Code-Behind

```csharp
public AlbumGalleryPage()
{
    InitializeComponent();
    DataContext = App.ViewModel;
}

private void LongListSelector_SelectionChanged(object sender, SelectionChangedEventArgs e)
{
    if (e.AddedItems.Count > 0)
    {
        App.ViewModel.CurrentPicture = e.AddedItems[0] as Microsoft.Xna.Framework.Media.Picture;
        NavigationService.Navigate(new Uri("/ViewPicturePage.xaml", UriKind.Relative));
    }
}
```

As you have probably guessed, we will be adding a new page, called ViewPicturePage, to the project. This page will contain an image control that is bound to the CurrentPicture object, which will also make use of the ThumbnailImageConverter. In this case, we will not be passing a ConverterParameter value, since we want the full-size image returned.

```xaml
<Image Width="480"
       Height="600"
       Grid.Row="1"
       Source="{Binding CurrentPicture,
           Converter={StaticResource thumbnailImageConverter}}" />
```

The ViewPicturePage's code-behind will only need to set the DataContext to our current view model instance. Once that is done, we can test the application. Go ahead and launch the application in the emulator. What do you notice? If you said, "There are no albums in my list," then you would be correct! On the initial launch of the emulator, your albums list will be empty, as shown in Figure 7-1.

Figure 7-1. *First launch of MyGalleryApp in the emulator*

Testing in the Emulator

To populate an album in the emulator with sample photos, you will need to launch the Photos Hub manually, by clicking Photos on the main screen or in the application list on the emulator. This information is discussed in the Windows Phone Emulator article on the MSDN site, under the section "Features that changed in the Windows Phone 8 emulator," located at http://msdn.microsoft.com/en-us/library/windowsphone/develop/ff402563(v=vs.105). aspx#BKMK_changedfeatures.

This means you will need to exit from your application by hitting the back button in the emulator. Next, tap the Photos tile on the main screen to launch the Photos Hub. Once the Photos Hub screen loads, hit the back button. Now you can go to the apps list in the emulator and relaunch MyGalleryApp. Notice that there is sample data on the main screen of the application now. Tap the Sample Pictures album to drill down into the album and view its collection of pictures (Figure 7-2). Then tap any picture on the album pictures grid to view the full-size image of the selected picture.

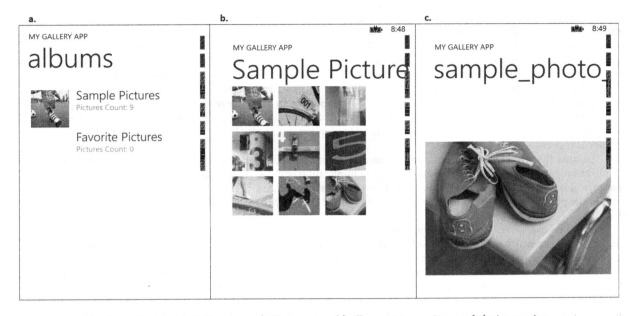

Figure 7-2. The three views in MyGalleryApp: a) albums view, b) album pictures view, and c) picture view

As we demonstrated in this recipe, it is easy to access photos on a device by creating a new instance of the MediaLibrary class, leveraging one of the available picture collections, and calling the GetImage or GetThumbnail method on the Picture object. Although we tested it only in the emulator, ideally you will want to test this application on a device that has many pictures in order to test performance.

7-2. Integrate Basic Photo Capture in Your App
Problem
You want to create an app that allows the user to take photos without having to leave the app.

Solution
Leverage the CameraCaptureTask from within the application to launch the device's native Camera application.

How It Works
The Windows Phone APIs include a CamaraCaptureTask, in the Microsoft.Phone.Tasks namespace, which you can use to incorporate photo capture from within your app. The CameraCaptureTask contains a single method, Show, which launches the device's Camera application. It also contains a single event, Completed, which is triggered when the photo capture has completed. The Completed event receives a PhotoResult object indicating whether the capture was successfully completed. The PhotoResult.TaskResult property is an enumerated value with the following options: OK, Cancel, None. If the photo capture completed as expected, the TaskResult will be set to the OK enumerated value, and the image data stream will be returned in the PhotoResult.ChosenPhoto property. If an error occurred on capture, the PhotoResult.Error object will return the exception that occurred.

Once a photo stream is returned in the `Completed` event of the `CameraCaptureTask`, it is already saved to the device's Camera Roll. Additionally, you can save it to isolated storage, save it to the device's Saved Pictures album, or even stream it to a web service, depending on the purpose of your application. However, because the `CameraCaptureTask` automatically saves the photo to the Camera Roll when the user accepts the photo, it would be courteous to give the user an indication beforehand that this is the behavior of your application. The user may have the Camera Roll set up to automatically sync to their SkyDrive account, and they may not want any photos they take through your application to be synchronized to that account. In the same respect, if you want to stream photos captured on the user's device to an alternate web service that hosts photos, make this abundantly clear to the user as well, keeping in line with Microsoft's requirement to obtain user consent before taking action on any of the user's personal content.

Another thing to note is that when the Camera application is launched using the `CameraCaptureTask`, your application may be deactivated. To ensure that your application will successfully receive the result of the camera capture, it is necessary to declare a class-level property for the `CameraCaptureTask` in the page's code-behind. And, within the page's constructor, create a new instance of the `CameraCaptureTask` and register its `Completed` event handler.

In this recipe, we will create a simple camera application that will allow the user to take a photo that will automatically be saved to the Camera Roll upon acceptance of the capture. Launch Visual Studio 2012 and create a new Windows Phone application. Since the application's sole purpose is to take pictures, we should ensure that the user has a rear-facing camera at a minimum. Go to the application manifest's Requirements tab and include the ID_REQ_REARCAMERA requirement. This ensures that the user's device must have a rear-facing camera at an absolute minimum in order to install this application. In this way, we will not need to conduct a check in code for this feature. If you are unsure how to include this requirement, go back to Chapter 1 and review Recipe 1-6.

The Code

In the MainPage markup, add a TextBlock control and an Image control to the ContentPanel grid, as shown in Listing 7-8. Also, include an application bar containing a single button that will be used to launch the Camera application.

Listing 7-8. MyCameraApp's MainPage Markup

```
<Grid x:Name="LayoutRoot" Background="Transparent">
    <Grid.RowDefinitions>
        <RowDefinition Height="Auto"/>
        <RowDefinition Height="*"/>
    </Grid.RowDefinitions>
    <TextBlock Text="MY CAMERA APP"
                    Style="{StaticResource PhoneTextNormalStyle}"
                    Grid.Row="0" Margin="12,17,0,28"/>

    <Grid x:Name="ContentPanel" Grid.Row="1">
        <Grid.RowDefinitions>
            <RowDefinition Height="Auto"/>
            <RowDefinition Height="*"/>
        </Grid.RowDefinitions>
        <TextBlock x:Name="statusMessage"
                    TextWrapping="Wrap"
                    Margin="10"
                    MaxWidth="450"
                    Text="Tap the camera button below to take a picture" />
```

```xml
        <Image Name="myPicture"
               Grid.Row="1" />
    </Grid>
</Grid>
<phone:PhoneApplicationPage.ApplicationBar>
    <shell:ApplicationBar>
        <shell:ApplicationBarIconButton
            IconUri="/Assets/feature.camera.png"
            Text="take a pic"
            Click="ApplicationBarIconButton_Click" />
    </shell:ApplicationBar>
</phone:PhoneApplicationPage.ApplicationBar>
```

In the MainPage code-behind, add a using directive for the `Microsoft.Phone.Tasks` namespace. Next, instantiate the CameraCaptureTask and attach an event handler to the CameraCaptureTask's `Completed` event. In the ApplicationIconBarButton's `Click` event, call the `Show` method of the CameraCaptureTask's instance. In the `Completed` event handler, convert the image data stream returned in the PhotoResult's `ChosenPhoto` property to a `BitmapImage` that will then be set as the Image control's `Source` property, provided the capture completed successfully. The resulting code is shown in Listing 7-9.

Listing 7-9. MainPage Code-Behind Instantiating the CameraCaptureTask and Launching It When the Application Bar Button Is Tapped

```csharp
using Microsoft.Phone;
using Microsoft.Phone.Controls;
using Microsoft.Phone.Tasks;

namespace MyCameraApp
{
    public partial class MainPage : PhoneApplicationPage
    {
        CameraCaptureTask camera;

        public MainPage()
        {
            InitializeComponent();
            camera = new CameraCaptureTask();
            camera.Completed += camera_Completed;
        }

        private void camera_Completed(object sender, PhotoResult e)
        {
            if (e.TaskResult == TaskResult.OK && e.Error == null)
            {
                System.Windows.Media.Imaging.BitmapImage image =
                    new System.Windows.Media.Imaging.BitmapImage();

                image.SetSource(e.ChosenPhoto);
```

```
            myPicture.Source = image;

            statusMessage.Text = "Photo captured using the CameraCaptureTask. Photo has been
saved to the Camera Roll.";
        }
    }

    private void ApplicationBarIconButton_Click(object sender, System.EventArgs e)
    {
        camera.Show();
    }

    }
}
```

Testing in the Emulator

That is all the code we need! Now we can launch the application in the emulator to take it for a test run. When the application is first launched, the user is prompted to tap the camera button in the application bar to take a picture (Figure 7-3).

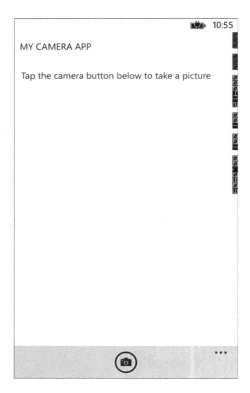

Figure 7-3. *MyCameraApp main screen on launch*

When the camera button is tapped, the native Camera application is launched in the emulator. When testing camera functionality in the emulator, the viewfinder will display a moving block along the edge of the viewfinder that changes colors intermittently. When the screen is tapped, the Camera application will capture the display in the viewfinder. The resulting photo will be the screen with a colored block at the location that the capture completed. You have the option to accept the photo capture or retake the photo, because this is the behavior of the native Camera application. Upon accepting a photo capture, you will automatically be returned to MyCameraApp's main page, and the Completed event is triggered. The image in Figure 7-4 will be displayed in the main page.

Figure 7-4. *Photo captured in emulator*

Remember that upon acceptance of the photo capture, the photo is saved to the device's Camera Roll. You can confirm this by launching the Photos Hub in the emulator and drilling down into the Camera Roll. You will notice that the photo that was captured through MyCameraApp is now in the Camera Roll as well.

7-3. Integrate Advanced Photo Capture in Your App
Problem

You want to create an app that allows the user to take photos without leaving the app.

Solution

Leverage the PhotoCamera class, in the Microsoft.Devices namespace, to launch the device's built-in camera capture feature.

How It Works

The `Microsoft.Devices.PhotoCamera` class allows you to include a camera that runs right within your Windows Phone application. It includes properties that allow you to have control of the camera's flash mode, resolution, and image capture. It also provides events for camera focus, image capture, image availability, and thumbnail availability, as shown in Figure 7-5.

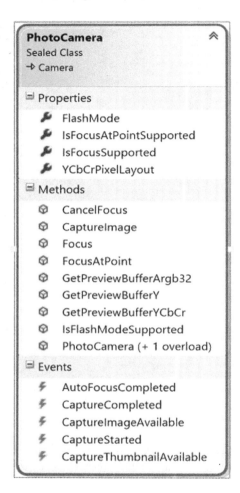

Figure 7-5. *PhotoCamera members*

To provide a true camera experience, we will also need to handle the events triggered when the device's hardware shutter button is pressed. The `CameraButtons` class, in the `Microsoft.Devices` namespace provides events for this purpose, as shown in Figure 7-6.

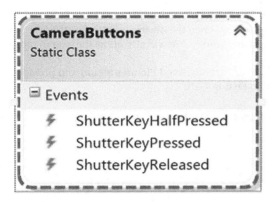

Figure 7-6. *CameraButtons events*

Now we can put the information we learned about PhotoCamera and CameraButtons to use. In this recipe, we will create a camera that runs within the application and allows for camera capture through both the tap of the screen and the device's shutter button. Once the capture is successful and an image is available, we will save the picture to the device's Saved Pictures album within the media library. We will also force navigation to another page to load the saved picture from the media library.

The Code

Launch Visual Studio 2012, and create a new Windows Phone App project named MyAdvancedCameraApp. Since we are providing an integrated camera capture experience, the first thing we need to do is add the ID_CAP_ISV_CAMERA capability in the application manifest file. We also plan on loading the saved photo from the MediaLibrary class, so we will need to include the ID_CAP_MEDIALIB_PHOTO capability as well. Last but not least, we will need to include the ID_REQ_REAR_CAMERA requirement in the manifest to specify that, at a minimum, the user's device must have a rear-facing camera.

In the MainPage markup, add a Canvas, named viewfinderCanvas, and a TextBlock, named cameraState, that will serve as our camera status message.

```
<Grid x:Name="LayoutRoot" Background="Transparent">
    <Grid.RowDefinitions>
        <RowDefinition Height="Auto"/>
        <RowDefinition Height="Auto" />
    </Grid.RowDefinitions>
    <Canvas x:Name="viewfinderCanvas"
                Width="480"
                Height="700"
                HorizontalAlignment="Left" >
        <Canvas.Background>
            <VideoBrush x:Name="viewfinderBrush" />
        </Canvas.Background>
    </Canvas>
    <TextBlock Name="cameraState" Grid.Row="1"
                Width="450"
                Margin="10"
                TextWrapping="Wrap"/>
</Grid>
```

In the MainPage code-behind, we will add code to ensure that we create a new instance of the PhotoCamera class and set the Canvas' Source to this instance. We will also register events to trap when the device's shutter button is pressed/released and register events to handle focus and image capture availability. We will also allow the user to tap the screen to initiate a photo capture.

As an added bonus, we will also save the captured image to the media library's Saved Pictures album and provide a full-size view of the captured image. The resulting code is displayed in Listing 7-10.

Listing 7-10. Instantiating a PhotoCamera Object and Registering Camera-Related Events in the MainPage Code-Behind

```
using System;
using System.Windows.Navigation;
using Microsoft.Devices;
using Microsoft.Phone.Controls;

namespace MyAdvancedCameraApp
{
    public partial class MainPage : PhoneApplicationPage
    {
        PhotoCamera myCamera;

        public MainPage()
        {
            InitializeComponent();
        }

        protected override void OnNavigatedTo(NavigationEventArgs e)
        {
            if (PhotoCamera.IsCameraTypeSupported(CameraType.Primary))
            {
                CameraButtons.ShutterKeyHalfPressed += CameraButtons_ShutterKeyHalfPressed;
                CameraButtons.ShutterKeyPressed += CameraButtons_ShutterKeyPressed;
                CameraButtons.ShutterKeyReleased += CameraButtons_ShutterKeyReleased;

                myCamera = new PhotoCamera(CameraType.Primary);
                myCamera.AutoFocusCompleted += myCamera_AutoFocusCompleted;
                myCamera.CaptureImageAvailable += myCamera_CaptureImageAvailable;

                this.Tap += MainPage_Tap;
                viewfinderBrush.SetSource(myCamera);

                cameraState.Text = "Tap the screen to focus and take a picture or press the hardware
camera button to take a picture";

            }
            else
            {
                cameraState.Text = "Camera not supported";
            }
        }
```

```csharp
void MainPage_Tap(object sender, System.Windows.Input.GestureEventArgs e)
{
    if (myCamera != null)
    {
        myCamera.Focus();
        SetCameraStateMessage("Camera focus initiated through screen tap");
    }
}

protected override void OnNavigatingFrom(NavigatingCancelEventArgs e)
{
    CameraButtons.ShutterKeyHalfPressed -= CameraButtons_ShutterKeyHalfPressed;
    CameraButtons.ShutterKeyPressed -= CameraButtons_ShutterKeyPressed;
    CameraButtons.ShutterKeyReleased -= CameraButtons_ShutterKeyReleased;

    myCamera.AutoFocusCompleted -= myCamera_AutoFocusCompleted;
    myCamera.CaptureImageAvailable -= myCamera_CaptureImageAvailable;

    myCamera.Dispose();
}

private void myCamera_CaptureImageAvailable(object sender, ContentReadyEventArgs e)
{
    string imageName = string.Format("MyAdvCam{0}.jpg", DateTime.Now.Ticks.ToString());

    using (Microsoft.Xna.Framework.Media.MediaLibrary library = new
Microsoft.Xna.Framework.Media.MediaLibrary())
    {
        //save picture to device's Saved Pictures album
        library.SavePicture(imageName, e.ImageStream);
    };

    this.Dispatcher.BeginInvoke(() =>
        {
            NavigationService.Navigate(new Uri("/PhotoDetailsPage.xaml?pic=" +
imageName, UriKind.Relative));
        });
}

private void myCamera_AutoFocusCompleted(object sender, CameraOperationCompletedEventArgs e)
{
    if (myCamera != null)
    {
        myCamera.CaptureImage();
        SetCameraStateMessage("Auto focus completed, camera capture initiated");
    }
}
```

```csharp
        private void CameraButtons_ShutterKeyReleased(object sender, EventArgs e)
        {
            if (myCamera != null)
            {
                myCamera.CancelFocus();
                SetCameraStateMessage("Camera focus cancelled");
            }
        }

        private void CameraButtons_ShutterKeyPressed(object sender, EventArgs e)
        {
            if (myCamera != null)
            {
                myCamera.CaptureImage();
                SetCameraStateMessage("Camera capture initiated");
            }
        }

        private void CameraButtons_ShutterKeyHalfPressed(object sender, EventArgs e)
        {
            if (myCamera != null)
            {
                myCamera.Focus();
                SetCameraStateMessage("Camera focus initiated");
            }
        }

        private void SetCameraStateMessage(string message)
        {
            this.Dispatcher.BeginInvoke(() =>
            {
                cameraState.Text = message;
            });
        }
    }
}
```

As shown in the code for the PhotoCamera's `CaptureImageAvailable` event, we will need to add a new page, named PhoneDetailsPage, to the project. Add an Image control, named myImage, and a TextBlock, named imageDetails, to the page.

```xml
<Image Name="myImage"
       Width="400"
       Height="500"
       Stretch="Fill"/>
<TextBlock Name="imageDetails"
           Width="450"
           Margin="10"
           Grid.Row="1"
           TextWrapping="Wrap" />
```

As shown in Listing 7-11, in the PhoneDetailsPage code-behind, we will simply override the OnNavigatedTo event. This will determine whether a picture name is being passed in so that it can be loaded from the Media Library.

Listing 7-11. Overriding the OnNavigatedTo Event in the PhoneDetailsPage Code-Behind

```
protected override void OnNavigatedTo(NavigationEventArgs e)
{
    if (NavigationContext.QueryString.ContainsKey("pic"))
    {
        string imageName = NavigationContext.QueryString["pic"];

        using (MediaLibrary myLibrary = new MediaLibrary())
        {
            Picture myPic = myLibrary.SavedPictures.Where(p => p.Name ==
imageName).FirstOrDefault();
            if (myPic != null)
            {
                BitmapImage bmp = new BitmapImage();
                bmp.SetSource(myPic.GetImage());
                myImage.Source = bmp;

                imageDetails.Text = string.Format("Image saved as {0} in album {1}", imageName,
myPic.Album.Name);
            }
        }
    }
}
```

If the NavigationContext's QueryString property contains the picture name, we will use the query string value to load the picture from the device's media library by name, render it as a BitmapImage, and display it in the Image control within the page.

Testing in the Emulator

We are now ready to run the application in the emulator to test our custom camera. When the application launches, our PhotoCamera object will be instantiated and attached to our viewfinderCamera canvas. Notice that we do not have to leave the application for the camera to work. It is currently functioning within our app. The viewfinderCamera canvas will display the rotating image in the emulator for our testing purposes, as shown in Figure 7-7. Tap the screen to initiate the photo capture.

Tap the screen to focus and take a picture or press
the hardware camera button to take a picture

Figure 7-7. *MyAdvancedCameraApp displays our in-app camera viewfinder on launch*

Upon a successful photo capture, the PhotoCamera's `CaptureImageAvailable` event is triggered, which returns the captured image, as shown in Figure 7-8. It is then saved to the Saved Pictures album on the device, and navigation to the PhotoDetailsPage occurs, passing the picture's saved name through the query string. The PhotoDetailsPage checks the query string for a picture name. If a name has been passed in, it retrieves the specified picture from the media library and displays it in the page.

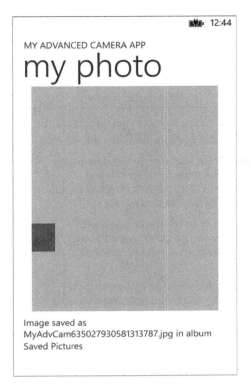

Figure 7-8. PhotoDetailsPage loads and displays the saved image that was captured by the app.

Incorporating an in-app camera requires a little more legwork than using the `CameraCaptureTask`, but it provides more control over the actions that are taken on the captured image within your application. It provides the added benefit that the application is not navigated away from to take a picture.

Another benefit of developing an in-application camera experience is that you will be able to extend your application as a Lens application. As this topic is beyond the scope of this book, you can learn more about Lens applications by reviewing the MSDN article "Lenses for Windows Phone 8" at
`http://msdn.microsoft.com/en-us/library/windowsphone/develop/jj206990(v=vs.105).aspx`.

7-4. Register Your App as a Media-Sharing App
Problem
You want to allow the user to load a photo by launching and displaying it in your app using the share option in Photos Hub.

Solution
Include the `Photos_Extra_Share` extension in the application manifest to register it as a media-sharing application, and leverage the `MediaLibrary` class in code to load the photo.

How It Works

When developing a Windows Phone application, you have the option to extend your application, using one or more extension points, as listed in Table 7-2.

Table 7-2. *Photos Extension Points*

Extension	Extension Name	End Result
Photos Hub	Photos_Extra_Hub	The application is listed under the apps list in the Photos Hub.
Share Picker	Photos_Extra_Share	The application is available for selection in the share picker list, when the user selects the share menu item when viewing a photo in the Photos Hub. QueryString will contain Action=ShareContent and FileId={picture token}.
Rich Media App	Photos_Rich_Media_Edit	The application is available as an open menu option in the application bar when viewing a photo in the Photos Hub. QueryString will contain Action=RichMediaEdit and token={picture token}.
Photo Edit Picker	Photos_Extra_Image_Editor	The application is available for selection in the edit picker list, when the user selects the edit menu item when viewing a photo in the Photos Hub. QueryString will contain Action=EditPhotoContent and FileId={picture token}.
Photo Apps Picker	Photos_Extra_Viewer	The application is available for selection.

The Code

Launch Visual Studio 2012 and open the MyCameraApp we developed in Recipe 7-2. We will extend this application as a photo-sharing app. To register this application as a media-sharing application, we will need to add the Photos_Extra_Share element to the application manifest.

```
<Extensions>
    <Extension ExtensionName="Photos_Extra_Share" ConsumerID="{5B04B775-356B-4AA0-AAF8-
6491FFEA5632}" TaskID="_default" />
</Extensions>
```

Next, we will need to override the OnNavigatedTo event in the MainPage code-behind. Within this event, we will check the NavigationContext.QueryString to determine whether the navigation was a result of the share menu item selection in the Photos Hub. As discussed in Table 7-2, we will check the query string for the Action key, with a value of ShareContent. We will then retrieve the picture token value from the FileId key in the query string. This token will be used to load the picture using the MediaLibrary's GetPictureFromToken method. Listing 7-12 shows the resulting code. If you are unfamiliar with the MediaLibrary or its related members, review Recipe 7-1.

Listing 7-12. Override the OnNavigatedTo Event in the MainPage Code-Behind to Check Whether the Current Navigation Is a Result of the Share Option Through Photos Hub

```
protected override void OnNavigatedTo(System.Windows.Navigation.NavigationEventArgs e)
{
    if (NavigationContext.QueryString.ContainsKey("Action") &&
        NavigationContext.QueryString["Action"] == "ShareContent")
    {
        using (MediaLibrary library = new MediaLibrary())
        {
            string token = NavigationContext.QueryString["FileId"];
            Picture sharedPicture = library.GetPictureFromToken(token);

            System.Windows.Media.Imaging.BitmapImage image =
            new System.Windows.Media.Imaging.BitmapImage();

            image.SetSource(sharedPicture.GetImage());

            myPicture.Source = image;

            statusMessage.Text = "Photo was loaded through the share menu option from Photos Hub.";
        }
    }
}
```

Once the Picture is loaded from the MediaLibrary, we will generate the BitmapImage from the Picture's image data stream and set the resulting BitmapImage to the Source of the MainPage's Image control.

At this point, we are ready to test the application in the emulator. When our newly extended application launches in the emulator, tap the back button to exit from the application. Tap the Photos tile to launch the Photos Hub, drill down into the Sample Albums, and select a picture to view. When a picture is displayed, click the ellipsis button in the application bar to display the application bar menu options. Tap the Share... menu item. This action will display a list of all applications that are registered as media-sharing applications. Select MyCameraApp.

Notice that MyCameraApp will load and the selected photo is displayed in the Image control right when the application is launched in this way. The TextBlock status message also indicates that the photo was loaded through the Share... menu item.

7-5. Enable Your Application to Play Background Audio

Problem

You want to create an application that allows the user to play music even when the app is not running in the foreground.

Solution

Create a Windows Phone Audio Playback Agent and reference it from your main app's project.

How It Works

The Windows Phone APIs include two types of background agents, within the Microsoft.Phone.BackgroundAudio namespace, that can be used to play audio when an application is not running in the foreground.

- AudioPlayerAgent: Use this agent to play audio files that are on the device even when the application is no longer running in the foreground. The AudioPlayerAgent class derives from the BackgroundAgent class and provides three methods that can be overridden.

  - OnPlayStateChanged: This method is invoked when the play state changes, except for the error state. Play state changes include actions such as buffering, playing, track ready, track ended, and shutdown, to name a few.

  - OnUserAction: This method is invoked when the user triggers an action on the application's audio playlist using controls provided through the foreground application or the Universal Volume Control.

  - OnError: This method is invoked when an error occurs with the audio playback.

    When overriding methods in the audio player agent, you must call the NotifyComplete or Abort method within 30 seconds.

- AudioStreamingAgent: Use this agent to stream audio within the application, through the use of a MediaStreamSource. When using this approach, you will need to create a class derived from MediaStreamSource to handle the streaming and decoding of audio. The AudioStreamingAgent also derives from the BackgroundAgent class and provides two methods.

  - OnBeginStreaming: This method is invoked when a new track requires audio streaming.

  - OnCancel: This method is invoked when the streaming is cancelled. When overriding this method in your background agent, be sure to call base.OnCancel to ensure all resources are released properly.

■ **Note**   When playing files within a background audio agent, you may access audio only from a URI or audio files that are saved in isolated storage. Songs in the device's media library cannot be accessed from the background audio agent.

When designing an application that supports playing audio in the background, you must design a foreground application that provides the user with the ability to trigger the audio playback. You will also need to create a background audio agent that performs the audio playback. The background audio agent includes methods that are invoked when the play state of a song has changed (in other words, started, stopped, paused, skipped, and so on). These actions may be driven through the application or through the Universal Volume Control on the device. The Universal Volume Control is the band that contains the set of playback when an audio file is playing. The Universal Volume Control is displayed at the top of the device's lock screen when audio is playing, as illustrated in Figure 7-9. It also appears at the top of the device screen when the user presses the volume control switch.

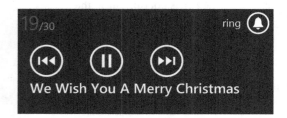

Figure 7-9. *Windows Phone Universal Volume Control*

Although it appears that the audio playback is executed from the background agent, there is an additional layer within the operating system, the Zune Media Queue, through which all media on the device is played. The background audio agent sends commands to the Zune Media Queue, which in turn performs the desired action on the audio file.

Within the foreground application, you can obtain a reference to the application's background audio agent through the BackgroundAudioPlayer.Instance property. The BackgroundAudioPlayer.Instance communicates with the Zune Media Queue to manipulate the playback of the audio files.

For a more in-depth look at the background audio architecture and details on the differences between an AudioPlayerAgent and AudioStreamingAgent, refer to the MSDN article "Background audio overview" at http://msdn.microsoft.com/en-us/library/windowsphone/develop/hh394039(v=vs.105).aspx.

Now that we have a basic understanding of what a background audio agent is and how it works, let's put it into action!

The Code

Launch Visual Studio 2012 and open the solution named MyBackgroundMusicApp, located within the \Chapter 7\MyBackgroundMusicAppStart directory. Notice that this project contains a few audio files that will be saved to isolated storage on application launch, if the files do not already exist in isolated storage. This will then make the audio files accessible from the background audio agent. In the App.xaml.cs file, we have already provided a method, CopyToIsolatedStorage, where we have handled this action. This method is called from the app constructor so that it is executed only on application launch.

Open the application manifest and ensure that the ID_CAP_MEDIALIB_AUDIO capability is included. Next, open the MainPage code-behind and include a using directive to the Microsoft.Phone.BackgroundAudio namespace. In the MainPage initializer, attach an event handler to the BackgroundAudioPlayer.Instance.PlayStateChanged event.

Within the PlayStateChanged event handler, add any code to handle UI state based on the current state of the audio player, as depicted in Listing 7-13.

Listing 7-13. Handling UI State in the BackgroundAudioPlayer's PlayStateChanged Event

```
void Instance_PlayStateChanged(object sender, EventArgs e)
{
    BitmapImage image = new BitmapImage();

    switch (BackgroundAudioPlayer.Instance.PlayerState)
    {
        case PlayState.Playing:
            //set the button image to a pause button
            //while a track is playing
            SetButtonImage(playTrack, "pause");
            break;
        case PlayState.Paused:
        case PlayState.Stopped:
            //set the button image to a play button
            //when there is no track playing
            SetButtonImage(playTrack, "play");
            break;
    }

    if (null != BackgroundAudioPlayer.Instance.Track)
    {
        App.ViewModel.CurrentTrackTitle = BackgroundAudioPlayer.Instance.Track.Title;
    }
}
```

Next, add the code necessary to the button Tap events for the buttons in the MainPage. For example, as shown in Listing 7-14, the previousTrack button should call the SkipPrevious method of the BackgroundAudioPlayer.Instance.

Listing 7-14. Main Page Button Events Will Trigger Audio Manipulation Through the BackgroundAudioPlayer to Reflect the User's Chosen Action

```
private void previousTrack_Tap(object sender, System.Windows.Input.GestureEventArgs e)
{
    BackgroundAudioPlayer.Instance.SkipPrevious();
}

private void playTrack_Tap(object sender, System.Windows.Input.GestureEventArgs e)
{
    if (PlayState.Playing == BackgroundAudioPlayer.Instance.PlayerState)
    {
        BackgroundAudioPlayer.Instance.Pause();
    }
    else
    {
        BackgroundAudioPlayer.Instance.Play();
    }
}

private void nextTrack_Tap(object sender, System.Windows.Input.GestureEventArgs e)
{
    BackgroundAudioPlayer.Instance.SkipNext();
}
```

Finally, in the OnNavigatedTo method, check the BackgroundAudioPlayer's current state and update the buttons in the UI accordingly, as shown in Listing 7-15. This is more for the benefit of when an application is relaunched after an audio playback is initiated. If the audio is then managed through the Universal Volume Control (either paused or stopped), the application needs to ensure its UI reflects the current state of the audio playback.

Listing 7-15. Ensure That the Application's MainPage UI Is Updated When Launched to Reflect the Current State of the Audio Playback

```
protected override void OnNavigatedTo(NavigationEventArgs e)
{
    if (!App.ViewModel.IsDataLoaded)
    {
        App.ViewModel.LoadData();
    }

    if (PlayState.Playing == BackgroundAudioPlayer.Instance.PlayerState)
    {
        SetButtonImage(playTrack, "pause");
        App.ViewModel.CurrentTrackTitle = BackgroundAudioPlayer.Instance.Track.Title;
    }
    else
    {
        SetButtonImage(playTrack, "play");
    }
}
```

Next, we will need to create our background audio agent that will handle the audio playback through the Zune Media Queue. Add a new project to the solution. In the Add New Project dialog, select the Windows Phone Audio Player Agent, as depicted in Figure 7-10. Name the project MyAudioPlayerAgent.

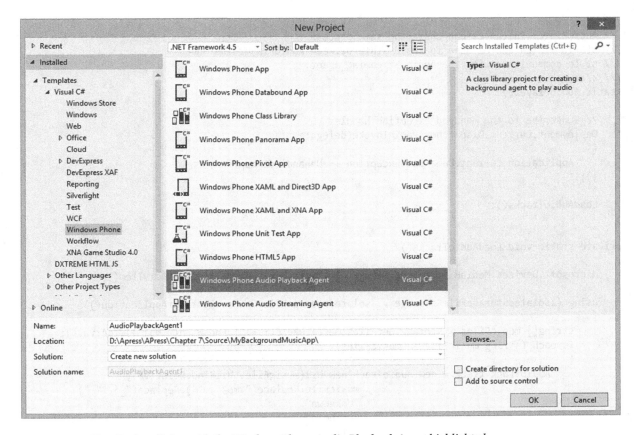

Figure 7-10. *New Project dialog with the Windows Phone Audio Playback Agent highlighted*

In the main application, add a reference to MyAudioPlaybackAgent.

Open the AudioPlayer class in the background audio agent project. Add the following using directives at the top of the AudioPlayer class:

```
using System.Collections.Generic;
using System.IO.IsolatedStorage;
using System.Linq;
```

Note that code has already been generated for the three available methods in the class. All we need to do is load our music files from isolated storage and track the current audio track so that when the user wants to skip forward or backward, we will be able to set the next track to the proper audio file. Refer to Listing 7-16 for the code needed to accomplish this action.

Listing 7-16. Load the Audio Files from Isolated Storage Within the Background Agent

```
static List<AudioTrack> tracks = new List<AudioTrack>();
static int songIndex = 0;

/// <remarks>
/// AudioPlayer instances can share the same process.
/// Static fields can be used to share state between AudioPlayer instances
/// or to communicate with the Audio Streaming agent.
/// </remarks>
static AudioPlayer()
{
    // Subscribe to the managed exception handler
    Deployment.Current.Dispatcher.BeginInvoke(delegate
    {
        Application.Current.UnhandledException += UnhandledException;
    });

    LoadAudioTracks();
}

private static void LoadAudioTracks()
{
    Microsoft.Devices.MediaHistoryItem item = new Microsoft.Devices.MediaHistoryItem();

    using (IsolatedStorageFile storage = IsolatedStorageFile.GetUserStoreForApplication())
    {
        string[] musicFiles = storage.GetFileNames().Where(f => f.EndsWith(".mp3")).ToArray();
        foreach (string musicFile in musicFiles)
        {
            AudioTrack track = new AudioTrack(new Uri(musicFile, UriKind.Relative),
                                    musicFile.Replace(".mp3", "").Replace("_", " "),
                                    "Unknown",
                                    "Unknown",
                                    null);

            tracks.Add(track);
        }
    }
}

private AudioTrack GetNextTrack()
{
    songIndex++;

    if (songIndex > tracks.Count-1)
        songIndex = 0;

    return tracks[songIndex];
}
```

```
private AudioTrack GetPreviousTrack()
{
    songIndex--;
    if (songIndex < 0)
        songIndex = tracks.Count-1;

    return tracks[songIndex];
}
```

Testing in the Emulator

Now we can test the application in the emulator. On the initial launch, the song list will display, and there is a visual indication that audio is not currently playing. When the play button is tapped, the button image changes to a pause button, and a text message displays the current song that is playing (Figure 7-11).

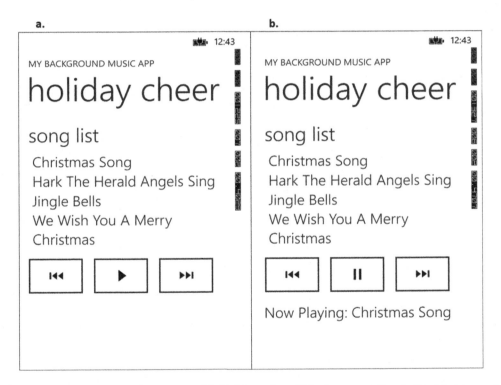

Figure 7-11. *Main application on a) initial launch and b) when an audio playback is triggered*

Press the back button in the emulator to exit from the application. The audio should continue playing at this point. Test the application on a device to access the Universal Volume Control (UVC) in order to manage the audio playback through the UVC. Launch the application after using the UVC to skip forward to the next track or to stop the playback altogether. The current state of the audio playback should be displayed in the application's UI.

CHAPTER 8

■ ■ ■

Maps, Location, and Routing

Windows Phone 8 ships with a new Maps control that is available in the `Microsoft.Phone.Maps.Controls` namespace. The Bing Maps control was browser-based and rendered in design mode. The new Map control is partially implemented in unmanaged code and therefore does not render in the Visual Studio designer. The new Map control is the same control used in the built-in applications, and it takes advantage of the new map platform that is included with the Windows Phone 8 OS. A nice design-time experience is certainly a plus, but the trade-offs in this case are well worth the price of admission. Some features enabled by the new control include offline map sharing, more responsive gestures, and vector-based high-frame-rate rendering.

Maps that are downloaded in any application are immediately available to any other application via shared map caching, which saves on bandwidth use. That's a big plus for those on a limited cellular data plan.

The recipes included in this chapter are as follows:

- 8-1. Using the Maps Task Launchers
- 8-2. Mapping the Current Location
- 8-3. Understanding Map Control Basics
- 8-4. Creating Map Overlays
- 8-5. Creating Routes and Directions

8-1. Using the Maps Task Launchers
Problem

You don't know where you are, where you are going, or how to get there.

Solution

Use the maps-related Launcher tasks in the `Microsoft.Phone.Tasks` namespace.

How It Works

Sure, you could launch one of the online mapping services or the built-in Maps application and navigate your way to the search and . . . well, you get the idea.

I'll admit that the problem statement is a little contrived, but sometimes it's tough to come up with a decent real-world scenario for such narrow topics. Of course, one of the overarching principles of Windows Phone 8 design is simplicity. Everything is focused around the experience of the user. Your application should allow users to accomplish their goals as quickly as possible. Generally speaking, it should do one thing, do it very well, and stay out of the way.

With those principles in mind, we'll create a small application that allows the user to enter the name of a place and locate it on a map, find themselves on the map, and see how to get there from here. Table 8-1 describes the tasks we'll be using.

Table 8-1. *Maps-Related Launcher Tasks*

Task	Description
MapsTask	This task searches around a specific location for items that match the search text. If no location is provided, the phone's current location is used as the center of the search area. It has the same internal implementation as the Windows Phone 7.*x* BingMapsTask.
MapsDirectionsTask	When given a destination as coordinates or as text, this task displays a map route and list of directions. If a starting point is not provided, directions begin with the phone's current location. It has the same internal implementation as the Windows Phone 7.*x* BingMapsDirectionsTask.
MapDownloaderTask	This task launches a user interface that provides a narrowing set of choices that allow the user to download maps for offline use.
MapUpdaterTask	This task examines the currently downloaded maps and retrieves any updates that might be available.

Let's get started. Create a new Windows Phone application in Visual Studio. The first thing you need to do is add the required capabilities to your project. Double-click the WPAppManifest.xaml file to open the editor. Select the Capabilities tab and then check the ID_CAP_MAPS and ID_CAP_LOCATION capabilities.

Next, let's set up a page that will let us launch each of these tasks. This sample uses the Windows Phone Toolkit, so you'll need to add a reference in your project using NuGet. Listing 8-1 provides the XAML for a simple UI.

Listing 8-1. XAML for the Maps-Related Tasks

```
<Grid x:Name="ContentPanel" Grid.Row="1" Margin="12,0,12,0">
    <Grid.RowDefinitions>
        <RowDefinition Height="Auto"/>
        <RowDefinition Height="Auto"/>
        <RowDefinition Height="Auto"/>
        <RowDefinition Height="Auto"/>
        <RowDefinition Height="Auto"/>
        <RowDefinition />
    </Grid.RowDefinitions>
    <Grid.ColumnDefinitions>
        <ColumnDefinition />
        <ColumnDefinition />
    </Grid.ColumnDefinitions>

    <toolkit:PhoneTextBox
        Grid.Column="0"
        Grid.ColumnSpan="2"
        Grid.Row="2"
        Hint="enter a location"
        x:Name="locationToFind"/>
```

```xml
<Button
    Click="WhereIsIt"
    Grid.Column="0"
    Grid.Row="1">
    <TextBlock
        Style="{StaticResource PhoneTextNormalStyle}"
        Text="where is it"/>
</Button>
<Button
    Click="HowToGetThere"
    Grid.Column="1"
    Grid.Row="1">
    <TextBlock
        Grid.Row="1"
        Style="{StaticResource PhoneTextNormalStyle}"
        Text="how to get there"/>
</Button>
<Button
    Click="WhereAmI"
    Grid.Column="0"
    Grid.ColumnSpan="2"
    Grid.Row="0">
    <TextBlock
        Grid.Row="1"
        Style="{StaticResource PhoneTextNormalStyle}"
        Text="where am I"/>
</Button>
<Button
    Click="DownloadMaps"
    Grid.Column="0"
    Grid.Row="3">
    <TextBlock
        Grid.Row="1"
        Style="{StaticResource PhoneTextNormalStyle}"
        Text="download maps"/>
</Button>
<Button
    Click="UpdateMaps"
    Grid.Column="1"
    Grid.Row="3">
    <TextBlock
        Grid.Row="1"
        Style="{StaticResource PhoneTextNormalStyle}"
        Text="update maps"/>
</Button>
</Grid>
```

MapsTask

The MapsTask has only three properties that you can set. You must set either the Center or SearchTerm (or both); otherwise, an InvalidOperationException will be thrown. Setting the ZoomLevel is optional. Table 8-2 describes the properties of the MapsTask.

Table 8-2. *Properties of the MapsTask Class*

Name	Description
Center	The location that will be used as the center point for the map. If this property is left empty, then the phone's current location is used as the center point of the search.
SearchTerm	The search term that is used to find and tag locations on the map. The search is centered on the Center coordinates or the phone's current location if no Center is specified.
ZoomLevel	The initial zoom level of the map. The property is of type Double and must be greater than zero with a range between 1 and 21.

Using the MapsTask is simple. Most commonly you will want to find something that is close by, so in Listing 8-2 we will just set the SearchTerm and ZoomLevel and then call the Show method.

Listing 8-2. Finding a Location Using the MapsTask

```
private void WhereIsIt(object sender, RoutedEventArgs e)
{
    if (string.IsNullOrEmpty(locationToFind.Text))
    {
        MessageBox.Show("Please enter a location.");
    }
    else
    {
        MapsTask mapTask = new MapsTask();
        mapTask.ZoomLevel = 15;
        mapTask.SearchTerm = locationToFind.Text;
        mapTask.Show();
    }
}
```

MapsDirectionsTask

Probably the most common use case for directions is the desire to be somewhere else. We've all had that feeling I'm sure. The MapsDirectionsTask makes it simple to plan your escape. The MapsDirectionsTask has only two properties, Start and End, both of which are of type LabeledMapLocation. See Table 8-3 for the specifics of the LabeledMapLocation class.

Table 8-3. *Properties of the LabeledMapLocation Class*

Name	Description
Label	This is the text label that identifies the associated geographic location and will be applied to the pushpin on the map. If a Location is not provided, then this value is used as a search term.
Location	The geographic coordinate that is associated with the labeled map location. The Label text is used as a search term if this property is not set.

The End property will be set to the phone's current location if it is not set to a valid LabeledMapLocation. The same applies to the Start property. The problem of both the Start and End properties being set to an invalid location is addressed by the task throwing an InvalidOperationException given that you are, in essence, asking it to route you from where you are currently located to your current location.[1]

MapDownloaderTask and MapUpdaterTask

The last two tasks are very simple to use and have no properties to set. They rely completely on the built-in functionality. Listing 8-3 and Listing 8-4 show their use, while Figures 8-1 and 8-2 show the respective results.

Listing 8-3. Using the MapDownloaderTask

```
private void DownloadMaps(object sender, RoutedEventArgs e)
{
    MapDownloaderTask mapDownloaderTask = new MapDownloaderTask();
    mapDownloaderTask.Show();

}
```

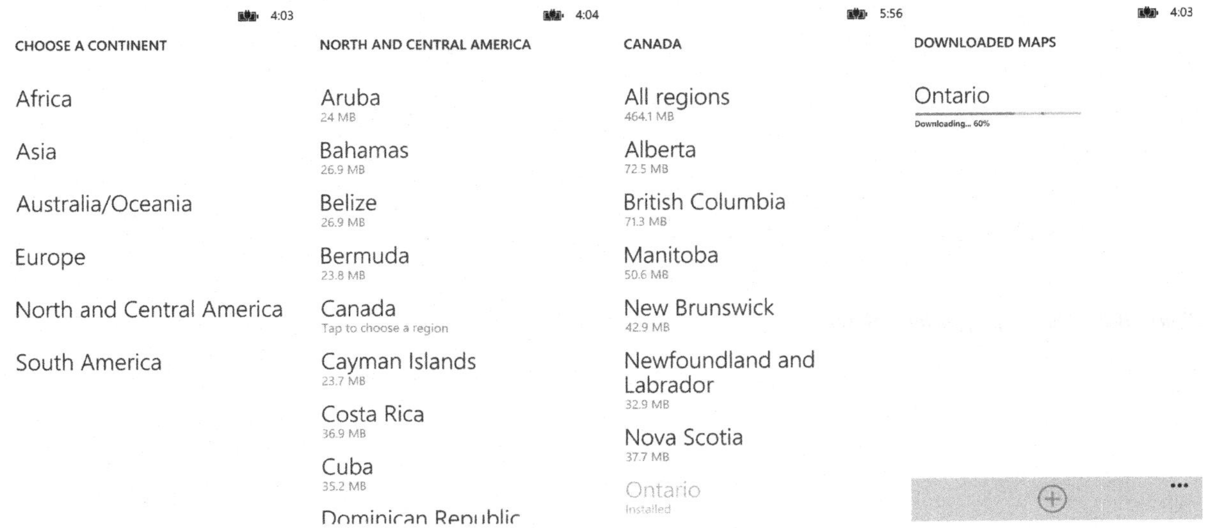

Figure 8-1. *The four possible map download screens*

---

[1]If I wrote that method, I'd just send them out in a western direction and route them around the globe back to their starting point. That's probably why I don't write mapping software.

Listing 8-4. Using the MapUpdaterTask

```
private void UpdateMaps(object sender, RoutedEventArgs e)
        {
            MapUpdaterTask mapUpdaterTask = new MapUpdaterTask();
            mapUpdaterTask.Show();
        }
```

◨ 4:04

MAPS

updates

All of your maps are up to
date.

Figure 8-2. *The MapUpdaterTask screen*

8-2. Mapping the Current Location

Problem

You still don't know where you are. (Hey, it happens.)

Solution

Use the `GetGeopositionAsync` method of the `Geolocator` class in the `Windows.Devices.Geolocation` namespace to get the phone's current `Geoposition`.

How It Works

Create a new project using the Windows Phone 8 App project template in Visual Studio. Two of the ingredients for this recipe are the capabilities[2] ID_CAP_MAPS and ID_CAP_LOCATION. Double-click the WMAppManifest.xml file so that it opens in the editor, and make sure these capabilities are selected. The `GetGeopositionAsync` method will throw an `UnauthorizedAccessException` if Location is disabled on the device or if you don't request the required capabilities.

Those of you who have read Recipe 8-1 will remember that it requires either the `SearchTerm` or `Center` property (or both) to be set to a valid value. Knowing this, we can simply set the `Center` to the phone's current location and leave out the `SearchTerm`.

Now that we have a project, let's add a button to the MainPage.xaml file. Replace the ContentPanel `Grid` with the XAML in Listing 8-5.

Listing 8-5. XAML for the "Where Am I" User Interface

```
<Grid x:Name="ContentPanel" Grid.Row="1" Margin="12,0,12,0">
    <Grid.RowDefinitions>
        <RowDefinition Height="Auto"/>
    </Grid.RowDefinitions>
    <Button
        Click="WhereAmI"
        Grid.Column="0"
        Grid.ColumnSpan="2"
        Grid.Row="0">
        <TextBlock
            Grid.Row="1"
            Style="{StaticResource PhoneTextNormalStyle}"
            Text="where am I"/>
    </Button>
</Grid>
```

■ **Note**   The sample source code for this recipe is in the Chapter08\WhereAmI project included in the Chapter 8 download.

---

[2]Eight chapters in and I'm just now using the word *ingredients* . . .?

The GetGeopositionAsync method of the Geolocator returns a Geoposition. The Coordinate property of GeoPosition gives us the Latitude and Longitude that we then use to create a GeoCoordinate. We then pass that to the MapsTask as the Center property value and leave the SearchTerm property empty. The GetGeopositionAsync method is awaitable, so first we'll create a private async method that returns a GeoCoordinate. Listing 8-6 has the code.

Lisitng 8-6. Awaitable Private Method for Retrieving the Phone's Current GeoCoordinate

```
private async Task<GeoCoordinate> GetCurrentCoordinate()
{
    Geolocator locator = new Geolocator();
    locator.DesiredAccuracy = PositionAccuracy.High;

    Geoposition position = await locator.GetGeopositionAsync();

    GeoCoordinate coordinate =
        new GeoCoordinate(position.Coordinate.Latitude, position.Coordinate.Longitude);
    return coordinate;
}
```

All that's left now is to add the code for the Click event of the Button. Make sure you add the async keyword to the method declaration since we'll be using await in our code. Listing 8-7 has the details, and Figure 8-3 shows the results.

Listing 8-7. Code-Behind to Launch the MapsTask and Display the Phone's Current Location

```
private async void WhereAmI(object sender, RoutedEventArgs e)
{
    try
    {
        GeoCoordinate coordinate = await GetCurrentCoordinate();

        MapsTask mapTask = new MapsTask();
        mapTask.ZoomLevel = 15;
        mapTask.Center = coordinate;
        mapTask.Show();
    }
    catch (UnauthorizedAccessException ex)
    {
        // this means that location is disabled on the device.
        MessageBox.Show("Location is disabled.");
    }
}
```

Figure 8-3. *Where am I? Right here, of course . . . or am I?*

8-3. Understanding Map Control Basics

Problem

You're creating an application that requires some mapping capability. You don't want to use the Maps-related tasks because they take the user out of your application and you would rather control the experience.

Solution

Use the `Map` control that can be found in the `Microsoft.Phone.Maps.Controls` namespace to allow the user to interact with the map.

How It Works

The beginning of this chapter introduced the new `Map` control that ships with Windows Phone 8, but it's a significant enough improvement that it bears repeating here. It can be found in the `Microsoft.Phone.Maps.Controls` namespace. The Bing Map control was browser-based and rendered in design mode. The new `Map` control is partially implemented in unmanaged code and therefore does not render in the Visual Studio Designer.

Some features enabled by the new control include offline map sharing, more responsive gestures, and vector-based high-frame-rate rendering. In addition, maps that are downloaded in any application are immediately available to any other application via shared map caching, which saves on bandwidth use. That's a big plus for those on a limited cellular data plan. Let's get cooking.

Start Visual Studio and create a new project using the Windows Phone App project template. Once the designer finishes loading the MainPage, open the ToolBox, and drag a Map control onto the design surface. The first thing you will notice is that the map does not render but rather just shows a placeholder image; however, if you run the application without doing anything else, you will see a zoomed-out image of North America and South America. Figure 8-4 shows the design-time and run-time views of the Map control.

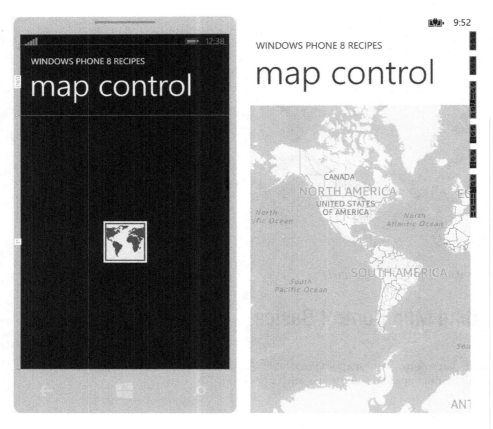

Figure 8-4. *The Windows Phone 8 Map control design-time and run-time views*

The Map control inherits from System.Windows.Controls.Control and as such inherits properties from UIElement, FrameworkElement, and Control. Table 8-4 describes the Map control–specific properties.

Table 8-4. *Map Control–Specific Properties*

Name	Description
CartographicMode	Gets or sets the MapCartographicMode of the Map control
Center	Gets or sets the center of the Map control
ColorMode	Gets or sets the MapColorMode of the Map control
Heading	Gets or sets the heading of the Map control
LandmarksEnabled	Gets or sets a value that indicates whether 3D landmarks are enabled on the Map control
Layers	Gets or sets a collection of MapLayer objects on the Map control
MapElements	Gets or sets the map elements on the Map control
PedestrianFeaturesEnabled	Gets or sets a value that indicates whether pedestrian features such as public stairs are enabled on the Map control
Pitch	Gets or sets the pitch of the Map control
TileSources	Gets or sets the TileSource collection of the Map control
TransformCenter	Gets or sets a value to which the center of the Map control is transformed
UniqueId	Gets the ID of the Map control
WatermarkMode	Gets or sets the watermark of the Map control
ZoomLevel	Gets or sets the zoom level of the map control

Let's set up a user interface with some controls that will allow us to change the properties of the map. We'll add a couple of Slider controls for the Pitch, ZoomLevel, and Heading. Listing 8-8 has the XAML you'll need.

To use the Map control, you'll need to declare the namespace at the top of your XAML or simply drag the Map control out of the ToolBox and drop it on the design surface.

```
xmlns:mapControls="clr-namespace:Microsoft.Phone.Maps.Controls;assembly=Microsoft.Phone.Maps"
```

Listing 8-8. XAML for the Map Control User Interface

```
<Grid x:Name="ContentPanel" Grid.Row="1" Margin="12,0,12,0">
    <Grid.RowDefinitions>
        <RowDefinition />
        <RowDefinition Height="Auto"/>
    </Grid.RowDefinitions>
    <mapControls:Map
        x:Name="theMap" />
    <Grid
        Grid.Row="1"
        Visibility="Visible"
        x:Name="settingsPanel">
        <Grid.RowDefinitions>
            <RowDefinition/>
            <RowDefinition/>
            <RowDefinition/>
        </Grid.RowDefinitions>
```

```xml
        <Grid.ColumnDefinitions>
            <ColumnDefinition/>
            <ColumnDefinition/>
        </Grid.ColumnDefinitions>
        <Slider
            Grid.Column="0"
            Grid.Row="0"
            Maximum="19"
            Minimum="1"
            ValueChanged="ZoomSliderValueChanged"
            X:Name="zoomSlider" />
        <Slider
            Grid.Column="1"
            Maximum="75"
            Minimum="0"
            ValueChanged="PitchSliderValueChanged"/>
        <Slider
            Grid.Row="1"
            Grid.ColumnSpan="2"
            Maximum="360"
            Minimum="0"
            ValueChanged="HeadingSliderValueChanged"/>
    </Grid>
</Grid>
```

■ **Note**   The sample project for this recipe is called BasicMapControl and is available with the Chapter 8 download.

We'll also add an ApplicationIconBarButton to show and hide the setting controls and another to refresh the current location. Listing 8-9 shows the XAML for the ApplicationBar.

Listing 8-9. XAML for the ApplicationIconBarButtons

```xml
<phone:PhoneApplicationPage.ApplicationBar>
    <shell:ApplicationBar>
        <shell:ApplicationBarIconButton
            Click="ShowSettings"
            IconUri="/Assets/feature.settings.png"
            Text="settings"/>
        <shell:ApplicationBarIconButton
            Click="UpdateLocation"
            IconUri="/Assets/refresh.png"
            Text="settings"
            x:Name="locationButton"/>
    </shell:ApplicationBar>
</phone:PhoneApplicationPage.ApplicationBar>
```

Listing 8-6 in Recipe 8-2 demonstrated how to get the phone's Geoposition and extract the coordinate information from it. Here is a reminder of that code:

```
private async Task<GeoCoordinate> GetCurrentCoordinate()
{
    Geolocator locator = new Geolocator();
    locator.DesiredAccuracy = PositionAccuracy.High;

    Geoposition position = await locator.GetGeopositionAsync();

    GeoCoordinate coordinate =
        new GeoCoordinate(position.Coordinate.Latitude, position.Coordinate.Longitude);
    return coordinate;
}
```

Add this method to MainPage.xaml.cs so that it's available. Next we'll add the event handlers for the Slider controls that will set the ZoomLevel, Pitch, and Heading properties of the Map control. Add the code in Listing 8-10 to the code-behind.

Listing 8-10. Event Handlers for the Slider Controls

```
private void ZoomSliderValueChanged(object sender,
    RoutedPropertyChangedEventArgs<double> e)
{
    if (theMap != null)
    {
        theMap.ZoomLevel = e.NewValue;
    }
}

private void PitchSliderValueChanged(object sender,
    RoutedPropertyChangedEventArgs<double> e)
{
    if (theMap != null)
    {
        theMap.Pitch = e.NewValue;
    }
}

private void HeadingSliderValueChanged(object sender,
    RoutedPropertyChangedEventArgs<double> e)
{
    if (theMap != null)
    {
        theMap.Heading = e.NewValue;
    }
}
```

The final code we need is for the app bar icon buttons and some code in the override of the OnNavigatedTo method to initialize our current location. Add the code in Listing 8-11 to your code-behind.

Listing 8-11. ApplicationIconBarButton Code and OnNavigateTo Override

```
private void ShowSettings(object sender, EventArgs e)
{
    settingsPanel.Visibility =
        settingsPanel.Visibility == Visibility.Visible ? Visibility.Collapsed :
                                                          Visibility.Visible;
}

private async void UpdateLocation(object sender, EventArgs e)
{
    try
    {
        ((ApplicationBarIconButton)sender).IsEnabled = false;
        GeoCoordinate coordinate = await GetCoordinate();
        theMap.Center = coordinate;
    }
    catch (Exception) // I meant to do that.
    {
        MessageBoxResult result = MessageBox.Show("Location services is not enabled.
Would you like to go to the settings page to enable it?", "Error", MessageBoxButton.OKCancel);
        if (result == MessageBoxResult.OK)
        {
            Launcher.LaunchUriAsync(new Uri("ms-settings-location:"));
        }
    }
    finally
    {
        ((ApplicationBarIconButton)sender).IsEnabled = true;
    }
}

protected async override void OnNavigatedTo(NavigationEventArgs e)
{
    try
    {
        theMap.Center = await GetCoordinate();
        zoomSlider.Value = 15;                }
    catch (Exception)
    {
        MessageBoxResult result = MessageBox.Show("Location services is not enabled.
Would you like to go to the settings page to enable it?", "Error", MessageBoxButton.OKCancel);
        if (result == MessageBoxResult.OK)
        {
            Launcher.LaunchUriAsync(new Uri("ms-settings-location:"));
        }
    }
}
```

Notice the addition of the async keyword in the method override declaration and the event handler for UpdateLocation. This is needed because we are going to be using await in our handler. Go ahead and build and run the project. If you are running in the emulator, you should be centered on the Microsoft campus in Redmond, Washington. If you are using your device, the map should be centered on your current location. There won't be a marker to show the location exactly. When using the Map control, you are in charge of everything. Recipe 8-4 will cover adding overlays to the map for things such as location marking.

■ **Note**   The observant reader will have noticed that Listing 8-11 catches the base System.Exception. This is not a Good Thing.[3] Unfortunately, this is what gets thrown when the Location service is disabled on the device, so we're left with no choice.

You will also note the use of the Windows.System.Launcher.LaunchUriAsync method to send the user to the Location settings page so that they can enable the Location service. LaunchUriAsync is a simple way to launch the built-in application rather than using one of the classes in Microsoft.Phone.Tasks, and there are some applications that are accessible only by using this technique. Table 8-5 describes a few of the others that are available.

Table 8-5. *Uri Schemes for Launching Built-in Applications*

URI Scheme	Description
http:[URL]	Launches the web browser and navigates to the specified URL.
mailto:[email address]	Launches the e-mail app and creates a new message with the specified e-mail address on the To line. Note that the e-mail is not sent until the user taps send.
ms-settings-accounts:	Launches the account Settings app.
ms-settings-airplanemode:	Launches theflight mode Settings app.
ms-settings-bluetooth:	Launches the Bluetooth Settings app.
ms-settings-cellular:	Launches the Cellular Settings app.
ms-settings-emailandaccounts:	Launches the e-mail and accounts settings app.
ms-settings-location:	Launches the location Settings app.
ms-settings-lock:	Launches the lock screen Settings app.
ms-settings-wifi:	Launches the WiFi Settings app.

We don't have the space to cover all of the properties, so we'll look at two of the more interesting ones: CartographicMode and ColorMode. They are controlled by their respective enumerations, and changing modes is as easy as setting the property. Listing 8-12 contains the XAML and code-behind.

---

[3]"I invented 'It's a good thing' before you were even born." —Martha Stewart

Listing 8-12. XAML for the MapCartographicMode and MapColorMode with Code-Behind

```
<Button
    Click="ToggleColorMode"
    Content="Dark"
    Grid.Row="2"/>
<Button
    Click="CycleMapCartographicMode"
    Content="Mode"
    Grid.Column="1"
    Grid.Row="2"/>

// code-behind for the color mode
private void ToggleColorMode(object sender, RoutedEventArgs e)
{
    ((Button)(sender)).Content = theMap.ColorMode.ToString();
    theMap.ColorMode = theMap.ColorMode == MapColorMode.Dark ? MapColorMode.Light :
                                                                MapColorMode.Dark;
}

// code-behind for the cartographic mode
private void CycleMapCartographicMode(object sender, RoutedEventArgs e)
{
    switch (theMap.CartographicMode)
    {
        case MapCartographicMode.Aerial:
            theMap.CartographicMode = MapCartographicMode.Hybrid;
            break;
        case MapCartographicMode.Hybrid:
            theMap.CartographicMode = MapCartographicMode.Road;
            break;
        case MapCartographicMode.Road:
            theMap.CartographicMode = MapCartographicMode.Terrain;
            break;
        case MapCartographicMode.Terrain:
            theMap.CartographicMode = MapCartographicMode.Aerial;
            break;
    }
}
```

As you experiment with the two settings, you will notice that the MapColorMode affects only what you see when the MapCartographicMode is set to MapCartographicMode.Road. Figure 8-5 shows the Light and Dark modes, and Figure 8-6 shows the four cartographic modes: Road, Terrain, Aerial, and Hybrid.

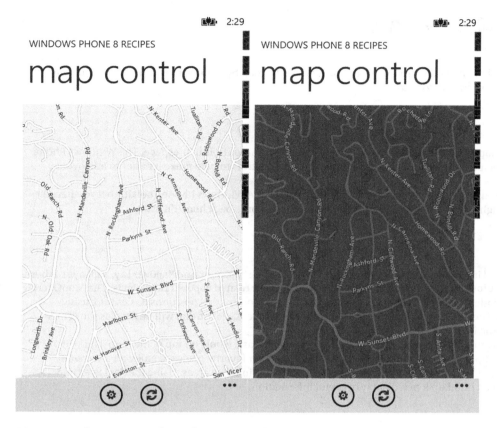

Figure 8-5. *The two MapColorMode settings: Light and Dark*

Figure 8-6. *The four cartographic modes of the Map control: Road, Terrain, Aerial, and Hybrid*

8-4. Creating Map Overlays

Problem

You have an application that allows the user to mark a location on the map by tapping it. You also want to display a marker showing the device's current location.

Solution

Use the MapLayer and MapOverlay classes in the Microsoft.Phone.Maps.Controls namespace. The Windows Phone Toolkit, first shown in Recipe 2-6, also includes several map-related controls to help make it easier to add overlay items to a Map control.

Recipe 2-6 contains instructions on how to obtain and work with the Windows Phone Toolkit, so if you haven't read that one yet, you might want to give it a quick read now and then come back here. I'll wait.

How It Works

Two main classes are used in the overlaying of visuals on the Map control: MapLayer and MapOverlay. MapLayer inherits from ObservableCollection<MapOverlay> and serves as a container for related MapOverlay objects. The MapOverlay class inherits from DependencyObject and serves as a custom content control that positions its Content using geographic coordinates. The PositionOrigin property is a System.Windows.Point that will be used as the center point when positioning the item.

Think of a layer as a group of related items that you want to display as a whole on top of the map. Figure 8-7 shows an example of multiple layers. The first layer could be a list of your favorite places to enjoy an afternoon out, and the top layer could be an overlay of current weather conditions in those areas. Using the MapLayer and MapOverlay classes you can build up a rich display of useful information.

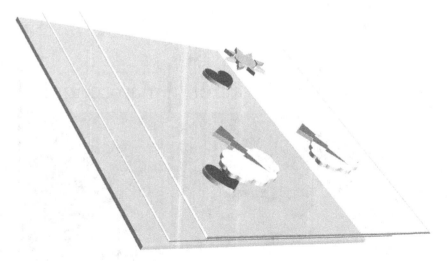

Figure 8-7. *An example of layering on the Map control*

Marking the Current Location

The Windows Phone Toolkit comes with a static class called MapExtensions that uses AttachedProperties to extend the functionality of the Map control. You can examine the source code that comes with the Windows Phone Toolkit to see how it works. The MapExtensions class basically takes each child item, wraps it in a MapOverlayItem, wraps that in a MapOverlay and then puts that into a MapLayer, and finally adds the item to the map. It's an exercise in convolution to be sure, but it works.

To mark the current location of the phone, we'll use the UserLocationMarker control that comes with the Toolkit. Create a new project using the Windows Phone App template and then use NuGet to add a reference to the Toolkit. As always, don't forget to add the ID_CAP_MAP and ID_CAP_LOCATION to the capabilities required by your application. Add the following namespace declaration to the top of the MainPage XAML and then replace the ContentPanel Grid with the XAML in Listing 8-13:

```
xmlns:toolKit="clr-namespace:Microsoft.Phone.Maps.Toolkit;assembly=Microsoft.Phone.Controls.Toolkit"
```

Listing 8-13. XAML for the ContentPanel Grid

```
<Grid x:Name="ContentPanel" Grid.Row="1" Margin="12,0,12,0">
    <mapControls:Map x:Name="theMap">
        <toolKit:MapExtensions.Children>
            <toolKit:UserLocationMarker
                Visibility="Collapsed"
                x:Name="UserLocationMarker"/>
        </toolKit:MapExtensions.Children>
    </mapControls:Map>
</Grid>
```

Next we'll add some code that you've probably already seen in the previous recipe that gets the current location of the device. We'll also add code to override OnNavigatedTo and set the location of the UserLocationMarker. Listing 8-14 has everything you need.

Listing 8-14. Code to Get and Set the Current Location

```
private async Task<GeoCoordinate> GetCoordinate()
{

    Geolocator locator = new Geolocator();
    GeoCoordinate coordinate;
    locator.DesiredAccuracy = PositionAccuracy.High;

    Geoposition position = await locator.GetGeopositionAsync();

    coordinate = new GeoCoordinate(position.Coordinate.Latitude,
        position.Coordinate.Longitude);
    return coordinate;
}

protected async override void OnNavigatedTo(NavigationEventArgs e)
{
    try
    {
        GeoCoordinate coordinate = await GetCoordinate();
        theMap.Center = coordinate;
        theMap.ZoomLevel = 15;
```

```
        this.UserLocationMarker =
                     (UserLocationMarker)this.FindName("UserLocationMarker");
        this.UserLocationMarker.GeoCoordinate = coordinate;
        this.UserLocationMarker.Visibility = System.Windows.Visibility.Visible;

    }
    catch (Exception)
    {
        MessageBoxResult result = MessageBox.Show("Location services is not enabled.  Would you like
to go to the settings page to enable it?", "Error", MessageBoxButton.OKCancel);
        if (result == MessageBoxResult.OK)
        {
            Launcher.LaunchUriAsync(new Uri("ms-settings-location:"));
        }
    }
}
```

You should now be able to run the application and see a marker at the current location of your phone or the current location of the emulator if you are using one. Figure 8-8 shows the results.

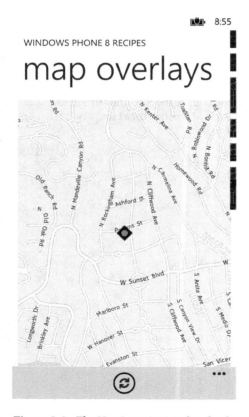

Figure 8-8. *The UserLocationMarker displayed on the map*

Adding Dynamic Overlays

For the sake of simplicity, let's imagine that you want to be able to mark some favorite places on the Map by tapping them. The process for doing this is straightforward. You can add pretty much anything you want as an overlay, but it's advisable to keep it simple.

We'll add our code in an event handler for the Tap event of the Map. The code in Listing 8-15 is well-commented to describe each step of the process. Add this code to the code-behind of the MainPage and then wire up the handler in XAML. In addition to the code in the listing, also add a private class-level variable to hold a MapLayer. Figure 8-9 shows the results of tapping on the Map.

```
private MapLayer layer;
```

Listing 8-15. Code to Add an Overlay to the Map at the Location Tapped by the User

```
private void TheMapTap(object sender, System.Windows.Input.GestureEventArgs e)
{
    // create an image using the favs icon
    // that comes with the SDK and add it to
    // a new MapOverlay
    Image image = new Image();
    image.Source = new BitmapImage(new Uri("Assets/footprint.png",
                            UriKind.RelativeOrAbsolute));

    MapOverlay overlay = new MapOverlay();
    overlay.Content = image;

    // get the position that the user tapped
    Point point = e.GetPosition(theMap);

    // the favs icon is 76 x 76 and we want to
    // center it on the point the user tapped
    // so we'll shift the point
    point.X -= 38;
    point.Y -= 38;

    // convert the ViewPort point into an actual GeoCoordinate value
    GeoCoordinate coordinate = theMap.ConvertViewportPointToGeoCoordinate(point);
    overlay.GeoCoordinate = coordinate;

    // the one and only layer that we
    // add all of the overlays to
    if (layer == null)
    {
        layer = new MapLayer();
        theMap.Layers.Add(layer);
    }
    layer.Add(overlay);
}
```

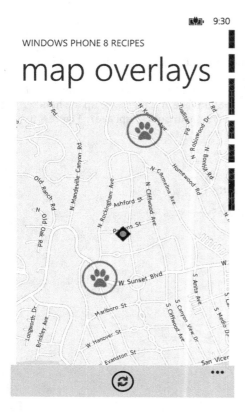

Figure 8-9. Footprints on my map. Who didn't wipe their feet?

8-5. Creating Routes and Directions

Problem

The MapsDirectionsTask is great, but what if you have more than one stop?

Solution

Use the GeocodeQuery and RouteQuery available in the `Microsoft.Phone.Maps.Services` namespace.

How It Works

The MapsDirectionsTask that we explored in Recipe 8-1 provides a fairly simple interface for getting directions, but sometimes you need more flexibility and power. It is a very nice implementation, and you get to reap the benefit of the investments made by Microsoft and Nokia. The built-in Maps application is really nice.

Having said that, there are certainly times when you need more fine-grained control of the information and overall experience. The MapsDirectionsTask, for example, supports only a single destination, and you may want to be able to display directions through several waypoints. The services available to you in the `Microsoft.Phone.Maps.Services` namespace provide you with these abilities and more.

Before we get started with the code, I want to make sure that we're all on the same page when it comes to what a GeocodeQuery is. I have to admit, I made some assumptions in the beginning, and it caused me some pain, so I want to be sure you don't suffer the same fate. This type of searching is about as far as you can get from a simple keyword search that you would do when Googling/Binging. A search for *coffee* may or may not go well.[4] A search for *coffee* using the MapsDirectionsTask from my current location will take me to Coffee County about 100 km outside of Nashville, Tennessee, in the United States. That is just over 1,228 km from where I am right now here in southwestern Ontario in Canada.

Geocoding

Geocoding is the process of discovering the geographic coordinates of a location, commonly expressed as latitude and longitude, based on other geographic data such as street addresses and postal/ZIP codes. This information is premapped in what is generically referred to as a Geographic Information System (GIS). These systems aren't always about street addresses; in fact, the first operational GIS was developed in the early 1960s by Dr. Roger Tomlinson in Ottawa, Canada, for the Canadian Land Inventory. It mapped things such as soils, recreation, wildlife, forestry, and land use. In the late 1980s CGIS was slowly being rendered obsolete by the emergence of commercial GISs. In the early 1990s, a team of volunteers was successful in extracting all of the CGIS information from tapes, and it's been made available for free on GeoGratis at http://geogratis.cgdi.gc.ca.

The best way to ensure good results with the GeocodeQuery is to give it as much information about the location you are seeking as possible. An exact and detailed address including a postal code will provide the best results. The other thing to note is that the search needs to be centered on a specific location. The results of the query will change depending on the location because it returns matches based on how close they are to that location. Notice also that I said "matches." The GeocodeQuery, at least in my experience, will return up to ten possible matches. There is also a MaxResultCount property that you can use to limit the number of results further if you so choose. The first result in the list may or may not be the one you are looking for if a possible match is found that is geographically closer to the GeoCoordinate you set as the center of the search.

Route

A *route* is the lists of waypoints, legs, and maneuvers that describe how to navigate between two or more locations. A route in Windows Phone 8 is represented by the Microsoft.Phone.Maps.Services.Route class. A Route is returned as the Result of a RouteQuery. A MapRoute instance is constructed by passing a Route to the constructor, and that is added to a Map control for display.

Waypoints

Most commonly we want to be somewhere else. We want to start "here" and go "there." Other times you may have more than one *point* along the *way* that you want to visit. Your starting point is included as a waypoint when configuring the RouteQuery, and the route is constructed based on the order in which the waypoints are added. It's up to you to determine the most efficient order in which to visit all of the waypoints given specific start and end points. There are advanced routing programs available that, given a start point, an end point, and a list of points in between, will calculate the optimal route through all waypoints. That is not the case with the RouteQuery.

A waypoint is represented by a System.Device.Location.GeoCoordinate. The RouteQuery.Waypoints property takes an IEnumerable<GeoCoordinate>.

---

[4]It's not entirely my fault. The sample for the MapsTask on MSDN sets the SearchTerm to *coffee*.

Legs

A *leg* consists of a list of maneuvers that are taken between one waypoint and the next. The number of legs is equal to the number of waypoints minus one. A trip from your home to the bank, the grocery store, and home again would have three legs because there are four waypoints. One of them, your home, is counted at the start and end points even though they are the same geographic location.

1.   Home ➤ Bank

2.   Bank ➤ Grocery store

3.   Grocery store ➤ Home

A leg is represented in code by the `Microsoft.Phone.Maps.Services.RouteLeg` class.

Maneuvers

Maneuvers are the actions that make up each leg of a route and are represented by the RouteManeuver class in the `Microsoft.Phone.Maps.Services` namespace. A maneuver contains the list of actions to be taken by a traveler for each leg of the route to get to the next waypoint. Table 8-6 describes the various properties of the RouteManeuver.

Table 8-6. *Properties of the RouteManeuver Class*

Name	Description
InstructionKind	A value from the `RouteManeuverInstructionKind` enumeration that identifies the basic type of the maneuver, such as `TurnLeft`, `TurnLightLeft`, `TurnHardLeft`, `FreewayEnterLeft`, and so on
InstructionText	Describes the action to take based on the InstructionKind followed by the target of the action, such as "Turn Left onto Main Street" or "Keep right onto Hwy 401"
LengthInMeters	The distance in meters to the start of the next maneuver
StartGeoCoordinate	The `GeoCoordinate` of the starting point of the maneuver

Bringing It All Together

Now that we know what all the moving parts are and how they relate to each other, let's take a look at how to tie them all together into something useful. The first step is to find your current location and set that as the first item in our list of waypoints. This will be the start of our route. We'll do this in the override of OnNavigatedTo in our MainPage.xaml.cs file, as shown in Listing 8-16.

Listing 8-16. Code to Determine and Set the Current Location of the Device

```
protected async override void OnNavigatedTo(NavigationEventArgs e)
{
    try
    {
        currentLocation = await GetCurrentLocation();
        App.ViewModel.WayPoints.Clear();
        App.ViewModel.WayPoints.Add(new LocationItem
```

```
        {
            Address = "My Location",
            Coordinate = currentLocation
        });

    }
    catch (Exception)
    {
        MessageBoxResult result = MessageBox.Show("Location services is not enabled.
Would you like to go to the settings page to enable it?", "Error", MessageBoxButton.OKCancel);
        if (result == MessageBoxResult.OK)
        {
            Launcher.LaunchUriAsync(new Uri("ms-settings-location:"));
        }
    }
}

private async Task<GeoCoordinate> GetCurrentLocation()
{
    Geolocator locator = new Geolocator();
    GeoCoordinate coordinate;
    locator.DesiredAccuracy = PositionAccuracy.High;

    Geoposition position = await locator.GetGeopositionAsync();

    coordinate = new GeoCoordinate(position.Coordinate.Latitude,
        position.Coordinate.Longitude);

    return coordinate;
}
```

The next step, now that we have our starting point, is to look up the GeoCoordinate of each of the destinations we want to add to our route. We do that by using the GeocodeQuery. Setting up and executing the GeocodeQuery is simple, as shown in Listing 8-17; dealing with the results, not so much.

Listing 8-17. Configuring and Executing a GeocodeQuery

```
codeQuery = new GeocodeQuery();
codeQuery.SearchTerm = App.ViewModel.SearchText;
codeQuery.GeoCoordinate = currentLocation;
codeQuery.QueryCompleted += GeocodeQueryQueryCompleted;
codeQuery.QueryAsync();
```

As discussed earlier, the more specific the information is that you pass in for the SearchTerm, the more accurate your results are going to be. Including a postal or ZIP code will almost guarantee a match. The GeocodeQuery uses an event-based asynchronous programming model and doesn't provide an awaitable version of the QueryAsync method. This is a shame since it makes our code more complicated. Listing 8-18 contains the code for our QueryCompleted handler.

Listing 8-18. QueryCompleted Event Handler for Our GeocodeQuery

```
void GeocodeQueryQueryCompleted(object sender,
    QueryCompletedEventArgs<IList<MapLocation>> e)
{
    App.ViewModel.LocationItems.Clear();
    if (e.Error != null || e.Result.Count == 0)
    {
        string errorText = string.Empty;
        if (e.Error != null)
        {
            GeocodeQueryHresult hresult = (GeocodeQueryHresult)e.Error.HResult;
            errorText = hresult.GetGeocodeQueryHresultDescription();

        }
        else
        {
            errorText = "Location not found";
        }

        App.ViewModel.LocationItems.Add(new LocationItem { Address = errorText });
    }
    else
    {
        App.ViewModel.LocationItems.Clear();
        foreach (var result in e.Result)
        {
            MapAddress address = result.Information.Address;
            string addressText = string.Format("{0} {1}, {2}",
                address.HouseNumber, address.Street, address.City);
            LocationItem item = new LocationItem
            {
                Address = addressText,
                Coordinate = result.GeoCoordinate
            };
            App.ViewModel.LocationItems.Add(item);
            App.ViewModel.SearchControlsEnabled = true;
        }
    }
    App.ViewModel.SearchControlsEnabled = true;
}
```

The first thing to do in our handler is to check the Error property of the returned event arguments, and if it's not null, something has gone wrong. Another thing that complicates our code is the fact that the Error is returned as an Exception—not as a specific exception cast to the base type, mind you, but just a plain old exception. You know, it's the one that you are never supposed to throw or catch. Adding injury to the insult is the fact that the only useful information that gets returned to you is an HResult. In other words, "Something bad happened. Please decode this cryptic value to find out what." Table 8-7 lists the possible HResult codes and their meaning. I suppose it's better than nothing but only just.

Table 8-7. *HResult Codes for the GeocodeQuery Results*

HResult	Symbolic Code
0x80041B58	EErrorBadLocation
0x80041B57	EErrorIndexFailure
0x80041B56	EErrorCancelled

Assuming that nothing has gone wrong and our search returned some results, we can now add each result to a list of items and allow the user to pick the one that corresponds to the destination that they are searching for. The Result property of the argument is of type MapLocation. The MapLocation class has a property of type LocationInformation, and from that we can access the Address property that is of type MapAddress.

I created my own LocationItem class that exposes a string used to display the address of the result and a property of type GeoCoordinate since that is all we need for our RouteQuery later. I simply create a new instance and add it a list of locations from which the user can pick the correct match.

```
MapAddress address = result.Information.Address;
string addressText = string.Format("{0} {1}, {2}",
address.HouseNumber, address.Street, address.City);
LocationItem item = new LocationItem
{
    Address = addressText,
    Coordinate = result.GeoCoordinate
};
App.ViewModel.LocationItems.Add(item);
```

The item selected by the user is then added to a list of waypoints that will be used in the RouteQuery. The RouteQuery, like the GeocodeQuery, is very simple to use. Listing 8-19 has the details.

Listing 8-19. Setting Up and Executing a RouteQuery

```
RouteQuery routeQuery = new RouteQuery();
coordinates = (from point in App.ViewModel.WayPoints
               select point.Coordinate).ToList();

routeQuery.Waypoints = coordinates;
routeQuery.QueryCompleted += RouteQueryQueryCompleted;
routeQuery.QueryAsync();
```

The QueryCompleted handler for the RouteQuery follows the same pattern as the GeocodeQuery right down to the use of the Exception and HResult. On the upside, there are quite a few result codes, and each has a fairly descriptive meaning. Table 8-8 lists the codes and their meaning. The sample code for this recipe contains a couple of enumerations I created to wrap up these HResult codes. I also created a couple of extension methods that allow you to get the description text for a particular code.

Table 8-8. *HResult Codes for the RouteQuery*

HResult	Symbolic Code	Description
0x80042328	EErrorGraphDisconnected	No route found.
0x80042327	EErrorGraphDisconnectedCheckOptions	No route found; some option (for example, disabled highways) may be prohibiting it.
0x80042326	EErrorNoStartPoint	Start point not found.
0x80042325	EErrorNoEndPoint	End point not found.
0x80042324	EErrorNoEndPointCheckOptions	End point unreachable; some option (for example disabled highways) may be prohibiting it.
0x80042323	EErrorCannotDoPedestrian	Pedestrian mode was set but cannot do pedestrian route (too long route).
0x80042322	EErrorRouteUsesDisabledRoads	Route was calculated but it uses roads, which were disabled by options. Note: this error is given also when start direction is violated.
0x80042321	EErrorRouteCorrupted	Corrupted route.
0x80042320	EErrorRouteNotReady	Route not ready.
0x8004231F	EErrorRouteNotReadyFailedLocally	Route not ready failed locally.
0x8004231E	EErrorRoutingCancelled	Routing was cancelled.

We'll use the LongListSelecor to display the results and use its grouping capability to display the maneuver list for each leg of the journey in a separate group. The features of the LongListSelector are covered in depth in Recipe 2-5 in Chapter 2. We'll make use of the ObservableLongListGroup class from that chapter to display our results.

The Result property of the QueryCompletedEventArgs is of type Route. The Legs property of Route contains one RouteLeg for each of the waypoints we provided to our query, and each RouteLeg contains the collection of RouteManeuver objects that direct us to that waypoint. The RouteLeg doesn't contain the address information, but since the Legs are in the same order as our list of waypoints, we can index into that list to retrieve the address for display in our group header. Listing 8-20 shows the code to create the ObservableLongListGroup items, and Listing 8-21 shows the XAML used to create the necessary templates and LongListSelector to display the directions.

Listing 8-20. Generating the ObservableLongListGroup Items

```
Route route = e.Result;
for (int j = 0; j < route.Legs.Count; j++)
{

    string wayPoint = App.ViewModel.WayPoints[j].Address;
    List<string> manuvers = (from man in route.Legs[j].Maneuvers
                        select man.InstructionText).ToList();

    App.ViewModel.Maneuvers.Add(
    new ObservableLongListGroup<string>(manuvers, wayPoint));
}
```

Listing 8-21. XAML for the LongListSelector and Related Templates

```
<phone:JumpListItemBackgroundConverter x:Key="BackgroundConverter"/>
<phone:JumpListItemForegroundConverter x:Key="ForegroundConverter"/>

<DataTemplate x:Name="ManeuverHeaderTemplate">
    <Border
        BorderThickness="1"
        Background="{Binding Converter={StaticResource BackgroundConverter}}">
        <TextBlock
            Foreground="{Binding Converter={StaticResource ForegroundConverter}}"
            Text="{Binding Key}"
            Style="{StaticResource LongListSelectorGroupHeaderStyle}"/>
    </Border>
</DataTemplate>

<DataTemplate x:Name="MaueverItemTemplate">
    <TextBlock
        Style="{StaticResource PhoneTextNormalStyle}"
        Text="{Binding}"/>
</DataTemplate>

    <phone:LongListSelector
        Grid.Row="3"
        IsGroupingEnabled="True"
        ItemTemplate="{StaticResource MaueverItemTemplate}"
        ItemsSource="{Binding Path=Maneuvers}"
        GroupHeaderTemplate="{StaticResource ManeuverHeaderTemplate}">
    </phone:LongListSelector>
```

Figure 8-10 shows the results of our efforts.

Figure 8-10. *The list of maneuvers with a group header showing the starting point*

CHAPTER 9

■ ■ ■

Communications and Speech

Windows Phone SDK 8 provides new APIs to enable wireless communication using Bluetooth technology and Near Field Communications (NFC). Additionally, the SDK includes APIs that make it easy for developers to incorporate speech recognition and voice commands within the application. This chapter will cover the essentials of integrating these APIs within a Windows Phone application to enhance the user experience.

In this chapter, we will walk through the following recipes:

- 9-1. Send Data Between Devices Using Bluetooth

- 9-2. Send Data Between Devices Using NFC

- 9-3. Launch Your App Using Voice Commands

- 9-4. Incorporate Speech Recognition Within Your App

9-1. Send Data Between Devices Using Bluetooth

Problem

You want to create a chat application that will allow Windows Phone users to connect and send chat messages to each other when they are in close proximity.

Solution

Leverage the Proximity API in your application.

How It Works

Bluetooth is a wireless communication technology that devices use to communicate with each other within a 10-meter (or 32 – 33 foot) range. Numerous Bluetooth-enabled devices on the market today provide unlimited potential to mobile app developers to build engaging and innovative mobile apps that can interact with these devices. The Windows Phone 8 SDK makes it even easier through its Proximity API, which contains classes that enable wireless communication from a Windows Phone 8 application.

Peer Discovery

The PeerFinder class is part of the Windows.Networking.Proximity namespace in the Windows Phone SDK. It enables discovery of devices and applications that are within close range, using the FindAllPeers method. This method returns a read-only collection of PeerInformation objects. A PeerInformation object contains information about a peer application or device.

The PeerFinder class also provides a mechanism for a Windows Phone 8 application to create a socket connection with a peer application or external device, in the form of a StreamSocket, as shown in Listing 9-1. The StreamSocket class is part of the Windows.Networking.Sockets namespace. It supports network communication using a TCP stream socket, which enables app-to-app and app-to-device communication.

Listing 9-1. Use PeerFinder to Discover Peer Applications and to Establish a Connection with a Selected Peer

```
StreamSocket socket;
public async void FindPeers()
{
    IReadOnlyList<PeerInformation> peers = await PeerFinder.FindAllPeersAsync();
    if (peers.Count > 0)
    {
        //establish connection with the first peer in the list
        socket = await PeerFinder.ConnectAsync(peer[0]);

        //now that a connection has been established
        //stop advertising to conserve battery life
        PeerFinder.Stop();
    }
}
```

App-to-Device Communication

App-to-device communication allows an application to interact with an external device using a Bluetooth connection to exchange messages. To enable app-to-device communication, devices must be paired before they are able to transmit data in either direction. This means that the device must have Bluetooth turned on so that it is discoverable by the application to initiate device pairing.

During the pairing process, the connection is authenticated, and a Bluetooth connection is provided to the application in the form of a StreamSocket that allows the application to communicate with the required service on the device. To enable app-to-device communication from your Windows Phone application, you must include the ID_CAP_PROXIMITY and ID_CAP_NETWORKING capabilities in your application manifest. In this recipe, we will focus on app-to-app communication.

App-to-App Communication

App-to-app communication allows two programs to interact using Bluetooth to exchange messages. Devices do not need to be paired when using app-to-app communication. Instead, the application searches for a device that is running an instance of itself. The application can wait for, and respond to, messages from another application.

An application can advertise itself as an application accepting connections by setting the DisplayName property on the PeerFinder class and then calling the PeerFinder.Start method, as shown in Listing 9-2.

Listing 9-2. Make the Application Discoverable Using PeerFinder

```
public void Advertise()
{
        //Set the DisplayName on the PeerFinder class to
        //the name of the app so that our peers can find it
        PeerFinder.DisplayName = appName;
```

```
        //Start advertising
        PeerFinder.Start();
}
```

The `PeerFinder` class exposes the `ConnectionRequested` event, which is raised when a communication request is received from another device. You must subscribe to this event within your application. When the event fires, the application can decide whether to accept the request and may display a confirmation to the user to indicate whether the connection was accepted. You can use the `PeerInformation` property of the event argument `ConnectionRequestedEventArgs` to determine who is attempting to connect to the application.

When the connection is accepted, use the `ConnectAsync` method on the `PeerFinder` class to create a `StreamSocket` to respond to messages from the incoming request (Listing 9-3). Also, you will want ensure that you call the `PeerFinder.Stop` method to stop advertising the application's service within your application to prevent any further incoming requests and to conserve battery life.

Listing 9-3. Use the StreamSocket Instance to Connect to the Peer Application

```
public MySampleApp()
{
    //Register for incoming connection requests
    PeerFinder.ConnectionRequested += PeerFinder_ConnectionRequested;
}

private void PeerFinder_ConnectionRequested(object sender, ConnectionRequestedEventArgs args)
{
    MessageBoxResult result = MessageBox.Show(
                string.Format("{0} is trying to connect. Would you like to accept?",
args.PeerInformation.DisplayName),
                "My Bluetooth Chat App",
                MessageBoxButton.OKCancel);

    if (result == MessageBoxResult.OK)
    {
        socket.Connect(args.PeerInformation);
    }
}
```

To enable app-to-app communication within your Windows Phone application, you must include the ID_CAP_PROXIMITY capability in your application manifest.

Now that you know how to establish a Bluetooth connection, you're probably thinking "That's great, but how do I actually put it to use to send and receive messages?" Well, that's a great question! Keep reading to find out more.

DataReader

The `DataReader` class, which is part of the `Windows.Storage.Stream` namespace, is used to read incoming messages that are transmitted from an external device or peer application. The `DataReader` class is used to load and read data from an input stream, as shown in Listing 9-4. To use the `DataReader` class within your application, you will need to perform the following steps:

1. Instantiate an instance of the `DataReader` class, passing in the `StreamSocket`'s `InputStream`.

2. Call the `DataReader`'s `LoadAsync` to retrieve the message size.

3. Call the LoadAsync method a second time to load the actual message input stream.

4. Call the ReadString method to extract the message sent by the external device.

Listing 9-4. Reading an Incoming Message Using the DataReader Class

```
DataReader dataReader = new DataReader(socket.InputStream);

//Get the size of the message
await dataReader.LoadAsync(4);
uint messageLen = (uint)dataReader.ReadInt32();

//Get the actual message
await dataReader.LoadAsync(messageLen);
string actualMessage = dataReader.ReadString(messageLen);
```

DataWriter

The DataWriter class is also part of the Windows.Storage.Stream namespace and is used to send outgoing messages to an external device or peer application, as shown in Listing 9-5. To use the DataWriter class within your application, you will need to perform the following steps:

1. Instantiate an instance of the DataWriter class, passing in the StreamSocket's OutputStream.

2. Set the message length in the OutputStream by calling the DataWriter's WriteInt32 method.

3. Call the StoreAsync method to transmit the data through the OutputStream.

4. Call the WriteString method to write the actual message that you want to send to the connected device or peer application.

5. Call the StoreAsync method a second time to send the message through the OutputStream.

Listing 9-5. Sending a Message Through an Established Connection Using the DataWriter Class

```
DataWriter dataWriter = new DataWriter(socket.OutputStream);

//Send the message length first
dataWriter.WriteInt32(message.Length);
await dataWriter.StoreAsync();

//Next, send the actual message
dataWriter.WriteString(message);
await dataWriter.StoreAsync();
```

Let's see a full working sample of the concepts discussed in this recipe. Launch Visual Studio 2012, and open the project named MyBluetoothChatApp, located in the \Chapter 9\MyBluetoothChatApp directory. This is a full working sample of a chat application using Bluetooth communication. As you look at the project files and source code, notice that the sample application is structured a bit differently than the code listings provided in this recipe, making use of a view model and including error handling where appropriate.

This is the point where you are probably chomping at the bit to test it, and if you are impatient, you may have already tried to launch it in the emulator. Here's where we break the bad news to you. You cannot test Bluetooth communication in the Windows Phone emulator.

Although you can see the Bluetooth settings page in the emulator, the setting itself is disabled. Attempting to run an app that requires a Bluetooth connection will fail miserably. The sample app that ships with this recipe checks whether Bluetooth is enabled and prompts the user to turn it on. In the emulator, the switch to turn on Bluetooth connections is disabled (Figure 9-1) because it is not supported.

Figure 9-1. *Bluetooth settings are disabled in the Windows Phone emulator*

This is the point in time where you will need to phone a friend, a Windows Phone 8 friend, that is, in order to fully test Bluetooth communication within your Windows Phone application.

9-2. Send Data Between Devices Using NFC
Problem

You want to create an app that will allow Windows Phone users to send messages to another device by tapping the two devices together.

Solution

Use the TriggeredConnectionStateChanged event handler on the PeerFinder class to register for incoming requests.

How It Works

Near Field Communication enables communication between electronic devices, over either a Bluetooth connection or a wireless network connection. Communication is often initiated by tapping the two devices together. Devices must be in very close proximity, no more than 3 to 5 centimeters (or 1 – 2 inches) of each other, to leverage Near Field Communication. The application must be running in the foreground to use NFC. Also, your application will need to include the ID_CAP_PROXIMITY and ID_CAP_NETWORKING capabilities in your application manifest in order to use NFC within your application.

As we discussed in Recipe 9-1, a StreamSocket is established when a connection between the two devices is successful. The socket is established on either a Wi-Fi connection using TCP/IP or a Bluetooth connection. The Proximity API determines which connection to establish based on the values of the PeerFinder.AllowBluetooth and PeerFinder.AllowInfrastructure properties. Both properties are set to True by default.

Note that communication between devices over a wireless network connection may be established only if both devices are on the same infrastructure network, with no IP conflicts and no firewalls blocking communication. Since Bluetooth offers a consistent user experience, it is recommended that you design your application to use Bluetooth communication if possible over a wireless network connection. You can set your application to exclusively use Bluetooth communications only by setting the PeerFinder.AllowInfrastructure property value to False in your application. It is also recommended that your application display a message to the user to confirm that Bluetooth is enabled on both devices before a tap attempt is initiated.

Tap to Connect

To provide a simple implementation of sharing data using a tap to connect devices through NFC, you will need to leverage the PeerFinder, StreamSocket, DataReader, and DataWriter classes. These classes were detailed in Recipe 9-1, so if you skipped that part, you may want to go back to read up on them.

On the PeerFinder class, you will need to subscribe to the TriggeredConnectionStateChanged event, rather than the ConnectionRequested event that was demonstrated in Recipe 9-1. However, you will want to subscribe to this event only if the current device supports NFC.

To determine whether the current device supports NFC, check the SupportedDiscoveryTypes property on the PeerFinder class.

```
if ((PeerFinder.SupportedDiscoveryTypes & PeerDiscoveryTypes.Triggered) == PeerDiscoveryTypes.Triggered)
{
    //Device supports NFC, so we can register for incoming connection requests
    PeerFinder.TriggeredConnectionStateChanged +=
        PeerFinder_TriggeredConnectionStateChanged;
}
```

When a tap between devices occurs, the PeerFinder_TriggeredConnectionStateChanged event is triggered. The order of states when a tap and subsequent successful connection between devices occur generally includes PeerFound, Connecting, Listening, and Completed. If the devices tap a second time, the Canceled state is initiated, and the connection is closed. You may want to handle the case in your application where an accidental secondary tap is triggered. You can choose to ignore the action or confirm with the user if they want to close the connection.

Listing 9-6 demonstrates an example of putting the TriggeredConnectionStateChanged event to use. When a connection is established, the application will send a random picture from the device's media library to the connected device, using the DataWriter and StreamSocket classes. When the application is not sending data, it is listening for any incoming messages. When a picture is received, it is retrieved from the StreamSocket's InputStream using the DataReader class to retrieve the picture's byte array data. It is then converted to a BitmapImage and displayed in the view. The full code implementation of this can be found in the sample application shipped with this book, located in the \Chapter 9\TapToShare directory.

Listing 9-6. Monitor NFC Connection Requests from the PeerFinder's TriggeredConnectionStateChanged Event

```
void PeerFinder_TriggeredConnectionStateChanged(object sender, TriggeredConnectionStateChangedEventArgs args)
{
    switch (args.State)
    {
        case TriggeredConnectState.Canceled:
            //This may have been triggered accidentally
            //so just ignore it. There is a way the user can
            //forcibly cancel the connection from the view
            break;
        case TriggeredConnectState.Completed:
            this.IsConnected = true;

            socket = args.Socket;
            StartRandomPictureShare();
            SetStatus(args.State.ToString());

            //Connection established, so we can stop advertising now
            PeerFinder.Stop();
            break;
        case TriggeredConnectState.Listening:
            this.IsConnected = true;

            socket = args.Socket;
            GetRandomPictureShare();
            SetStatus(args.State.ToString());

            //Connection established, so we can stop advertising now
            PeerFinder.Stop();
            break;
        default:
            //set the connected flag to false and display the state in the view
            SetStatus(args.State.ToString());
            this.IsConnected = false;

            //Connection is closed, so we can start advertising again
            PeerFinder.Start();
            break;

    }
}
```

Close Proximity Communication

To obtain information on a device that is within close proximity, you can leverage the ProximityDevice class. The ProximityDevice class, which is part of the Windows.Networking.Proximity namespace, enables you to publish messages to devices in close proximity, as well as subscribe to messages from those devices. Table 9-1 describes the methods available on the ProximityDevice class, including the various publish and subscribe methods. Publish and subscribe actions should be used only when sending or receiving small blocks of data. When you need to transmit larger amounts of data, use the PeerFinder and StreamSocket classes, as discussed in the "Tap to Connect" section, earlier in this recipe.

Table 9-1. *ProximityDevice Methods*

Method	Description
FromId	Creates an instance of the ProximityDevice class, using the DeviceInformation ID of the device that is in close proximity, and activates the specified proximity device interface.
GetDefault	Creates an instance of a ProximityDevice class and activates the default proximity provider. If the proximate device does not support NFC, a NULL value will be returned.
GetDeviceSelector	Returns the class selection string that you can use to enumerate proximity devices.
PublishBinaryMessage	Publishes a message that contains binary data to subscribers of the specified message type. You may optionally specify a handler that will be called when the message has been transmitted.
PublishMessage	Publishes a message to subscribers of the specified message type. You may optionally specify a handler that will be called when the message has been transmitted.
PublishUriMessage	Publishes a Uniform Resource Identifier (URI) to a proximate device. You may optionally specify a handler that will be called when the message has been transmitted.
StopPublishingMessage	Stops publishing a message.
StopSubscribingForMessage	Cancels a message subscription.
SubscribeForMessage	Creates a subscription for a specified message type.

The ProximityDevice class also exposes two events: DeviceArrived and DeviceDeparted. The DeviceArrived event is triggered when a device enters in close range for Near Field Communication. The DeviceDeparted event is triggered when the device leaves the proximate range for Near Field Communication. As mentioned earlier, devices are close in proximity when they are within 3 to 5 centimeters of each other.

The Code

Launch Visual Studio 2012, and open the project named TapToShare, located in the \Chapter 9\TapToShare directory. This application demonstrates two simple NFC implementations:

- Establishing a connection between devices when the devices are tapped together. Once connected, the app sends a random picture from the user's device to share with the connected device. Step through the PictureShare markup and code-behind, along with the PictureShareViewModel class, to see how it all ties together.

- A simple message exchange between two devices in close proximity, using the publish-subscribe actions available within the ProximityDevice class. Step through the MessageShare markup and code-behind, along with the MessageShareViewModel class.

Proximity Tapper

If you are anxious to play around with NFC in your application but you don't have multiple devices to test with, we have some good news to share! Proximity Tapper allows you to test your NFC application within the Windows Phone emulator.

Proximity Tapper is an open source project available on CodePlex at `http://proximitytapper.codeplex.com`. This tool allows you to test NFC apps in the Windows Phone emulator by enabling the tap to connect functionality between two separate running instances of the Windows Phone emulator on a single machine. When first launching the Proximity Tapper tool, you will receive a Windows Firewall prompt. You must select all of the check boxes in the prompt to allow the tool to communicate through the firewall; otherwise, the tool will silently fail.

The simplest way to launch your application in separate running instances of the Windows Phone emulator is to launch two separate instances of Visual Studio 2012 and load your project in each one. Set the emulator resolution in the first instance to any resolution and launch it in the emulator. In the second Visual Studio 2012 project instance, set the emulator to a different resolution, and then launch. If you have the Proximity Tapper running at this point, you will notice both emulator instances will appear in the Proximity Tapper window within ten seconds of launch, as illustrated in Figure 9-2.

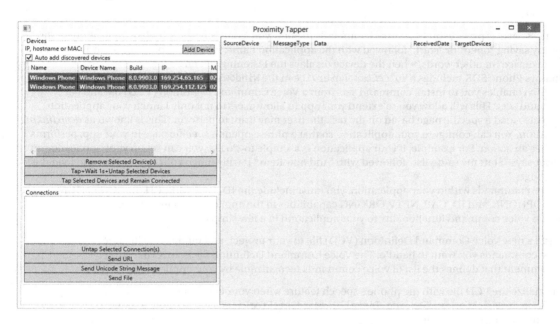

Figure 9-2. *Proximity Tapper tool displaying two running Windows Phone emulator instances in the Devices pane*

If all is well with the emulator instances, then both lines will appear green in the Proximity Tapper window. At this point, you can select both instances in the window, holding down the Ctrl key as you click each row to ensure both remain highlighted. You can then click the Tap Selected Devices and Remain Connected button to initiate a tap action and establish a connection. Connection information is displayed in the text field within the Connections group in the left pane, below the Devices list. The right pane contains information about any attempted data transmission.

When testing the sample application in the emulators, note that for the publish-subscribe feature, you will need to set one application as a subscriber by clicking the subscribe button. Once the application is subscribing, enter a message in the second emulator window, and tap the publish button. You should see the message appear in both windows.

When testing the picture share feature in the emulators, you will need to use this tool to simulate the tap between the two devices. We found that the Proximity Tapper is a good tool, but oftentimes the connection would be refused or the one instance would be stuck in a "Connecting..." state without successfully establishing the connection. Ideally, you will want to test your application on multiple devices to ensure it is working as expected, prior to submitting the app to Windows Phone Store.

9-3. Launch Your App Using Voice Commands

Problem

You want to provide a way for users to launch your application and load a specific page simply by saying a phrase.

Solution

Leverage the VoiceCommandService in your application.

How It Works

Windows Phone 8 devices provide built-in voice commands to allow you to launch any installed application on the device, simply by saying "open" or "start," followed with the application name, when the Voice Command prompt is activated on the device (in other words, when the device displays the Listening screen).

The Windows Phone SDK includes a VoiceCommandService in the Windows.Phone.Speech.VoiceCommands namespace, which enables you to install command sets from a Voice Command Definition (VCD) file and get installed command sets. This will allow you to extend your app to allow users to not only launch your application using voice but also load a specific page based on the task the user may want to perform. This is known as *deep linking* into the application. You can configure your application so that a phrase opens a specific page in your app, performs a task, or initiates an action. For example, if your application is a simple to-do list, you can set up your application so that when a user says "Start my to-do list" followed with "Add new item," it will launch your application and load the Add New Item page.

To use voice commands within your application, you must include the ID_CAP_SPEECH_RECOGNITION, ID_CAP_MICROPHONE, and ID_CAP_NETWORKING capabilities in the application manifest file.

You can add voice command functionality to your application in a few simple steps:

1. Add a new Voice Command Definition (VCD) file to your project, and modify it to include the commands you want to handle. The Voice Command Definition file is an XML document that defines the list of voice commands recognizable by your application.

2. Initialize the VCD file with the phone's speech feature when your application launches by calling the VoiceCommandService.InstallCommandSetsFromFileAsync method, passing in the URI to your VCD file.

3. Add code to determine whether the page was loaded through a voice command. If so, you will need to handle navigation and execute the desired commands accordingly.

Adding the Voice Command Definition File

You can add a new Voice Command Definition file in your project by clicking Add ➤ New Item . . . and selecting Voice Command Definition File in the Add New Item dialog, as shown in Figure 9-3.

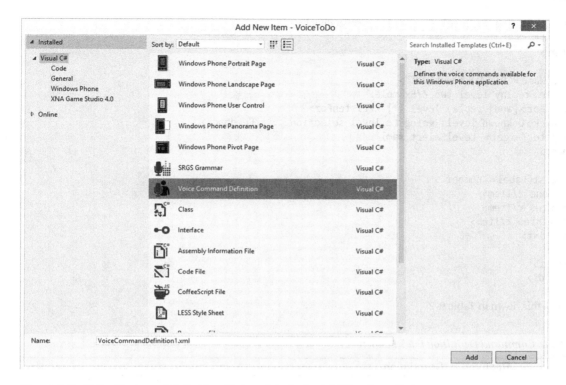

Figure 9-3. *Voice Command Definition file template in the Add New Item dialog*

When the file is added to your project, be sure to set the Build Action property to Content. Set the Copy To Output Directory property to Copy if newer. Take a moment to examine the default content that is generated in the VCD file (Listing 9-7). It provides some good examples of what the file layout and information should contain.

Listing 9-7. Voice Command Definition File Sample Content

```
<?xml version="1.0" encoding="utf-8"?>

<VoiceCommands xmlns="http://schemas.microsoft.com/voicecommands/1.0">
  <CommandSet xml:lang="en-US">
    <CommandPrefix>Contoso Rodeo</CommandPrefix>
    <Example>play a new game </Example>

    <Command Name="PlayGame">
      <Example>play a new game </Example>
      <ListenFor>[and] play [a] new game </ListenFor>
      <ListenFor>[and] start [a] new game </ListenFor>
      <Feedback>Starting a new game... </Feedback>
      <Navigate />
    </Command>

    <Command Name="PlayLevel">
      <Example>replay level two </Example>
      <ListenFor>replay level {number} </ListenFor>
```

```
    <Feedback>Going to level {number}... </Feedback>
    <Navigate />
  </Command>

  <Command Name="PlayUnknownLevel">
    <Example>replay level two </Example>
    <ListenFor>[and] replay level {*} </ListenFor>
    <Feedback>Unknown level; going to level selection... </Feedback>
    <Navigate Target="LevelSelect.xaml" />
  </Command>

  <PhraseList Label="number">
    <Item>one </Item>
    <Item>two </Item>
    <Item>three </Item>
  </PhraseList>

  </CommandSet>
</VoiceCommands>
```

Let's break this down in Table 9-2.

Table 9-2. *Voice Command Definition File's Elements*

Element	Required	Description
VoiceCommands	Yes	This is the root element of the VCD file. It must include the attribute xmlns = "http://schemas.microsoft.com/voicecommands/1.0". You may define only one VoiceCommand element per VCD file.
CommandSet	Yes	This defines a group of commands that are recognized by the application in a specific language. The xml:lang attribute must be included in the element, which indicates the language of the commands included in the group. If you want to modify the CommandSet programmatically, you must also include the Name attribute with a unique name value to identify the CommandSet. A file may have many CommandSets in order to support voice commands in different languages. However, you may not define multiple CommandSets for a single language.
CommandPrefix	No	When included, it must be the first child of the CommandSet element. Include this element to specify a user-friendly name for your application that will be spoken by the user when initiating a voice command for the application. You may define only one CommandPrefix per CommandSet.
Command	Yes	This defines a valid voice command that will be recognized by the application. Used in conjunction with its required child elements, it specifies an example for users to understand how to use the command and determines which phrase to listen for, which response to provide back to the user, and which page in your application to navigate to. You may define up to 100 Commands per CommandSet.
Example	Yes	This element must be the first child of the Command element. It provides an example of what the user must say to initiate the voice command. This phrase is listed on the "What can I say?" screen, the Listening screen, and the "Did you know?" screen. Only one Example may be defined per Command.

(continued)

Table 9-2. *(continued)*

Element	Required	Description
ListenFor	Yes	This element must follow the Example child element. The ListenFor element contains a word or phrase that will be recognized by your application when spoken by the user. You can use square brackets around any words that are optional within a phrase: `<ListenFor>[and] play [a] new game </ListenFor>`. You may also want to recognize any one of a set of phrases defined in a PhraseList by including the PhraseList name surrounded by curly braces: `<ListenFor>replay level {number} </ListenFor>`. You may also include wildcard searches to handle words that are not configured in the command file by including an asterisk surrounded by curly braces: `<ListenFor>[and] replay level {*} </ListenFor>`. Each Command must have at least one ListenFor element. You may define up to ten ListenFor elements per Command.
Feedback	Yes	This element contains the response text that will be displayed and read back to the user when the command is recognized. You may also refer to a PhraseList in the Feedback element, provided that the same PhraseList is used in any one of the configured ListenFor elements for the Command. You may specify only one Feedback element within a Command.
Navigate	Yes	This specifies the page that the application will navigate to when the voice command is spoken by the user. If the Navigate element is left empty, it will simply launch the application, loading its default main page. If a `Target` attribute is specified, its value should contain a valid URI pointing to a page in the application. In this way, the application will load and navigate directly to the page indicated. You may also include query string parameters in the Target URI value. You may specify only one Navigate element within a Command.
PhraseList	No	This defines list items, each of which may include a single word or phrase that may be used in a Command. You must specify a unique value for the PhraseList's `Label` attribute, because it is this value that is specified in curly braces within a ListenFor or Feedback element. The Voice Command Definition file may contain multiple PhraseLists, provided the combined total of Item elements is not exceeded.
Item	No	Defines a single word or phrase that will be recognized by the application when spoken by the user. A single Voice Command Definition file may contain up to 2,000 Item elements combined, across all configured PhraseLists.

Initializing the VCD File

The `VoiceCommandService.InstallCommandSetsFromFileAsync` method installs the CommandSet elements that are defined in the application's Voice Command Definition file. The `VoiceCommandService` is part of the `Windows.Phone.Speech.VoiceCommands` namespace. To execute this command, simply pass in the URI of the application's VCD file when calling the method, as shown in Listing 9-8. Although you can execute this command at any time from within the application, I prefer to handle it when the application first launches.

Listing 9-8. Initialize the Voice Command Definition File

```
using Windows.Phone.Speech.VoiceCommands;

private async void InitializeVoiceCommand()
{
    Uri vcdUri = new Uri("ms-appx:///MyVoiceCommands.xml");
    await VoiceCommandService.InstallCommandSetsFromFileAsync(vcdUri);
}

private void Application_Launching(object sender, LaunchingEventArgs e)
{
    InitializeVoiceCommand();
}
```

Handling Navigation and Command Execution

To handle navigation and command execution for voice commands within your application, override the OnNavigatedTo event in each page that is expected to be a target of a voice command action. Within the OnNavigatedTo event, check to see whether the NavigationContext.QueryString contains the voiceCommandName key. If so, the value of the voiceCommandName will be set to the Command that was initiated by the user. In this way, you can handle the action that was triggered accordingly. Listing 9-9 demonstrates an example of how this can be handled for simple voice commands.

Listing 9-9. Check Whether a Voice Command Initiated the Navigation Within the OnNavigatedTo Event

```
protected override void OnNavigatedTo(NavigationEventArgs e)
{
    if (NavigationContext.QueryString.ContainsKey("voiceCommandName"))
    {
        string voiceCommand = NavigationContext.QueryString["voiceCommandName"];

        switch (voiceCommand)
        {
            case "ViewTravel":
                //add code here to filter items by travel
                break;
            case "ViewRestaurant":
                //add code here to filter items by restaurant
                break;
            default:
                //add code here to filter items by the default view
                break;
        }
    }
}
```

The Code

Launch Visual Studio 2012, and open the project named VoiceBucketList, located in the \Chapter 9\VoiceBucketList directory. This application allows the user to view three bucket lists: Movie, Travel, and Restaurants. The user can also add new items to any of those three lists. We have decided to extend this application to allow the user to launch the application in a specific view by voice command. The user can also launch into the "Add Item page by voice" command.

The first thing we will look at is the application manifest file for this application. Notice that the three required capabilities (ID_CAP_SPEECH_RECOGNITION, ID_CAP_MICROPHONE, and ID_CAP_NETWORKING) have been included in this file, as depicted in Figure 9-4.

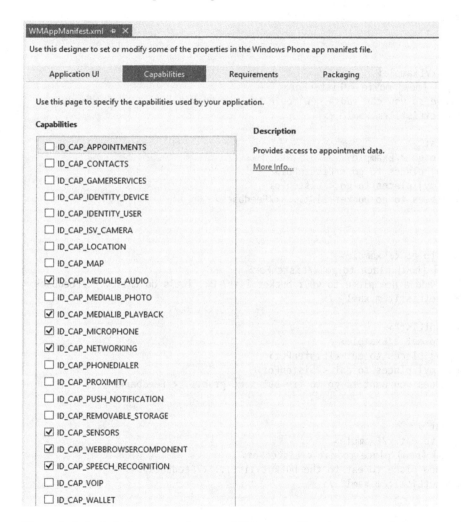

Figure 9-4. *Include the appropriate capabilities to enable voice commands in your application*

Next, take a moment to examine the Voice Command Definition file called MyVoiceCommands.xml (Listing 9-10). Within this command file, the recognizable commands by this application allow the user to view any one of the three valid bucket lists (i.e., movie, restaurants, and travel), as well as allowing the user to directly launch into the Add Item page for any of those lists.

Listing 9-10. VoiceBucketList's VCD File

```xml
<VoiceCommands xmlns="http://schemas.microsoft.com/voicecommands/1.0">
  <CommandSet xml:lang="en-US">
    <CommandPrefix>Voice Bucket List</CommandPrefix>
    <Example>view my movie bucket list </Example>
    <Command Name="ViewMovieList">
      <Example>view my movies </Example>
      <ListenFor>[and] view [my] movies </ListenFor>
      <ListenFor>[and] manage [my] movies </ListenFor>
      <Feedback>Loading your movie bucket list... </Feedback>
      <Navigate />
    </Command>
    <Command Name="AddMovie">
      <Example>add a new movie </Example>
      <ListenFor> [and] add [a] [new] movie </ListenFor>
      <Feedback>Loading the page so you can add a new movie to your bucket list... </Feedback>
      <Navigate Target="AddBucketListItem.xaml" />
    </Command>
    <Command Name="ViewTravelList">
      <Example>view my places to go </Example>
      <ListenFor>[and] view [my] places to go </ListenFor>
      <ListenFor>[and] manage [my] places to go </ListenFor>
      <Feedback>Loading your places to go bucket list... </Feedback>
      <Navigate />
    </Command>
    <Command Name="AddTravel">
      <Example>add a new place to go </Example>
      <ListenFor> [and] add [a] [new] place to go </ListenFor>
      <Feedback>So, you want to add a new place to your bucket list? Ok, let's do this... </Feedback>
      <Navigate Target="AddBucketListItem.xaml" />
    </Command>
    <Command Name="ViewRestaurantList">
      <Example>view my places to eat </Example>
      <ListenFor>[and] view [my] places to eat </ListenFor>
      <ListenFor>[and] manage [my] places to eat </ListenFor>
      <Feedback>Loading the places you want to go to try out some grub... </Feedback>
      <Navigate />
    </Command>
    <Command Name="AddRestaurant">
      <Example>add a new place to eat </Example>
      <ListenFor> [and] add [a] [new] place to eat </ListenFor>
      <Feedback>Time to add a new place to eat to the bucket list... </Feedback>
      <Navigate Target="AddBucketListItem.xaml" />
    </Command>
  </CommandSet>
</VoiceCommands>
```

Now, open the App.xaml.cs code-behind file. In it, we have included the call to initialize the Voice Command Definition file when the application is launched. This is the same code that was displayed in Listing 9-6 earlier in this chapter.

Last but not least, let's examine the navigation and command execution in the code-behind for both the MainPage and AddBucketListItem pages.

The MainPage simply displays a pivot list, where each pivot item represents each of the three bucket lists. When the user initiates an action to load the application to a specific list, we simply set the SelectedIndex of the pivot list to the desired view, as shown in Listing 9-11.

Listing 9-11. Handling Navigation and Command Execution in the MainPage of the Application

```
protected override void OnNavigatedTo(NavigationEventArgs e)
{
    if (NavigationContext.QueryString.ContainsKey("voiceCommandName"))
    {
        string voiceCommand = NavigationContext.QueryString["voiceCommandName"];

        switch (voiceCommand)
        {
            case "ViewTravelList":
                pivotList.SelectedIndex = 1;
                break;
            case "ViewRestaurantList":
                pivotList.SelectedIndex = 2;
                break;
            default:
                pivotList.SelectedIndex = 0;
                break;
        }
    }
}
```

The AddBucketListItem page simply creates a new bucket list item, setting its type based on the user's voice command, as shown in Listing 9-12. The user then just needs to enter a name for the new item and then tap the save button to add the item to the corresponding list.

Listing 9-12. Handling Navigation and Command Execution in the AddBucketListItem Page

```
protected override void OnNavigatedTo(NavigationEventArgs e)
{
    if (NavigationContext.QueryString.ContainsKey("voiceCommandName"))
    {
        string voiceCommand = NavigationContext.QueryString["voiceCommandName"];

        switch (voiceCommand)
        {
            case "AddTravel":
                App.ViewModel.NewItem = new Models.BucketListItem { ItemType = BucketListItemType.Travel };
                App.ViewModel.PageTitle = BucketListItemType.Travel.ToString();
                break;
            case "AddRestaurant":
                App.ViewModel.NewItem = new Models.BucketListItem { ItemType = BucketListItemType.Restaurant };
                App.ViewModel.PageTitle = BucketListItemType.Restaurant.ToString();
                break;
```

```
            default:
                App.ViewModel.NewItem=new Models.BucketListItem { ItemType=BucketListItemType.Movie };
                App.ViewModel.PageTitle=BucketListItemType.Movie.ToString();
                break;
        }

    }
}

private void AddItem_Tap(object sender, System.Windows.Input.GestureEventArgs e)
{
    //force lost focus to occur on textbox so that the value gets updated in the binding
    var binding=itemToAdd.GetBindingExpression(TextBox.TextProperty);
    binding.UpdateSource();

    //let the viewmodel handle adding the item to the appropriate list based on item type
    App.ViewModel.AddNewItem();

    MessageBox.Show("The item has been added to the bucket list!");

    if (NavigationService.CanGoBack)
    {
        NavigationService.GoBack();
    }
    else
    {
        NavigationService.Navigate(new Uri("/MainPage.xaml", UriKind.RelativeOrAbsolute));
    }
}
```

You can run the application in the Windows Phone emulator to test it, provided you have a working microphone so that the emulator can hear your commands. Launch the application in the emulator but then hit the Back button once the application loads to return to the device's Start screen.

Once you are at the Start screen, tap and hold the Start button. If this is the first time you are running the voice command feature in the emulator or on a device, the "What can I say" screen is displayed, as shown in Figure 9-5. Tap the accept button to allow access to speech recognition going forward.

Figure 9-5. *"What can I say?" screen*

At this point, you'll see the Listening screen, as illustrated in Figure 9-6.

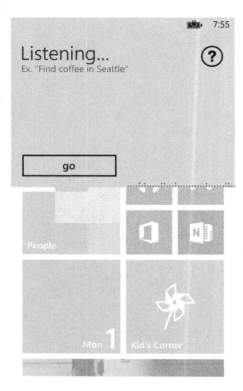

Figure 9-6. *At the Listening screen, speak a command to launch the desired application*

With the Listening screen initiated, speak your desired command. You can say "Open [app name]" or "Start [app name]" to launch the application with the main page in view, as shown in Figure 9-7.

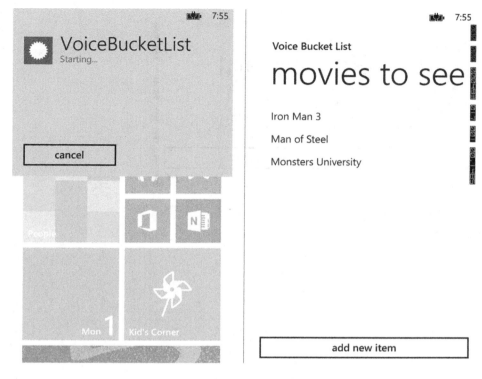

Figure 9-7. *Launch Voice Bucket List using a simple start command*

Go ahead and run a test with the following phrases to see what happens:

1. Open Voice Bucket List.

2. Open Voice Bucket List and add a new place to eat.

3. Open Voice Bucket List and view places to go.

You may also use alternate commands to deep-link into the application or execute another command when the app is launched, as shown in Figure 9-8. In this case, we have launched the Voice Bucket List using a start command along with an action phrase from the CommandSet in the VCD file. Notice the Feedback phrase that is displayed and read back is from the Feedback element associated to the spoken command.

Figure 9-8. *Launch Voice Bucket List using a start command along with an action phrase from the VCD file*

As demonstrated in this recipe, it is quite easy to add voice commands to enhance your application for the user. By allowing the user to launch the application and drill down to specific pages using voice commands, you will make the experience more pleasurable for the user!

9-4. Incorporate Speech Recognition Within Your App

Problem

You want to enhance your Windows Phone 8 application by allowing users to give voice commands to complete tasks within the application.

Solution

Leverage the Windows.Phone.Speech.Recognition API within your application.

How It Works

Speech recognition is similar to the voice command feature in that it allows the user to initiate actions or commands through speech. However, speech recognition is used within the application after it is launched, while voice commands are used to launch an application. To incorporate speech recognition within your application, you must include the ID_CAP_SPEECH_RECOGNITION, ID_CAP_MICROPHONE, and ID_CAP_NETWORKING capabilities in the application manifest.

Speech recognition in Windows Phone 8 is driven by grammars. Within your application, you may include support for predefined dictation grammar, which is the simplest implementation when providing support for speech recognition within your application. You may also choose to include support for custom grammar by including a grammar file that is created using the industry-standard Speech Recognition Grammar Specification (SRGS).

To make your application speech-ready, you must incorporate one of the speech recognizer objects within your application. This allows your user to initiate a speech recognition operation within the application. The `Windows.Phone.Speech.Recognition` API contains two objects, each which contain its own method for initiating a speech recognition operation.

- `SpeechRecognizerUI`: Use the method `RecognizeWithUIAsync` to trigger a recognition operation, displaying the built-in Windows Phone 8 speech recognition-related screens during the recognition process.

  When using predefined dictation or web search grammar, the user will be presented with the Listening screen, the Thinking screen, and either the "Heard you say" screen or an Error screen, all in that order. When using custom grammar, the user will be presented with the Listening screen, the Did You Say screen, and either the "Heard you say" screen or an Error screen.

  The `RecognizeWithUIAsync` method returns a `SpeechRecognitionUIStatus` value to indicate the result of its speech recognition session. The potential values include `Succeeded`, `Busy`, `Cancelled`, `Preempted`, and `PrivacyPolicyDeclined`.

- `SpeechRecognition`: This object contains the method, `RecognizeAsync`, to trigger a recognition operation, without displaying the built-in Windows Phone 8 speech recognition-related screens.

To load predefined or custom grammar within your application, you must use one of the three available `AddGrammar` methods in the `Windows.Phone.Speech.Recognition.SpeechGrammarSet` class, as listed in Table 9-3.

Table 9-3. *SpeechGrammarSet Methods for Loading Predefined or Custom Grammar into the Application*

Method	Description
AddGrammarFromList (string key, IEnumerable < string > phrases)	Creates a `SpeechGrammar` object from the string array of values that are passed into the method and adds it to the speech grammar set.
AddGrammarFromPredefinedType (string key, SpeechPredefinedGrammar predefinedGrammarType)	Creates a `SpeechGrammar` object based on the predefined grammar type passed into the method and adds it to the speech grammar set. Possible values for the `SpeechPredefinedGrammar` parameter include `Dictation` or `WebSearch`.
AddGrammarFromUri (string key, Uri grammarUri)	Creates a `SpeechGrammar` object from the SGRS grammar file that is passed in through the `Uri` parameter and adds it to the speech grammar set.

These methods are available through the `Recognizer.Grammars` collection, which is accessible from the `SpeechRecognitionUI` and `SpeechRecognition` objects. Here's an example:

```
SpeechRecognizerUI speechRecognizerUI = new SpeechRecognizerUI();
speechRecognizerUI.Recognizer.Grammars.AddGrammarFromPredefinedType("myAppGrammar",
SpeechPredefinedGrammar.Dictation);
```

You can also customize the listen prompt and example text that is displayed on the Listening screen by modifying the ListenText and ExampleText properties on the Settings class, which is accessible from both speech recognizer objects. Here's an example:

```
speechRecognizerUI.Settings.ListenText = "What are you searching for?";
speechRecognizerUI.Settings.ExampleText = "coffee shop";
```

The Code

Launch Visual Studio 2012, and open the project named VoiceBucketListWithSpeech, located in the \Chapter 9\VoiceBucketListWithSpeech directory. This application is an extension of the application we developed in Recipe 9-3. If you skipped Recipe 9-3, now is the time to head back there to get ramped up on the application that we are working with now.

You will notice that this application has been enhanced to include speech recognition from within the application, when adding new items to the bucket list. All of our enhancements were performed in the AddBucketListItem page's code-behind. Within the code-behind, you will notice that we instantiate a SpeechRecognizerUI object when the page is initialized (Listing 9-13). We also load a predefined dictation grammar set and ensure that the voice readout is enabled, and the confirmation message is displayed by setting the ReadoutEnabled and ShowConfirmation properties of the Settings class. If we want to turn voice readout off or bypass the confirmation dialog, simply set these properties to false.

Listing 9-13. Initializing the SpeechRecognizerUI Object in the AddBucketListItem Page

```
using Windows.Phone.Speech.Recognition;
...

SpeechRecognizerUI speechRecognizerUI;

public AddBucketListItem()
{
    InitializeComponent();
    DataContext = App.ViewModel;

    InitializeSpeechRecognizer();
}

private void InitializeSpeechRecognizer()
{
    speechRecognizerUI = new SpeechRecognizerUI();

    // Use the short message dictation grammar with the speech recognizer
    speechRecognizerUI.Recognizer.Grammars.AddGrammarFromPredefinedType("voiceBucketListKeywords",
    SpeechPredefinedGrammar.Dictation);

    speechRecognizerUI.Settings.ReadoutEnabled = true;
    speechRecognizerUI.Settings.ShowConfirmation = true;

}
```

Next, we decided to customize the Listen text and Example text that is displayed on the speech recognition screens, based on the type of item the user is currently adding to their bucket list, and then initiate the speech recognition UI, as shown in Listing 9-14.

Listing 9-14. Customize the Listen and Example Text Within the SpeechRecognizerUI.Settings Object

```
protected override void OnNavigatedTo(NavigationEventArgs e)
{
    if (NavigationContext.QueryString.ContainsKey("voiceCommandName"))
    {
        string voiceCommand=NavigationContext.QueryString["voiceCommandName"];

        switch (voiceCommand)
        {
            case "AddTravel":
                App.ViewModel.NewItem=new Models.BucketListItem { ItemType=BucketListItemType.Travel };
                App.ViewModel.PageTitle=BucketListItemType.Travel.ToString();

                speechRecognizerUI.Settings.ListenText="Which place do you want to add?";
                speechRecognizerUI.Settings.ExampleText="New York City";
                break;
            case "AddRestaurant":
                App.ViewModel.NewItem=new Models.BucketListItem { ItemType=BucketListItemType.Restaurant };
                App.ViewModel.PageTitle=BucketListItemType.Restaurant.ToString();

                speechRecognizerUI.Settings.ListenText="Which restaurant do you want to add?";
                speechRecognizerUI.Settings.ExampleText="McDonalds";
                break;
            default:
                App.ViewModel.NewItem=new Models.BucketListItem { ItemType=BucketListItemType.Movie };
                App.ViewModel.PageTitle=BucketListItemType.Movie.ToString();

                speechRecognizerUI.Settings.ListenText="Which movie do you want to add?";
                speechRecognizerUI.Settings.ExampleText="Spiderman";
                break;
        }

        PromptUserToSpeak();

    }
}

private async void PromptUserToSpeak()
{
    try
    {
        SpeechRecognitionUIResult recognitionResult =
            await speechRecognizerUI.RecognizeWithUIAsync();
```

```
        if (recognitionResult.ResultStatus == SpeechRecognitionUIStatus.Succeeded)
        {
            App.ViewModel.NewItem.Name = recognitionResult.RecognitionResult.Text;
        }
    }
    catch (Exception ex)
    {
        MessageBox.Show(ex.Message);
    }
}
```

When a successful result is received, the spoken word or phrase is set within the text box in the page. At this point, the user can tap the add button to add the item to the appropriate bucket list.

With just a few lines of code added, we have made the AddBucketListItem page speech-enabled. Let's run this in the emulator to see what happens. Launch the application in the emulator and then hit the Back button to return to the Start screen. Initiate a deep-link to the application's Add Bucket List Item screen by saying "Open VoiceBucketList and add a new movie." The voice command response feedback will display, and the application will launch directly into the AddBucketListItem page. However, when the page loads, it will immediately initiate the speech recognition screen, prompting the user to say the name or description of the item they want to add, as depicted in Figure 9-9.

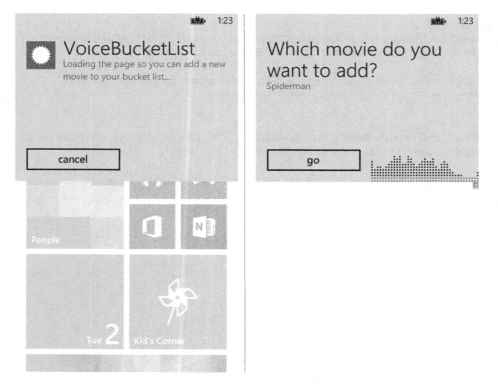

Figure 9-9. Use voice commands to launch the VoiceBucketList app and load the page to add a new bucket list item

When the user speaks a word or phrase, the speech recognition process then displays the Thinking screen while it processes the user's speech. Once it locates a match within the predefined grammar collection, it will then display the "Heard you say" screen with the word or phrase displayed, as illustrated in Figure 9-10.

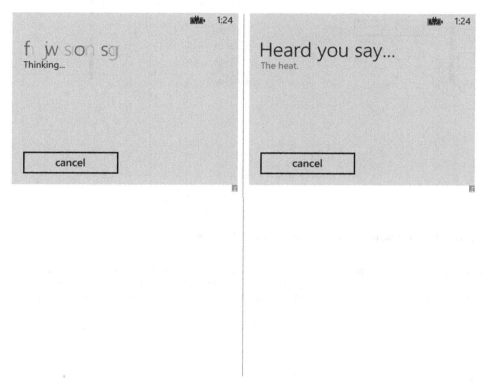

Figure 9-10. *Once a command is heard, the Thinking screen displays, followed by the "Heard you say" screen*

Next, the application sets the text box to the Text value of the RecognitionResult. At this point, the user needs only to tap the Add Movie button to add the new movie to a bucket list (Figure 9-11).

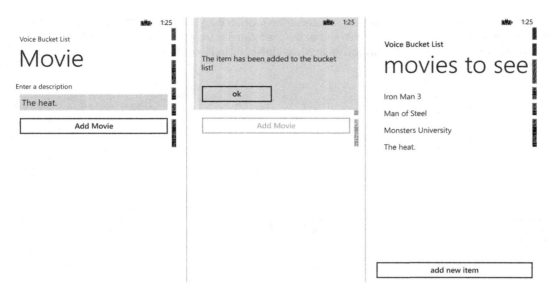

Figure 9-11. *The resulting phrase is added to the text box in the AddBucketListItem page*

As we demonstrated in this recipe, you can enhance the application experience for your users by incorporating speech recognition within the application in just a few lines of code. Speech recognition simplifies the tedious task of inputting information into a Windows Phone 8 application and will more than likely make the process more enjoyable for your user base.

■ ■ ■

CHAPTER 10

Launching and Resuming Apps

To pass the Windows Store certification requirements, developers must understand how to properly handle app activation and deactivation and how to preserve and restore both page state and application state. This chapter will provide you with the information you need to know to ensure that these tasks are handled, as well as how to enable fast app resume within your application. This chapter will wrap up with a recipe on how to launch other Windows Phone 8 apps from within your own app.

In this chapter, we will walk through the following recipes:

- 10-1. Preserve and Restore State

- 10-2. Enable Fast Application Resume Within Your App

- 10-3. Launch a Built-in Windows Phone 8 App from Your App

- 10-4. Launch Another Published App from Your App

10-1. Preserve and Restore State

Problem

The users of your application are complaining that the app experiences data loss when they launch other apps while your app is still running. When they return to the app to continue working within it, the app just relaunches the main screen, instead of the page that was last viewed.

Solution

Leverage the application and page navigation events to preserve and restore application state.

How It Works

Before understanding how to manage state using events, let's review the application states of a Windows Phone application.

Application States

There are three states of a Windows Phone application:

- *Running*: This state is pretty self-explanatory. An application is running when the user launches a new instance of that application from the Windows Phone Start screen (in other words, tapping a tile, using a voice command, tapping the name in the application list, and so on) and the application is in the foreground.

- *Dormant*: This occurs when the application is no longer running in the foreground because the user navigated away from the app, without exiting the app itself. Some examples include tapping the Start button to return to the Start screen to launch another app, tapping the Search button, receiving a phone call, or engaging the lock screen. Note that in all of these cases, the app was not terminated by the user (in other words, the Back button was not tapped to exit the application). When an app is dormant, its application state is preserved in memory. When a dormant app is resumed, application and page states are restored automatically.

- *Tombstoned*: This occurs when a dormant application is terminated by the operating system because another application requires more memory to run. The operating system will tombstone up to five apps to release memory for the currently running application. A tombstoned app will have its state information preserved, but the app itself is not preserved in memory. Instead, the State dictionary of the PhoneApplicationPage object is stored. In this case, when a user navigates to an app that has been tombstoned, the developer will need to perform a little extra legwork to ensure that the app retrieves the data stored in the State dictionary to restore page state.

It is important to note that Windows Phone devices can run only one application at a time in the foreground. So, if your user is entering in data and a phone call comes in, the phone call takes over the foreground, and your application is sent to the background in a dormant state. When the user finishes the phone call, the user may end up launching other applications or performing tasks that require more memory before returning to your app. This, in turn, will cause the device operating system to tombstone your application. If you did not take the proper precautions to preserve and restore both page state and application state, your user may lose data that was being entered at the point in time that the application was interrupted.

▪ **Note**   Application state refers to data that needs to be stored to ensure the application continues running as expected when resumed from a tombstoned state without experiencing any delays, such as an authentication key or a web service result. Page state refers to data that was modified by the user in a specific view in the application, such as changing control state or entering values in an input field.

As a developer, the best thing you can do to mitigate against data loss is to manage page state and application state during the small window of opportunity that is made available to you by the API to prepare for the scenario where your application is tombstoned by the device's operating system. This includes storing any unsaved data in the State dictionary, as the application is being deactivated.

It also provides you with the ability to restore page state and application state as the application is brought back to the foreground again, or reactivated. This gives the illusion to the user that your Windows Phone app was simply "minimized" while they were working within other applications. Application and page state need to be restored only when the application has been tombstoned. At this point, you're probably wondering how you can tell when an app has been tombstoned and requires the extra work to restore both page state and application state.

The first hint is to check the IsApplicationInstancePreserved property on the ActivatedEventArgs parameter that is passed in during the Application_Activated event. Refer to the "Application Events" section later in this recipe.

Also, an app that is resumed from a tombstoned state will reconstruct the application's page when launched, whereas a dormant app will not. Therefore, when a page constructor is called within your application, this is the point where you should check the State dictionary for your page's view model. If the page's view model was successfully retrieved from the State dictionary, then your app has been restored from a tombstoned state. If not, then a new instance of your application has been launched.

Application Events

When you create a new Windows Phone application, the template that is used to create your Windows Phone project automatically generates Application events in the App code-behind file in your project, as listed in Table 10-1. Code is automatically generated within these events that handles the app's initialization process, as well as loading and setting up language resources, when creating a Windows Phone App project using one of the built-in templates. Take a moment to look through the App code-behind file in a newly created Windows Phone project.

Table 10-1. *Application Life-Cycle Events*

Event	Event Triggered...	Application State
Application_Launching (object sender, LaunchingEventArgs e)	When launching a new instance of the application (for example, tapping the app tile).	Running
Application_Activated (object sender, ActivatedEventArgs e)	When the user returns to a dormant or tombstoned app. Check the result of the boolean property ActivatedEventArgs.IsApplicationInstancePreserved to determine which state the app is being resumed from. A value of True indicates the app is being resumed from a dormant state. Otherwise, the app is being resumed from a tombstoned state.	Running
Application_Deactivated (object sender, DeactivatedEventArgs e)	Just before the app is moved from the foreground to background. Check the Reason property on the DeactivatedEventArgs parameter to determine why the app is being deactivated. It will indicate one of the following DeactivatedReason enumeration values: ApplicationAction, PowerSavingModeOn, ResourcesUnavailable, UserAction.	Dormant, but may be tombstoned by OS if needed
Application_Closing (object sender, ClosingEventArgs e)	Just before the application is closed. At this point, the application is no longer running.	Closed

You can include your own code within these events to perform additional actions for any of the steps in the application's life cycle. However, note that anything you do within these events must execute quickly. And by quickly, I mean in a few seconds or less. All application events and page navigation events that are executed, when either launching, activating, or deactivating an app, must all execute in ten seconds or less, and that's a combined total. That means there is a very small window of opportunity for you, as the developer, to perform some housekeeping before the application is "put to sleep." If you have long-running code that exceeds that time frame, your app will be terminated. For more tips on how to handle application state, review the article "Activation and deactivation best practices for Windows Phone" at http://msdn.microsoft.com/en-us/library/windowsphone/develop/ff817009(v=vs.105).aspx.

Preserving and Restoring Application State

To preserve application state, you may use persistent storage, such as isolated storage and/or a local database. Since we have not yet touched on these topics, we will not delve too far into this approach. Just note that you can save data to, and load data from, either of these storage methods in order to preserve application state. One example of application state would be in the implementation of a Settings page to store user preferences that control how the application will look and feel. The user's desired settings will be loaded whenever a new instance of the application is loaded or when an application is being resumed from a tombstoned state. Refer to the recipes in Chapter 11 to learn more about data storage and retrieval.

Page Navigation Events

The Windows Phone 8 APIs provide page navigation events that can be overridden within your page's code-behind in order to perform custom actions within your application, as listed in Table 10-2.

Table 10-2. *Page Navigation Override Events*

Method	Triggered When..	Override When..
OnNavigatedTo (NavigationEventArgs)	Navigating to the current page.	You need to prepare the page on load, such as retrieving data or setting the state of visual elements in the page.
OnNavigatedFrom (NavigationEventArgs)	Navigating away from the current page.	You need to perform some sort of action on the page when it has become inactive. For example, you may want to save data to isolated storage or a local database.
OnNavigatingFrom (NavigationCancelEventArgs)	A navigation action is initiated to move away from the current page but the page is not yet inactive. Navigation may be cancelled.	You want the option to cancel the event based on navigation mode, or you want to perform other actions on the page before it becomes inactive.

The NavigationEventArgs object contains read-only properties that provide information about the navigation request, including the target URI, the navigation mode, and whether the current application was the navigation target.

The NavigatingCancelEventArgs object provides the same information as the NavigationEventArgs class, along with two properties related to navigation cancellation: IsCancelable and Cancel.

IsCancelable is a read-only boolean property that indicates whether the current navigation request can be cancelled. Cancel is a read-write boolean property. When Cancel is set to True, the navigation request is cancelled, and the application remains on the current page.

The NavigationMode property on both NavigationEventArgs and NavigatingCancelEventArgs is an enumerated value that is set to one of the following possible values:

- Back: The current navigation request is going back to the last-visited page in the back stack.

- Forward: The current navigation request is navigating forward to a page in the call stack.

- New: The current navigation request is navigating to a new page.

- Refresh: The current navigation request is reloading the current page.

- Reset: The current navigation request is reloading the current page, but the application should also conduct checks to determine whether it is necessary to clear the back stack based on the navigation target page.

Preserving and Restoring Page State

To preserve and restore page state, simply design your application using the MVVM pattern and leverage two-way bindings to display data in your View. The controls in your View should be bound to properties in the view model. Furthermore, make your view models serializable so that they can be stored in the State dictionary of the PhoneApplicationPage object. To make a view model serializable, use the DataContract attribute on the class definition, and use the DataMember attribute on all properties that will need to be preserved. These attributes allow the class and its properties to be used in serialization and deserialization procedures by the DataContractSerializer.

Within the view model's corresponding View (in other words, the page), override the OnNavigatedFrom event in the code-behind to store the current state of the View model in the State dictionary.

Override the OnNavigatedTo event to restore the view model from the State dictionary. Also, remember to distinguish whether the page constructor was called prior to the event's execution. This can simply be accomplished through a boolean class-level variable that will serve as the indicator.

Let's create a simple application where we can demonstrate the techniques discussed here.

The Code

Launch Visual Studio 2012 and create a new project, and select the Windows Phone Databound App template in the New Project dialog. Name the project ManagingState. We will simply leverage the test data that is in place in order to focus on the important details of managing both page state and application state. Therefore, we will make a few simple modifications to this project. In the DetailsPage markup, replace the TextBlock control in the ContentPanel to a TextBox control instead, as follows:

```
<Grid x:Name="ContentPanel" Grid.Row="1" Margin="12,0,12,0">
    <TextBox
        Text="{Binding LineThree, Mode=TwoWay}"
        TextWrapping="Wrap"
        AcceptsReturn="True" />
</Grid>
```

Next, modify the DetailsPage code-behind to override the OnNavigatedTo and OnNavigatedFrom events, as we discussed in the section "Preserving and Restoring Page State." Listing 10-1 shows the full modifications.

Listing 10-1. DetailsPage Code Modifications to Preserve and Restore Page State

```
using System.Windows.Navigation;
using Microsoft.Phone.Controls;
using ManagingState.ViewModels;

namespace ManagingState
{
    public partial class DetailsPage : PhoneApplicationPage
    {
        private ItemViewModel itemViewModel = null;
        private bool pageReconstructed = false;

        public DetailsPage()
        {
            InitializeComponent();
            pageReconstructed = true;
        }
```

```
protected override void OnNavigatedTo(NavigationEventArgs e)
{
    //If the page constuctor has been called, check State dictionary for
    //the page's view model. If one exists, restore the page state.
    //If not, then this is a new instance.
    if (pageReconstructed)
    {
        if (itemViewModel == null)
        {
            if (State.Count > 0)
            {
                itemViewModel = (ItemViewModel)State["ViewModel"];
            }
            else
            {
                string selectedIndex = "";
                if (NavigationContext.QueryString.TryGetValue("selectedItem", out selectedIndex))
                {
                    int index = int.Parse(selectedIndex);
                    itemViewModel = App.ViewModel.Items[index];
                }
            }
        }
        DataContext = itemViewModel;
    }

    pageReconstructed = false;
}

protected override void OnNavigatedFrom(System.Windows.Navigation.NavigationEventArgs e)
{
    //If this is a back navigation, just skip over it since the page will be discarded anyway
    if (e.NavigationMode != System.Windows.Navigation.NavigationMode.Back)
    {
        //Save the ItemViewModel in the page's State dictionary.
        State["ViewModel"] = itemViewModel;
    }
}
    }
}
```

Now let's run the application to see how this code performs when put to the test.

Testing in the Emulator

Since preserving page state is needed only when the application is tombstoned, we need to ensure that we can force our application into a tombstoned state in the emulator. To debug tombstoning behavior within the Windows Phone emulator, you will need to enable it within your project's debug settings. To accomplish this, right-click your project in the Solution Explorer in Visual Studio and select Properties from the context menu.

Within the Properties page, select the Debug section, and select the "Tombstone upon deactivation while debugging" check box, as depicted in Figure 10-1. Essentially, this will force your application into a tombstoned state within the emulator as soon as you move away from the app without closing it, which simplifies the testing process.

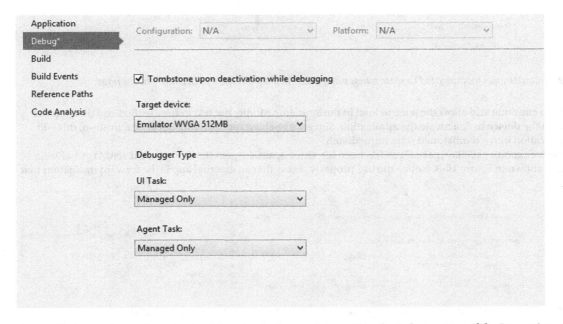

Figure 10-1. *Enable tombstoning for debugging in the emulator within the Debug section of the Properties page*

Next, place breakpoints on the opening brace for each of the following:

1. In the App code-behind file:

    a. App constructor

    b. Application_Launching event

    c. Application_Activated event

    d. Application_Deactivated event

2. In the DetailsPage code-behind file:

    a. DetailsPage constructor

    b. OnNavigatedTo event

    c. OnNavigatedFrom event

Launch the application in the Windows Phone emulator. With the breakpoints in place, take note of the application flow when the app is launched as a new instance, and then press F5 to continue with code execution as you hit each breakpoint. In this case, you would see that the App constructor and Application_Launching event were called.

When the application is loaded in the emulator, tap any item in the list to navigate to the item's details page. The next breakpoint is then hit within the OnNavigatedTo event. Take a moment to inspect the NavigationEventArgs object, as shown in Figure 10-2.

```
    protected override void OnNavigatedTo(NavigationEventArgs e)
                                                              e [System.Windows.Navigation.NavigationEventArgs]
        //If the page constuctor has been called, check State dict    base      {System.Windows.Navigation.NavigationEventArgs}
        //the page's ViewModel. If one exists, restore the page st     Content   {ManagingState.DetailsPage}
        //If not, then this is a new instance.                         IsNavigationInitiator  true
        if (pageReconstructed)                                         NavigationMode  New
        {                                                              Uri       {/DetailsPage.xaml?selectedItem=1}
            if (itemViewModel == null)                                 Static members
            {                                                          Non-Public members
                if (State.Count > 0)
                {
```

Figure 10-2. *DetailsPage OnNavigatedTo state when page is launched from the application's main page*

Press F5 to continue and allow the page to load in the emulator. Modify the text in the TextBox and then tap the Start button on the device to deactivate the application. Since we enabled tombstoning upon deactivation, this will force the application into a tombstoned state immediately.

Now, the breakpoint at OnNavigatedFrom has been hit. Once again, inspect the NavigationEventArgs before proceeding, as shown in Figure 10-3. Notice the Uri property shows that an external app is the forward navigation that is taking place.

```
    protected override void OnNavigatedFrom(System.Windows.Navigation.NavigationEventArgs e)
                                                                  e [System.Windows.Navigation.NavigationEventArgs]
        //If this is a back navigation, just skip over it since the page will be discarded an  base  {System.Windows.Navigation.NavigationEventArgs}
        if (e.NavigationMode != System.Windows.Navigation.NavigationMode.Back)                 Content  null
        {                                                                                      IsNavigationInitiator  false
            //Save the ItemViewModel in the page's State dictionary.                           NavigationMode  New
            State["ViewModel"] = itemViewModel;                                                Uri      {app://external/}
        }                                                                                      Static members
                                                                                               Non-Public members
100 %
```

Figure 10-3. *DetailsPage OnNavigatedFrom state when user navigates away from the application*

When the breakpoint stops at the Application_Deactivated event, take note of the DeactivatedEventArgs, namely, the Reason property, as shown in Figure 10-4. Press F5 to continue with the debugging.

```
    // Code to execute when the application is deactivated (sent to background)
    // This code will not execute when the application is closing
    private void Application_Deactivated(object sender, DeactivatedEventArgs e)
                                                              e [Microsoft.Phone.Shell.DeactivatedEventArgs]
    }                                                              base    {Microsoft.Phone.Shell.DeactivatedEventArgs}
                                                                   Reason  UserAction
    // Code to execute when the application is closing (eg, user hit Back)  Non-Public members
    // This code will not execute when the application is deactivated
```

Figure 10-4. *The DeactivedEventArgs shows that the reason for application deactivation is because of user action*

At this point, you should be at the Start screen of the emulator. Click the Back button to return to your application. When it loads, notice that the App constructor is executed again, but then the Application_Activated event is called this time. With the breakpoint still at the open brace of the Application_Activated event, inspect the ActivatedEventArgs. You will see that the IsApplicationInstancePreserved property is set to False, as shown in Figure 10-5. This demonstrates that the application was in fact tombstoned. Press F5 to continue running the application.

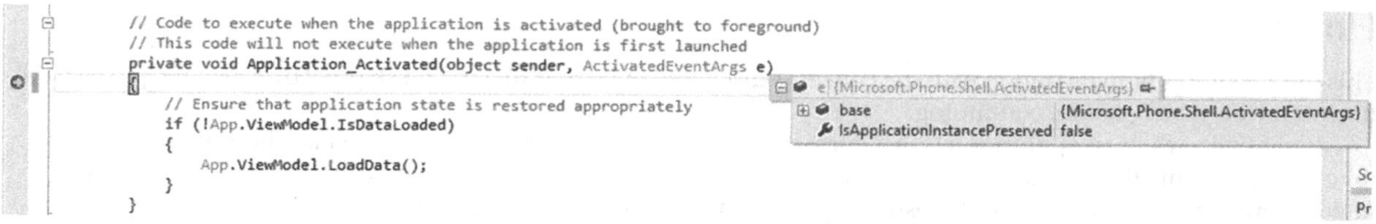

```
      // Code to execute when the application is activated (brought to foreground)
      // This code will not execute when the application is first launched
      private void Application_Activated(object sender, ActivatedEventArgs e)
      {                                                  ┌─ e {Microsoft.Phone.Shell.ActivatedEventArgs} ─┐
          // Ensure that application state is restored approp│ ⊞ ● base                    {Microsoft.Phone.Shell.ActivatedEventArgs}│
          if (!App.ViewModel.IsDataLoaded)                   │  ⚲ IsApplicationInstancePreserved  false │
          {                                                  └──────────────────────────────────────────┘
              App.ViewModel.LoadData();
          }
      }
```

Figure 10-5. *The ActivatedEventArgs shows that the application instance was not preserved, which is the case for tombstoned applications*

Press F5 to continue running the application. You will notice that the next breakpoint that is hit is the DetailsPage constructor (Figure 10-6). Again, press F5 to continue application execution. When the breakpoint stops at the OnNavigatedTo event again, take a moment to inspect the NavigationEventArgs. Did you notice the difference?

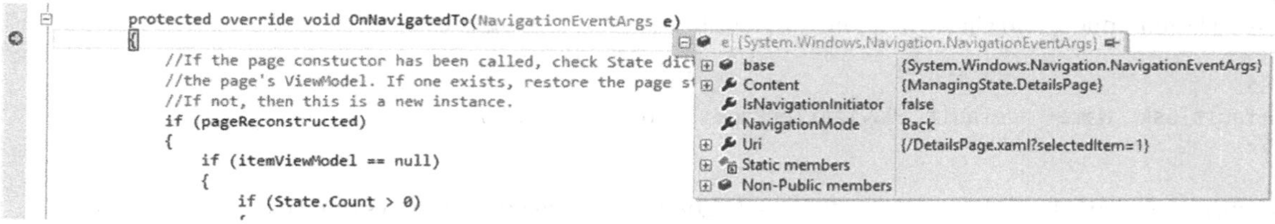

```
      protected override void OnNavigatedTo(NavigationEventArgs e)
      {                                                 ┌─ e {System.Windows.Navigation.NavigationEventArgs} ─┐
          //If the page constuctor has been called, check State dic│ ⊞ ● base          {System.Windows.Navigation.NavigationEventArgs}│
          //the page's ViewModel. If one exists, restore the page s│ ⊞ ⚲ Content       {ManagingState.DetailsPage}│
          //If not, then this is a new instance.                   │  ⚲ IsNavigationInitiator  false │
          if (pageReconstructed)                                   │  ⚲ NavigationMode  Back │
          {                                                        │ ⊞ ⚲ Uri          {/DetailsPage.xaml?selectedItem=1}│
              if (itemViewModel == null)                           │ ⊞ °⊟ Static members │
              {                                                    │ ⊞ ● Non-Public members │
                  if (State.Count > 0)                             └──────────────────────────────────┘
```

Figure 10-6. *NavigationEventArgs property values are different when resuming an application*

The NavigationMode is now displayed as Back instead of New, and the IsNavigationInitiator is now False. At this point, you can press F10 to step through code execution to see that the View model is in fact being loaded from the State dictionary of the PhoneApplicationPage. Once you have completed stepping through the OnNavigatedTo event, the page will be loaded in the emulator. Notice that the modified text is displayed exactly as it was when you left the application.

To fully understand the difference in behavior of an application in a dormant state vs. an application in a tombstoned state, it is a good idea to uncheck the "Tombstone upon deactivation while debugging" box in the Debug section of the project's Properties page and then run through the same tests discussed in this section, making sure to inspect the various event arguments along the way.

As we demonstrated in this recipe, the Windows Phone 8 operating system automatically preserves our application in memory when the application moves to a dormant state, which requires no extra work on our part when the application is resumed. When resuming from a tombstoned state, the implementation to preserve and restore page state is pretty straightforward. The code required is minimal within each page, as long as your application adheres to the MVVM design pattern and you ensure that your View models are serializable.

10-2. Enable Fast Application Resume Within Your App
Problem

You handled application state in your Windows Phone 8 app, but users are complaining that when they try to resume the app by tapping its pinned tile on the Start screen, it reloads the application as a new instance, and all is lost.

Solution

Modify the DefaultTask element within the application manifest to include the ApplicationPolicy attribute with a value of Resume.

How It Works

This topic requires familiarization with the concepts discussed in Recipe 10-1. If you skipped over that recipe, take the time to review it now, before continuing.

Essentially, when an application is in a dormant state and is resumed by pressing the Back button on the device to return to the app, then the application reactivates and is loaded where the user left off, with page state and data intact. However, if the user decides to resume the application by tapping the app's pinned tile on the Start screen, for example, then the suspended instance of the application is destroyed, and a new instance is launched, causing the user to start all over again. Ideally, in this circumstance, you would prefer to have the suspended instance reactivate, because you would like the user to pick up where they left off, if possible. To accomplish this, you will need to open your application manifest in an XML editor.

Enabling Fast Resume in the Application Manifest

Within Visual Studio, right-click the application manifest file, and click Open With... in the context menu. Select the XML (Text) Editor option, and click OK. In the XML file, locate the following entry:

```
<Tasks>
    <DefaultTask  Name="_default" NavigationPage="MainPage.xaml" />
</Tasks>
```

Modify the DefaultTask element by adding the ActivationPolicy attribute and setting its value to Resume, as follows:

```
<Tasks>
    <DefaultTask Name="_default" NavigationPage="MainPage.xaml" ActivationPolicy="Resume"/>
</Tasks>
```

■ **Note** Fast application resume kicks in only if there is an instance of your application sitting in a dormant state on the device. If not, it will simply load a new instance.

Once you have added the entry in the application manifest, you also need to make some minor changes within your code to manage the application's back stack.

Managing the Back Stack

Windows Phone apps will maintain the history of pages that the user has visited within the app in what is referred to as the *back stack*. This is because the user will be able to navigate back through the previously visited pages by clicking the Back button. In most cases, this is the ideal and expected behavior. However, there may be instances where this is not desired and will create an awkward experience for the user. Enabling fast resume within the application is one of those cases.

With fast application resume enabled, the system creates a new page instance for the page that is to be launched and places it on the top of the page's existing back stack. This could provide a confusing user experience if the target page to be launched is the application's default page. If the user was last visiting a page deeper in the application, then the user's back stack will consist of the following when fast resume is used to launch the application:

Page 1 (the default page) ➤ Page 2 ➤ Page 1 (new instance created during fast resume)

In this case, if the user presses the Back button from the new instance of Page 1, the user will be returned to Page 2. Tapping the Back button a subsequent time will return the user to the original instance of Page 1. Finally, another tap of the Back button will exit the application. This is not the behavior the user is expecting. The user simply expects that pressing the Back button from the default page will exit the application. To maintain a consistent user experience upon fast resume with the target being the default page, you will need to clear the application's back stack and load the new instance of the default page.

Another scenario that the user may encounter when using fast application resume is the expectation to return to the last-viewed page when resuming the application. By attempting to relaunch a running instance of the app by tapping a pinned tile in the Start screen or selecting the app in the installed apps list, this will in effect launch the application with the current back stack intact. In this case, you will simply cancel navigation to the target launch page so that the user is returned to the most recent page in the application back stack.

The Importance of the PhoneApplicationFrame

Similar to page navigation events that were discussed in Recipe 10-1, the PhoneApplicationFrame of the application also contains navigation events, as shown in Table 10-3. These events can be used to determine whether the current application is being launched as a new instance or whether the application is resumed from a current instance preserved in memory.

Table 10-3. *PhoneApplicationFrame Navigation Events*

Method	Triggered when..
Navigating (NavigatingCancelEventArgs)	A new navigation request is initiated.
Navigated (NavigationEventArgs)	The navigation target has been loaded.
NavigationFailed (NavigationFailedEventArgs)	An error has occurred while attempting to navigate to the target.
NavigationStopped (NavigationEventArgs)	The navigation has been forcibly terminated, or another instance of the navigation request has been requested, causing the current request to stop.

Note that these events are not overridden. Instead, you will need to register event handlers for them in the usual fashion. The good news here is that when you create a new Windows Phone app from one of the built-in templates, much of the necessary code to wire up the event handlers for the PhoneApplicationFrame is already generated for you, as shown in Listing 10-2.

Clearing the Back Stack

To determine whether the back stack should be cleared, you will need to check the value of the NavigationMode property within the NavigationEventArgs object that is passed in. If the NavigationMode is set to Reset, this indicates the application is being relaunched. To clear the back stack, simply call the RemoveBackEntry method on the PhoneApplicationFrame object to remove each entry individually, until the back stack is cleared. This part is already generated in the App code-behind file when a new Windows Phone App project is created, which is also shown in Listing 10-2.

Listing 10-2. Autogenerated Code in App Code-Behind File to Initialize RootFrame, Wire Up Navigation Events, and Clear Back Stack on Reset

```
/// <summary>
/// Provides easy access to the root frame of the Phone Application.
/// </summary>
/// <returns>The root frame of the Phone Application.</returns>
public static PhoneApplicationFrame RootFrame { get; private set; }
```

```
private void InitializePhoneApplication()
{
    if (phoneApplicationInitialized)
        return;

    // Create the frame but don't set it as RootVisual yet; this allows the splash
    // screen to remain active until the application is ready to render.
    RootFrame = new PhoneApplicationFrame();
    RootFrame.Navigated += CompleteInitializePhoneApplication;

    // Handle navigation failures
    RootFrame.NavigationFailed += RootFrame_NavigationFailed;

    // Handle reset requests for clearing the backstack
    RootFrame.Navigated += CheckForResetNavigation;

    // Ensure we don't initialize again
    phoneApplicationInitialized = true;
}

private void CheckForResetNavigation(object sender, NavigationEventArgs e)
{
    // If the app has received a 'reset' navigation, then we need to check
    // on the next navigation to see if the page stack should be reset
    if (e.NavigationMode == NavigationMode.Reset)
        RootFrame.Navigated += ClearBackStackAfterReset;
}

private void ClearBackStackAfterReset(object sender, NavigationEventArgs e)
{
    // Unregister the event so it doesn't get called again
    RootFrame.Navigated -= ClearBackStackAfterReset;

    // Only clear the stack for 'new' (forward) and 'refresh' navigations
    if (e.NavigationMode != NavigationMode.New && e.NavigationMode != NavigationMode.Refresh)
        return;

    // For UI consistency, clear the entire page stack
    while (RootFrame.RemoveBackEntry() != null)
    {
        ; // do nothing
    }
}
```

Cancelling Navigation

In the case where you will want to preserve the back stack and return to the last-viewed page in the back stack rather than loading a new page, you will simply need to cancel navigation. The reason is that the page at the top of the back stack will receive the navigation events in this order: OnNavigatedTo, OnNavigatingFrom, OnNavigatedFrom. At this point, you can choose to cancel any forward navigation.

To cancel forward navigation, you will simply need to wire up the Navigating event on the RootFrame in the App code-behind file and conduct a check to determine whether the NavigationMode value is set to Reset. If it is, then we will set a class-level boolean variable to indicate that the next new navigation request must be cancelled. In this way, on the next execution of this event, we will set the Cancel property on the NavigatingCancelEventArgs parameter to True if the NavigationMode value is New. This will cancel the navigation request to the new instance of the default page and leave the current page in view, as demonstrated in Listing 10-3. This works because the RootFrame_Navigating event is triggered anytime navigation request is triggered in the app. In the case of application resume, this event is triggered once for the reset navigation, and then it is triggered a second time when it attempts to create a new instance of the default page.

Listing 10-3. Canceling Page Navigation on Application Resume

```
private bool cancelNewNavigation = false;

private void InitializePhoneApplication()
{
    if (phoneApplicationInitialized)
        return;

    // Create the frame but don't set it as RootVisual yet; this allows the splash
    // screen to remain active until the application is ready to render.
    RootFrame = new PhoneApplicationFrame();

    //ADDED THIS LINE
    //We need to handle the navigating event to ensure we cancel new navigation on app resume
    RootFrame.Navigating += RootFrame_Navigating;

    RootFrame.Navigated += CompleteInitializePhoneApplication;

    // Handle navigation failures
    RootFrame.NavigationFailed += RootFrame_NavigationFailed;

    // Handle reset requests for clearing the backstack
    RootFrame.Navigated += CheckForResetNavigation;

    // Ensure we don't initialize again
    phoneApplicationInitialized = true;
}

//ADDED THIS EVENT HANDLER
private void RootFrame_Navigating(object sender, NavigatingCancelEventArgs e)
{
    if (e.NavigationMode == NavigationMode.Reset)
    {
        cancelNewNavigation = true;
    }

    if (e.NavigationMode == NavigationMode.New && cancelNewNavigation)
    {
        e.Cancel = true;

        //reset the flag so that we don't block any new navigation after the app loads
        cancelNewNavigation = false;
    }
}
```

The Code

Load the application located in the directory \Chapter 10\ManagingStateWithFastResume. Once the project is loaded, open the application manifest file with the XML editor. Notice that we enabled fast resume by modifying the DefaultTask element to set its ActivationPolicy property to Resume, as was discussed in the section "Enabling Fast Resume in the Application Manifest."

Next, drill down into the DetailsPage code-behind. Here you will notice that we added an override event, OnNavigatingFrom, to provide us with the opportunity in the app to cancel the current navigation request, as was discussed in the section "Cancelling Navigation."

Testing in the Emulator

Before we launch the application in the emulator, place breakpoints on the opening brace for each of the following:

1. In the App code-behind file:

   a. App constructor

   b. RootFrame_Navigating event

2. In the MainPage code-behind file:

   a. MainPage constructor

   b. OnNavigatedTo event

   c. OnNavigatedFrom event

3. In the DetailsPage code-behind file:

   a. DetailsPage constructor

   b. OnNavigatedTo event

   c. OnNavigatedFrom event

Launch the application in the Windows Phone emulator. With the breakpoints in place, take note of the application flow when the app is launched as a new instance, and then press F5 to continue with code execution as you hit each breakpoint. When the app is loaded in the emulator, tap an item in the list to load the details page for the selected item. Modify the text in the TextBox and then tap the Start button to return to the Start screen in the emulator and force the application into a dormant state.

Instead of resuming the application by pressing the Back button, go to the installed apps list in the emulator, and launch the application by selecting its entry in the apps list. When the application resumes, you will notice that the RootFrame_Navigating method is triggered twice during the resume, as we discussed earlier. The first time the event is triggered, the NavigationMode is set to Reset. At this point, the cancelNewNavigation flag is set to True. The next time this event is triggered, the NavigationMode is set to New, and its Uri is set to the MainPage. However, we forcibly cancel the navigation request so the page that is loaded upon resume is the page that was last viewed by the user before the app went into a dormant state.

As we demonstrated in this recipe, with a few simple modifications to an existing app, it is easy to enable the application to resume a previously loaded instance, even if the user launches the application through an app tile or through the installed apps list.

10-3. Launch a Built-in Windows Phone 8 App from Your App

Problem

You want to create a simple utility application that provides the user with easy access to the device's settings, such as Wi-Fi, Bluetooth, cellular, and location settings.

Solution

Use the LaunchUriAsync method in the Windows.System.Launcher class, with the proper URI scheme, to load the desired app.

How It Works

The Windows.System.Launcher class provides two methods that allow you to launch another Windows Phone 8 application through a file or URI association, as listed in Table 10-4.

Table 10-4. *Launcher Methods*

Method	Description
LaunchFileAsync(Windows.Storage.IStorageFile file)	Launches the Windows Phone 8 application that is associated with the file that is passed into the method
LaunchUriAsync(Uri uri)	Launches the Windows Phone 8 application that is associated with the URI scheme that is passed into the method

Windows Phone 8 has a number of reserved file types and URI associations that are associated with a number of built-in apps, such as image files, the web browser, Bing search, and an e-mail client, to name a few. When attempting to open a file or launch an app with a reserved file type or URI association, using the methods provided in the Launcher class, the built-in Windows Phone application will load accordingly. This is a simple way to extend your application's functionality using only a few lines of code.

When the URI specified is a web URL, for example www.stackoverflow.com, the device's web browser will automatically load and navigate to the web address provided.

In the same respect, when the URI begins with the mailto: URI scheme, the device's e-mail client will load and the To: field will be populated with the e-mail address that is indicated in the URI.

Since the Windows Phone 8 device settings are actually separate apps, they can be independently launched using any one of the ms-settings- series of URI schemes available, as listed in Table 10-5.

Table 10-5. *Device Settings URI Schemes*

URI Scheme	Launches...
ms-settings-airplanemode:	Airplane Mode Settings
ms-settings-bluetooth:	Bluetooth Settings
ms-settings-cellular:	Cellular Settings
ms-settings-location:	Location Settings
ms-settings-lock:	Lock Screen Settings
ms-settings-wifi:	Wi-Fi Settings

To launch the device's lock screen from your application when the user taps a button, you would simply include the following code in the button's Tap event:

```
bool success = await Windows.System.Launcher.LaunchUriAsync( "ms-settings-lock:");
```

The method will return true if the application associated with the URI scheme was launched. It will return false if a failure occurred attempting to launch the URI scheme specified. A failure will occur when the URI scheme specified is not recognized.

To view the complete list of reserved file types and URI associations for Windows Phone 8, review the MSDN article at http://msdn.microsoft.com/en-us/library/windowsphone/develop/jj207065(v=vs.105).aspx.

The Code

Now that we know how to launch a built-in Windows Phone 8 app, let's put it into practice! Launch Visual Studio 2012, create a new Windows Phone project, and name the project MyDeviceSettingsApp.

Within the MainPage markup, add four buttons to the page, labelled Wi-Fi, Bluetooth, Cellular, and Location. Set the Tag property of each button to its related URI scheme. For example, the Wi-Fi button's Tag property will be set as follows: Tag="ms-settings-wifi:". Refer to Listing 10-4 for the changes that were made to the ContentPanel Grid markup in the MainPage.

Listing 10-4. ContentPanel Grid in the MainPage XAML File

```
<Grid x:Name="ContentPanel" Grid.Row="1" Margin="12,0,12,0">
    <Grid.RowDefinitions>
        <RowDefinition />
        <RowDefinition />
    </Grid.RowDefinitions>
    <Grid.ColumnDefinitions>
        <ColumnDefinition />
        <ColumnDefinition />
    </Grid.ColumnDefinitions>
    <Button Content="Wi-Fi"
            Tag="ms-settings-wifi:"
            Tap="SettingsButton_Tap"
            Grid.Row="0" Grid.Column="0" />
    <Button Content="Bluetooth"
            Tag="ms-settings-bluetooth:"
            Tap="SettingsButton_Tap"
            Grid.Row="0" Grid.Column="1" />
    <Button Content="Cellular"
            Tag="ms-settings-cellular:"
            Tap="SettingsButton_Tap"
            Grid.Row="1" Grid.Column="0" />
    <Button Content="Location"
            Tag="ms-settings-location:"
            Tap="SettingsButton_Tap"
            Grid.Row="1" Grid.Column="1" />
</Grid>
```

Notice that we added a Tap event handler in each button's markup, which will be wired up to the same event, SettingsButton_Tap. In the MainPage code-behind, add the code for the SettingsButton_Tap event handler, as shown in Listing 10-5.

Listing 10-5. Tap Event Handler for the Buttons That Will Launch an App Using a URI Association

```
private async void SettingsButton_Tap(object sender, System.Windows.Input.GestureEventArgs e)
{
    bool success = false;
    Button buttonTapped = (Button)sender;
    if (buttonTapped.Tag != null)
    {
        Uri uri = new Uri(buttonTapped.Tag.ToString());
        success = await Windows.System.Launcher.LaunchUriAsync(uri);
    }

    if (success == false)
    {
        MessageBox.Show("Failed to launch the app");
    }
}
```

Since the LaunchUriAsync method is awaitable, we used the async/await keywords here. With that in place, our application is now ready to be tested!

Testing in the Emulator

Launch the app in the emulator. When the app loads, tap a button and notice that the desired device settings app is launched accordingly. Notice that when you tap the Back button, you are returned to your application. This provides a seamless experience to the user, making it feel as though the device settings are integrated within the application.

For example, in Figure 10-7, the main page of the app simply consists of four buttons, each of which launches a built-in Windows Phone 8 app. Tapping a button launches the desired app shown on the right, in this case the Wi-Fi app. A Back button press will close the built-in app and return the user to the main page of the launcher app. That's all there is to it!

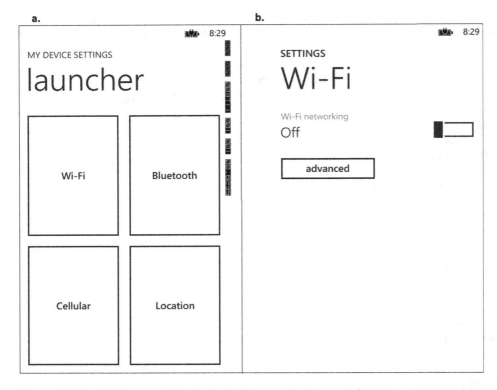

Figure 10-7. *a) Main page of My Device Settings application and b) Wi-Fi app launched from My Device Settings*

As we just demonstrated, with a few lines of code, you created a simple utility application that allows your user to launch a built-in Windows Phone 8 app. To view the completed project that ships with this book, open the Windows Phone project that is contained within the \Chapter 10\MyDeviceSettingsApp directory.

10-4. Launch Your Published Apps from Your Current App

Problem

You want to create a one-stop launcher app that will launch any one of your published apps, if they are installed on the current device.

Solution

Leverage APIs from the Windows.Phone.Management.Deployment namespace to determine whether any of your published apps are installed on the device and to launch them.

How It Works

The Windows.Phone.Management.Deployment namespace contains the InstallManager class, which can be used to search the device for any installed applications that were developed by the current app's publisher (that is, any apps installed under the same publisher ID as the current app). This is accomplished by executing a call to the FindPackagesForCurrentPublisher method. If any of the current publisher's applications are installed on the device, the method will return a collection of app packages. Each app package is represented as a Windows.Application.Model.Package.

The Windows.Application.Model.Package class provides information about an application, including the date the application was installed on the device, the install location, and a token to the image on the device that is the application's thumbnail image. Pertinent information is also available about the application through the Id property on the Package class. The Id property returns a PackageId object. Refer to Table 10-6 for the app information that can be retrieved from the PackageId class.

Table 10-6. *PackageId Properties*

Property	Type	Description
Author	String	The name of the author. This is the value that is set in the Author field in the Packaging section within the application's manifest file.
Name	String	The name of the application. This is the value that is set in the Display Name field in the Application UI section within the application's manifest file.
ProductId	String	Unique product identifier. This is the value that is set in the Product ID field in the Packaging section within the application's manifest file.
Publisher	String	The publisher name. This is the value that is set in the Publisher field in the Packaging section within the application's manifest file.
Version	PackageVersion	Contains the Major, Minor, and Revision information of the application. This is the value that is set in the Version field in the Packaging section in the application's manifest file.

Additionally, the Package class contains a Launch method, which is used to launch the specified application. The Launch method accepts a single string parameter, which serves as the navigation URI to deep-link into the application. If you want to simply load the default page on application launch, pass in an empty string.

The Code

Launch Visual Studio 2012, and create a new Windows Phone Databound App project. Set the name of the project to MyAppsLauncher.

Drill down into the ViewModels folder and delete the ItemsViewModel class. As well, delete the Sample Data folder and its contents. Next, open the MainViewModel class, and modify the class as follows:

1. Remove all the sample properties that were automatically generated in the class, except for IsDataLoaded.

2. Add the following using directives to the class:

   ```
   using Windows.ApplicationModel;
   using Windows.Phone.Management.Deployment;
   using System.Linq;
   ```

3. Add a new property called InstalledApps, which is of type ObservableCollection<Package>.

4. Modify the LoadData method to load the list of installed apps published by the current app's publisher, and exclude the current app from the list.

```
public void LoadData()
{
    //use Linq to exclude the current application from the selection list
    IEnumerable<Package> appPackages = InstallationManager.
FindPackagesForCurrentPublisher()
            .Where(p => p.Id.Name != "MyAppsLauncher")
            .AsEnumerable<Package>();
    this.InstalledApps = new ObservableCollection<Package>(appPackages);

    this.IsDataLoaded = true;
}
```

Listing 10-6 shows the final code result.

Listing 10-6. MainViewModel Class

```
using System;
using System.Collections.ObjectModel;
using System.ComponentModel;
using MyAppsLauncher.Resources;
using System.Collections.Generic;
using Windows.ApplicationModel;
using Windows.Phone.Management.Deployment;
using System.Linq;

namespace MyAppsLauncher.ViewModels
{
    public class MainViewModel : INotifyPropertyChanged
    {
        public MainViewModel()
        {
            this.Items = new ObservableCollection<Package>();
        }

        private ObservableCollection<Package> items;
        public ObservableCollection<Package> Items
        {
            get
            {
                return items;
            }
            set
            {
                items = value;
                NotifyPropertyChanged("Items");

            }
        }
```

```
    public bool IsDataLoaded
    {
        get;
        private set;
    }

    public void LoadData()
    {
        //use Linq to exclude the current application from the selection list
        IEnumerable<Package> appPackages = InstallationManager.FindPackagesForCurrentPublisher()
            .Where(p => p.Id.Name != "MyAppsLauncher")
            .AsEnumerable<Package>();
        this.Items = new ObservableCollection<Package>(appPackages);

        this.IsDataLoaded = true;
    }

    public event PropertyChangedEventHandler PropertyChanged;
    private void NotifyPropertyChanged(String propertyName)
    {
        PropertyChangedEventHandler handler = PropertyChanged;
        if (null != handler)
        {
            handler(this, new PropertyChangedEventArgs(propertyName));
        }
    }
  }
}
```

Next, open the MainPage's markup, and modify the MainLongListSelector so that its ItemSource is bound to the InstalledApps collection. Modify the DataTemplate so that its TextBlock controls display the application's name and install date, as shown in Listing 10-7.

Listing 10-7. MainLongListsSelector Modified Markup in the MainPage.xaml File

```
<phone:LongListSelector
    x:Name="MainLongListSelector"
    Margin="0,0,-12,0"
    ItemsSource="{Binding InstalledApps}"
    SelectionChanged="MainLongListSelector_SelectionChanged">
    <phone:LongListSelector.ItemTemplate>
        <DataTemplate>
            <StackPanel Margin="0,0,0,17">
                <TextBlock
                    Text="{Binding Id.Name}"
                    TextWrapping="Wrap"
                    Style="{StaticResource PhoneTextExtraLargeStyle}"/>
```

```
            <TextBlock
                Text="{Binding InstallDate, StringFormat='Installed On: {0:MM/dd/yyyy}'}"
                TextWrapping="Wrap" Margin="12,-6,12,0"
                Style="{StaticResource PhoneTextSubtleStyle}"/>
        </StackPanel>
    </DataTemplate>
</phone:LongListSelector.ItemTemplate>
</phone:LongListSelector>
```

Drill down into the MainPage code-behind, and modify the event as shown in Listing 10-8.

Listing 10-8. Modified SelectionChanged Event in the MainPage Code-Behind

```
private void MainLongListSelector_SelectionChanged(object sender, SelectionChangedEventArgs e)
{
    // If selected item is null (no selection) do nothing
    if (MainLongListSelector.SelectedItem == null)
        return;

    Package appPackage = (Package)MainLongListSelector.SelectedItem;
    appPackage.Launch("");

    // Reset selected item to null (no selection)
    MainLongListSelector.SelectedItem = null;
}
```

Testing in the Emulator

Launch the app in the emulator. Notice when the app loads, there are no applications listed. To get some applications to show up in that list when testing in the emulator, we need to create applications using the same publisher ID that the current app is set to. Essentially, we have to fake it in the emulator. When your app gets published to the Windows Phone Store, the publisher ID will be overwritten by the publisher ID in your Windows Phone Dev Center account, which will be different from the ID that the project generates in the application manifest file. Therefore, never hard-code any checks for the generated publisher ID in your application.

To set up our emulator such that we have multiple applications installed for the same publisher ID, copy the publisher ID from this project's application manifest file and paste it into the Publisher ID within another project's application manifest. For this example, let's use the project that we created in Recipe 10-3. If you skipped Recipe 10-3, you can use the completed project that shipped with this book, which is located in the \Chapter 10\MyDeviceSettingsApp directory. Once you have set the MyDeviceSettingsApp's publisher ID to the same publisher ID of our current project, launch the application in the emulator. Once the main page of the application loads, stop debugging, but leave the emulator instance running.

Next, relaunch MyAppsLauncher in the emulator. Now you will notice that My Device Settings appears in the list, as shown in Figure 10-8. Tap the app name in the list, and notice that the application launches as expected! Click the Back button in the emulator to return to the current app.

Figure 10-8. *The main page of the app loads the list of installed apps by the current publisher*

Similar to Recipe 10-3, we created a simple app that allows the user to launch your published apps that are installed on the device using minimal code. To view the completed project that ships with this book, open the Windows Phone project in the \Chapter 10\MyAppsLauncher directory.

CHAPTER 11

■ ■ ■

Data Storage

Without the ability to store and retrieve data, many Windows Phone applications would serve a limited purpose. Most real-world apps need to store and retrieve data to increase their usefulness and add appeal to the intended user. The Windows Phone 8 SDK provides APIs that allow developers to create files and folders, access the phone's external storage, store data in a local database, and encrypt sensitive data that is stored on the device.

In this chapter, we will go over the following recipes:

- 11-1. Read from and Write to a Local Text File
- 11-2. Read Data from an SD Card
- 11-3. Store and Retrieve Data from a Local Database
- 11-4. Encrypt Data Using the Data Protection API
- 11-5. Store Application Settings in Isolated Storage

11-1. Read from and Write Data to a Local File

Problem

You want to be able to read and write file data from within a Windows Phone app.

Solution

Utilize the StorageFolder and StorageFile classes to perform file and folder management.

How It Works

The StorageFolder and StorageFile classes, which belong to the Windows.Phone.Storage namespace, provide methods for file and folder management within a Windows Phone application. The StorageFile class represents a local file and contains information about the file and its content. It also contains methods that provide for further file manipulation.

The StorageFolder class can be used to read from and write to a local file. This class also contains methods to obtain the list of files or subfolders within a local folder, as well as to create, rename, or delete folders. Table 11-1 describes the methods available in the StorageFolder class related to file and folder management. This is not the complete list of methods that are exposed in this class. Rather, we have listed the methods that are relevant for the purpose of this topic.

Table 11-1. *Folder and File Management Methods in the StorageFolder Class*

Method	Description
CreateFileAsync (string desiredName, CreationCollisionOptions options)	Creates or updates a file in the local storage folder. CreationCollisionOptions is an enumerated value that specifies what to do if a file with the desired name already exists. Options include FailIfExists, GenerateUniqueName, OpenIfExists, and ReplaceExisting. Returns a StorageFile object if successful.
CreateFolderAsync (string desiredName, CreationCollisionOptions options)	Creates or updates a subfolder in the local storage folder, using the name that is passed into the method. The action that takes place depends on the CreationCollisionOptions value, in the same way that is described for CreateFileAsync. Returns a StorageFolder object if successful.
DeleteAsync (StorageDeleteOption option)	Deletes the local storage folder or filegroup. StorageDeleteOption indicates whether the folder/filegroup is a permanent delete. Options include Default and PermanentDelete. This parameter is optional. No value is returned when the method completes.
GetFileAsync(string name)	Gets a single file from the local storage folder that matches the name passed into the method. Returns a StorageFile object if a file exists in the local folder with the name indicated.
GetFilesAsync	Gets a collection of files from the local storage folder. Returns a read-only collection of StorageFile objects if the local folder contains files.
GetFolderAsync(string name)	Gets a single subfolder from the local storage folder that matches the name passed into the method. Returns a StorageFolder object if a subfolder exists in the local folder with the name indicated.
GetFoldersAsync	Gets a collection of subfolders from the local storage folder. Returns a read-only collection of StorageFolder objects if the local folder contains subfolders.
GetItemAsync	Gets a single file or folder that matches the name passed into the method. Returns an IStorageItem object if a file or subfolder exists with the name indicated. Use the IsOfTypeOf method to determine whether the item is a StorageFile or StorageFolder.
GetItemsAsync	Gets a collection of storage items from the local storage folder. Returns a read-only list of IStorageItem objects if the local folder contains files or subfolders. Use the IsOfTypeOf method on each item in the collection to determine whether the item is a StorageFile or StorageFolder.
IsOfType(StorageItemTypes type)	Determines whether the current object is a valid storage item object. StorageItemTypes is an enumerated value that determines the object type to match the current storage item against. Options include File, Folder, and None. Returns a boolean value indicating whether the current item matches the storage item type enumerated value.
OpenStreamForReadAsync (string relativePath)	Retrieves a Stream object that can be used to read data from a file. The desired file name must be specified in the relativePath parameter.

(continued)

Table 11-1. (*continued*)

Method	Description
OpenStreamForWriteAsync (string relativePath, CreationCollisionOptions option)	Retrieves a `Stream` object that can be used to write data to a file. The desired file name must be specified in the relativePath parameter. The action that takes place depends on the `CreationCollisionOptions` value, in the same way that is described for `CreateFileAsync`.
RenameAsync(string desiredName, NameCollisionOption option)	Renames the current local storage folder with the name passed into the method. Optionally, specify a `NameCollisionOption` to indicate the action to take if a folder with the desired name already exists. `NameCollisionOption` is an enumerated value with the following options: `FailIfExists`, `GenerateUniqueName`, and `ReplaceExisting`.

To be able to perform any type of file or folder management, we first need to obtain a handle to a local storage folder. This can be accomplished by accessing the `LocalFolder` property for the current application data store instance.

```
StorageFolder folder = ApplicationData.Current.LocalFolder;
```

With a handle to the root folder of the current app's data store, we can now perform various file and folder management tasks using the methods that are exposed on the `StorageFolder` object. Since we are interested in reading from a file, we will need to call the `OpenStreamForReadAsync` method to obtain a stream of the file data. We will then use the `StreamReader` class, from the `System.IO` namespace, to read the file contents, as shown in Listing 11-1.

Listing 11-1. Read Data from a Specified File Using OpenStreamReadForAsync in Conjunction with StreamReader

```
public async Task<bool> LoadFile(string fileName)
{
    this.FileName = fileName;

    //Get the local folder for the current application
    StorageFolder local = Windows.Storage.ApplicationData.Current.LocalFolder;

    if (local != null)
    {
        try
        {
            //Load the specified file
            Stream file = await local.OpenStreamForReadAsync(this.FileName);

            //Read the entire file into the FileText property
            using (StreamReader streamReader = new StreamReader(file))
            {
                FileText = streamReader.ReadToEnd();
            }

            file.Close();
        }
```

```
        catch (FileNotFoundException ex)
        {
            //file doesn't exist
            return false;
        }
    }

    return true;
}
```

Similarly, to write data to a text file, we can use the CreateFileAsync method on the StorageFolder object. However, a simple call to this method will not write the data to the file. It will simply create an empty file. We will need to call the OpenStreamForWriteAsync method to obtain a stream that we can use to write the contents to the file. Refer to Listing 11-2 for an example of how this is accomplished.

Listing 11-2. Create a File and Write Data to It Using CreateFileAsync and the Stream Class

```
public async Task<bool> SaveFile()
{
    try
    {
        //Convert the file text to a byte array
        byte[] fileBytes = Encoding.UTF8.GetBytes(FileText.ToCharArray());

        //Get the local folder for the current application
        StorageFolder local = ApplicationData.Current.LocalFolder;

        if (local != null)
        {
            //Create a new file, or update file if one already exists with the same name
            StorageFile file = await local.CreateFileAsync(this.FileName,
CreationCollisionOption.ReplaceExisting);

            //Write the file contents
            Stream fileStream = await file.OpenStreamForWriteAsync();
            fileStream.Write(fileBytes, 0, fileBytes.Length);
            fileStream.Flush();
            fileStream.Close();
        }
    }
    catch (Exception ex)
    {
        return false;
    }

    return true;
}
```

The asynchronous methods within the StorageFolder and StorageFile classes are "awaitable." As such, it is necessary to execute these calls using the async and await keywords. If you are not familiar with how to implement asynchronous calls using the async and await keywords in C#, refer to the article "Asynchronous Programming with Async and Await" on the MSDN site at http://msdn.microsoft.com/en-ca/library/vstudio/hh191443.aspx.

To view this recipe's code in its entirety, open the project named FileManagement within the directory \Chapter 11\FileManagement. The file management code can be found in the FileViewModel class. The app contains an additional bonus feature, which lists the files that currently exist in the app's local folder. This list was obtained by calling the GetFilesAsync method on the StorageFolder object, as shown in Listing 11-3.

Listing 11-3. Obtain the List of Files That Exist in the Local Storage Folder

```
public ObservableCollection<StorageFile> Files { get; set; }

public async Task GetFiles()
{
    StorageFolder folder = ApplicationData.Current.LocalFolder;
    IReadOnlyCollection<StorageFile> files = await folder.GetFilesAsync();
    Files = new ObservableCollection<StorageFile>(files);
}
```

Run the app in the emulator to see the file and folder management methods put into action. When the application first loads, you will notice a single button, called "create new file," as shown in Figure 11-1.

Figure 11-1. FileManagement app main screen

Tap the button to create a new text file that will be stored in a folder within the application's local data store. Enter the desired text, specify a file name, and tap the Save button in the application bar. Do this a few times, and notice that the files display within a list on the main screen, as illustrated in Figure 11-2.

Figure 11-2. *The files list is obtained through the GetFilesAsync method call*

Tap a file name in the list to view or update the file's text, as shown in Figure 11-3.

Figure 11-3. *View or update the content of an existing file*

When the save is initiated, the app will execute the same method call that was used when creating a new file. The current file will be overwritten through a call to the CreateFileAsync method, which will overwrite the file, since we passed in the ReplaceExistingFile creation collision option to the method. This will result in an overwrite of the existing file in the event that a file with the same name already exists.

As we demonstrated in this recipe, file access is simplified for developers thanks to the Windows.Phone.Storage API, which allows us to incorporate powerful file and folder management capabilities within a Windows Phone app using only a few lines of code.

11-2. Read Data from an SD Card
Problem
You want to develop an app that will allow the user to read data from an external media card.

Solution
Leverage the set of ExternalStorage classes, available within the Microsoft.Phone.Storage APIs.

How It Works

The Microsoft.Phone.Storage namespace includes the following set of classes that can be used to access and read from external storage:

- *ExternalStorage*: A static class that is used to obtain a handle to an external media card, if one is available on the device. It contains only a single method, GetExternalStorageDevicesAsync, which returns an ExternalStorageDevice object.

- *ExternalStorageDevice*: Exposes a property, RootFolder, which provides a handle to the root folder on the SD media card, which is an ExternalStorageFolder object.

- *ExternalStorageFolder*: Used to obtain the list of files or subfolders within a folder on the media card. Table 11-2 lists the methods available in the ExternalStorageFolder class related to file and folder retrieval.

- *ExternalStorageFile*: Used to open a stream to read the contents of the current file through the method OpenForReadAsync.

Table 11-2. *File and Folder Retrieval Methods in the ExternalStorageFolder Class*

Method	Description
GetFilesAsync	Gets a collection of files from the external storage folder. Returns a read-only collection of ExternalStorageFile objects if the folder contains files.
GetFolderAsync(string name)	Gets a single subfolder from the external storage folder that matches the name passed into the method. Returns an ExternalStorageFolder object if a subfolder exists with the name indicated.
GetFoldersAsync	Gets a collection of subfolders from the external storage folder. Returns a read-only collection of ExternalStorageFolder objects if the folder contains subfolders.

Note that there are not methods to create or update files on an external media card. The APIs currently allow only read-only access to files.

To read a file from an SD card, the app must incorporate the following modifications in the app manifest file:

1. Include the ID_CAP_REMOVABLE_STORAGE capability.

2. Register for a file association to declare what file types the app can handle. Listing 11-4 shows an example of how to do this. This must be done in Code View of the app manifest file.

Listing 11-4. File Associations Must Be Included in the App Manifest File

```
<Extensions>
  <FileTypeAssociation TaskID="_default" Name="txt" NavUriFragment="fileToken=%s">
    <SupportedFileTypes>
      <FileType ContentType="application/txt">.txt</FileType>
    </SupportedFileTypes>
  </FileTypeAssociation>
</Extensions>
```

Not all Windows Phone devices have microSD expansion slots. Therefore, before attempting to retrieve folder content or read from a file on an SD card, we will need to check to ensure external storage is available on the current device by calling the GetExternalStorageDeviceAsync method on the ExternalStorage class.

```
IEnumerable<ExternalStorageFile> files;
ExternalStorageDevice sdCard = (await
ExternalStorage.GetExternalStorageDevicesAsync()).FirstOrDefault();
if (sdCard != null)
{
    files = await sdCard.RootFolder.GetFilesAsync();
}
else
{
        //An SD card was not detected
}
```

If an external storage device was returned, we can obtain a handle to the root folder using the RootFolder property on the ExternalStorageDevice object. Next, we can retrieve a list of files in the root folder by calling the GetFilesAsync method on the RootFolder.

To read data from an existing file, we will need to call the OpenForReadAsync method on the ExternalStorageFile class to obtain a stream of the file data. We will then make use of the System.IO.StreamReader class to read the file contents, as shown in Listing 11-5.

Listing 11-5. MainViewModel

```
ExternalStorageDevice sdCard = (await ExternalStorage.GetExternalStorageDevicesAsync()).
FirstOrDefault();
if (sdCard != null)
{
    IEnumerable<ExternalStorageFile> files = await sdCard.RootFolder.GetFilesAsync();
    ExternalStorageFile file = files.Where(f=> f.Name.EndsWith(".txt")).FirstOrDefault();
    System.IO.Stream fileStream = await SelectedFile.OpenForReadAsync();

    //Read the entire file into the FileText property
    using (StreamReader streamReader = new StreamReader(fileStream))
    {
        FileText = streamReader.ReadToEnd();
    }

    fileStream.Close();
}
```

▓ **Note** Testing external storage file access within the Windows Phone emulator is not available. A Windows Phone device with a microSD expansion slot is required to test code that accesses media on an external storage card.

With only a few lines of code and a couple of configuration settings in the app manifest, we have easily incorporated reading files from external storage within a Windows Phone app.

To view the code related to this recipe, open the project named ExternalFileManagement within the directory \Chapter 11\ExternalFileManagement. The file management code can be found in the MainViewModel class. Similar to Recipe 11-1, the main page of the application will list the files that currently exist in the root folder of the device's SD card. When a file on the main screen is tapped, the LoadSelectedFile method on the view model will execute, which will load the file contents. Note that although you can run this app in the emulator, you will simply receive the error message that an SD card could not be found. The Windows Phone emulator does not provide support for testing external storage access. To fully test the functionality of this application, you will need to test it on a Windows Phone device that has a microSD expansion card and an SD card with relevant files to test against.

11-3. Store and Retrieve Data from a Local Database

Problem

You are in the midst of developing an app that allows the user to enter a list of books they have read. In addition to that, the user can add one or more personal notes/remarks on each book. You are looking for an efficient way to store relational data for this purpose.

Solution

Use LINQ to SQL to define the database schema and to access data in a local database.

How It Works

There are four namespaces that contain classes that provide a mechanism to define a database schema, create/delete a local database, and perform standard CRUD operations (in other words, create, retrieve, update, and delete) against the data in the database from a Windows Phone application: System.Data.Linq, System.Data.Linq.Mapping, Microsoft.Phone.Data.Linq, and Microsoft.Phone.Data.Linq.Mapping.

It is important to become familiar with data contexts, entities, and the LINQ to SQL runtime when working with a local database for Windows Phone.

- *Data context*: An object that is the main entry point for accessing a database using LINQ to SQL. It defines the connection string to the local data file. In this class, you will expose public properties of type Table<T> to provide a handle to each table in the database that you want to access in your application. The following are noteworthy methods that are available on a data context object:

    - *CreateDatabase*: Creates a database in the application's isolated storage

    - *DatabaseExists*: Conducts a check to determine whether the database already exists in isolated storage

    - *SubmitChanges*: Commits any changes that occurred on the database-related objects

- *Entity*: An object that represents a table in the database. To designate a class as an entity, the Table attribute must be included before the class declaration. Within the entity, one or more properties may be defined to represent columns in the table. In this case, each property that is to be included in the table must include the Column attribute before the property declaration. Additionally, it is possible to define foreign key to primary key relationships within an entity using the Association attribute on an EntitySet or EntityRef property in the parent and child entities, respectively. The following are data insertion and deletion methods that are available on Table objects:

- *InsertOnSubmit and InsertAllOnSubmit*: These add the entity object or collection of objects to the data context in a pending insert state.

- *DeleteOnSubmit and DeleteAllOnSubmit*: These add the entity object or collection of objects to the data context in a pending insert state.

To update data in an existing entity object, simply modify the data for the entity object that is exposed through the data context. The change will be picked up by the current data context and will be committed to the database when SubmitChanges is called on the data context.

- *LINQ to SQL runtime*: Provides object-relational mapping capabilities that map the objects defined in code to their respective representations in the database (in other words, table, column, index, and associations). It also provides the mechanism to perform basic database operations to select, insert, update, or delete data within the application.

Table 11-3 describes the database mapping attributes that are most often used when defining a database schema. These attributes are in the System.Data.Linq.Mapping namespace.

Table 11-3. *Mapping Attributes*

Name	Attribute Properties	Description
TableAttribute	Name: String value defining the name of the table in the database.	Associates the class with a table in the database.
ColumnAttribute	IsPrimaryKey: Boolean value indicating whether the column is a primary key. IsDbGenerated: Boolean value indicating whether the column values are automatically generated by the database on insert. DbType: String value that defines the data type. CanBeNull: Boolean value indicating whether the column allows null values. AutoSync: Enumerated value indicating when to retrieve the value when an insert or update is performed. Options are Always, Never, OnInsert, and OnUpdate.	Associates the class member with a column in its table.
IndexAttribute	Columns: String value that lists the columns that make up the index. IsUnique: Boolean value indicating whether the index is unique. Name: String value defining the name of the index.	Table-level attribute that designates indexes on the table and can include one or more columns.
AssociationAttribute	Name: String value defining the name of the association. Storage: String value that indicates the name of the private property that will hold the value of the column. ThisKey: String value that indicates the key in the current table that will be used in the relationship association OtherKey: String value that indicates the key in the associated table that will be used in the relationship association	Defines an association between two tables, such as a foreign key to primary key association. An EntitySet property is designated as an association in both the parent and child table definitions.

Listing 11-6 shows an example of the usage of the mapping attributes, which is part of the recipe's sample application, MyBookList. The Book entity is used to define a table that will store basic details of a book, such as author and title. It also defines a one-to-many relationship with a child table called BookNotes, which allows one or more notes to be associated to a single book.

Listing 11-6. Book Entity with an Association to a BookNotes Table

```
[Table(Name = "Book")]
public class Book : INotifyPropertyChanged, INotifyPropertyChanging
{
        #region Constructor
        public Book()
        {
            _notes = new EntitySet<BookNote>(
                    note =>
                    {
                        NotifyPropertyChanging("BookNotes");
                        note.Book = this;
                    },
                    note =>
                    {
                        NotifyPropertyChanging("BookNotes");
                        note.Book = null;
                    }
                );
        }
        #endregion

        #region Columns
        private int _bookId;
        [Column(IsPrimaryKey = true,IsDbGenerated = true, DbType = "INT NOT NULL Identity",
CanBeNull = false, AutoSync = AutoSync.OnInsert)]
        public int BookId
        {
            get { return _bookId; }
            set
            {
                if (_bookId != value)
                {
                    NotifyPropertyChanging("BookId");
                    _bookId = value;
                    NotifyPropertyChanged("BookId");
                }
            }
        }

        private string _title;
        [Column(DbType = "nvarchar(255)", CanBeNull = false)]
        public string Title
        {
            ...
        }
```

```
        private string _author;
        [Column(DbType = "nvarchar(255)", CanBeNull = false)]
        public string Author
        {
            ...
        }
        #endregion
        #region Book Notes Association (Child Table)
        private EntitySet<BookNote> _notes;
        [Association(Name = "FK_Book_Notes", Storage = "_notes", ThisKey = "BookId",
OtherKey = "BookId")]
        public EntitySet<BookNote> Notes
        {
            get
            {
                return _notes;
            }
            set
            {
                _notes.Assign(value);
            }
        }

        #endregion

        #region INotifyPropertyChanged, INotifyPropertyChanging Members
        ...
        #endregion
    }
}
```

The BookNote entity is used to define a table that will store notes for a book. Just as the Book entity defines the child association, the BookNote entity must define its parent association, as shown in Listing 11-7.

Listing 11-7. Parent Table Association to the Book Table Within the BookNote Entity

```
#region Parent Table Association
private EntityRef<Book> _book;
[Association(Name = "FK_Book_Notes", Storage = "_book", ThisKey = "BookId",
OtherKey = "BookId", IsForeignKey = true)]
public Book Book
{
    get
    {
        return _book.Entity;
    }
    set
    {
        NotifyPropertyChanging("Book");
        _book.Entity = value;
```

```
        if (value != null)
        {
            _bookId = value.BookId;
        }

        NotifyPropertyChanged("Book");

    }
}
#endregion
```

Once the entities are defined, we can proceed to create the DataContext that will provide the entry point to accessing data within the local database. The data context will expose properties that will contain table data and will initialize each table property by calling the GetTable<TEntity> method on the DataContext for each entity, as depicted in Listing 11-8.

Listing 11-8. Book DataContext

```
public class BookDataContext : DataContext
{
    public const string ConnectionString = "isostore:/Books.sdf";

    public BookDataContext(string connectionString)
        : base(connectionString)
    {
        this.Books = this.GetTable<Book>();
        this.BookNotes = this.GetTable<BookNote>();
    }

    public Table<Book> Books { get; set; }
    public Table<BookNote> BookNotes { get; set; }
}
```

With the entities and data context in place, we can continue to develop the remainder of the application, ensuring that the data context is initialized. As well, we will need to handle the initial database creation and retrieve and store data through the application. In the MyBookList project that is included with this chapter, the MainViewModel handles the data context instance initialization, as well as the initial database creation. As shown in Listing 11-9, a check is conducted to determine whether a database exists with the current database file name, which is defined through the connection string. If the target database does not exist in the application's isolated storage, the CreateDatabase method is called on the DataContext, which will then create the database based on the defined tables, columns, indexes, and primary key/foreign key relationship associations. SubmitChanges is then called to commit the changes to the database.

Listing 11-9. MainViewModel Initializes the Data Context and Creates a Local Database If One Does Not Exist

```
private BookDataContext CurrentDataContext;
public ObservableCollection<Book> Books { get; private set; }
public bool IsDataLoaded { get; private set; }

public MainViewModel()
{
    this.Books = new ObservableCollection<Book>();
    CurrentDataContext = new BookDataContext(BookDataContext.ConnectionString);
```

```
    if (!CurrentDataContext.DatabaseExists())
    {
        CurrentDataContext.CreateDatabase();
        CurrentDataContext.SubmitChanges();
    }
}
```

To view the sample application code that demonstrates the concepts in this recipe, open the project in the \Chapter 11\MyBookList directory. Let's perform a test run on this application to see it in action. Hit F5 to launch the app in the Windows Phone emulator.

The main screen will not contain any data to start since the database has been newly created on the initial run of the application. Tap the add button in the application bar to add a new book to the database in the details page, as illustrated in Figure 11-4. Enter a title and author and then hit the save button.

Figure 11-4. *Book details are stored in the database*

Once the save is successful, the add button on this page will become enabled to allow one or more notes to be added for a book. Go ahead and add a few notes for the book and then return to the main screen. Notice that the book is now displayed in the list, as shown in Figure 11-5. It also displays the book ID, which was generated by the database. If you recall, the BookId member in the Book entity was explicitly defined to act in this way.

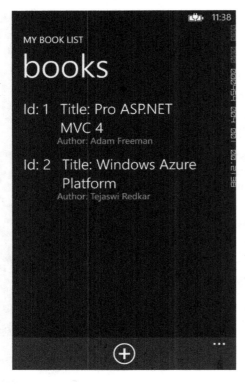

Figure 11-5. *List of books retrieved from the database using LINQ to SQL*

And just like that, we have developed an app that provides for relational data storage within a Windows Phone app! Keep in mind that although a Windows Phone local database seems to mirror the behavior of a standard client-server database, it differs from a typical database in the following ways:

- A Windows Phone local database does not run as a background service. Instead, it runs within the Windows Phone app's process.

- A Windows Phone local database resides in the local folder of the Windows Phone app; therefore, it can be accessed only by its corresponding app. It cannot be accessed by any other app on the device.

- LINQ to SQL must be used for data access. Transact-SQL is not directly supported.

11-4. Encrypt Data Using the Data Protection API

Problem

You are developing an app that will store sensitive data within a file that will be saved to isolated storage. You want to ensure the file data is encrypted as an additional security measure.

Solution

Leverage the Data Protection API to encrypt/decrypt sensitive file data.

How It Works

The Windows Phone Data Protection API provides a mechanism to encrypt and decrypt sensitive data using a unique decryption key that is created when the app is run for the first time. Cryptographic key generation is built into the API and removes the need for a developer to explicitly define a key for this purpose.

The Data Protection API includes the `ProtectedData` class (part of the `System.Security.Cryptography` namespace), which contains two methods.

- *Protect*: Encrypts the data that is passed into the method. The data must be passed in as a byte array. The encrypted data is returned as a byte array.

- *Unprotect*: Decrypts the data that is passed into the method. The data must be passed in as a byte array. The decrypted data is returned as a byte array.

For this recipe, we have created a sample application that allows the user to enter emergency contact information and save it to a file in isolated storage. Prior to writing the data to the file, the application leverages the Data Protection API to encrypt the information. To view the code for this application, open the project MyEmergencyInfo in the directory \Chapter 11\MyEmergencyInfo. Listings 11-10 and 11-11 demonstrate the use of the `Protect` method and `Unprotect` method, respectively.

Listing 11-10. Use the Protect Method on the ProtectedData Class to Encrypt Sensitive Data Prior to Saving

```
//EmergencyInfoData is a string property in the ViewModel
byte[] emergencyInfoByteArray = Encoding.UTF8.GetBytes(EmergencyInfoData.ToString());
byte[] encryptedEmergencyInfoByteArray = ProtectedData.Protect(emergencyInfoByteArray, null);

// Create a file in the application's isolated storage.
IsolatedStorageFile file = IsolatedStorageFile.GetUserStoreForApplication();
IsolatedStorageFileStream writestream = new IsolatedStorageFileStream(filePath, FileMode.Create,
FileAccess.Write, file);

Stream writer = new StreamWriter(writestream).BaseStream;
writer.Write(encryptedEmergencyInfoByteArray, 0, encryptedEmergencyInfoByteArray.Length);
writer.Close();
writestream.Close();
```

Listing 11-11. Use the Unprotect Method to Decrypt Data

```
IsolatedStorageFile file = IsolatedStorageFile.GetUserStoreForApplication();
IsolatedStorageFileStream readstream = new IsolatedStorageFileStream(filePath, FileMode.Open,
FileAccess.Read, file);

if (readstream != null)
{
    Stream reader = new StreamReader(readstream).BaseStream;
    byte[] encryptedEmergencyInfoByteArray = new byte[reader.Length];

    reader.Read(encryptedEmergencyInfoByteArray, 0, encryptedEmergencyInfoByteArray.Length);
    reader.Close();
    readstream.Close();
```

```
    byte[] emergencyInfoByteArray = ProtectedData.Unprotect(encryptedEmergencyInfoByteArray, null);

    string emergencyInfoData = Encoding.UTF8.GetString(emergencyInfoByteArray, 0,
emergencyInfoByteArray.Length);
    EmergencyInfoData = new EmergencyInfo(emergencyInfoData);
}
```

The decryption key that is generated for an application is used behind the scenes each time a call is made to either of these two methods. Note that the decryption key will remain the same even when updates to the app are installed.

■ **Note** The Data Protection API for encryption/decryption is best used on small amounts of data. To encrypt data in a local database, simply set the Password parameter within the connection string of the database, rather than using this approach.

Open the sample application, MyEmergencyInfo, within Visual Studio. Launch the app in the Windows Phone emulator. The application allows the user to enter emergency contact details as well as allergy and medication information. Enter values for each field and then hit the save button. A confirmation message will appear if the data was encrypted and saved to a local file without error, as shown in Figure 11-6.

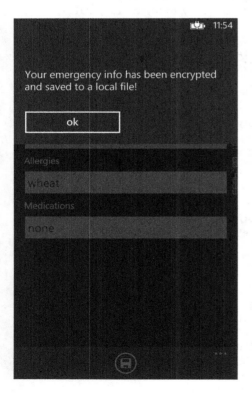

Figure 11-6. *Confirmation message displayed after data is encrypted and saved*

As demonstrated in this recipe, the Data Protection API provides a simple and straightforward approach to data encryption within a Windows Phone application.

11-5. Store Application Settings

Problem

You want to include application-specific settings in your Windows Phone application that the users can change from within the app.

Solution

Store the values of each setting within isolated storage and provide a UI that will allow the user to change these settings from within the application.

How It Works

The `IsolatedStorageSettings` class, within the `System.IO.IsolatedStorage` namespace, can be used to store key-value pairs in the application's isolated storage. The `ApplicationSettings` property retrieves the current instance of the `IsolatedStorageSettings` dictionary for the application, or it creates a new one if one does not yet exist.

Table 11-4 lists the methods available on the `IsolatedStorageSettings` object, which simplifies management of the key-value pairs within its settings collection.

Table 11-4. IsolatedStorageSettings Methods

Method	Description	Example
Add(key, value)	Adds an entry to the `IsolatedStorageSettings` collection.	IsolatedStorageSettings.ApplicationSettings.Add("MyKey", 1)
Clear()	Removes all items from the `IsolatedStorageSettings` collection.	IsolatedStorageSettings.ApplicationSettings.Clear()
Contains(key)	Conducts a check to determine whether an element exists in the collection for the specified key. Returns true if an element is found.	bool itemExists = IsolatedStorageSettings.ApplicationSettings.Contains("MyKey");
Remove(key)	Removes the item associated to the specified key from the dictionary.	IsolatedStorageSettings.ApplicationSettings.Remove("MyKey");
Save()	Saves the changes made within the collection to isolated storage.	IsolatedStorageSettings.ApplicationSettings.Save()

To allow for application-level settings management through the app, we will need to create a page that will serve as the Settings page. When the user navigates to the page, any existing settings should be loaded from the `IsolatedStorage.ApplicationSettings` collection. If no settings exist, then it would be ideal to display default values for each setting. A class should be created to handle defining the application-level settings that will be available for configuration, along with defining default values for each setting. In this way, we can simply bind the settings to the controls on the Settings page.

Furthermore, you can choose to update the settings automatically when a property changes, or you can expose a method that will save changes, only if the user chooses to do so (i.e., through the action of tapping a Save button).

The sample application provided with this recipe demonstrates the first approach, which forces a save to occur each time a change occurs on a setting. To view the code related to this recipe, open the project named MyAppSettings within the directory \Chapter 11\MyAppSettings.

Be sure to handle those pages in your application that depend on application-level settings. The setting values that are saved in isolated storage need to be retrieved and applied to the areas of the application where it makes sense. For example, if your application allows the user to change the font size within the app, then you will need to apply the new font size value across all fields that display text within your app.

Open the sample application MyAppSettings in Visual Studio and launch the application in the emulator. The main page displays the default setting values on the first run, since there are no saved values for these settings. Tap the settings button in the application bar to navigate to the Settings page. As shown in Figure 11-7, the Settings page simply contains a username and a check box to turn sounds on/off. We don't really have a sound file included in this app, but we will display the value of this setting on the main page.

Figure 11-7. *Settings page*

Notice that we have not included a save button on the Settings page. The reason is that we've chosen to automatically save any changes that occur on either of the setting fields, which will automatically be triggered through the magic of data binding. Refer to Listing 11-12 for an example of how this was implemented in the sample application.

Listing 11-12. Settings Page Markup

```
<StackPanel x:Name="ContentPanel" Grid.Row="1" Margin="12,0,12,0">
    <TextBlock
        Margin="10 0"
        Text="user name"
        Style="{StaticResource PhoneTextLargeStyle}" />
    <TextBox Text="{Binding UserName, Mode=TwoWay}" />
    <CheckBox
        Content="Play Sounds"
        IsChecked="{Binding PlaySounds, Mode=TwoWay}" />
</StackPanel>
```

In this way, the Settings page code-behind is pretty barren. The only code that needed to be included was to set the data context of the page to the main view model, as shown in Listing 11-13.

Listing 11-13. MainViewModel Used to Expose Settings Properties to Enable Data Binding

```
public class MainViewModel : INotifyPropertyChanged
{

    private MyAppSettings.Models.Settings _settings = new MyAppSettings.Models.Settings();

    public string UserName
    {
        get
        {
            return _settings.UserNameSetting;
        }
        set
        {
            _settings.UserNameSetting = value;
            NotifyPropertyChanged("UserName");
        }
    }

    public bool PlaySounds
    {
        get
        {
            return _settings.PlaySoundSetting;
        }
        set
        {
            _settings.PlaySoundSetting = value;
            NotifyPropertyChanged("PlaySounds");
        }
    }
```

```
    public event PropertyChangedEventHandler PropertyChanged;
    private void NotifyPropertyChanged(String propertyName)
    {
        PropertyChangedEventHandler handler = PropertyChanged;
        if (null != handler)
        {
            handler(this, new PropertyChangedEventArgs(propertyName));
        }
    }
}
```

Enter any value in the username field, and return to the main page. Notice that the "Hello" message has changed to include the new username that was entered in the Settings page, as shown in Figure 11-8. Exit the application in the emulator without shutting down the emulator. Now, relaunch the app within the emulator. The last values that were saved for the username and play sounds settings are reflected in the main page.

Figure 11-8. The main page displays the current value of each setting

CHAPTER 12

■ ■ ■

Windows Azure Mobile Services

Windows Azure Mobile Services (WAMS) at its core is a ready-made combination of a database and a web site through which CRUD operations can be performed on the data. Hosting these services in the Windows Azure infrastructure provides stability and scalability as well as ready access to this data from virtually any client platform. WAMS also provides various other supporting services including integration with various federated identity providers (Microsoft Account, Facebook, Google, and Twitter) as well as easy integration with the Windows, Apple, and Google push notification services. Direct integration with these types of services can be challenging at best, so having all of the heavy lifting done for you in advance is a huge advantage.

The first thing you will need to get started integrating your own applications with WAMS is an Azure account. Microsoft offers a free trial[1] of the service, and MSDN subscription holders have various amounts of free Azure services included with their subscriptions.[2] For all the details including pricing information, you should check out the Azure site at www.windowsazure.com.

■ **Note**   Recipes 12-1 and 12-2 introduce you to the WAMS portal and how to create a mobile service. If you are unfamiliar with navigating the portal, you should work through those recipes first. Also, if you haven't registered your application with at least one authentication provider and set the proper permissions on your tables, the scripts that use the user object are going to fail. Recipe 12-4 covers authentication.

Let's do some science! Here are the recipes we'll be reviewing:

- 12-1. Create a Mobile Service
- 12-2. Work with Data
- 12-3. Work with Server-Side Scripts: Validation and Access Control
- 12-4. Work with Authentication Providers
- 12-5. Work with Push Notifications

---

[1]www.windowsazure.com/en-us/pricing/trial/
[2]www.windowsazure.com/en-us/pricing/member-offers/msdn-benefits/

12-1. Create a Mobile Service

Problem

You want to take advantage of the functionality provided by WAMS.

Solution

Create a mobile service using the Windows Azure Management Portal.

How It Works

Open your browser and navigate to www.windowsazure.com. Click the Portal link at the top right of the page to be taken to the Windows Azure Management Portal. There is also a link on the home page to sign up for a free trial if you don't already have an account. Enter the Microsoft account ID and password to log into the management portal for the account associated with that ID. Figure 12-1 shows the Azure home page.

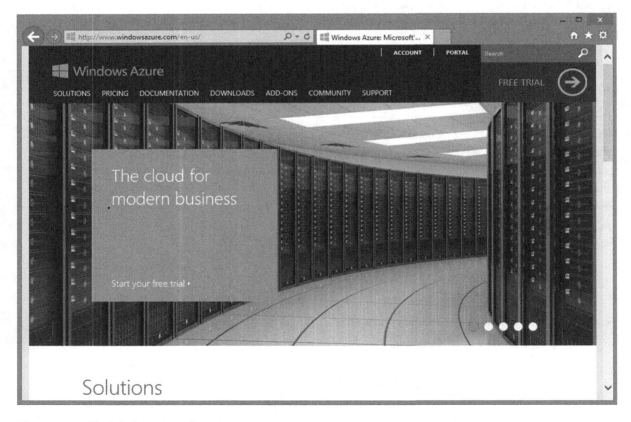

Figure 12-1. *The Windows Azure home page*

You will find all of the various Azure services available to you listed down the left side of the portal page. The one we are concerned with here is the Mobile Services tab. You will be presented with the default page advising you that you have no mobiles services (assuming this is your first time working with WAMS). Click the CREATE A NEW MOBILE SERVICE link to begin the process. See Figure 12-2.

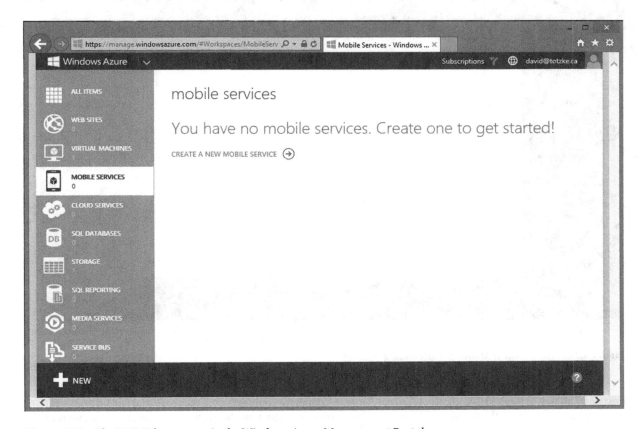

Figure 12-2. *The WAMS home page in the Windows Azure Management Portal*

The Create a Mobile Service dialog requires you to supply a URL for your service, choose a database, link this service to an Azure subscription (you can have more than one associated with your account) for billing purposes, and choose a deployment region. The domain `.azure-mobile.net` will be appended to the URL you supply. The name you choose must be unique across all of WAMS, so you may need to get a little creative here. The region you choose for deployment should be the one that is physically closest to the bulk of people who will be using your service. You can choose from East US, West US, Northern Europe, and East Asia. Figure 12-3 shows the dialog filled in for this recipe.

Figure 12-3. *The Create a Mobile Service dialog*

Click the right-pointing arrow in the bottom right of the dialog to be taken to the next step in the process. This next page, shown in Figure 12-4, allows you to configure the database settings for the database that will be used with this service. The name of the database, like the URL in the previous step, must be unique. The dialog will automatically validate the database name as you type and will display a green circle with a check mark in it if all is well. You database will be hosted on an instance of SQL Server that is dedicated to your account. You can choose an existing server from your account in the drop-down list if you have already set one up, or you can choose to create a new one. You will need to enter a login name and password for the new database server. There is the ability to specify some advanced database settings, but the defaults are fine for our needs. When you have entered everything, click the check at the bottom right of the dialog to complete the new mobile service creation process. Figure 12-5 shows the results.

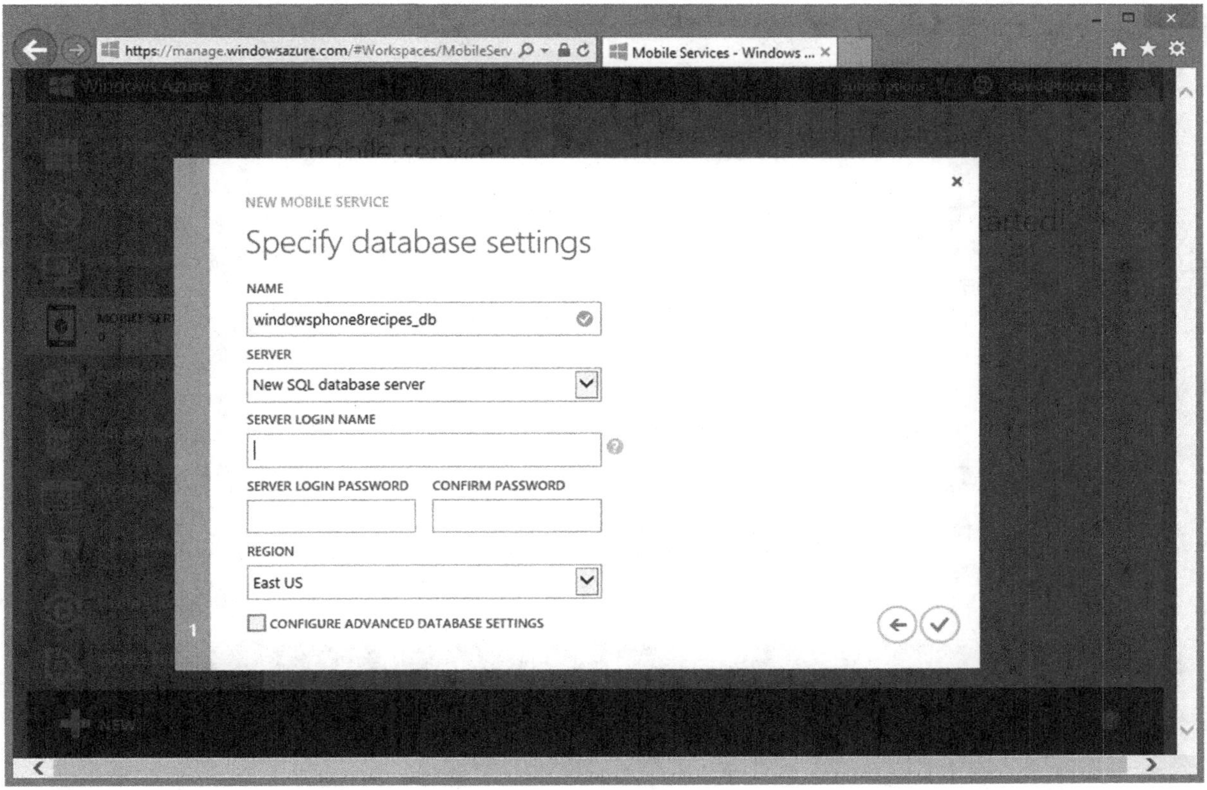

Figure 12-4. Database and server settings

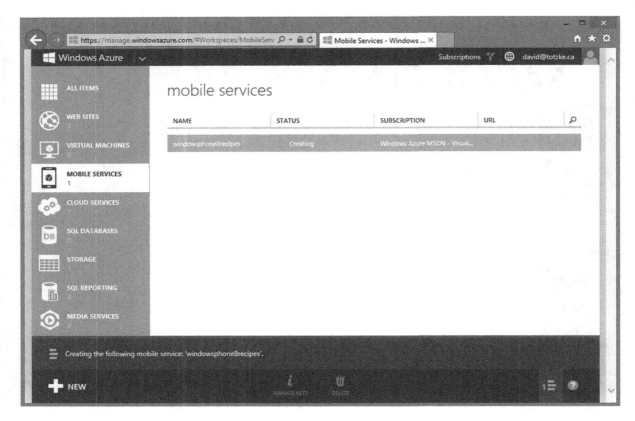

Figure 12-5. You are returned to this screen after completing the wizard. Note how it says "Creating" in the STATUS column

---

■ **Note**   Generally speaking, there is a cost associated with almost everything you have running in Azure. The costs are reasonable, there is a certain amount that is free, and by default there is a spending limit in place to avoid massive charges. Still, you should make yourself aware of these costs and how they may be incurred.

It won't take long, usually just a few minutes, until your service is ready; you will see the STATUS column says "Ready." The URL column, as shown in Figure 12-6, now contains a URL to your service. Click the link to be taken to the status page for your new service. Clicking the name of your new service will take you to the default landing page shown in Figure 12-7.

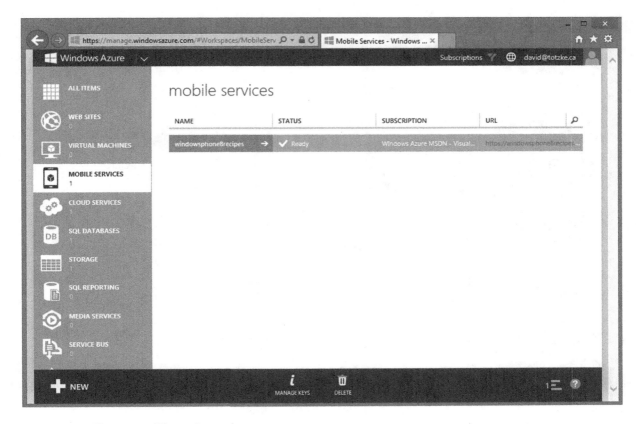

Figure 12-6. *The new mobile service ready to go*

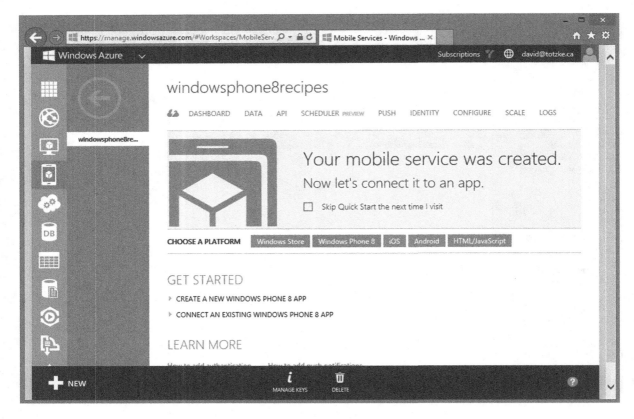

Figure 12-7. The default landing page for a new mobile service

From this landing page you can download a sample application that is preconfigured to work with your new service. Samples are available for Windows Store and Windows Phone 8 as well as iOS, Android, and HTML/JavaScript.

12-2. Work with Data

Problem

You keep "losing" the list of tasks your spouse has set for you. You need a more robust solution for tracking these items.

Solution

Use a WAMS service to store the list items in an Azure database so that they can be updated and added to from multiple client devices.

How It Works

As discussed in the introduction, the core purpose of WAMS is to enable easy storage and manipulation of data. In fact, the creation of a new mobile service requires that it be associated with a database. Recipe 12-1 covers the creation of a new mobile service, so if you don't already have one, you can follow the instructions there to create one and then return here. Before we continue, there are a few basic aspects of the interaction between your application and WAMS that you should understand. Table 12-1 shows the JSON and CLR data types and how they map to SQL Azure Table data types. The third column is how the data type is displayed when viewing the table schema in the WAMS Management Console.

Table 12-1. Data Type Mappings

JSON/CLR Data Type	T-SQL Type in Azure Table	Displayed As
Numeric values (integer, decimal, floating-point)	float(53) the highest-precision data type	Number
Boolean	Bit	Boolean
DateTime	DateTimeOffset	Date
String	nvarchar(max)	String

The default dashboard for your new service allows you to create a new basic application that you can immediately compile and run. I find that many people, including myself, learn and retain new skills by doing, so rather than just examining a sample, we'll build our own. The other advantage to this approach is that you will learn how to connect any existing applications you may have to a new service to enhance their features. Open Visual Studio 2012, create a new Windows Phone 8 application, and call it HoneyDo.

Defining the Data

The first thing we will need is a reference to the Windows Azure Mobile SDK. The SDK is no longer available as a separate installation but is now provided as a NuGet package. Right-click your new solution and select Manage NuGet Packages for Solution. You can then search online for *WindowsAzure.MobileServices*; finally, click INSTALL and follow the instructions.

Next we're going to need an object to represent a task that we've been given. This object will also be used to send our items across the wire for storage in the database. We'll keep it simple; Listing 12-1 shows a suitable class.

Listing 12-1. The HoneyDoThis Class Definition

```
public class HoneyDoThis
{
    public int Id { get; set; }
    public string Instructions { get; set; }
    public bool DidYouDoIt { get; set; }
}
```

Dynamic schema generation is enabled by default for WAMS, and as such, the first time you submit an object for insertion, WAMS will inspect the JSON sent over the wire and automatically create the table for you. The name of the class becomes the table name, and each public property becomes a column name. Data types are mapped as outlined in Table 12-1. There is no need to apply attributes to your class definition, but I like to be explicit about these things. Listing 12-2 shows our HoneyDoThis class with the DataTable and DataMember attributes applied.

■ **Note** The DataMember attribute is the same one used when defining a WCF data contract and is found in the System.Runtime.Serialization namespace. The DataTable attribute, however, is found in the Microsoft.WindowsAzure.MobileServices namespace.

Listing 12-2. The HoneyDoThis Class Definition with Attributes Applied

```
[DataContract]
[DataTable("HoneyDoThis")]
public class HoneyDoThis
{
    [DataMember(Name = "Id")]
    public int Id { get; set; }

    [DataMember(Name = "Instructions")]
    public string Instructions { get; set; }

    [DataMember(Name = "DidYouDoIt")]
    public bool DidYouDoIt { get; set; }

    [IgnoreDataMember]
    public string DoNotSaveThis { get; set; }
}
```

■ **Note** You'll notice that the class definition in Listing 12-2 contains an Id property of type int. Any class that is going to be used with WAMS must have an Id property of type integer. This property is then mapped to an Identity column in the SQL Azure table that is created for it. Although GUIDs would also work as a unique identifier, the WAMS implementation requires that you use integer. There is no way to change this.

The DataTable attribute constructor has a required string parameter used to pass in the name of the target table. It can be the same or different from the actual class name. You could use this to map a class onto an existing table, for example. The DataMember attribute has a parameter-less constructor; however, you can use named parameters to set a name that you want used for the column name. Again, this can be the same or different from the property name on the class.

You'll notice the addition of another property in Listing 12-2 from the previous class definition. This property demonstrates the use of the IgnoreDataMember attribute. A column for any property decorated with this attribute will not be created, and the data will not be serialized on the wire. Next, we'll need a table in which to store our data.

Log into your account at http://manage.windowsazure.com and click the mobile icon on the left side of the page to see a list of your mobile services. Click the service to which you want to connect to be taken to the dashboard. If you are taken to the Quick Start page, click **DATA** in the top navigation. On the toolbar at the bottom of the browser, you will see the **CREATE** button. Click the button and then enter **HoneyDoThis** in the TABLE NAME text box. Leave the default permissions, and then click the check mark. See Figure 12-8.

Figure 12-8. *Creating a new table in WAMS*

Setting Up the Client

The CRUD permissions for any new table that is created in a mobile service are set to only allow callers with the application key to be able to perform those operations. The first thing you are going to need then, in order to be able to communicate with your mobile service, is the application key. You can obtain the application key by downloading the sample application available from the management portal, but it's important that you know where to retrieve the keys directly within the portal. You will also need the site URL.

Log into your account at http://manage.windowsazure.com and then click the mobile icon on the left side of the page to see a list of your mobile services. Click the service to which you want to connect to be taken to the dashboard. If you are taken to the Quick Start page, click **DASHBOARD** in the top navigation. Figure 12-9 shows the dashboard, and you can see the mobile service URL at the bottom right of the picture. Make note of this URL.

Figure 12-9. WAMS dashboard showing the mobile service URL

On the toolbar at the bottom of the browser, as shown in Figure 12-10, you will see the MANAGE KEYS button. Clicking that button opens a dialog wherein you can retrieve both the application key and the master key. The master key is used by a calling application to identify itself as having greater authority. The master key will map the caller to the administrator role. Figure 12-10 shows the Manage Access Keys dialog. Don't bother, I've already changed them. Make note of the application key.

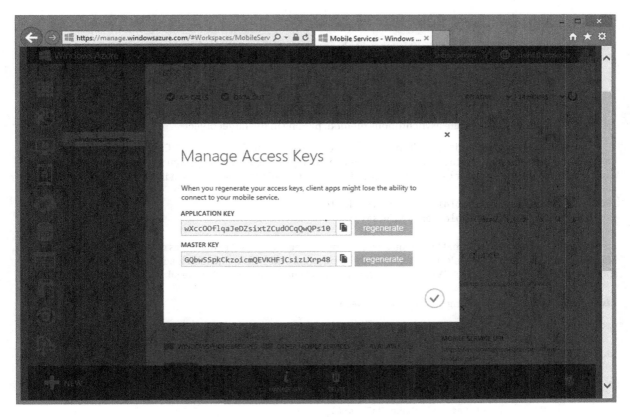

Figure 12-10. *The Manage Access Keys dialog*

Now that we have the site URL and the application key, we can return to our HoneyDo project and configure a MobileServiceClient that will allow us to communicate with WAMS. Open the App.xaml.cs file for editing and then add the code from Listing 12-3 at the top of the App class.

Listing 12-3. Declaration of a MobileServiceClient Property

```
private static readonly MobileServiceClient mobileClient =
    new MobileServiceClient("https://windowsphone8recipes.azure-mobile.net/",
"KpkRfKXGTXkeDFtiyfhd452ANMQfWQ64");

public static MobileServiceClient MobileClient
{
    get
    {
        return mobileClient;
    }
}
```

You'll recognize the two values passed into the constructor of the MobileServiceClient, with the first being the mobile service URL and the second one being the application key you retrieved earlier. Make sure to replace the values in the code listing with those from your own service.

Now that we have the client configured, we're ready to start interacting with our service.

Working with the Client Proxy

Interaction with the WAMS service client is remarkably easy. Retrieving an object follows a slightly different pattern, so we'll cover that separately. Inserting, deleting, and updating data all follow the same operational pattern.

1. Create or retrieve the target object.

2. Get a reference to the target data table.

3. Await the appropriate asynchronous method, passing in the target object.

Creating an object is simplicity itself; you simply "new" one up. The MobileServiceClient provides a generic GetTable method that you use to get a reference to the target table. The generic parameter you provide is the type associated with the table. In our example, this would be the HoneyDoThis type, as shown in the following line of code:

```
IMobileServiceTable<HoneyDoThis> honeyDoThisTable =
    App.MobileClient.GetTable<HoneyDoThis>();
```

Listing 12-4 contains code that first creates a new item and then updates it to mark it as done. Add this code to the MainPage.xaml.cs file in your project and then run the application. After the application loads and the code executes, you should be able to return to the **DATA** section in the Azure portal and see the record in the table, as shown in Figure 12-11.

Listing 12-4. Inserting, Updating, and Deleting a Record

```
protected async override void OnNavigatedTo(NavigationEventArgs e)
{
    HoneyDoThis thingToDo = new HoneyDoThis();
    thingToDo.Instructions = "Take out the garbage";

    IMobileServiceTable<HoneyDoThis> honeyDoThisTable =
        App.MobileClient.GetTable<HoneyDoThis>();
    await honeyDoThisTable.InsertAsync(thingToDo);

    // the instance will now have an Id so we
    // can simply modify it and submit the update
    thingToDo.DidYouDoIt = true;

    await honeyDoThisTable.UpdateAsync(thingToDo);

}
```

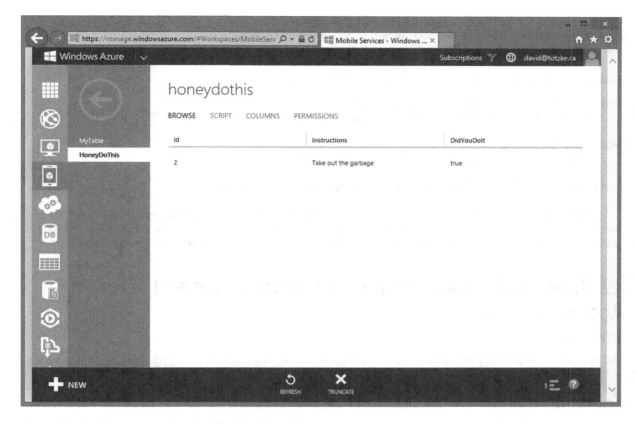

Figure 12-11. *The new record updated in the data table*

Deleting the new record is simply a matter of creating an instance of the HoneyDoThis class, setting its Id property to the ID of the record you want to delete, and then passing it into the DeleteAsync method on the MobileServicesClient. Listing 12-5 shows the code to accomplish this.

Listing 12-5. Deleting a Record from the Data Table

```
HoneyDoThis deleteThis = new HoneyDoThis();
deleteThis.Id = 2;
await honeyDoThisTable.DeleteAsync(deleteThis);
```

Now, it's unlikely that you will update an object immediately after creating it, so it would probably be helpful to be able to retrieve a specific record at a later time. As mentioned earlier, retrieving records from the data table uses a different pattern than the other three operations. You still start by getting a reference to a data table using the GetTable method of the MobileServicesClient, but the similarity ends there.

```
IMobileServiceTable<HoneyDoThis> honeyDoThisTable =
    App.MobileClient.GetTable<HoneyDoThis>();
```

The GetTable method returns an instance of a type that is an implementation of IMobileServiceTable<T>. This interface exposes a Where method. You simply provide the Where method with a lambda expression that will be used to filter the records that will be returned. Listing 12-6 shows an example that will return all HoneyDoThis items that

313

are not complete yet. The first thing you'll notice is that the Where method does not return an IEnumerable<T> but rather an IMobileServiceTableQuery<T>. To retrieve the results of the query, you must call either ToListAsync or ToEnumberableAsync.

Listing 12-6. Querying the Data Table for Unfinished Items

```
IMobileServiceTable<HoneyDoThis> honeyDoThisTable =
    App.MobileClient.GetTable<HoneyDoThis>();

IMobileServiceTableQuery<HoneyDoThis> thingsToDoQuery =
    honeyDoThisTable.Where(hdt => hdt.DidYouDoIt == false);

List<HoneyDoThis> thingsToDo = await thingsToDoQuery.ToListAsync();
```

This recipe covered the basic data interactions you have access to using the MobileServicesClient. Recipe 12-3 will cover server-side scripts that you can use to validate data before it is inserted, updated, or deleted as well as storing and working with per-user data. Recipe 12-4 will cover integrating your mobile service with an authentication provider.

12-3. Work with Server-Side Scripts: Validation and Access Control

Problem

You want to ensure that only valid data gets saved into the database while also controlling who has access to that data.

Solution

Implement server-side scripts that validate data as it is inserted or updated as well as filter the data based on the current user.

How It Works

It is a widely accepted principle that we should validate incoming data whenever it crosses a trust boundary. You may think that because our application owns, so to speak, both sides of the boundary that there is an implicit trust between client and service. This is true, to a point, but because WAMS can be accessed via REST as well as via the MobileServicesClient, we can't depend on the validation we included in our client-side application. Someone could easily craft a request using a web page or other medium and completely bypass our validation. This is where server-side scripting comes into play.

WAMS provides you with the ability to add a script for each of the insert, update, delete, and read functionalities. The scripts are written in JavaScript using a basic editor provided in the WAMS portal. The scripts are table-specific, so you have to validate each table's data separately and they cannot be shared between two or more tables. You can create and define functions to organize your code within each operational script, but these functions cannot be shared across operations. Any function you want to use in another script will have to be copied into it.

Log into the WAMS portal, click the Mobile Services icon in the left navigation, and then click your service to get to the dashboard. Click the **DATA** item in the top menu and then click the name of the table for which you want to add scripts. Once on the page for your table, click **SCRIPT** in the top menu. Figure 12-12 shows the script authoring page. The **OPERATION** drop-down list allows you to select the operation you want to script (insert, update, delete, and read). We'll examine each of the four operations in turn and then bring everything together by examining the techniques required to control the operations on a per-user basis.

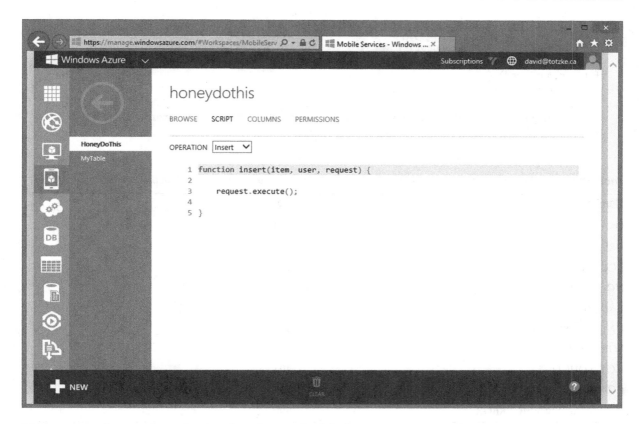

Figure 12-12. *The WAMS portal script editor showing the default insert operation script*

The script for each operation is executed before the actual operation itself, which provides you with the opportunity to add or modify the incoming data, cancel the operation entirely, or even do something entirely different. It's worth calling out here that, at a minimum, each script *must* call one of either request.execute() or request.respond() on every code path. Failure to do so will result in the mobile service not sending a response to the caller. This will be evidenced on the client by a timeout of the call to the service.

This is a fairly long recipe because there is a lot to cover for what on the surface seems to be a relatively simple set of tasks.

Insert

The script for each operation takes three parameters. The last two parameters, user and request, are the same for each operation. Only the first parameter is different. Figure 12-12 shows the default insert function, the first parameter of which is the actual item that is to be inserted into the table. The function as it stands now amounts to a NOOP, and the record is simply inserted into the table. Let's modify it a little bit to do some basic validation and cancel the insert if validation fails. Listing 12-7 shows our new insert script. For the purposes of demonstration, we'll continue with our theme, introduced in Recipe 12-2, of a list of items that have been assigned by our "honey." Now, I'm certainly not going to do anything unless it has approval. Happy wife, happy life, and all that. We'll add an Approved property to our HoneyDoThis object, and we want to insert the record only if it has been approved. The script checks the approved property, and if it's true, it then calls the execute method of the request object. If the item is not approved, the script calls the respond method, passing in a status and a message describing the error. The statusCodes object is an enumeration that represents a subset of HTTP response codes that are supported by WAMS. Table 12-2 lists the valid response codes.

Listing 12-7. Basic Insert Validation Script That Cancels the Operation If Validation Fails

```
function insert(item, user, request) {

    if (item.Approved) {
        request.execute();
    } else {
            request.respond(statusCodes.FORBIDDEN, "This task has not been approved.");
    }
}
```

Table 12-2. *Members of the statusCodes Scripting Enumeration for Use with the Respond Method of the Request Object*

Member	Code
OK	200
CREATED	201
ACCEPTED	202
NO_CONTENT	204
BAD_REQUEST	400
UNAUTHORIZED	401
FORBIDDEN	403
NOT_FOUND	404
CONFLICT	409
INTERNAL_SERVER_ERROR	500

Now that we are validating that only approved tasks are being saved, we should also ensure that we can track the tasks on a per-user basis because the WAMS database is shared by all the users of this application. From an object design perspective, the userId of the person to whom the task is assigned isn't really an attribute because it's obviously the person to whom the phone belongs. Devices aren't generally used by more than a single person and I don't know of a way that you can even switch between different users. Our HoneyDoThis class therefore now looks something like this:

```
public class HoneyDoThis
{
    // attributes have been omitted for clarity.
    public int Id { get; set; }
    public string Instructions { get; set; }
    public bool DidYouDoIt { get; set; }
    public bool Approved { get; set; }
}
```

We could modify the class to include a `userId` property, but then we are still dependent on the client application setting that value when it submits a `HoneyDothis` record. Also, since this is a service, it could be used by any number of clients and not just our application. Now we are relying on additional client applications to submit the `userId`. An arguably better approach would be to make use of the `user` object that gets passed to our server-side script. We don't even need to change our class definition.

Given the dynamic nature of JavaScript and the underlying WAMS data architecture, we can simply "pretend" that the `UserId` property exists on our `HoneyDoThis` class and set its value using the `user` object passed to the insert function. WAMS will automatically map this additional property to a column in the data table and as an added bonus will create the column if it doesn't already exist.

In reality, the dynamic schema creation functionality should be disabled in a production deployment of your application. It's very useful during development but could lead to trouble and perhaps even open you up to a denial-of-service attack when someone figures out that they can add columns at will to your data tables.

Listing 12-8 shows the modified version of the insert script.

Listing 12-8. The New Insert Script That Records the userId of the Purchaser

```
function insert(item, user, request) {

    if (item.Approved) {
        item.UserId = user.userId;
        request.execute();
    } else {
            request.respond(statusCodes.FORBIDDEN, "You can only insert approved items.");
    }
}
```

Update

The update script is the same as the `insert` script in that it has the `item`, `user`, and `request` objects as parameters and simply calls the execute method on the `request`, which translates to a NOOP. In addition to performing some type of validation before allowing the record to be updated, you could also use this script to add some auditing information to it, something like a last-updated time and date, for example. Listing 12-9 shows the script to accomplish this.

Listing 12-9. Adding a Last-Updated Date to the Object Before Updating the Record

```
function update(item, user, request) {

    item.Instructions = "Hello from the script."
    item.LastUpdate = new Date();
    request.execute();
}
```

Notice once again that because of the dynamic nature of JavaScript combined with the dynamic schema creation of WAMS, the `LastUpdated` property does not need to exist on the actual object that is being passed to the server for update. WAMS just figures it out and does the right thing. This script also demonstrates the fact that you can modify the properties of the object passed into it or even change it altogether. Figure 12-13 shows the results of our script.

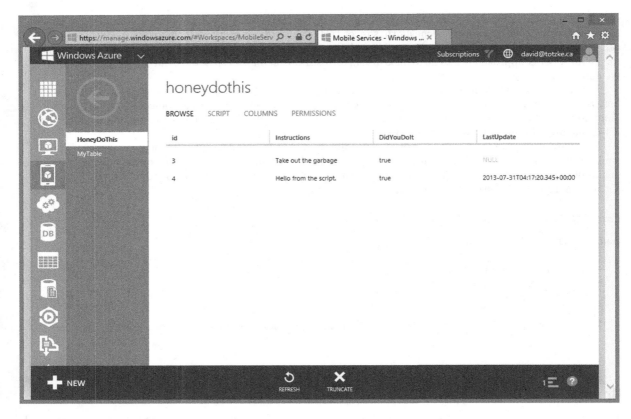

Figure 12-13. The results of the update script from Listing 12-9

You will notice in Figure 12-13 that the record with the id set to 3 has a value of NULL for the LastUpdate column. This is because the record existed prior to the implementation of the update script and there is no way to provide a default value for existing records. You would need to update any existing records and set their values individually.

One other validation that is important here is to make sure the user actually owns the record they are trying to modify. We can't examine the incoming object because the client can send us anything it wants and, besides that, our implementation doesn't include a client-side user identifier anyway. What we need to do is retrieve the existing record from the database and then test the UserId of it. We'll cover how to do that in the **Managing Per-User Data Operations** section.

Delete

The delete script still has the user and request objects as its second and third parameters, respectively, but differs from the insert and update scripts in that only the id of the record to be deleted gets passed in. The first thing you'll notice about the delete script, shown in Listing 12-10, is that it's actually named del. This is because *delete* is a reserved word in JavaScript. The default script is all you need if you want to let the delete just happen.

Listing 12-10. The Default Delete Script

```
function del(id, user, request) {

    request.execute();

}
```

There isn't really much validation you can do in the delete script since you have only the ID of the record to work with. If you are of a sadistic nature, you might want to make every second request fail silently by testing the ID to see whether it is divisible by two, as shown in Listing 12-11. The client code will have no idea if the `statusCodes.OK` was the result of the request being successfully executed or if it was simply returned as the response from the script. While this is clearly the work of a madman, it does illustrate an interesting aspect of the server-side scripts. Failing silently is sometimes a legitimate response, but `statusCodes.FORBIDDEN` or `statusCodes.UNAUTHORIZED` is a likely better response depending on the circumstances.

Listing 12-11. Failing Silently Only for Even-Numbered Records

```
function del(id, user, request) {

    if(id % 2 === 0) {
        request.respond(statusCodes.OK, "Everything went fine.");
    } else {
        request.execute();
    }

}
```

Now, admittedly, this isn't exactly useful. It would be useful to retrieve the corresponding record first to ensure it actually exists and, second, to examine it and apply any rules prior to deletion. The `insert` script in Listing 12-8 added a `UserId` property to our table and set its value to that of the caller provided by the `user` parameter of the function. We'll get to that shortly, but first let's take a look at the `read` script.

Read

The read script is the last of the operations in the CRUD quartet. Like the functions for `insert`, `del`, and `update`, the read script is passed the `user` and `request` objects as its second and third parameters, respectively. The first parameter is somewhat different in that it is not the object or its ID but rather the incoming query itself. This query object already contains any predicates, ordering, or projections that were applied on the client side. Any additional modifications we make to the query here will be additive. In the "Working with the Client Proxy" section of Recipe 12-2, we saw how we could retrieve only items that were not completed.

```
IMobileServiceTableQuery<HoneyDoThis> thingsToDoQuery =
    honeyDoThisTable.Where(hdt => hdt.DidYouDoIt == false);
```

The query object passed into the read script will already contain this filter. Keep this in mind as you develop your server-side scripts.

Probably the most useful and common application of the read script is to apply one or more filters to the incoming query that you want applied to every read. Filtering the data so that a client can only ever see their own records is a prime example. We not only remove the burden of filtering from the client but in so doing also ensure that no one ever sees anyone else's data.

The query parameter of the read script function has a where method with two overloads. The first overload accepts a JSON object as input. This JSON object defines the criteria that should be applied to the query. Listing 12-12 shows how we can add a filter to the query so that only records that match the userId of the client making the request get returned. Keep in mind that JavaScript is a case-sensitive language, so make sure you get that right.

Listing 12-12. Filtering Records by userId Using JSON

```
function read(query, user, request) {
    query.where({ UserId: user.userId, Approved: true});
    request.execute();
}
```

Just to make sure we're all on the same page here, Listing 12-12 is roughly the equivalent of writing the following SQL query:

```
SELECT * FROM TableName
WHERE UserId = user.userId AND Approved = true;
```

The where method returns an object of type query, which means we can use the result to compose our query as a series of method calls. Listing 12-13 shows three ways of writing the query defined in Listing 12-12. All three are semantic equivalents.

Listing 12-13. Variations on a Theme: All Three Statements Are Semantic Equivalents

```
function read(query, user, request) {
    query.where({ UserId: user.userId, Approved: true});
    request.execute();
}

function read(query, user, request) {
    query.where({ UserId: user.userId});
    query.where({ Approved: true});
    request.execute();
}

function read(query, user, request) {
    query.where({ UserId: user.userId})
        .where({ Approved: true});
    request.execute();
}
```

The final method of applying additional criteria to the incoming query is provided by the second overload of the where method. This version takes a JavaScript function as a parameter. This is similar to the way you can pass a lambda expression to the Where extension method in LINQ. Listing 12-14 shows two examples of how to use a JavaScript function as a filter.

Listing 12-14. Filtering Using a JavaScript Function

```
function read(query, user, request) {
    query.where(function(currentUserId){
    return this.UserId == currentUserId;
    }, user.userId);
    request.execute();
}
```

```
function read(query, user, request) {
    query.where(function(currentUserId){
    return this.UserId == currentUserId && this.Approved == true;
    }, user.userId);
    request.execute();
}
```

There is an important limitation that is imposed on the function that you pass to the where method of the query. It can contain only a single statement, and that statement must be a return. While the script in Listing 12-15 will pass validation by the rudimentary editor in the portal and the script will save, the client will get a MobileServiceInvalidOperationException.

Listing 12-15. This Script Will Fail

```
function read(query, user, request) {
    query.where(function(currentUserId){
        var x = true;
        return this.UserId == currentUserId && this.Approved == x;
    }, user.userId);
    request.execute();
}
```

Managing Per-User Data Operations

The ability to manage application data on a per-user basis is arguably one of the most common requirements when dealing with a shared data environment. We've already seen how we can record the identity of the user making the request in the section on the insert script. The section on the read script showed us how to filter the stored data at the service layer so that each client sees only their own data. We'll cover the update and del scripts together in this section because they require a similar technique in their implementation.

When an update or delete request arrives at the service, there is no guarantee that the associated item belongs to the user who is requesting the operation. An authenticated user with malicious intent can easily craft a request using the REST interface and supply an arbitrary identifier. For both operations then, you need to retrieve the existing object from the database and compare the userId that was associated to it.

■ **Note**   It's extremely important to keep the REST interface in mind when writing your server-side scripts. A malicious REST request is ludicrously easy to craft, and the dynamic nature of JavaScript means you need to be careful how you handle incoming data.

The first thing we'll need then is a reference to the table that contains the record in question. The WAMS scripting environment exposes several intrinsic objects that you can use to perform various operations. One of these objects is the tables object. The tables object exposes a getTable method that we can use to get a reference to the HoneyDoThis table. With the table in hand, we can use the where and read methods to retrieve the record and examine it. Listing 12-16 contains an example update script.

Listing 12-16. Retrieving and Updating an Existing Record

```
function update(item, user, request) {
    var table = tables.getTable('HoneyDoThis');
    table.where({ id: item.id }).read({
```

```
            success: function (results) {
                if (results.length) {
                    var existingItem = results[0];
                    if (existingItem.UserId === user.userId) {
                        request.execute();
                    } else {
                        request.respond(statusCodes.BAD_REQUEST, "Invalid user");
                    }
                } else {
                    request.respond(statusCodes.NOT_FOUND);
                }
            }, error: function () {
                request.respond(statusCodes.NOT_FOUND);
            }
        });
}
```

The script's logic should be fairly self-evident. Let's walk through it one step at a time. A reference to the HoneyDoThis table is retrieved, and the filter for the item's id is added to the where method.

```
var table = tables.getTable('HoneyDoThis');
table.where({ id: item.id })
```

The read method is then chained to the where, and a function is passed to the success parameter. The success function checks that a result was returned and, if so, retrieves the first element in the result set. The UserId of that element is tested against the userId of the caller. The request is executed if they match. Just before the call to the execute method is also a good place to put any additional validation logic.

```
.read({
    success: function (results) {
        if (results.length) {
            var existingItem = results[0];
            if (existingItem.UserId === user.userId) {
                request.execute();
            }
```

In the case that the user IDs do not match, a BAD_REQUEST status code is returned to the client.

```
else {
    request.respond(statusCodes.BAD_REQUEST, "Invalid user");
}
```

Finally, if no matching item is found in the table, a NOT_FOUND status code is returned to the client.

```
} else {
    request.respond(statusCodes.NOT_FOUND);
```

The only difference between this update script and that needed for the del script, aside from the name, is that the del script only gets the id of item and not the item itself. Listing 12-17 contains a sample del script.

Listing 12-17. Sample Script for Per-User Delete Operation

```
function del(id, user, request) {
    var table = tables.getTable('HoneyDoThis');
    table.where({ id: id }).read({
        success: function (results) {
            if (results.length) {
                var existingItem = results[0];
                if (existingItem.UserId === user.userId) {
                    request.execute();
                } else {
                    request.respond(statusCodes.BAD_REQUEST, "Invalid user");
                }
            } else {
                request.respond(statusCodes.NOT_FOUND);
            }
        }, error: function () {
            request.respond(statusCodes.NOT_FOUND);
        }
    });
}
```

The user object that is provided to every server-side script has another useful property called level. The level property is set to one of three values: anonymous, authenticated, or master. The master key, found along with the application key, as shown in Recipe 12-1, must be present in the request in order for the user object level to be set to master. Guard the master key carefully; it opens all the doors.

Many other server-side scripting objects are available to you, and I encourage you to investigate them all so that you can enrich the functionality of your applications. You can find documentation of the scripting objects on the Microsoft site at http://msdn.microsoft.com/en-us/library/windowsazure/jj554226.aspx.

12-4. Work with Authentication Providers

Problem

You have an application that requires the user to log on so that you can manage user-specific information, but you don't want the burden of managing user accounts and credentials.

Solution

Register with and connect your application to one of the authentication providers supported by Windows Azure Mobile Services.

How It Works

I have always found the management of user accounts and credentials to be one of the most annoying parts of creating an application. Almost every new application requires the same functionality to a greater or lesser degree. Fortunately, there is a better way that has been around for a long time but has only been gaining wide acceptance in the last few years. It is what is known as *federated identity*.

Now, a full discussion of federated identity and the workings thereof is enough to fill a book of its own and is certainly well beyond the scope of this one.[3] However, a brief introduction to the concept is appropriate to aid in your understanding of what is going on in this recipe.

Federated Identity: What Is It?

You can think of federated identity as off-loading the responsibility for verifying the identity of a specific person or entity to a trusted third-party, *trust* being the key. Perhaps an example from the physical world will help in understanding.

When traveling to another country, you need to be able to identify yourself, especially when returning home. You need to be able to prove that you are you. We use a passport to accomplish this. The passport has been issued to you by the government of your country. Each authority that wants to verify your identity trusts that the issuing government has done its due diligence in verifying your identity, that reasonable steps have been taken to prevent large-scale forgery, and that the document can be *trusted*. The passport is a kind of *token* that you can present as proof of identity. The requesting authority doesn't need to contact the issuer directly because of the *trust relationship* that the two share. The token is enough. Although not as universally accepted, a driver's license is another token of identity issued by a trusted provider.

Back in software-land, we have the same need for identity. This is where identity providers come into play. WAMS, at least at the time of this writing,[4] has support for four identity providers.

- Microsoft Account (formerly Microsoft Live ID)
- Google
- Facebook
- Twitter

Registering Your Application

The first thing you need to do in order to use one of these third-party identity providers is to establish a trust relationship between your application and the provider. This functionality is exposed by something called a *secure token service*. You need to know when a valid token is being presented to your application. This relationship hinges on two things: an application ID and a shared secret.

The application ID...well...identifies your application to the provider, and the shared secret is used to secure communications. The underlying plumbing that makes all of this happen is complex to say the least, but it is thankfully hidden from us. All four of the providers work in the same manner, and registration is a simple matter of obtaining a developer account and then registering your application to obtain the application ID and secret. We'll cover only the Microsoft account provider in detail in this recipe.

Microsoft Account Provider Registration

Log into the Live Connect Developer Center at `http://dev.live.com`. The sign-in page provides a link to register for a Microsoft account (formerly Live ID) if you don't already have one. Once you are signed in, click the "My apps" link at the top left of the page. You should arrive at the page shown in Figure 12-14.

---

[3]"Fill its own book and beyond the scope of this one." I can think of no cliché more worthy to be the last one I write...at least in this book.

[4]OK, that's the last one.

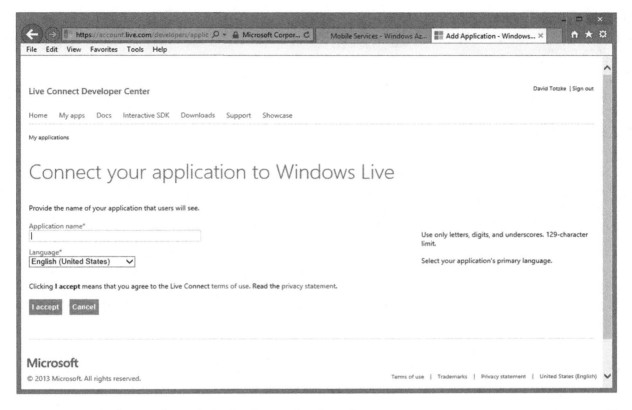

Figure 12-14. *The "My apps" page in the Live Connect Developer Center*

Enter the name of your application, and select its primary language. Review the terms of use and the privacy statement and then click the button labeled "I accept." Figure 12-15 shows the API Settings page for your application, which will appear next.

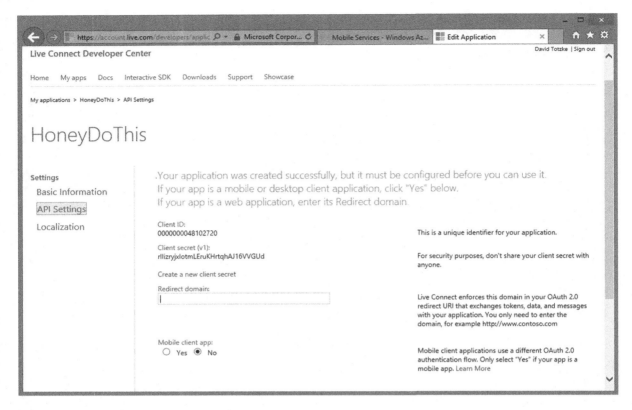

Figure 12-15. *The application API Settings page in Live Connect Developer Center*

Make a note of the client ID and client secret because you will need these values later.

You need to enter one more piece of information before your application is fully configured: the redirect domain. You might be thinking "I'm doing Windows Phone, so this is a mobile client app," but that isn't the case. We're actually establishing the trust relationship between the mobile service and the provider, and the mobile service is a web application. Enter the domain you assigned to your service when you created it and then click the Save button.

Configuring Authentication for Your Service

Now that you have registered your application with one or more identity providers, you need to configure the settings in your mobile service. Log into the WAMS Management Portal, click the Mobile Services icon in the left navigation pane, and then click the name of the service you want to configure. Along the top of the page there is an **IDENTITY** link. Click that to be taken to the page shown in Figure 12-16. There is a section for each of the four identity providers where you can enter the client ID and shared secret.

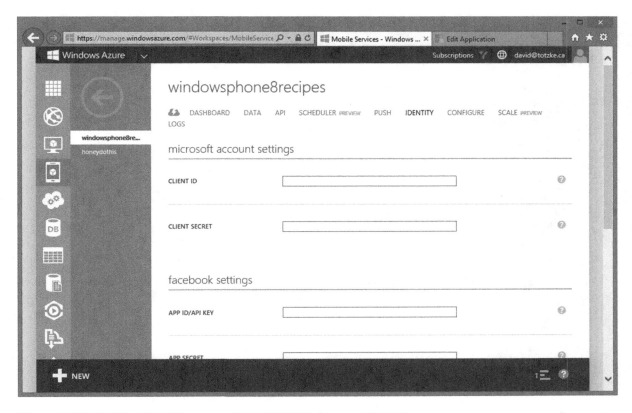

Figure 12-16. *The Identity Settings screen in the WAMS Management Portal*

The last thing we need to do is configure our table security to limit access to only those users who have been authenticated. Navigate to the page for your table in the WAMS portal and click the PERMISSIONS link at the top. For each of the operations, select Only Authenticated Users from the drop-down and then click the Save button in the bottom toolbar. Figure 12-17 shows the result.

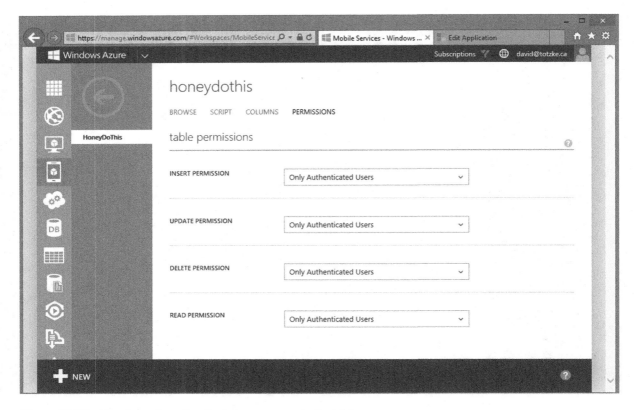

Figure 12-17. *Allowing only authenticated users access to the table*

With all of that out of the way, we are now ready to enable authentication in our client application.

Authentication in the Client

So far, getting our service up and running hasn't been too much trouble. There are a lot of moving parts that need to be connected, and we had to write some JavaScript,[5] but it hasn't been a particularly arduous journey. You might be thinking, as I was, that the client-side code is going to be just completely ugly to compensate for that. Against all expectations, it's arguably the easiest part of the entire process.

If you refer to Listing 12-3 in Recipe 12-2, you'll see that we exposed a static property of type `MobileServiceClient` on the App class and used that to interact with our mobile service. The `MobileServiceClient` class has a method called `LoginAsync`. The `LoginAsync` method takes a single parameter of the enumeration type `MobileServiceAuthenticationProvider`. This one line of code is all it takes:

```
await App.MobileClient.LoginAsync(MobileServiceAuthenticationProvider.MicrosoftAccount);
```

The call to `LoginAsync` will then display the user interface that is appropriate for the specified provider. You don't even need to provide a UI to enter a username and password. How cool is that? Figure 12-18 shows an initial opt-in screen for the Microsoft account provider if this is the first time you are connecting. Beside it is the actual sign-in page.

---

[5]My eyes! The goggles do nothing!

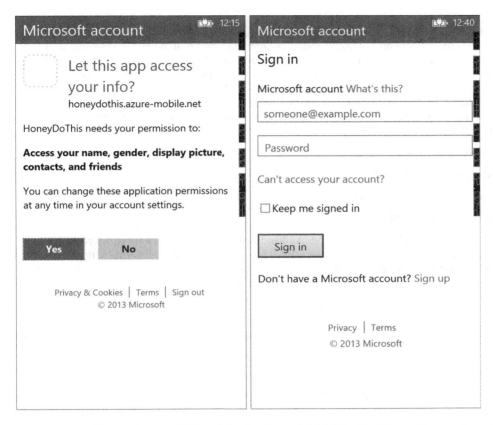

Figure 12-18. *The opt-in page (left) and the sign-in page (right) for the Microsoft account provider*

And that's all there is to it. You'll want to wrap the call in a try/catch to trap the InvalidOperationException, which gets thrown if the authentication fails for any reason and makes it nice for the user, of course, but that's easy.

12-5. Work with Push Notifications

Problem

You have an application that helps people track their to-do items, and you want to be able to periodically send productivity tips to anyone running the application.

Solution

Register your application with one of the push notification services that is supported by Windows Azure Mobile Services. Your application can then register the client device with your mobile service to receive notifications.

How It Works

There are two basic approaches to architecting a periodic update system: push and pull. While there are certainly situations where polling for an update and pulling down the data is appropriate, it can be a fairly inefficient method. This is especially true if the updates are infrequent and polling will create a lot of unnecessary network traffic. Users who have a metered connection are not going to be happy with your application.

The push or, more commonly, publish-subscribe pattern is far more efficient. Clients subscribe to a channel, and the service publishes the information to all subscribers. WAMS has built-in support for several of the most popular push notification services. The four supported providers are as follows:

- Microsoft Push Notification Service (MPNS)

- Windows Notification Service (WNS)

- Apple Push Notification Services (APNS)

- Google Cloud Messaging (GCM)

Windows devices will interact with either MPNS or WNS. Android and iOS devices that want to interact with your mobile service will do so via either the Apple or Google service. We'll be working through registering with and using WNS; however, the flow of interactions is the same for all the services. Figure 12-19 illustrates the various interactions involved.

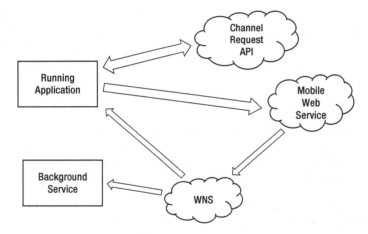

Figure 12-19. *Interactions between client applications, WAMS, and WNS*

Push notifications can be received by two components of a Windows Phone application: the application itself if it's running and a background task. You can send two types of notifications from your service: XML and raw (Binary). XML notifications are by far the easiest to use and require very little client-side processing. Raw notifications, on the other hand, require your application to provide 100 percent of the message processing and do everything needed to display the message on the device.

■ **Note** Push notifications are triggered in one of two ways: from one of the server-side scripts attached to a table or from a script that is associated with a scheduled job.

Registering Your Application

Just as you did in Recipe 12-4, you need to register your application with one of the supported service providers. The steps are virtually the same. A unique application identifier and shared secret need to be generated for your application, and then you need to configure this information in the WAMS Management Portal.

We're going to concern ourselves only with the Windows Push Notification Service, but the basic procedure will be roughly the same for the Apple and Google services.

■ **Note** The Microsoft Push Notification Service does not require you to authenticate your service in order to send push notifications. Notification volume is limited to 500 notifications per user per day. It's an easy choice with no configuration overhead if you have modest notification needs.

Windows Notification Service Registration

The first thing you will need in order to register your application is a developer account in the Windows Dev Center at http://msdn.microsoft.com/en-us/windows/apps. There is a cost associated with this account; however, it's not hugely expensive, and you do need to have it if you want to publish applications to the Windows Store.

Once you are logged in to the developer center, click the DASHBOARD link at the top right of the page and then click the "Submit an app" link in the left navigation. Figure 12-20 shows the page you should now be seeing.

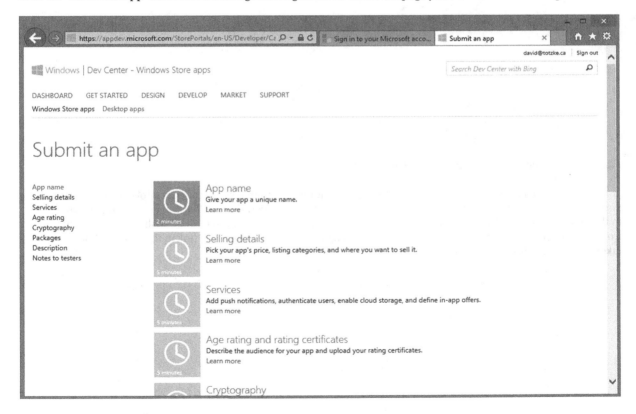

Figure 12-20. The "Submit an app" landing page in the Dev Center

Click the "App name" icon and then enter a name for your application in the text box on the page that comes up next; then click the "Reserve app name" button. The next page will confirm the name registration, assuming that the name is available. Click the Save button. Figure 12-21 shows the final application page you should land on assuming everything went well.

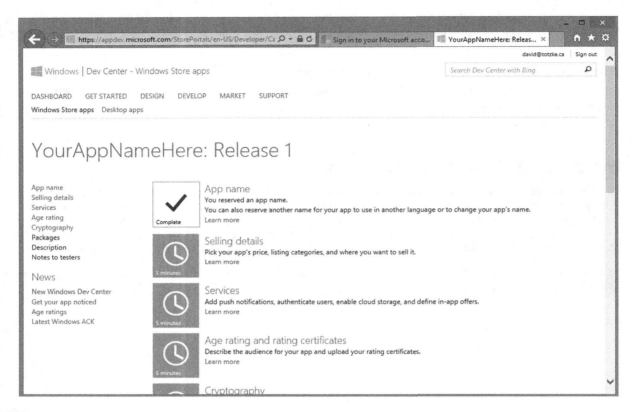

Figure 12-21. *The app submission details page showing a reserved name*

The next step is to retrieve the unique application identifier and shared secret for your application. Click the Services icon to start the process. The page that appears next is a little confusing. What you are looking for is the link to the Live Services site. I've highlighted it in Figure 12-22. That link will land you on the "Push notifications and Live Connect services info" page shown in Figure 12-23. Click the "Identifying your app" link in the WNS section to be taken to the page shown in Figure 12-24.

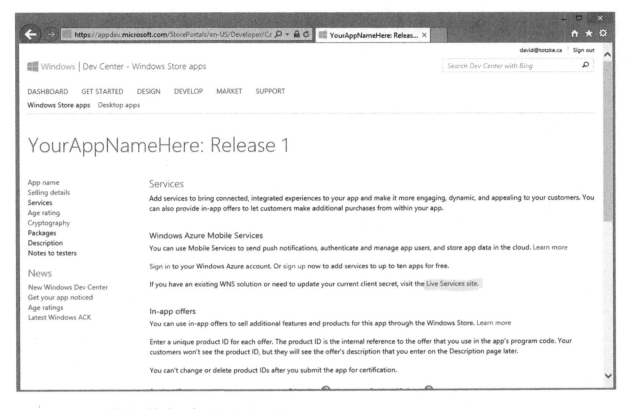

Figure 12-22. *Highlighted link to the Live Services site*

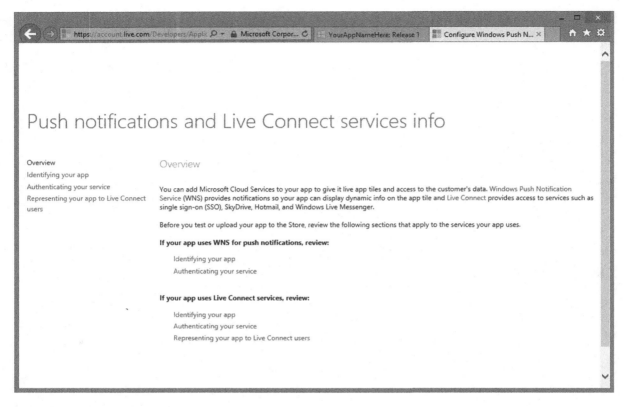

Figure 12-23. *"Push notifications and Live Connect services info" page*

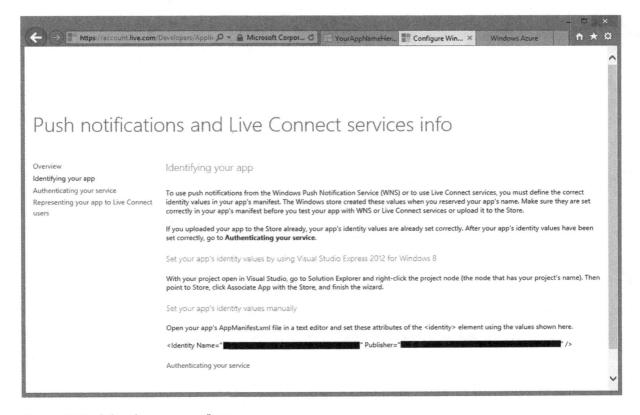

Figure 12-24. *"Identifying your app" page*

Take heart, dear reader, for we are nearly there. Click the **"Authenticating your service"** link at the bottom of the page shown in Figure 12-24, and you will finally be presented with the information you need. Figure 12-25 shows the page that displays your package security identifier (SID) and the client secret.

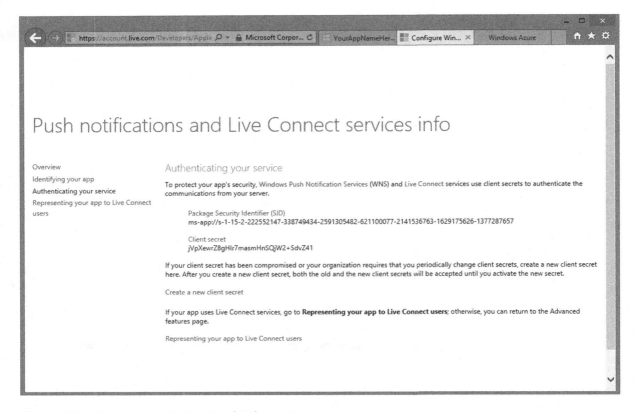

Figure 12-25. *Package security identifier (SID) and client secret page*

Make a note of the identifier and secret so that you can enter them in the WAMS portal.

Configuring Your Service for Push

The final step in the process of setting up your mobile service to support push notifications is to enter the package security identifier and client secret you retrieved in the previous step into the configuration of your mobile service. Those of you who have worked through Recipe 12-4 will note the similarity.

Log into the WAMS portal and then click the Mobile Services icon in the left navigation. Click the name of the mobile service you want to configure and then click PUSH in the top navigation links. This should land you on a page similar to the one in Figure 12-26. Enter the client secret and package SID from the previous step into the boxes in the "windows application credentials" section and then click Save in the bottom toolbar.

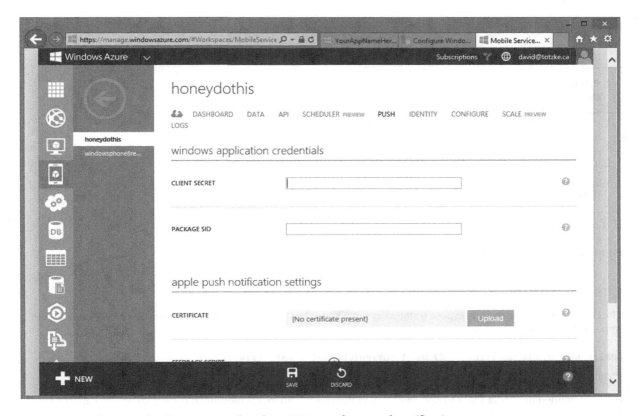

Figure 12-26. *Entering the client secret and package SID to configure push notifications*

Application Functionality

The problem statement for this recipe says that we want to be able to send periodic tips to all the users of the application. Now that we have our mobile service configured to authenticate with the Windows Push Notification Service, we can work on implementing the rest of the application logic.

Figure 12-27 recalls an image we saw earlier. When the application first starts, it requests a notification channel. The URI of that channel is what the mobile service will use to communicate with the client device to deliver the notification. The client registers the URI with the mobile service by inserting it into a table. When it's time for a notification to be sent, the mobile service simply loops through all the registered clients and sends a notification to each one. The Windows Push Notification Service is then responsible for delivering the message to the devices.

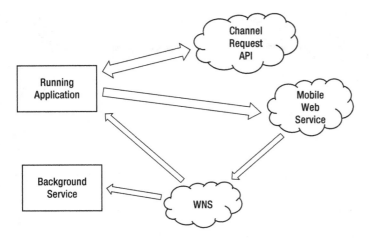

Figure 12-27. *Push Notification Service interactions*

Channel Surfing

The first thing we need to do is expose a static CurrentChannel property on the App class. Add this line of code to the App.xaml.cs file of your application:

```
public static HttpNotificationChannel CurrentChannel { get; private set; }
```

Next we'll add code that runs when the application is launched that will request a channel instance. Add the function defined in Listing 12-18 to App.xaml.cs and then add a call to this method in the Application_Launching method.

Listing 12-18. The AcquirePushChannel Method

```
private async void AcquirePushChannel()
{
    CurrentChannel = HttpNotificationChannel.Find("MyPushChannel");

    if (CurrentChannel == null)
    {
        CurrentChannel = new HttpNotificationChannel("MyPushChannel");
        CurrentChannel.Open();
        CurrentChannel.BindToShellToast();
    }

    IMobileServiceTable<Channel> channelTable =
        App.MobileClient.GetTable<Channel>();
    List<Channel> existingRegistration = await channelTable
        .Where(r => r.PublisherHostId == HostInformation.PublisherHostId).ToListAsync();

    if (existingRegistration.Count == 0)
        await registrationTable.InsertAsync(new Channel()
```

```
    {
        Uri = CurrentChannel.ChannelUri.ToString(),
        PublisherHostId = HostInformation.PublisherHostId
    });
else
    if (existingRegistration[0].Uri != CurrentChannel.ChannelUri.ToString())
    {
        existingRegistration[0].Uri = CurrentChannel.ChannelUri.ToString();
        await registrationTable.UpdateAsync(existingRegistration[0]);
    }
}
```

Let's walk through the AcquirePushChannel code. To obtain a channel reference, we simply call the static Find method of the HttpNotificationChannel class, passing in a name for the channel. The name can be any arbitrary string. The result of the method call is assigned to our static CurrentChannel property. Take note of the following line of code in the method:

```
CurrentChannel.BindToShellToast();
```

Normally when an application exits, any channel that it had open would become invalid. A push channel persists after an app exits only if it has been bound to Tile or Toast notifications so that these notifications can still be received even though the app is not running. Since our application will be sending Toast notifications, we call BindToShellToast.

A notification channel will remain valid for a period of 30 days from the time of its creation. The mobile service will error if it tries to send a notification to an invalid channel and there's no way for the service to request a new channel on behalf of the client. The client needs to manage updating the service should the ChannelUri change, and that's exactly what the next bit of code does. Our application defines a Channel class that it uses to send a unique device identifier and channel URI to the mobile service. Listing 12-19 shows the Channel class.

Listing 12-19. The Channel Class Definition

```
[DataContract]
[DataTable("Channel")]
public class Channel
{
    [DataMember]
    public int Id { get; set; }

    [DataMember]
    public string PublisherHostId { get; set; }

    [DataMember]
    public string Uri { get; set; }
}
```

■ **Note**   You'll need to create a Channel table in your mobile service. You can also create a ProductivityTip table while you're there since we'll be needing that next. Refer to Recipe 12-2 for information on creating a table in the WAMS Management Portal.

The code queries the Channel table using the unique device identifier, and if no match is found, a new Channel record is inserted. If a matching record is found, the existing ChannelUri is compared to the CurrentChannel's ChannelUri. The URI is then updated if they don't match. In this way, the service will (well, should) always have a valid URI to work with for each client.

A Hot Tip

As mentioned earlier, push notifications can be sent only via server-side scripts. There is no client API. For this problem, we'll use the insert script on a ProductivityTip table to trigger the push. Inserting a record into this table will trigger code that sends the new tip to all of the registered client channels. The ProductivityTip class is defined in Listing 12-20. Recipe 12-2 demonstrates inserting records into a table using the client proxy.

Listing 12-20. The ProductivityTip Class Definition

```
[DataContract]
[DataTable("ProductivityTip")]
public class ProductivityTip
{
    [DataMember]
    public int Id { get; set; }

    [DataMember]
    public string Content { get; set; }
}
```

Broadcast Time

Our goal for this application is to send a notification whenever a new productivity tip is inserted into the database. We'll do this by adding an insert script to the ProductivityTip table. Log into the WAMS portal and navigate to the script editor for the ProductivityTip table and then select insert from the drop-down. Listing 12-21 has the required JavaScript for the insert.

Listing 12-21. The Insert Script for the ProductivityTip Table

```
function insert(item, user, request) {
    request.execute({
        success: function() {
            request.respond();
            sendNotifications();
        }
    });
}
function sendNotifications() {
    var channelTable = tables.getTable('Channel');
    channelTable.read({
        success: function(channels) {
            channels.forEach(function(channel) {
                push.wns.sendToastText01(channel.uri, {
                    text: item.Content
                }, {
```

```
                success: function(pushResponse) {
                    console.log("Sent push:", pushResponse);
                }
            });
        });
    }
});
}
}
```

The script is very straightforward. The list of subscribed clients is retrieved from the Channel table, and then we use one of the startlingly numerous send methods of the push.wns object to send the actual notification.

There is one particular aspect of this script that is worth calling out specifically. Take a look at the first few lines of the insert function:

```
function insert(item, user, request) {
    request.execute({
        success: function() {
            request.respond();
            sendNotifications();
```

You'll notice that the request is immediately executed, which would normally end things right there. In this case, we've added a function call to the success option. The very first thing that the success function does is to call respond on the request. This allows the client that submitted the new item to get on with its life, and the rest of the script executes asynchronously on the server.

It's been a long journey, but once all of the moving parts are connected, supporting push notifications in your Windows Phone 8 application is remarkably simple.

CHAPTER 13

■ ■ ■

Using the Microsoft Live SDK

The Microsoft Live SDK is a set of APIs that allow developers to integrate a user's Windows Live account and related services within a Windows Phone application. This chapter will walk through the necessary steps to download and install the SDK, as well as how to incorporate the Live Connect APIs to authenticate a user, retrieve a user's list of Hotmail contacts and calendar information, and access files in a user's SkyDrive[1] account.

In this chapter, we will go over the following recipes:

- 13-1. Install the Live SDK
- 13-2. Register Your Windows Phone App with the Live Connect Developer Center
- 13-3. Authenticate a User Within Your Windows Phone App
- 13-4. Manage the User's Outlook Calendar Information
- 13-5. Download Files from SkyDrive

13-1. Install the Live SDK
Problem

You want to develop an app that allows the user to log in using a Microsoft Live account.

Solution

Download and install the Live SDK v5.4.

How It Works

The Microsoft Live SDK v5.4 comes packaged with a set of controls and APIs that provide you with the ability to incorporate the Microsoft Live user experience within your Windows Phone 8 app. Along with basic user authentication, you can upload or retrieve files from SkyDrive, manage a user's Hotmail contacts list or calendar, integrate in-app chat, and more.

---

[1]By the time you read this, SkyDrive may be called something completely different due to a trademark infringement case that was filed by a British company against Microsoft over the use of the word sky. The latest reports indicate that Microsoft settled the case and will rebrand SkyDrive. (www.pcworld.com/article/2045634/microsoft-to-rename-skydrive-after-losing-trademark-suit.html/). For now, we will continue to use SkyDrive to refer to Microsoft's cloud storage product until a new name has been announced.

To download and install the Live SDK, go to www.microsoft.com/en-us/download/details.aspx?id=39304, and click the Download button. Select the check box next to the file named LiveSDK.msi, and then click the Next button.

The minimum requirements for this installation are pretty simple. It must be installed on a system that is running on Windows 7, Windows 8, Windows 8.1 Preview, Windows Server 2008, or Windows Server 2012. The Live SDK may be leveraged in Windows Phone 7.1, Windows Phone 8, Windows 8, and Windows 8.1 Preview application development, and it requires .NET 4.5.

Since we already have our machines configured for Windows Phone 8 application development, it is safe to say that we have met the minimum requirements for the Live SDK, and we should proceed with the installation once the MSI file has been downloaded.

The main screen of the Live SDK Setup application provides the SDK license agreement, as shown in Figure 13-1. Read and accept the terms of the license agreement; then click Install.

Figure 13-1. *Live SDK installation*

Once the installation completes successfully, launch Visual Studio 2012, and create a new Windows Phone app. There will not be a noticeable visual indication that the Live Connect controls and APIs were installed. The libraries are available on your machine, which you will be able to reference from your project. To add these libraries in your Windows Phone project, right click on the project name in Visual Studio, and select Add Reference... from the context menu to launch the Reference Manager dialog.

You will now see that the Microsoft.Live and Microsoft.Live.Controls are available for inclusion in your project, as depicted in Figure 13-2. This is something we will discuss in more detail in Recipe 13-3. For now, we just wanted to quickly demonstrate that the Live SDK was in fact installed properly, even though it is not something that is immediately apparent when you are creating or updating a Windows Phone project.

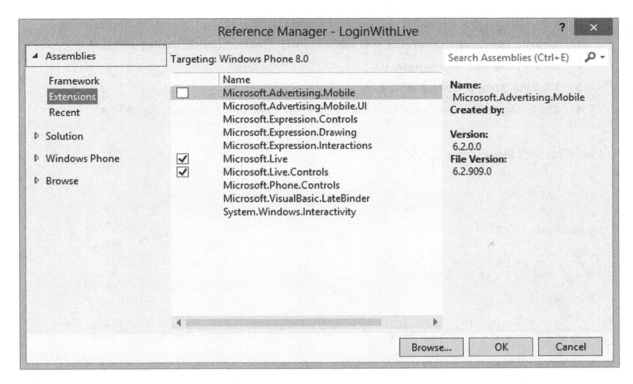

Figure 13-2. *Add a reference to the Microsoft Live libraries in your Windows Phone app*

13-2. Register Your Windows Phone App with the Live Connect Developer Center

Problem

You've installed the Live SDK, and you want to develop an app that leverages the Live Connect APIs.

Solution

Register the app online at the Live Connect Developer Center.

How It Works

If you want to include features and functionality that is available through the Live Connect APIs within a Windows Phone app, you will need to obtain a unique client ID from the Live Connect Developer Center. This means you must log in to the Live Connect Developer Center and register your app. Once your application is properly registered, it is assigned a client ID. You must register each Windows Phone app that will be using the Live Connect APIs separately in your Live Connect Developer Center account.

Perform the following steps to register your Windows Phone app with the Live Connect Developer Center:

1. Go to the Live Connect Developer Center web site at http://msdn.microsoft.com/en-us/live/.

2. Sign in using your Microsoft Live ID.

3. Click the "My apps navigation" link.

4. On the "My applications" page, click the "Create application" link, as shown in Figure 13-3.

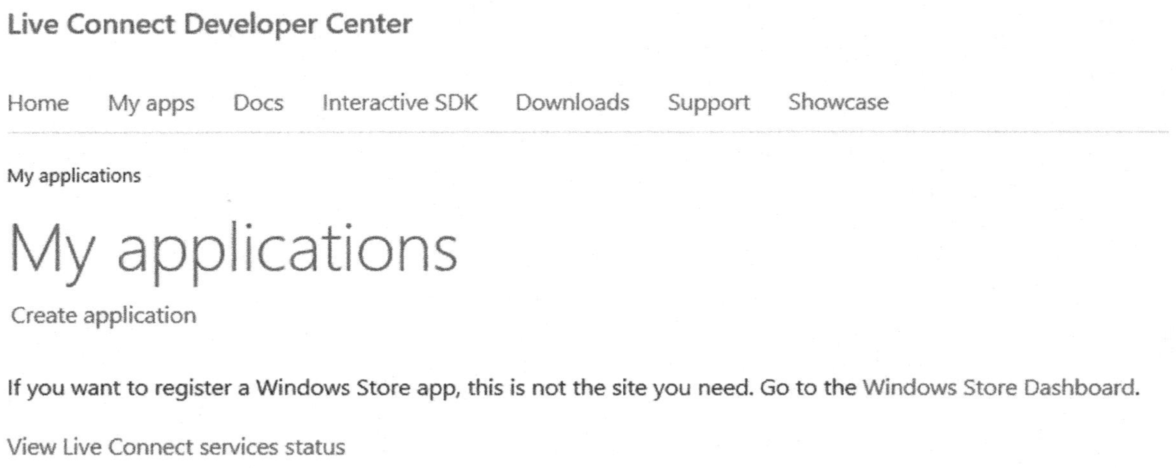

Live Connect Developer Center

Home   My apps   Docs   Interactive SDK   Downloads   Support   Showcase

My applications

My applications

Create application

If you want to register a Windows Store app, this is not the site you need. Go to the Windows Store Dashboard.

View Live Connect services status

Figure 13-3. Register an application by clicking the "Create application" link on your Live Connect Developer Center "My applications" page

5. The next step will prompt you to enter your application name and select the application's primary language, as shown in Figure 13-4. You must also read and accept the terms of use.

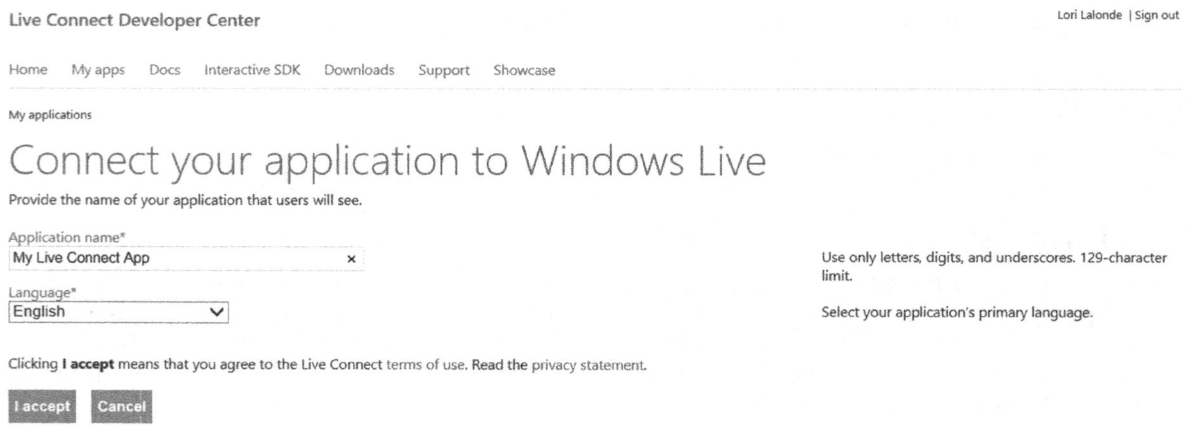

Live Connect Developer Center   Lori Lalonde | Sign out

Home   My apps   Docs   Interactive SDK   Downloads   Support   Showcase

My applications

Connect your application to Windows Live

Provide the name of your application that users will see.

Application name*

| My Live Connect App   × |

Use only letters, digits, and underscores. 129-character limit.

Language*

| English   ∨ |

Select your application's primary language.

Clicking **I accept** means that you agree to the Live Connect terms of use. Read the privacy statement.

| I accept | | Cancel |

Figure 13-4. Provide an application name and set your application's primary language

Upon acceptance of the terms of use, your application is assigned a client ID and client secret. At this point, you will notice a message indicating that the application requires further configuration, as shown in Figure 13-5.

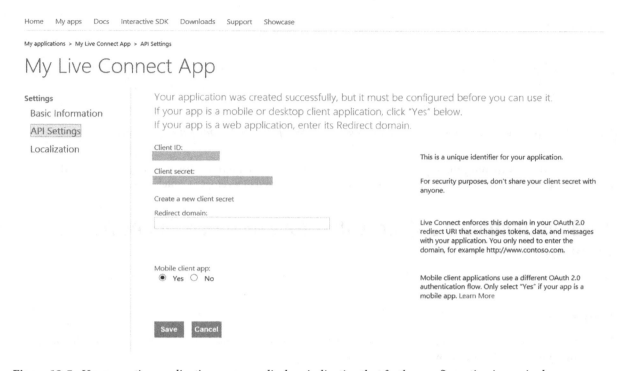

Figure 13-5. *Upon creating application, message displays indicating that further configuration is required*

Note that I have grayed out the client ID and client secret intentionally. This is a private key that you will use to enable use of the Live Connect features within your application. It is not to be shared.

On this page, select the Yes radio button to indicate that the app we just registered is a mobile client app. This distinction is necessary because the OAuth 2.0 authentication flow used in a mobile client application is different from the flow used in a web application. If you are unfamiliar with OAuth 2.0, visit the OAuth 2.0 site at http://oauth.net/2/ and review the specifications.

Save your changes on this screen. At this point, we can now create the intended Windows Phone application using the client ID provided.

If you return to the "My applications" page in your Live Connect Developer Center dashboard, you will notice that not only can you view the list of applications that are registered, but you can also track daily and monthly users (Figure 13-6). If you are the type of developer who cares about tracking analytics for your application, this feature is provided with your Live Connect Developer Center account. Bookmark this site and ensure that you visit it regularly to monitor your application's usage.

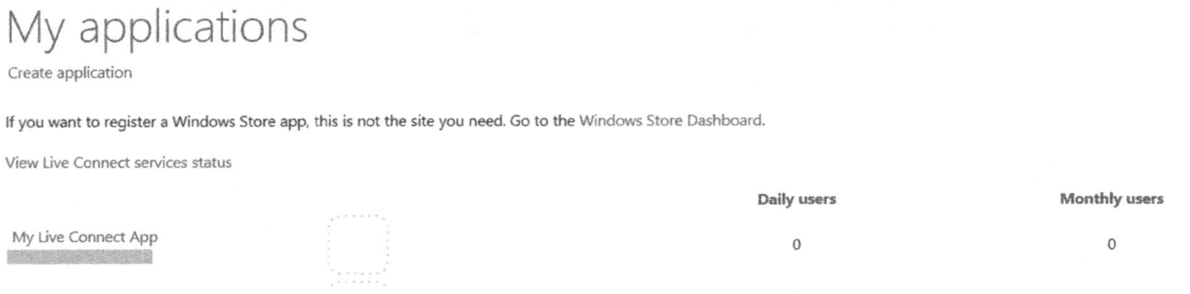

My applications

Create application

If you want to register a Windows Store app, this is not the site you need. Go to the Windows Store Dashboard.

View Live Connect services status

		Daily users	Monthly users
My Live Connect App		0	0

Figure 13-6. *The "My applications" dashboard displays a snapshot of daily and monthly users for each registered application*

You can drill down into your application registration page to view or modify settings. You can also view detailed analytics in chart form or delete your application from the Live Connect Developer Center.

13-3. Authenticate a User Within Your Windows Phone App

Problem

You want to incorporate a quick and easy way to authenticate a user from your Windows Phone app.

Solution

Leverage the Identity API, available as part of the Live Connect APIs, to provide a simple way to incorporate user authentication and single sign-in within the application.

How It Works

The LiveConnectClient class exposes a set of methods that execute the REST API calls to manage a user's Microsoft account. The Identity API is a subset of the Live Connect APIs, which allows us to include basic authentication within a Windows Phone app.

As we discussed in Recipe 13-2, a client ID must be registered with the Live Connect Developer Center in order to leverage the Live Connect APIs. Additionally, we must obtain consent from the user to access any of the Microsoft Live account features within the application. This is accomplished by defining the type of access that is required when attempting to create a new LiveConnect session. Essentially, we must define the scope of the request.

The Live Connect APIs provide two scope types: core and extended. Core scopes provide sign-in capabilities as well as access to the user's profile and basic contact information. The core scopes are as follows:

- wl.basic: Provides read-only access to the user's profile information and contacts list.

- wl.offline_access: Allows the app to access or update the user's info whether or not the user is signed in to their Live account.

- wl.signin: Enables the user to sign in within the app using Live ID credentials. The sign-in process will prompt for credentials on the application's first sign-in attempt. After that, the sign-in will occur automatically.

Extended scopes provide access to additional information and functionality, such as accessing calendars, photos, and SkyDrive contents, to name a few. We will be utilizing a handful of the available scopes as we progress through the remaining recipes in this chapter. To view a full list of extended scopes and the type of access each scope provides, read the MSDN article on scopes and permissions at http://msdn.microsoft.com/en-us/library/live/hh243646.aspx.

In this recipe, we will create a simple app that allows a user to sign in using Live ID credentials, and we will build on this app to include additional functionality in the following recipes in this chapter. If you have not registered your app with the Live Connect Developer Center yet, go back to Recipe 13-2 and walk through the steps to register your app and obtain a client ID for your application.

The Code

Launch Visual Studio 2012, and open the project located within the \Chapter 13\MyLiveConnectAppStart directory. Add a reference to the Microsoft.Live and Microsoft.Live.Controls libraries, which we briefly touched upon at the end of Recipe 13-1 and depicted in Figure 13-2.

Open the MainPage XAML file, and add a namespace declaration for the Microsoft.Live.Controls library within the phone:ApplicationPage element:

```
xmlns:live="clr-namespace:Microsoft.Live.Controls;assembly=Microsoft.Live.Controls"
```

The only control available to add to the MainPage from the Microsoft.Live.Controls library is the SignInButton, which will be used to initiate the sign-in process of the user's Microsoft account. Within the MainPage markup, replace the comment <!-- Add the Live Signin button here --> with a SignInButton as follows:

```
<live:SignInButton
        Name="signInButton"
        Grid.Row="1"
        ClientId="{Binding ClientId, Mode=OneTime}"
        Scopes="wl.signin wl.basic wl.birthday"
        Branding="MicrosoftAccount"
        TextType="SignIn"
        SessionChanged="signInButton_SessionChanged"/>
```

The SignInButton allows us to specify the scopes we want to use right within the button's markup. To specify multiple scopes, enter them in the Scopes property, making sure to separate each scope with a single space. For this example, we will request the user to enable sign-in, as well as enable access to the user's birthday, basic profile information, and contacts information from within the application.

The Branding property allows us to select which logo to display on the SignInButton. There are four available logos: Messenger, MicrosoftAccount, Outlook, and SkyDrive. TextType allows us to select which text to display: Connect, Custom, Login, and Signin. If Custom is selected, then we will need to provide text for two additional properties, SigninText and SignoutText, on the SignInButton. You can choose whichever branding and text type you prefer. They are simply cosmetic changes and do not affect the behavior of the SignInButton.

Additionally, we will need to include an event handler for the button's SessionChanged event. This will be the event that will be raised when the session is instantiated. Within the ContentPanel grid, add a few TextBlock controls to display the user's name, birthday, and current sign-in state. Add a HyperlinkButton so that we can provide a link to the user's online profile page.

In the MainPage code-behind, we will first need to add the following using directives:

```
using Microsoft.Live;
using Microsoft.Live.Controls;
```

Next, we will need to include code within the SessionChanged event handler to check whether a Live Connect session was successfully connected (Listing 13-1). If the session is connected, this means the user entered valid Live ID credentials during the authentication process and the user consented to enable access to the information requested within the application.

Listing 13-1. Check to Determine Whether We Are Successfully Connected in the SessionChanged Event of the SignInButton

```
private LiveConnectClient client;
private async void signInButton_SessionChanged(object sender, LiveConnectSessionChangedEventArgs e)
{
    try
    {
        if (e.Status == LiveConnectSessionStatus.Connected)
        {
            client = new LiveConnectClient(e.Session);
            LiveOperationResult operationResult = await client.GetAsync("me");
            App.ViewModel.LoadUserInfo((dynamic)operationResult.Result);
        }
        else
        {
            App.ViewModel.ResetUserInfo();
        }
    }
    catch (LiveConnectException exception)
    {
        App.ViewModel.ResetUserInfo();
        MessageBox.Show("An error occurred signing in: " + exception.Message);
    }
}
```

Notice that we did not have to write any code to handle user login or to manage the authentication flow. This is all handled for us within the SignInButton. We simply need to track the current state of the Live Connect session. As well, we can easily obtain the Session, Status, and Error information from the LiveConnectSessionChangedEventArgs parameter that is passed into the SessionChanged event.

We simply check the Status to determine whether the session was successfully connected and make the appropriate calls to the Live Connect APIs to obtain the information we need within the application.

The LiveConnectClient encapsulates the web service calls to the available REST APIs to manage a user's Live account. The LiveConnectClient class includes async methods (Figure 13-7) for each of the HTTP verbs that are used with REST-based services: GET, POST, PUT, MOVE, DELETE, and COPY.

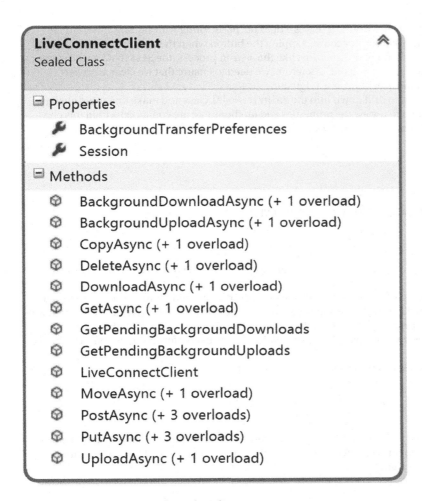

Figure 13-7. *LiveConnectClient class diagram*

As shown in Listing 13-1, to obtain the user's profile information, we instantiated the LiveConnectClient using the current Session object: client = new LiveConnectClient(e.Session).

To retrieve the user's profile information, we called the GetAsync method on the LiveConnectClient instance. The GetAsync method expects a string parameter that points to the REST API's object path. In this case, we want the user's profile information, so we will pass in "me". This is a valid object path that maps to the user's profile. Review the online REST reference article to view the full list of available object paths at http://msdn.microsoft.com/en-us/library/live/hh243648.aspx#objectdata.

The GetAsync method returns a dynamic object in the Result property of the LiveOperationResult object. The dynamic object contains all combined fields that are returned based on the object path passed into the GetAsync method, along with the scopes defined for application access during sign-in. In this case, the dynamic object is a User object. To view the list of fields returned in the User object, review the Live Connect REST API article online at http://msdn.microsoft.com/en-us/library/live/hh243648.aspx#user.

Finally, to serve as good developer citizens, we added exception handling to trap for the exception LiveConnectException. If an error occurred while attempting to communicate with the Microsoft Live services, then we can gracefully handle it and display a friendly message to the user.

This is a good place to mention that the SignInButton serves a dual purpose. Along with signing a user in, the button is also used to sign a user out of the Microsoft account. Tapping the button when the session is connected will trigger a sign-out process that is handled behind the scenes. Just like the sign-in process, the SessionChanged event will be triggered once the sign-out process has completed. Therefore, we need to ensure that we clear any user-specific information from the page when the user chooses to sign out.

Before we test the application, we need to drill down into the MainViewModel class and make one more change. Load the MainViewModel and take a moment to review the properties and methods that are contained within this class.

Notice that the ClientId property is not filled in with a valid ID:

```
public string ClientId
{
    get
    {
        return "TO DO: REGISTER YOUR APP FOR A CLIENT_ID ONLINE";
    }
}
```

You will need to modify this property to return the client ID that was generated in your Live Connect Developer Center account for this application.

Take a moment to review the LoadUserInfo method and the ResetUserInfo method. Both methods are called from the MainPage code-behind. The LoadUserInfo method accepts the LiveOperationResult.Result value that was returned when we requested the user's profile information through the LiveConnectClient's GetAsync method. It simply sets the properties within the view model, which in turn will display the user information in the view through the power of data binding.

At this point, we are ready to test the user sign-in process within our app!

Testing in the Emulator

Run the application in the emulator so that we can see what happens when the SignInButton is tapped and to observe the authentication flow that takes place. On initial launch, you will see the "Sign in" button and the status that indicates we are not signed in, as shown in Figure 13-8.

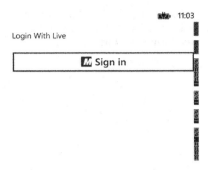

You are not signed in.

Figure 13-8. *Live "Sign" in button, branded with the Microsoft Live account logo*

Tap the "Sign in" button to initiate user authentication. Notice that the sign-in page displayed prompts for your Microsoft Live ID credentials (Figure 13-9). Enter your credentials and then tap "Sign in."

Figure 13-9. *The Live sign-in process prompts for credentials*

Upon successful verification of your credentials, the user consent page is displayed, as depicted in Figure 13-10. The permissions list that is displayed on this page reflect the scopes that we included in the SignInButton's Scopes property. Tap the Yes button to give the application permission to your basic profile information, birthday, and contacts information.

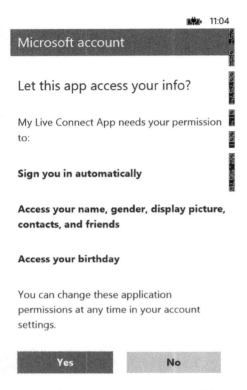

Figure 13-10. *User consent is required for access to the user's Live account info*

Once user consent is obtained, the SessionChanged event will be triggered. At this point, our code will execute, which will conduct an async call to obtain the user's profile information and display it in the MainPage, as shown in Figure 13-11.

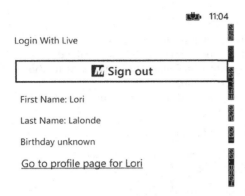

Figure 13-11. *Once the user is signed in, the requested Live account information is available within the application*

As you can see, we were able to include user authentication within our Windows Phone application simply by adding the SignInButton from the `Microsoft.Live.Controls` library, setting the ClientId to a valid ID that was generated specifically for your application, and defining the scope of the desired access within the application. That is how easy it is to include a sign-in process within your Windows Phone application!

To view the completed application, open the solution MyLiveConnectApp in the `\Chapter 13\ MyLiveConnectAppFinished` directory.

13-4. Manage the User's Outlook Calendar Information
Problem
You want to develop an app that allows a user to manage their Outlook calendar events within the application.

Solution
Leverage the Hotmail API, available as part of the Live Connect APIs, to access the user's calendar information.

How It Works

Similar to the concept that was discussed in Recipe 13-3, the Hotmail APIs packaged within the Live Connect APIs provide access to the user's online calendar. The `LiveConnectClient` will be used to retrieve the user's calendar information. We will simply need to pass in the object path `me/calendars` in the `LiveConnectClient`'s async methods to accomplish this goal. We can either `GET` or `POST` data to the user's Outlook calendar.

In addition to that, we will need to include one or more of the following extended scopes to ensure we obtain user consent so that our application can access the user's Outlook calendars:

- `wl.calendars`: Provides read-only access to the user's calendars and events

- `wl.calendars_update` : Provides read-write access to a user's calendars and events. This scope also provides the ability to create new calendars and delete calendars.

- `wl.events_create`: Allows the application to create events within the user's default calendar.

■ **Note**   Microsoft recently rebranded its popular Hotmail calendar to Outlook. However, the term *Hotmail* is still used in the Live Connect API documentation when referring to the Microsoft online calendar and contacts. In this chapter, we will refer to it as Outlook to conform to the recent rebranding. If you are searching the Live SDK documentation, keep in mind it may still be labeled as Hotmail.

When retrieving calendar data through the `LiveConnectClient`'s `GetAsync` method, the result that is returned is a `Calendar` object. To view the list of fields available in the `Calendar` object, review the Live Connect REST API article online at `http://msdn.microsoft.com/en-us/library/live/hh243648.aspx#calendar`.

The Code

Launch Visual Studio 2012 and open the project in the `\Chapter 13\ MyLiveConnectAppWithCalendar` directory. Notice that it is similar to the MyLiveConnect app discussed in Recipe 13-3 but has some additional tweaks. The most significant change was that we moved the user profile information to a separate page.

In addition, within the MainPage markup, notice that the `wl.calendar` scope has been added to allow the application to access the user's calendar data. The `wl.calendars_update` scope has been included as well so that we can update the user's calendar information from within the application.

Furthermore, HubTiles from the Windows Phone Toolkit are used in the MainPage, which will serve as our navigation menu. Notice in the MainPage code-behind, when a HubTile is tapped, it will navigate to the page that we specified in the HubTile's Tag property.

```
private void HubTile_Tap(object sender, System.Windows.Input.GestureEventArgs e)
{
    if (App.ViewModel.IsConnected)
    {
        HubTile selectedTile = (HubTile)sender;
        Uri pageUri = new Uri(string.Format("/{0}.xaml", selectedTile.Tag.ToString()),
UriKind.Relative);
        NavigationService.Navigate(pageUri);
    }
    else
    {
        MessageBox.Show("You must sign in first.");
    }
}
```

The Calendar HubTile will load the Calendars page, listing the user's Outlook calendars, as shown in Listing 13-2.

Listing 13-2. Retrieve the User's List of Outlook Calendars When the Calendars Page Loads

```
private async void Calendars_Loaded(object sender, RoutedEventArgs e)
{
    try
    {
        if (App.ViewModel.IsConnected)
        {
            LiveOperationResult operationResult = await App.ViewModel.LiveClient.GetAsync("me/calendars");
            dynamic eventsResult = ((dynamic)operationResult.Result).data;
            App.ViewModel.LoadCalendars(eventsResult);
        }
    }
    catch (LiveConnectException ex)
    {
        MessageBox.Show("Error occurred loading calendars: " + ex.Message);
    }
}
```

With the calendar information at hand, we can drill down to view events that are contained within a calendar by calling the LiveConnectClient's GetAsync method and passing in the object path of [calendarId]/events, where calendarId is the unique ID for the selected calendar.

In the Calendars page code-behind, notice that the SelectionChanged event for the LongListSelector control passes the selected calendar ID to the Events page on navigation.

```
        private void LongListSelector_SelectionChanged(object sender, System.Windows.Controls.
SelectionChangedEventArgs e)
            {
                LiveConnectCalendar selectedCalendar = calendarList.SelectedItem as LiveConnectCalendar;
                NavigationService.Navigate(new Uri("/Events.xaml?id=" + selectedCalendar.Id,
UriKind.RelativeOrAbsolute));
            }
```

Within the Events code-behind file, we simply retrieve the ID value from the NavigationContext's QueryString and use that in our object path when requesting the events list for the selected calendar, as shown in Listing 13-3. The result returned will be a list of Event objects. To view the list of fields available in the Event object, review the Live Connect REST API article online at http://msdn.microsoft.com/en-us/library/live/hh243648.aspx#event.

Listing 13-3. On Navigation to the Events Page, Retrieve a Specific Calendar's List of Events

```
protected override void OnNavigatedTo(System.Windows.Navigation.NavigationEventArgs e)
{
    LoadEvents();
}

private async void LoadEvents()
{
    try
    {
        if (NavigationContext.QueryString.ContainsKey("id") && App.ViewModel.IsConnected)
```

```
        {
            string calendarId = NavigationContext.QueryString["id"];
            LiveOperationResult operationResult = await App.ViewModel.LiveClient.GetAsync(string.
Format("{0}/events", calendarId));
            dynamic eventsResult = ((dynamic)operationResult.Result).data;
            App.ViewModel.LoadEvents(eventsResult);
        }
    }
    catch (LiveConnectException ex)
    {
        MessageBox.Show("Error occurred loading events: " + ex.Message);
    }
}
```

Also, since we included the `wl.calendars_update` scope, we can also create new calendars, update information on existing calendars, and delete calendars, provided the user has the either owner, co-owner, or read-write permissions on the calendar. Within the Calendars page, we have included a single button that creates a new calendar with some sample information when it is first selected. We were able to add a new calendar to the user's calendars list by calling the `PostAsync` method, passing in the object path of `me/calendars`, and passing in a new `Calendar` object. Listing 13-4 shows the call that is made to create the calendar.

Listing 13-4. Add a New Calendar to the User's Calendars List

```
Dictionary<string, object> newCalendar = new Dictionary<string, object>();
                newCalendar.Add("name", "My New Calendar");
                newCalendar.Add("description", "Sample to demonstrate adding and deleting
calendars");
                LiveOperationResult operationResult = await App.ViewModel.LiveClient.
PostAsync("me/calendars", newCalendar);
```

Once the calendar has been created, the calendars list is updated, and the button changes to a delete button, which will simply the delete the calendar we just added the next time the button is tapped. To delete a calendar, we simply call the `LiveConnectClient`'s `DeleteAsync` method, passing in only the unique calendar ID.

```
LiveOperationResult operationResult = await App.ViewModel.LiveClient.DeleteAsync(calendarId);
```

Testing in the Emulator

As we mentioned in Recipe 13-3, modify the `ClientId` property in the `MainViewModel` to the application ID you generated in your Microsoft Live account so that you can properly test this in the emulator. Once that is in place, launch the application in the emulator. When the application launches, sign in. Once connected, navigate to the calendars page. It will display a list of the calendars you currently have configured in your Outlook account (Figure 13-12).

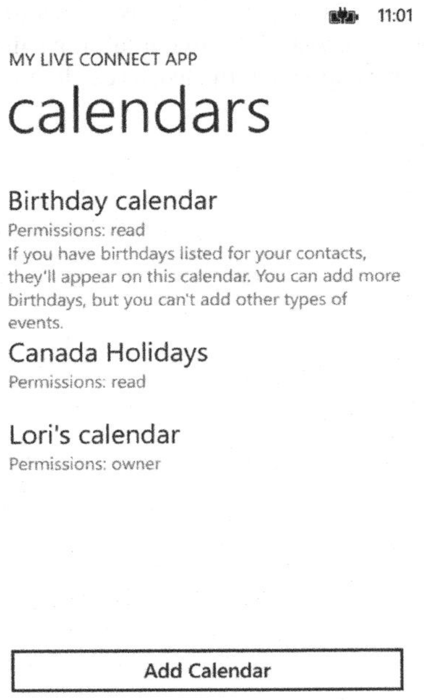

11:01

MY LIVE CONNECT APP

calendars

Birthday calendar
Permissions: read
If you have birthdays listed for your contacts,
they'll appear on this calendar. You can add more
birthdays, but you can't add other types of
events.

Canada Holidays
Permissions: read

Lori's calendar
Permissions: owner

Add Calendar

Figure 13-12. *Calendars list from the user's online Outlook account*

Next, click the Add Calendar button to create a new calendar. If the calendar has been created successfully, the list will refresh with the new calendar added to the list, as shown in Figure 13-13.

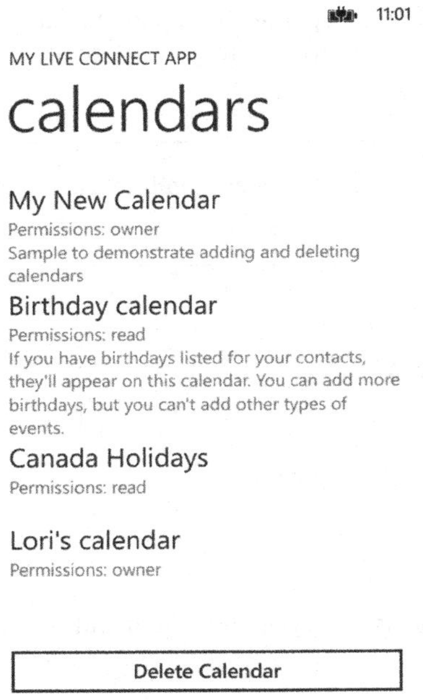

11:01

MY LIVE CONNECT APP

calendars

My New Calendar
Permissions: owner
Sample to demonstrate adding and deleting
calendars

Birthday calendar
Permissions: read
If you have birthdays listed for your contacts,
they'll appear on this calendar. You can add more
birthdays, but you can't add other types of
events.

Canada Holidays
Permissions: read

Lori's calendar
Permissions: owner

Delete Calendar

Figure 13-13. *New calendar added to the user's Outlook calendars*

To prove that this calendar was not just created locally, launch Internet Explorer, go to http://outlook.com, and sign in. Navigate to your Calendars view, and click the Settings button. This action will display a menu containing a list of calendars configured as part of your Outlook account. Notice that the new calendar appears in the list, as depicted in Figure 13-14.

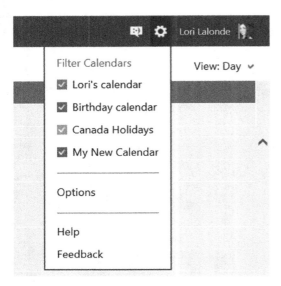

Figure 13-14. *The newly created calendar is accessible when logging into* Outlook.com

If you want to add or delete events from a calendar, the same concepts that we went over with GetAsync, PostAsync, and DeleteAsync apply, as we discussed in the calendars demonstration, except the object path that must be specified in the GetAsync and PostAsync calls will need to indicate me/events and the wl.events_create scope must be included in the sign-in process.

■ **Note**   A bonus project is packaged with this chapter in the directory \Chapter 13\MyLiveConnectAppWithContacts, which demonstrates the same concepts discussed in this recipe but against the Outlook Contacts list.

13-5. Download Files from the User's SkyDrive
Problem

You want to develop an app that allows the user to access and manage the user's SkyDrive files.

Solution

Leverage the SkyDrive API, available as part of the Live Connect APIs, to access the user's SkyDrive account and download files.

How It Works

Following the pattern of Recipes 13-3 and 13-4, the LiveConnectClient will be used to retrieve the user's SkyDrive contents. Before attempting to access the SkyDrive through the APIs available, we will need to include the extended scope, wl.skydrive, to obtain permission from the user to get a read-only list of SkyDrive contents, as well as download files from the user's SkyDrive account.

To retrieve the list of contents in the SkyDrive root folder or child folders, we will once again leverage the LiveConnectClient's GetAsync method call, passing in the relevant object path. To view a list of valid object paths for SkyDrive access, refer to the SkyDrive API article online at http://msdn.microsoft.com/en-us/library/live/jj680723.aspx.

To download a file from SkyDrive, we will leverage the DownloadAsync method call, passing in the unique ID of the file we want to download. This method writes the file content to a stream, at which point you can do what you want. Some common options include saving the file to isolated storage and loading the file content into the app.

For this recipe, our application will use the object path me/skydrive/files to load the top-level files and folders available in the SkyDrive account when the SkyDrive Contents page is first loaded. The page will display the list of folders and files in a list. Selecting a folder will drill down to display the folder contents. Selecting a file will prompt the user to download the file.

The Code

Launch Visual Studio 2012 and open the project within the \Chapter13\ MyLiveConnectAppWithSkyDrive directory.

Note that we added the wl.skydrive scope to the SignInButton Scopes property in the MainPage markup. As well, there is a new HubTile, which allows us to navigate to the SkyDrive Contents page. On initial load of this page, we retrieve the list of items at the top level in the user's SkyDrive account, as shown in Listing 13-5.

Listing 13-5. SkyDriveContents Page Retrieves Top-Level SkyDrive Items During Load

```
private async void SkyDriveContents_Loaded(object sender, RoutedEventArgs e)
{
    try
    {
        if (App.ViewModel.LiveClient != null)
        {
            LiveOperationResult operationResult = await App.ViewModel.LiveClient.GetAsync("me/
skydrive/files");
            dynamic skyDriveResult = ((dynamic)operationResult.Result).data;
            App.ViewModel.LoadSkyDriveContents(skyDriveResult);
        }
    }
    catch (LiveConnectException ex)
    {
        MessageBox.Show("Error occurred loading files from SkyDrive: " + ex.Message);
    }
}
```

Within the SelectionChanged event for the LongListSelector control, if the selected item is a folder, another call is made to the GetAsync method call, passing in the object path [folder_id]/files, in order to load the folder's contents (Listing 13-6).

Listing 13-6. *SkyDriveContents Page Retrieves the Selected Folder Contents or Downloads the Selected File*

```
private async void LongListSelector_SelectionChanged(object sender, SelectionChangedEventArgs e)
{
    LiveConnectSkyDriveItem selectedItem = this.skyDriveList.SelectedItem as
LiveConnectSkyDriveItem;
    if (!selectedItem.IsFolder)
    {
        MessageBoxResult result = MessageBox.Show("Would you like to download this file?", "",
MessageBoxButton.OKCancel);
        if (result == MessageBoxResult.OK)
        {
            LiveConnectClient client = App.ViewModel.LiveClient;
            LiveDownloadOperationResult operationResult = await
App.ViewModel.LiveClient.DownloadAsync(selectedItem.Id);

            MessageBox.Show("Download completed. Now saving to IsolatedStorage...");

            ...
        }
    }
    else
    {
        LiveOperationResult operationResult = await
App.ViewModel.LiveClient.GetAsync(string.Format("{0}/files", selectedItem.Id));
        dynamic filesResult = ((dynamic)operationResult.Result).data;
        App.ViewModel.LoadSkyDriveContents(filesResult);
    }

}
```

If the selected item is a file, the application will prompt the user to download the file. If the user agrees to download the file, the LiveConnectClient's DownloadAsync method is called, passing in the file's unique ID. Once the download completes, the file content will be returned in the LiveDownloadOperationResult object's Stream property. Within the sample application in this chapter, the application conducts a save of the file stream to isolated storage. If you are not familiar with isolated storage or how to save files to isolated storage on a Windows Phone device, you may want to revisit Chapter 11's Recipe 11-1, which discusses this topic in detail.

The SkyDrive APIs provide extensive functionality for accessing photos, videos, files, and folders in a user's SkyDrive account. In this recipe, we demonstrated a simple file download; however, you could also add the ability to upload files, move files and folders, copy files, and delete files and folders, among many other actions. Visit the SkyDrive API page at http://msdn.microsoft.com/en-us/library/live/hh826521.aspx to learn more about how to manage a user's SkyDrive account from within a Windows Phone application.

Testing in the Emulator

As we mentioned in Recipe 13-3, modify the ClientId property in the MainViewModel to the application ID you generated in your Microsoft Live account so that you can properly test this in the emulator. Once that is in place, launch the application in the emulator. When the application launches, sign in.

Once connected, navigate to the SkyDrive page. It will display a list of folders you created in your SkyDrive, along with any files you have uploaded. For my account, I have two folders at the top level: Blog and CTTDNUG (Figure 13-15).

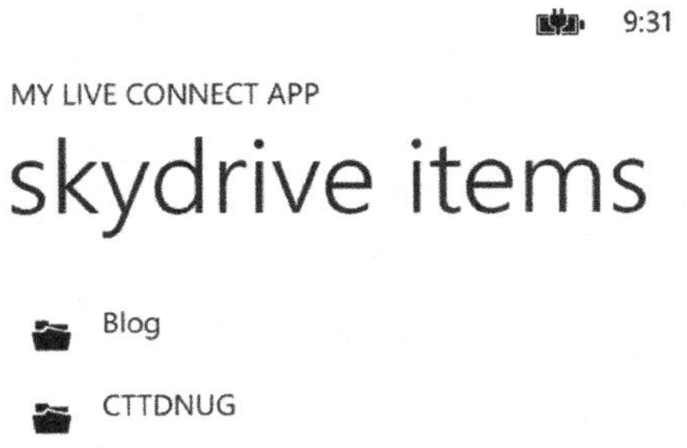

📶 9:31

MY LIVE CONNECT APP

skydrive items

📁 Blog

📁 CTTDNUG

Figure 13-15. *SkyDrive folders list from the user's online Outlook account*

Click a folder to view its contents. I have chosen to drill down into the CTTDNUG folder, where I store slide decks for my user group, as shown in Figure 13-16.

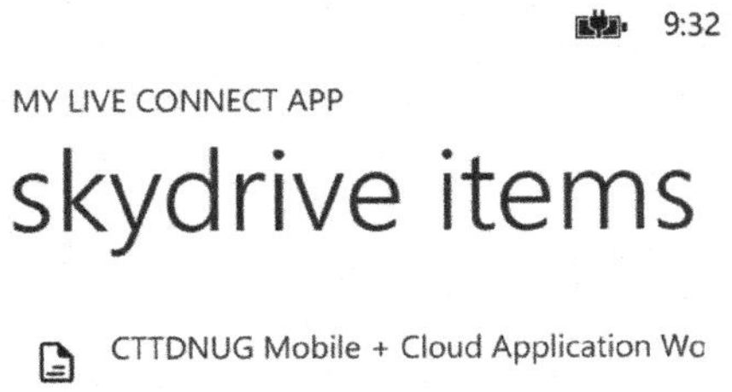

📶 9:32

MY LIVE CONNECT APP

skydrive items

📄 CTTDNUG Mobile + Cloud Application Wo

Figure 13-16. *SkyDrive files*

In this case, I have one slide deck from a "Mobile and Cloud" workshop we hosted for our user group members. If you have a file in your list, click it to initiate the file download. You will be prompted to confirm the file download (Figure 13-17). This was a prompt we included in the code when a user selected a file in the LongListSelector control. Refer to Listing 13-6 to see where this was added.

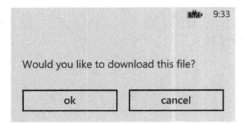

Figure 13-17. *Prompt the user to confirm the file selected for download*

Click the "ok" button to proceed with the file download. You will see a few more messages indicating that the file was downloaded and then saved successfully. If you so desire, you can enhance this application by launching the file in the appropriate application after it is saved to the device.

CHAPTER 14

■ ■ ■

Publishing Your App

Now that you are equipped with the skills to build mobile apps for Windows Phone, you are ready to become a full-fledged mobile app publisher! In this chapter, we will discuss how you can monetize your applications, provide trial versions of paid applications, and walk through the steps necessary to officially submit your application for publication to the Windows Phone Store!

In this chapter, we will walk through the following recipes:

- 14-1. Monetize your application using in-app advertisements

- 14-2. Provide a trial version of your Windows Phone 8 app

- 14-3. Submit your mobile app to the Windows Phone store

14-1. Monetize Your Application Using In-App Advertisements
Problem

You plan to publish a free app to the Windows Phone Store but would like to still find a way to make money from your app.

Solution

Create a Microsoft pubCenter account, and leverage the Microsoft Advertising SDK in your application.

How It Works

Microsoft's pubCenter enables Windows Phone developers to monetize their applications by equipping them with the controls to quickly and easily incorporate ads within their applications. When users click on these ads, the developer earns money from the advertiser through Microsoft's Mobile Ad Exchange. The Mobile Ad Exchange enables multiple advertisers to buy ads within your apps, by bidding on impressions generated by your users, which maximizes the revenue opportunity for you, the developer. When you create a pubCenter account, you must register each application in which you plan to provide advertisements, along with each ad unit you plan to include in the application. Each ad unit allows you to define the guidelines for the types of ads that will appear in your application. In this way, ads that are relevant to the target audience of your application will appear in your application, thereby increasing the potential of click-through rates by your users.

To enable delivery of these ads within your applications, Microsoft has conveniently packaged the controls you will need within yet another SDK! The Microsoft Advertising SDK for Windows Phone is installed along with the Windows Phone 8 SDK (that's right, it's an SDK within an SDK) and includes controls which display the ads that are served up through the Microsoft pubCenter. The ads that are delivered to your application are based on the ad unit configuration settings that you defined in pubCenter. Is that clear as mud? Don't worry! You will realize how this all ties together as we progress through this recipe.

The ad controls included in the SDK support the display of either text or image-based advertisements and support actions such as Click to Web, Click to Call, and Click to Marketplace. Since the Microsoft Advertising SDK is tightly coupled with your Microsoft pubCenter account, one benefit you receive as the Windows App publisher, is having access to real-time reporting on ad performance within your application. Another benefit is that you will be able to tweak your ad unit configuration and keyword selection to maximize your revenue earning potential. So, let's get started!

Create a Microsoft pubCenter Account

To create your pubCenter account, login to your Windows Phone Developer Center account and go to the Account Summary page. Under the Ad Network heading, you will see a link to create your pubCenter account. Click the link to get started.

Alternatively, you may go to http://pubcenter.microsoft.com and sign up by clicking the Sign up now button. However, you will need to be sure to go back to your Dev Center account and input your pubCenter Account number there to ensure that you properly tie the two accounts together. From the pubCenter site, click the Sign up now button as shown in Figure 14-1.

Make money by including ads in your applications

Advertisers will pay to present ads that your users will see. Learn more.

Sign up for pubCenter   Sign up now

Application developers

 Windows 8

Add advertising to your Windows 8 application with a few easy steps. Learn more.

 Windows Phone

Add advertising to your Windows Phone application with a few easy steps. Learn more.

Figure 14-1. *Microsoft pubCenter main page*

You will then be prompted for your Windows Live ID login credentials (Figure 14-2). If you do not have a Windows Live ID account, you may create one by clicking the link, "Sign up for a new Windows Live ID now."

Enable ads for your Windows Phone or Windows 8 applications in 3 easy steps

Three easy steps: 1. Sign in with your Windows Live ID 2. Sign up with pubCenter   3. Register your first application and create an ad unit (optional)

1 Sign in with your Windows Live ID

If you have a Hotmail, Messenger, or Microsoft Office Live account, you have a Windows Live ID (example555@hotmail.com).

Sign up for a new ♫ Windows Live ID now

Sign in to Microsoft PubCenter   Help

Email address: [ ]

Password: [ ]
                                Forgot your password?

                                        Sign in

○ Save my email address and password
○ Save my email address
● Always ask for my email address and password

♫ Windows Live ID
Works with Windows Live, MSN, and Microsoft Passport sites
Account Services | Privacy Statement | Terms of Use
©2013 Microsoft

Figure 14-2. *Sign in using your Live ID*

Upon entering your Live ID credentials on the pubCenter sign up page, click the Sign In button.

At this point, you will have the opportunity to enter information about your business. If you signed up directly on the pubcenter.com site, outside of the Developer Center Dashboard, take note of your pubCenter account ID. Login to your Windows Phone Developer Center Account, go to the Account summary page, and enter in your pubCenter account ID to associate the two accounts.

Create Application Ad Units

Once you have a pubCenter account associated with your Windows Phone Developer Center account, you can create ad units for your application within your Windows Phone Developer Center Dashboard when you initiate a new application submission. Prior to the pubCenter account integration within the Windows Phone Developer Center, you were able to register your application and create the related ad units through pubCenter, incorporate the ads in your application, and then submit your application to the Windows Phone store. This, in my opinion, seemed to follow a natural order.

Now, you will notice that you will need to "start" your application submission process before you are ready to submit your application simply to generate your ad unit Ids that you will need to include in your application. This requires you to pause the submission process, go back to your app, and incorporate the related application Id and ad unit Ids that were generated for your in-app advertisements. At that point, you can revisit your application submission to complete the process by uploading your new XAP file and related images.

To create ad units for your application, click the Submit App link in your dashboard. On the Submit app page, click the App info link (Figure 14-3).

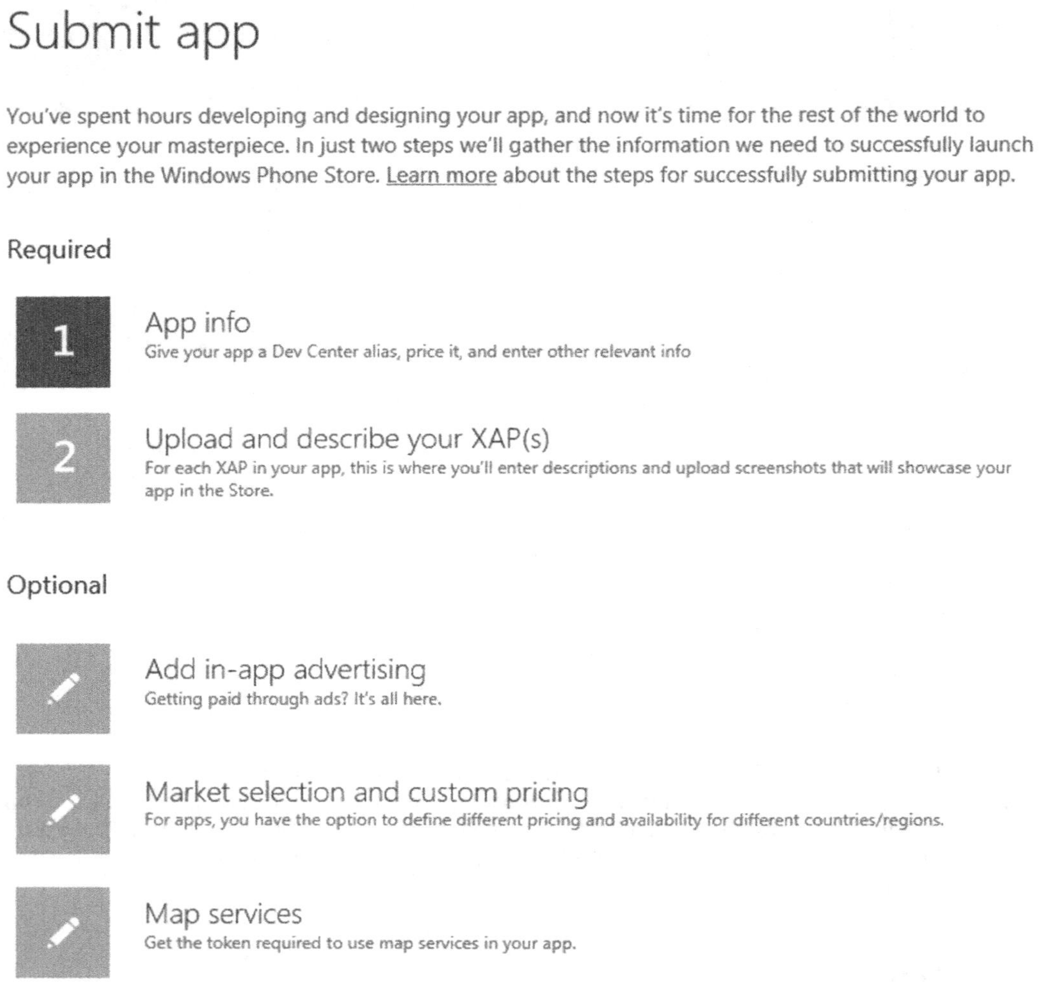

Submit app

You've spent hours developing and designing your app, and now it's time for the rest of the world to experience your masterpiece. In just two steps we'll gather the information we need to successfully launch your app in the Windows Phone Store. Learn more about the steps for successfully submitting your app.

Required

App info
Give your app a Dev Center alias, price it, and enter other relevant info

Upload and describe your XAP(s)
For each XAP in your app, this is where you'll enter descriptions and upload screenshots that will showcase your app in the Store.

Optional

Add in-app advertising
Getting paid through ads? It's all here.

Market selection and custom pricing
For apps, you have the option to define different pricing and availability for different countries/regions.

Map services
Get the token required to use map services in your app.

Figure 14-3. Submit app page

On the App info page, enter a name for your application and select a category. The name entered here is simply the name associated to your application in your Dev Center Dashboard, so don't get hung up on trying to select the perfect app name just yet. The application name the customer sees is the one defined in your application project. We will discuss the app submission process in detail in Recipe 14-3. However, the category you select is important, as well as the related subcategory (when applicable), as this will determine the type of advertisements that are delivered to your application and displayed in the AdControl. Once you save the app info and return to the Submit app page, you will be able to select the Add in-app advertising link. Click this link to navigate to the in-app advertising page, as shown in Figure 14-4.

Add in-app advertising

A mobile application ad unit defines the size and types of ads that appear in your app. Learn more about ad units.

pubCenter app alias*
This name is used to refer to your app in pubCenter.

My Windows Phone App

pubCenter Application ID

None

To create new ad units, add a name and select Generate ad unit ID.*

Ad unit name   Size   ID

MyWPAppAd_300X50   300x50   Generate ad unit ID
                            480x80
                            480x640
                            480x800
                            480x853

Close

Figure 14-4. Create ad units for your application during your app submission process

The first thing that you will define is an alias for your application. To simplify things, you will likely use your application's name or the name you defined as the app alias for your Dev Center account (back in the App info page).

Next, you will want to generate one or more ad units for your application. Note that you may define multiple ad units, of different sizes, for a single application. The dropdown list provides the following ad sizes:

- 300 X 50

- 480 X 80

- 480 X 640

- 480 X 800

- 480 X 853

Microsoft guidelines recommend using an ad size of 480 X 80 for mobile applications. The larger sizes are meant for non-Windows Phone applications. The smaller ad size of 300 X 50 is provided for backward compatibility. However, the smaller ad size should still be rendered in an AdControl with a size of 480 X 80.

To generate an ad unit, enter a name in the Ad unit name text box, select a size from the Size dropdown list, and then click the Generate ad unit ID link. Once your first ad unit Id is generated, notice that your pubCenter Application ID will change from "None" to a GUID. This GUID is unique to your application and will remain the same across all ad units that you generate for this application. Your application Id and ad unit Ids are unique to your application and should not be shared.

Use the Microsoft AdControl

The Microsoft AdControl is contained within the Microsoft.Advertising.Mobile.UI namespace. You must include the following capabilities in your Application Manifest when incorporating in-app ads using the Microsoft AdControl: ID_CAP_PHONEDIALER, ID_CAP_IDENTITY_USER, and ID_CAP_MEDIALIB_PHOTO.

To include an AdControl on your page, simply drag-and-drop the AdControl from your toolbox to your page. Alternatively, you can manually enter the necessary XAML markup, which requires including the following namespace declaration within the PhoneApplicationPage element, xmlns:UI="clr-namespace:Microsoft. Advertising.Mobile.UI;assembly=Microsoft.Advertising.Mobile.UI", as well as the AdControl markup:

```
<UI:AdControl
    x:Name="myAdControl"
    IsAutoRefreshEnabled="True"
    Width="480"
    Height="80"
    ApplicationId="INSERT YOUR APPLICATION ID HERE"
    AdUnitId="INSERT YOUR AD UNIT ID HERE"
    ErrorOccurred="AdControl_ErrorOccurred" />
```

Within the markup, you must explicitly set the Width and Height of your AdControl to the recommended size of 480 X 80. You must also enter the ApplicationId and AdUnitId values in the markup. Attempting to bind these properties to a ViewModel property will crash. It doesn't seem to take binding very well. Also note that you will need to handle the ErrorOccurred event, because the AdControl is notorious for crashing unexpectedly. Handling the ErrorOccurred event will give you the opportunity to recreate the instance of the AdControl programmatically and possibly recover gracefully, as shown in listing 14-1.

Listing 14-1. Reinstantiate the AdControl Within the ErrorOccurred Event

```
private string applicationId = "INSERT YOUR APPLICATION ID HERE";
private string adUnitId = "INSERT YOUR AD UNIT ID HERE";
private void AdControl_ErrorOccurred(object sender, Microsoft.Advertising.AdErrorEventArgs e)
{
    myAdControl = new AdControl(applicationId, adUnitId, true);
}
```

Handling the ErrorOccurred event alone will not necessarily rectify scenarios where ads are not displaying as expected in your application. There may be instances where the AdControl will not render at all due to a lack of ad availability. This may be a result of low ad inventory in the Mobile Ad Exchange for your application's selected category and/or related subcategory. The availability of ads is dependent on advertisers' actively participating in the marketplace. As well, the categories configured for your ad units may not have ads available, which may require you to modify the application's defined category, or associated subcategory, within your Dev Center Account to allow your application to receive ads from a broader market.

When incorporating the AdControl in your application, note that you must test the application on a device in order to view the ads in your application. Applications running within the emulator will not receive live ads. Alternatively, for testing within the emulator, you may use the Application Id of test_client and one of the following ad unit Ids: TextAd, Image480_80, or Image300_50.

■ **Note** The AdControl can be used in standard Windows Phone 7.x and Windows Phone 8 applications. When developing XNA games, you must use the DrawableAd and AdGameComponent classes to incorporate in-app advertisements.

When designing your application with in-app advertisements, it is good practice to adhere to the recommended usage guidelines, as follows:

1. Ensure your AdControl is configured at the the recommended size of 480 X 80, and ad units are generated at this size only.

2. Place the AdControl at the top or bottom of the page

3. When a page contains a ScrollViewer control, place the AdControl outside of the ScrollViewer so that the ad always remains in view.

4. When a page contains a Pivot control, place the AdControl outside of the Pivot control so that the ad always remains in view or place a separate AdControl within each pivot item to display different ads.

5. When a page contains a Panorama control, place the ad outside of the Panorama control so that the ad always remains in view, or place a separate AdControl within each panorama page to display different ads.

6. Ensure that if your application uses alternate foreground and background colors, instead of the standard system colors, that the AdControl's border and text content are readable when the device theme is set to either light or dark theme.

Let's take a look at how this all comes together. Launch Visual Studio 2012 and open the sample project in the \Chapter 14\MyWindowsPhoneApp directory. Double-click the MyAdPage.xaml file to view the XAML markup. You will notice that AdControl markup is similar to the markup that was depicted earlier in this section, with the only modification being that we have specified the use of the test application Id and ad unit Id, so that we can view the ad in the emulator. Open the code behind for this page, to see that the only code on this page is that which handles the AdControl's ErrorOccurred event. The majority of the work involved when including ads within your app are primarily in the application and ad unit configuration in your Windows Phone Developer Center account.

Launch the application in the emulator to see how in-app advertisements will look within the application. As shown in Figure 14-5, the first page simply contains 3 buttons: Single Page, Pivot Page, and Panorama Page. The Single Page displays the ads at the top of the page.

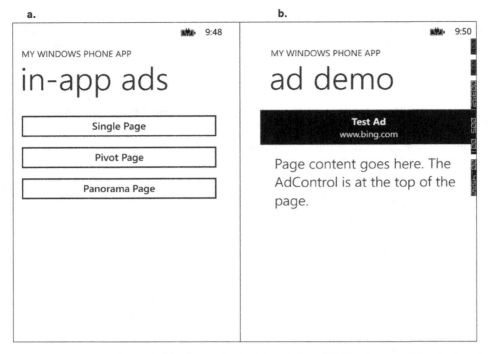

Figure 14-5. *Example usage of in-app ads: a) Main page, and b) Single page with ads placed at the top of the page*

Tap each one of these buttons to view how the AdControl placement works within each page. Figure 14-6 depicts the ad placement within a panorama page.

Figure 14-6. *Panorama control with a separate AdControl placed in each panorama page*

As you can see, it is very easy to incorporate in-app advertisements within your Windows Phone application. Through your Windows Phone Developer Center account and pubCenter account integration, along with the Microsoft Advertising SDK, you can include in-app advertisments in your existing app in no time and with minimal code.

14-2. Provide a Trial Version of Your App

Problem

You plan to publish a paid app to the Windows Phone store. You would like to provide a trial version to entice users to try the app with limited features to encourage downloads and potentially increase app sales.

Solution

Use the `Microsoft.Phone.Marketplace.LicenseInformation` class to limit features when your app is running as a trial version.

How It Works

The Windows Phone SDK makes it easy for developers to provide trial versions of their apps without the need to create two separate applications. The `Microsoft.Phone.Marketplace` namespace contains the `LicenseInformation` class that allows you to provide a limited feature set in your existing application simply by calling the method, `IsTrial`. This method returns a boolean value to indicate if the application is currently running as a trial version. You can make use of this method's return value to limit the available features when your app is running as a trial version. It is best to give some thought to which features will be excluded within the trial version. In this way, you can include code within your application to hide or disable these features when the app is running in trial mode.

■ **Note** When developing games using the XNA Framework, you will need to use the `GamerServices.Guide` class instead, as it comes with built-in trial and purchase simulation features. For more information, refer to the MSDN article, Simulating Trial Mode for Marketplace Content, at `http://msdn.microsoft.com/en-us/library/dd282459.aspx`.

When providing a trial version of your application, you should also allow the user to purchase the full version right from within your application. This can be accomplished by incorporating a button that launches the application product page in the Windows Phone Store, through a call to the `MarketplaceDetailTask.Show` method.

Finally, when it is time to submit your application to the Windows Phone Store, you will need to indicate that your app will offer free trials by including a checkmark in the box, "Offer free trials of this app," during the application submission process in the Windows Phone Developer Center (Figure 14-7).

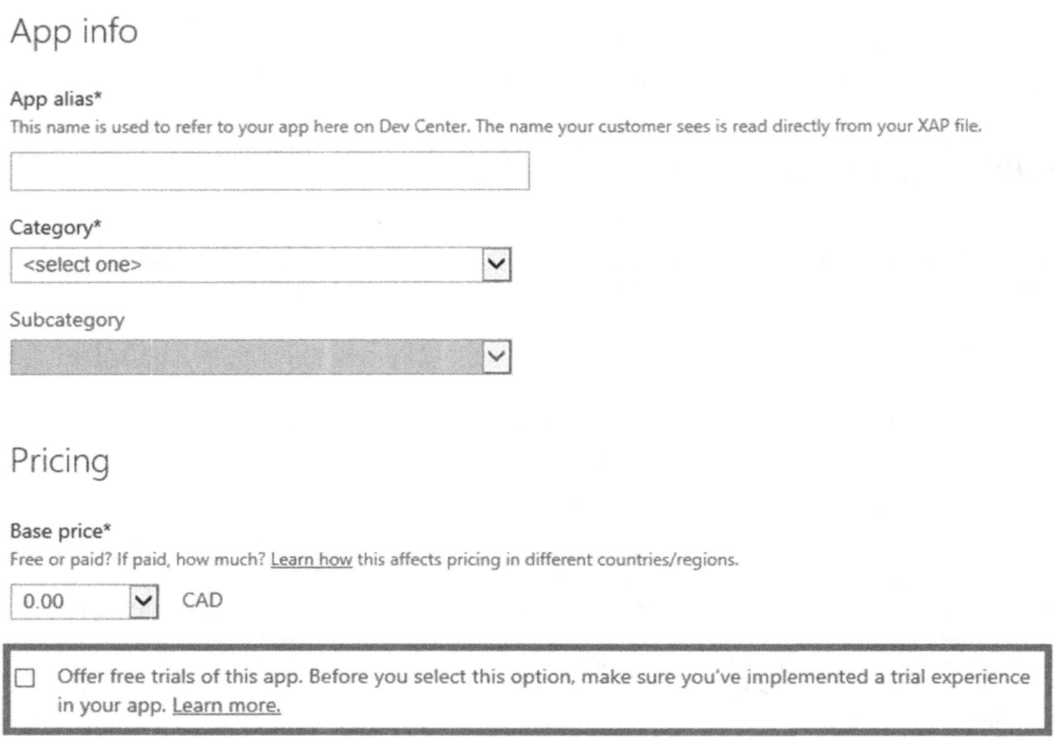

App info

App alias*

This name is used to refer to your app here on Dev Center. The name your customer sees is read directly from your XAP file.

[   ]

Category*

[<select one>   ▼]

Subcategory

[▼]

Pricing

Base price*

Free or paid? If paid, how much? Learn how this affects pricing in different countries/regions.

[0.00   ▼] CAD

☐ Offer free trials of this app. Before you select this option, make sure you've implemented a trial experience in your app. Learn more.

Figure 14-7. *Indicate that your app offers free trials during the submission process*

This ensures that when your app is published, Microsoft will make both a trial and full license available for your application. As well, a `Try` button will be displayed within your application's product page in the Store. When the user purchases the application, the trial license is simply replaced with a full license.

Trial licenses do not expire, so it is not a good idea to provide a time-based trial offering of your application. It is best to include limited functionality that provides just enough functionality to allow your user to test out the application but leaves them wanting for more. This will hopefully entice your users to eventually purchase the full version.

Now that we have discussed what you need to do to create a trial version of an application, let's walk through the process and see how it all comes together!

The Code

Launch Visual Studio 2012, and open the TrafficView application located in the \Chapter 14\TrafficViewWithTrialStart directory. In the App.xaml.cs file, include the following using directive: using `Microsoft.Phone.Marketplace;`

Next, we need to add a new static property that will contain a new instance of the LicenseInformation object, along with a new static boolean property that we will use to store the return value of the `LicenseInformation.IsTrial` method call. We will also create a method called CheckLicense, which will be called from the `Application_Launching` and `Application_Activated` events, as shown in Listing 14-2.

Listing 14-2. Cache the Check for Trial Version License in the App Code Behind

```
private static LicenseInformation licenseInfo = new LicenseInformation();
private static bool isTrial = true;
public static bool IsTrial
{
    get
    {
        return isTrial;
    }
    set
    {
        isTrial = value;
    }
}

private void CheckLicense()
{
#if DEBUG
    IsTrial = true;
#else
    IsTrial = licenseInformation.IsTrial();
#endif
}

private void Application_Launching(object sender, LaunchingEventArgs e)
{
    CheckLicense();
}

private void Application_Activated(object sender, ActivatedEventArgs e)
{
    CheckLicense();
}
```

Note that we also included a special check using #if DEBUG...#else...#endif to set the IsTrial property to True when running in Debug mode. Since there is no license information available when running within the emulator, this is how we will simulate a trial mode experience for testing purposes.

Next, open the MainPage.xaml file and add a button to the bottom of the page, which will allow the user to buy the full version of the application, and include an event handler for the Tap event. This button will only display only when the application is running as a trial version:

```
<Button Name="trialButton"
        Content="buy the full version"
        Tap="trialButton_Tap"/>
```

In the MainPage code behind, override the OnNavigatedTo event, and set the Visibility of the button to display only when the IsTrial static property within the App class is set to True. As well, include a call to the view model's LoadTrafficList event, so that we can be sure to refresh the list with a limited number of traffic views.

Also, we will need to instantiate a new MarketplaceDetailTask object and store it in a class level variable in the MainPage code behind. Within the trialButton_Tap event, we simply need to call the Show method on the instance of the MarketplaceDetailTask object. The resulting code is shown in Listing 14-3.

Listing 14-3. Managing the UI Based on Whether the App is Running in Trial Mode

```
protected override void OnNavigatedTo(System.Windows.Navigation.NavigationEventArgs e)
{
    trialButton.Visibility = (App.IsTrial) ? System.Windows.Visibility.Visible :
System.Windows.Visibility.Collapsed;
    App.ViewModel.LoadTrafficList();
}
MarketplaceDetailTask task = new MarketplaceDetailTask();
private void trialButton_Tap(object sender, System.Windows.Input.GestureEventArgs e)
{
    task.Show();
}
```

Finally, within the `TrafficViewModel` class, we need to modify the `LoadTrafficList` method to ensure that only two of the four traffic views are loaded in the dropdown list when running in trial mode, as shown in Listing 14-4.

Listing 14-4. Limit Traffic View Options When Running in Trial Mode

```
public void LoadTrafficList()
{
    TrafficItems = new ObservableCollection<TrafficItemViewModel>();
    TrafficItems.Add(new TrafficItemViewModel { Description = "E.C. Row near Lauzon Pkwy",
ImageName = "loc27.jpg" });
    TrafficItems.Add(new TrafficItemViewModel { Description = "Howard near Hwy 3",
ImageName = "loc10.jpg" });

    if (App.IsTrial == false)
    {
        //only include the additional views when it's a full version application
        TrafficItems.Add(new TrafficItemViewModel { Description = "Hwy 401 near Hwy 3",
ImageName = "loc89.jpg" });
        TrafficItems.Add(new TrafficItemViewModel { Description = "St. Clair College near Hwy 3",
ImageName = "loc08.jpg" });
    }

    LoadLastAppState();
}
```

With that in place, we can now run our application in the emulator to see what the user experience will be like when the application is installed as a trial. Notice that the "buy full version" button appears at the bottom, and our dropdown list of traffic views only lists 2 possible views, as illustrated in Figure 14-8.

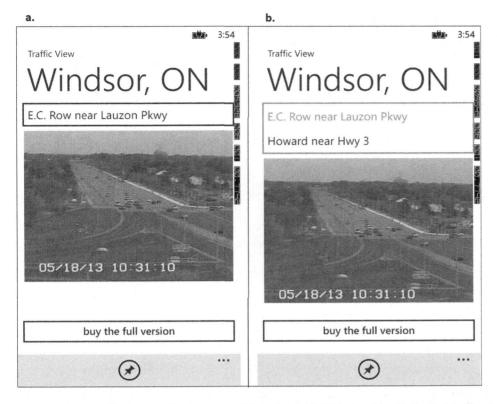

Figure 14-8. *TrafficView application as a trial version: a) initial view, b) with limited traffic view selections*

Tap the buy button to simulate the experience the user will have when attempting to purchase the full featured version of the application. As depicted in Figure 14-9, you can see a shadow of a product page in the emulator, but an error is displayed indicating that there was a problem with the request. If the error code listed is 805a0194, then this indicates a "successful" execution of the MarketplaceDetailTask.Show method in the emulator.

Figure 14-9. *Error code 805a0194 indicates a successful call in the emulator for the MarketplaceDetailTask.Show method*

When the application is actually running as a trial application that was downloaded from the Windows Phone Store onto an actual device, the buy action will launch the application's product page, allowing the user to buy the full version of the application.

That is all it takes to include a trial version of your application! In my opinion, I think it's a pretty sweet deal that Microsoft handles the license management for Windows Phone publishers, which in turn simplifies life tremendously for the average developer turned publisher. You only need to create a single app and include simple boolean checks to turn on/off features to provide a trial mode of your application. If this doesn't knock your socks off, then I don't know what else will!

14-3. Submit Your App to the Windows Phone Store

Problem

You have fully functional mobile app that is ready to be published to the Windows Phone Store.

Solution

Prepare your application for submission, then login to your Windows Phone Developer Center account and submit your app to the Windows Phone Store.

How It Works

Submitting your application to the Windows Phone Store can seem like a daunting task. There is a list of things you will need to ensure are completed before you can even begin the app submission process. First and foremost, Microsoft defines a slew of certification requirements that must be met for your application to pass testing and to be published to the Windows Phone Store. The list is quite extensive, and many of the requirements may not apply to your application specifically. It is important that you take the time to review the app certification requirements for Windows Phone at http://msdn.microsoft.com/en-us/library/windowsphone/develop/hh184843(v=vs.105).aspx.

This article contains subarticles, which contain quite a lot of information, and is not for the faint of heart. But for those developers who are serious about publishing Windows Phone applications, this is something you will want to use as a reference when submitting your applications. It is a good idea to bookmark this link and refer to it whenever you are ready to submit a new application to the Windows Phone Store.

Some of the common checks you should perform include, but are not limited to, the following:

- Test your application in both dark and light themes within the emulator to verify all text displays as expected.

- Create a custom app icon and tile images and associate them with your application from within the Application Manifest.

- Verify that your application's XAP file is no larger than 1 GB in size.

- Build your application using the Release configuration in Visual Studio

- Verify the Application Manifest information is configured properly.

- Provide at least one screenshot for each of the resolutions your application will support.

Application Manifest Configuration

Verify the settings within your Application Manifest are configured properly across all sections: Application UI, Capabilities, Requirements, and Packaging.

- Application UI tab: This tab is where you will define your application's display name, description, app icon, and tile images.

- Capabilities tab: The appropriate capabilities must be included in your manifest to ensure that your application runs properly.

- Requirements tab: You may also specify minimum hardware requirements to ensure that users can only install your application if their device is able to execute the features within it (e.g., a camera application should require that a device has a rear-facing camera, at a minimum).

- Packaging tab: This tab is where you will specify your author name, publisher name, version number, default language, and supported languages. Note that your Windows Phone 8 app will fail certification if the Default Language is not set.

Capturing Screenshots for Application Submission

You will need to ensure that you have taken at least one screenshot of your application in each of the supported resolutions, which will be uploaded during the application submission process.

To capture the necessary screenshots for the app submission process, build your application in Visual Studio 2012 using the Release configuration, select the emulator for the desired resolution that you wish to simulate, then select "Deploy [app name]" from the Build menu to install your application within the emulator. Once it is successfully deployed, you should launch your application in the emulator through the application list in the emulator.

Next, click the ➤➤ button in the sidebar that appears to the right of the emulator. This will cause the Additional Tools screen to display, as shown in Figure 14-10.

Figure 14-10. *Use the Additional Tools within the emulator to capture screenshots of the application*

Click on the Screenshot tab. You will notice that the tab page contains two buttons: Capture and Save. As well, notice that the resolution of the screen is displayed in the bottom left corner of the page. Click the Capture button. An image of your screenshot will appear in the Screenshot page (Figure 14-11).

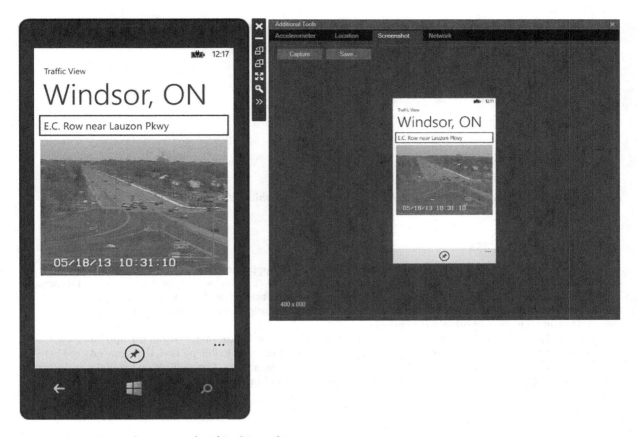

Figure 14-11. Screenshot captured within the emulator

Click Save... to launch the Windows Save As dialog box. Select the directory location where you wish to keep your screenshots contained within, and provide a unique name for the image. When generating screenshots for multiple resolutions, I prefer to create subdirectories for each of the resolutions that I will be supporting, and store the respective screenshots in the proper directories. This simplifies the application submission process when it comes time to upload the necessary screenshots for each resolution.

Submitting Your Application to the Windows Phone Store

Once you have confirmed that the Application Manifest is configured properly, build a Release version of your application in Visual Studio. This will be the XAP file that you will submit to the Store.

Windows Phone Developer Center Dashboard

Navigate to http://dev.windowsphone.com and login using your Developer Center Account credentials. Upon login, your Dashboard will appear within the browser window. To the left of the Dashboard, you will notice navigation links, including one labeled Submit App as depicted in Figure 14-12. Click this link to start the application submission process.

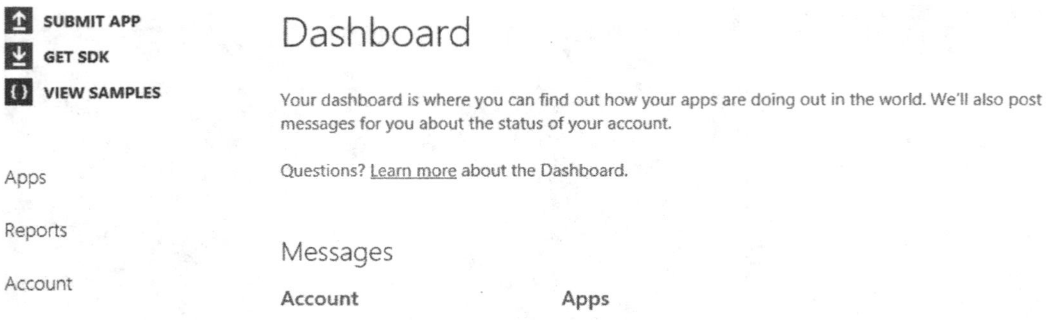

↑ **SUBMIT APP**

↓ **GET SDK**

{} **VIEW SAMPLES**

Apps

Reports

Account

Dashboard

Your dashboard is where you can find out how your apps are doing out in the world. We'll also post messages for you about the status of your account.

Questions? Learn more about the Dashboard.

Messages

Account   **Apps**

Figure 14-12. *Initiate the application submission process from the Dashboard*

App Submission Page

On the Submit app page, you will be provided with links to enter your application information, and submit your application's XAP file. These two actions are required. Refer to Figure 14-3, in Recipe 14-1, for a screenshot of this page.

In addition to that, you may include in-app advertisements, limit market availability, set custom pricing per region, and generate tokens for map services, if used within the application. These actions are optional and not required to complete the app submission process.

Click the App info link to navigate to the App info page as shown in Figure 14-13. Within the App info page, enter a name for your application and select a category. As we touched upon in Recipe 14-1, the name entered here is simply the name associated to your application in your Dev Center Dashboard. The application name the customer sees is the Display Name defined in your Application Manifest file, within the Application UI tab.

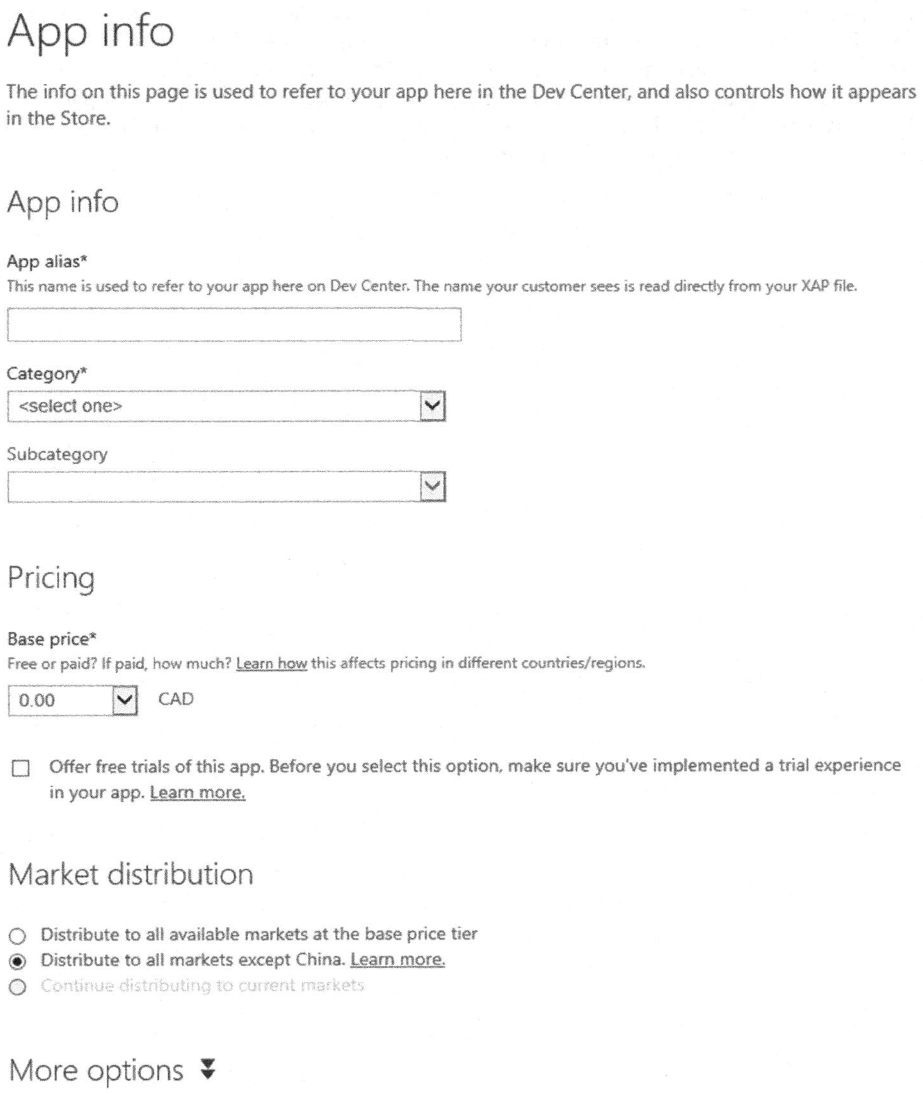

App info

The info on this page is used to refer to your app here in the Dev Center, and also controls how it appears in the Store.

App info

App alias*
This name is used to refer to your app here on Dev Center. The name your customer sees is read directly from your XAP file.

[   ]

Category*
[<select one>   ⌄]

Subcategory
[⌄]

Pricing

Base price*
Free or paid? If paid, how much? Learn how this affects pricing in different countries/regions.

[0.00   ⌄] CAD

☐ Offer free trials of this app. Before you select this option, make sure you've implemented a trial experience in your app. Learn more.

Market distribution

○ Distribute to all available markets at the base price tier
◉ Distribute to all markets except China. Learn more.
○ Continue distributing to current markets

More options ⬇

Figure 14-13. *Step 1 of the app submission process*

The category you select here determines the category grouping that your application will appear within in the Windows Phone Store. If a subcategory is available for the selected category, its dropdown list will become enabled. You may optionally select a subcategory.

At this point, you will want to give careful consideration to pricing. If you choose to provide a free app, you do not need to modify this value. You can leave it at the default value of 0.00. If you choose to charge your users to install your application, you will need to set a price here. If you have incorporated in-app advertisements, do NOT charge users to download your app. That is an unspoken rule of sorts. There's no easier way to turn off users from your app than to include advertisements within a product that they paid for.

When you are charging users to install your app, as we discussed in Recipe 14-2, it is a good idea to offer a trial version. Remember that you will need to checkmark the "Offer free trials" checkbox if you have set up your application to leverage the LicenseInformation.IsTrial check within your application to limit features for trial mode.

If you expand the More options list (Figure 14-14), you will note that there are options to submit your app to the Public Store or only provide it as a Beta release. When submitting an application as a Beta release, you are able to specify which users are able to receive your app for free to test your application.

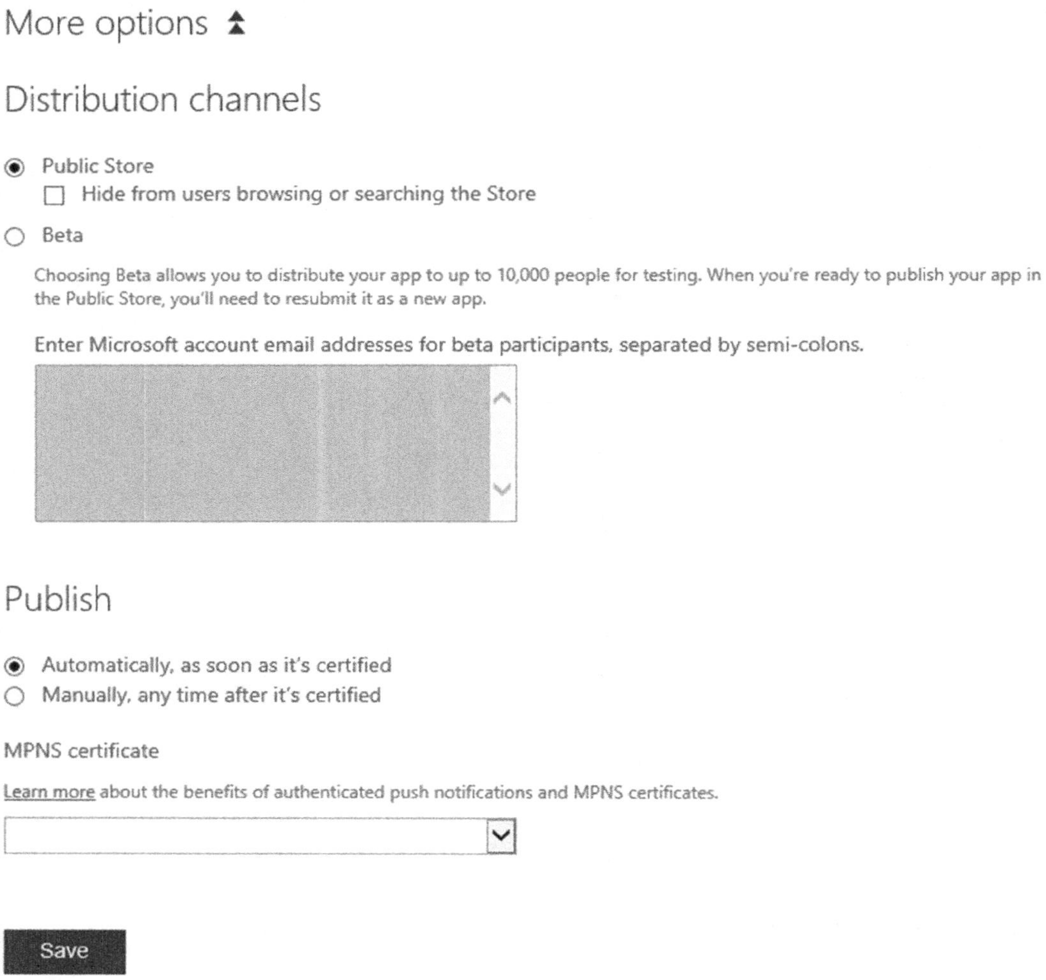

More options ▲

Distribution channels

⦿ Public Store
  ☐ Hide from users browsing or searching the Store

◯ Beta

   Choosing Beta allows you to distribute your app to up to 10,000 people for testing. When you're ready to publish your app in the Public Store, you'll need to resubmit it as a new app.

   Enter Microsoft account email addresses for beta participants, separated by semi-colons.

Publish

⦿ Automatically, as soon as it's certified
◯ Manually, any time after it's certified

MPNS certificate

Learn more about the benefits of authenticated push notifications and MPNS certificates.

Save

Figure 14-14. *App info page - More options section*

You must include at least one Microsoft email address account that is associated to a user's Windows Phone device. In this way, the user will receive an e-mail with a download link from which they can download and install your Beta release onto the device. The maximum limit of Beta testers that you may set up for a single application is 10,000 users.

As well, you may choose to have your app published automatically, once it has passed testing. Note, that it generally takes between 24 and 48 hours for an application to appear in the Windows Phone Store once it has been certified. You will receive an e-mail once testing has completed, with a status to indicate if your app has passed or failed the testing phase. If there is a problem with your application that was uncovered in testing, the cause of the failure will be included in your application status e-mail. If this happens, be sure to review it carefully, review the certification and submission requirements, and address any issues that were listed. Once you have corrected the issues, you may resubmit your application to the Store.

Finally, if your app is configured to receive Push Notifications from an authenticated web service, you will need to upload the web service's TLS cetificate to your Windows Phone Developer Center account. This can be found by clicking the Certificates link, which is available from your Account page. When you are submitting an application, any previously uploaded TLS certificates will appear in the MPNS certificate dropdown list within the App info page. Select the appropriate TLS certificate, if it is required by your application. When you are satisfied with the information entered on the App info page, hit the Save button to return to the main app submission page to continue on to the next step.

Upload Your XAP File

Upon saving the application information, you will be able to upload your XAP file, set up the Store listing, configure relevant keywords, and upload screenshots of the application. Click on the Upload and describe your XAP link. The first thing you must do within the Upload page is to do just that, and upload the Release version of your application's XAP file. Click the Add new link to launch a File Explorer that you will use to browse and select the XAP file to upload (Figure 14-15).

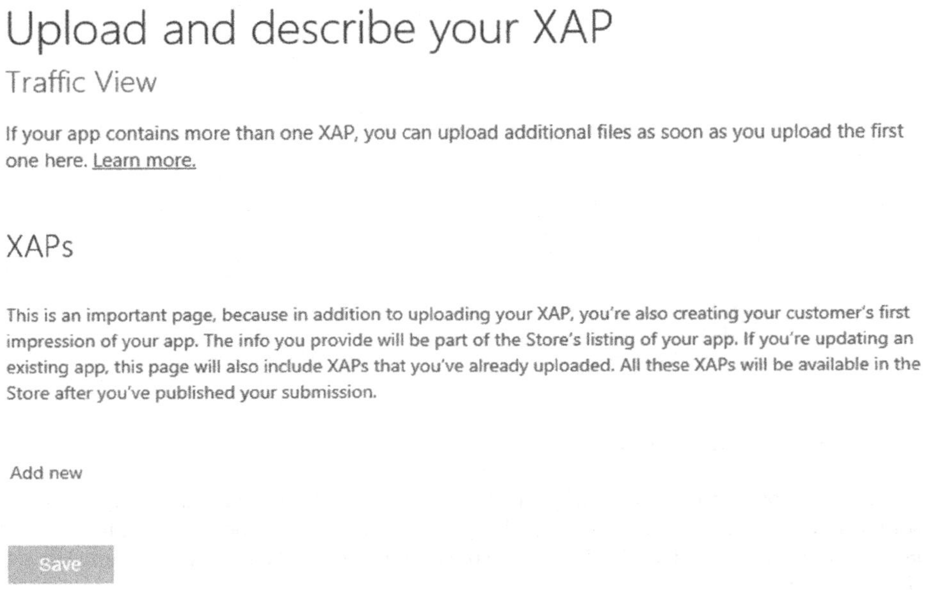

Upload and describe your XAP

Traffic View

If your app contains more than one XAP, you can upload additional files as soon as you upload the first one here. Learn more.

XAPs

This is an important page, because in addition to uploading your XAP, you're also creating your customer's first impression of your app. The info you provide will be part of the Store's listing of your app. If you're updating an existing app, this page will also include XAPs that you've already uploaded. All these XAPs will be available in the Store after you've published your submission.

Add new

Save

Figure 14-15. *Step 2 of the app submission process - Upload and describe your XAP*

Once you have selected the file, click Open in the File Explorer dialog to initiate the upload process. A progress indicator will display as the XAP file is uploaded. Once the upload has completed successfully, the Upload page will refresh and will then display information about the uploaded XAP file, as shown in Figure 14-16.

XAPs

This is an important page, because in addition to uploading your XAP, you're also creating your customer's first impression of your app. The info you provide will be part of the Store's listing of your app. If you're updating an existing app, this page will also include XAPs that you've already uploaded. All these XAPs will be available in the Store after you've published your submission.

XAP name	Version	OS	Resolution	Language		
● TrafficView.xap	1.0.0.0	8.0	WVGA, 720P, WXGA	English	Replace	Delete

Add new

Select a XAP above to view or edit its Store listing and other info.

XAP version number*　　　　　　　　　　　　　　　　　　　　　　　　　　　　　More XAP options ▼

| 1 | . | 0 | . | 0 | . | 0 |

XAP details detected from file ▲

File name	TrafficView.xap
File size	189 KB
Supported OS	8.0
Resolution(s)	WVGA
	720P
	WXGA
Language(s)	English
Capabilities	ID_CAP_MEDIALIB_AUDIO
	ID_CAP_MEDIALIB_PLAYBACK
	ID_CAP_NETWORKING
	ID_CAP_SENSORS
	ID_CAP_WEBBROWSERCOMPONENT
	ID_RESOLUTION_HD720P
	ID_RESOLUTION_WVGA
	ID_RESOLUTION_WXGA

Figure 14-16. *Additional info displayed once XAP is uploaded*

As you can see, the capabilities that you configured within your Application Manifest now appear in this page, along with the supported resolutions, XAP file size, and version number. This information will be displayed in your application's product page listing in the Store, once it is published. The only thing that you can manually change in this section is the application version number.

Once you have confirmed the information about your XAP file is accurate, scroll down to the XAP's Store listing info section, as depicted in Figure 14-17. This is the where you will provide a description about your application, which will appear in the application's product page when published to the Windows Phone Store. You may also specify keywords which makes it easier for users to find your app when they are searching the Windows Phone Store using any of the keywords that you provide here. As well, you should include a URL that points to a legal disclaimer and privacy policy that you have hosted on your own website, along with a support e-mail address for your application. Notice that you can enter this information in multiple languages. The languages provided here correspond to the supported languages that you selected in the Packaging tab within your Application Manifest.

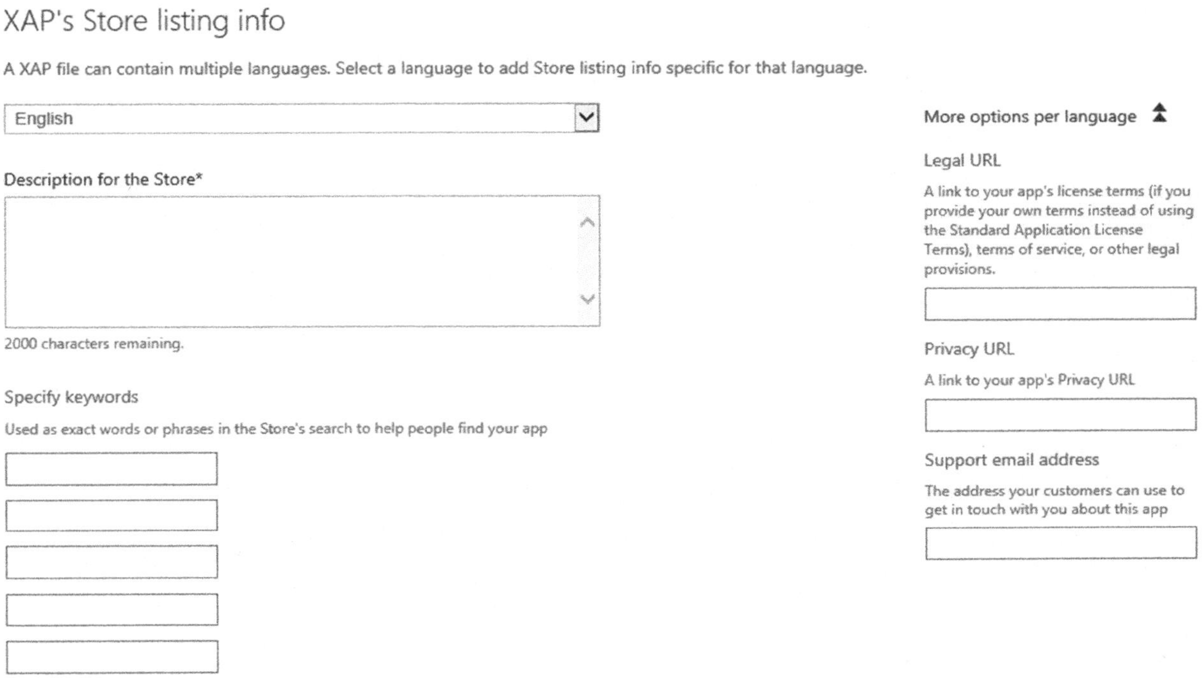

XAP's Store listing info

A XAP file can contain multiple languages. Select a language to add Store listing info specific for that language.

English ▾

Description for the Store*

2000 characters remaining.

Specify keywords

Used as exact words or phrases in the Store's search to help people find your app

More options per language ▲

Legal URL

A link to your app's license terms (if you provide your own terms instead of using the Standard Application License Terms), terms of service, or other legal provisions.

Privacy URL

A link to your app's Privacy URL

Support email address

The address your customers can use to get in touch with you about this app

Figure 14-17. Enter a description, keywords, legal URL, privacy URL, and support e-mail address for each language your application will support

Upload Images

The next thing that you will discover, as you scroll down the page further, is that this is the page where you will upload your application's app tile icon, background image, and at least one screenshot for each supported resolution (Figure 14-18). You may click the Upload All link to browse and select all of the images at once. Alternatively, you may upload each image separately by clicking on each image placeholder.

Upload images*

Use this link to upload all the images in one step, or upload them separately by clicking on each image placeholder below.

Upload all

* App tile icon 300 x 300 px

Background image 1000 x 800 px

☑ Automatically create lower resolution screenshots from WXGA

WXGA | 720p | WVGA

* We'll use these screenshots to showcase your app.
  For WXGA they must be 768 x 1280 px or 1280 x 768 px. Learn more.

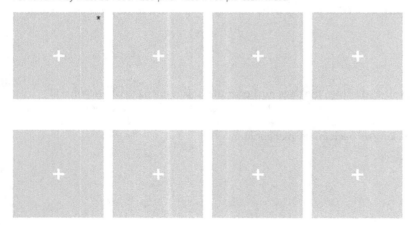

Figure 14-18. *Upload an app tile icon, background image, and screenshots for each resolution your application will support*

Once you are satisfied with the information provided in the Upload page, hit Save to commit these changes, and return to the main application submission page. At this point, you have fulfilled the basic submission requirements and you can proceed to submit your app to the Windows Phone Store.

However, there are 3 optional links that allow you to further configure your application: Add in-app advertising, Market selection and custom pricing, and Map services.

In-app advertising should have been configured and incorporated into your application prior to uploading the XAP file. We discussed this topic in Recipe 14-2.

Market Selection and Pricing

If you wish to make your application available only to specific markets and/or if you wish to define custom pricing per region, drill down into the Market selection and custom pricing link. This will load the Define market pricing page as shown in Figure 14-19. In this page, you can uncheck any markets that you do not want to your application being distributed within. For example, if you are developing an application that is specific to a region, such as a Transit application for a single city, then make that application available only in the country in which that transit application applies to. It doesn't make sense to make the application availabe for download by users across the world. Unfortunately, this page does not have an "Uncheck all" option, and the list of markets is quite extensive. So in the case where the application is very limited to a smaller market, this could be a painstaking task to go through.

Define market pricing

Traffic View

Change where your app is available and how much it will cost in those individual markets.

- ○ Distribute to all available markets at the base price tier
- ○ Distribute to all markets except China. Learn more.
- ● Continue distributing to current markets

ⓘ These countries\regions have more restrictions for app or in-app product content. Learn more.

☑ Afghanistan ⓘ	0.00	USD	☑ Lithuania	0.00	LTL
☑ Albania ⓘ	0.00	USD	☑ Luxembourg	0.00	EUR
☑ Algeria ⓘ	0.00	DZD	☑ Macao SAR	0.00	USD
☑ Andorra	0.00	EUR	☑ Macedonia FYRO	0.00	USD
☑ Angola	0.00	USD	☑ Madagascar	0.00	USD
☑ Antigua and Barbuda	0.00	USD	☑ Malawi	0.00	USD
☑ Argentina	0.00	ARS	☑ Malaysia ⓘ	0.00	MYR
☑ Armenia	0.00	USD	☑ Maldives ⓘ	0.00	USD
☑ Australia	0.00	AUD	☑ Mali ⓘ	0.00	USD
☑ Austria	0.00	EUR	☑ Malta	0.00	EUR

***Figure 14-19.** Optionally, you can limit the markets that your app is available within or set custom pricing for each market*

Also, make sure to familiarize yourself with the restrictions that some countries may have. If your application should not be distributed to those markets due to the type of content it includes, make sure to exercise due diligence and remove those markets from your app distribution list. Those countries that contain a small icon to the right of the name include special restrictions. Review the restrictions and other content policies on MSDN at the following URL: http://msdn.microsoft.com/library/windowsphone/develop/hh184842(v=vs.105).aspx. As well, you can define custom pricing for each region within this page, if you so desire.

Map Services

Finally, if your application uses Map services, you will need to generate a map service Application ID and token, as shown in Figure 14-20. Similar to in-app advertisements, this should have been done prior to uploading the application's XAP file, as this information must be incorporated within the application code. Refer to the recipes provided within Chapter 8 for more information on location and map services.

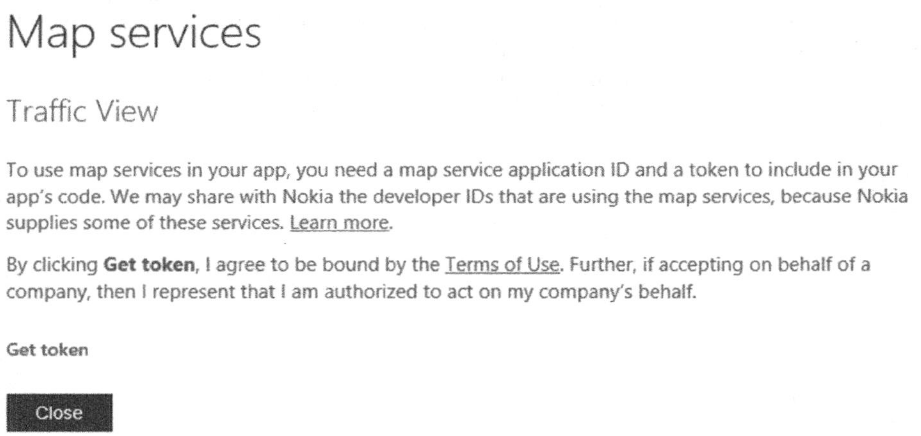

Map services

Traffic View

To use map services in your app, you need a map service application ID and a token to include in your app's code. We may share with Nokia the developer IDs that are using the map services, because Nokia supplies some of these services. Learn more.

By clicking **Get token**, I agree to be bound by the Terms of Use. Further, if accepting on behalf of a company, then I represent that I am authorized to act on my company's behalf.

Get token

Close

Figure 14-20. *Generate a map service application ID and token to include in your application if it leverages map services*

Completing the Submission Process

At this point, you may choose to proceed with the application submission process or leave your submission information as an in-progress submission. In-progress submissions will appear in your Dashboard with a state of Not submitted, as depicted in Figure 14-21.

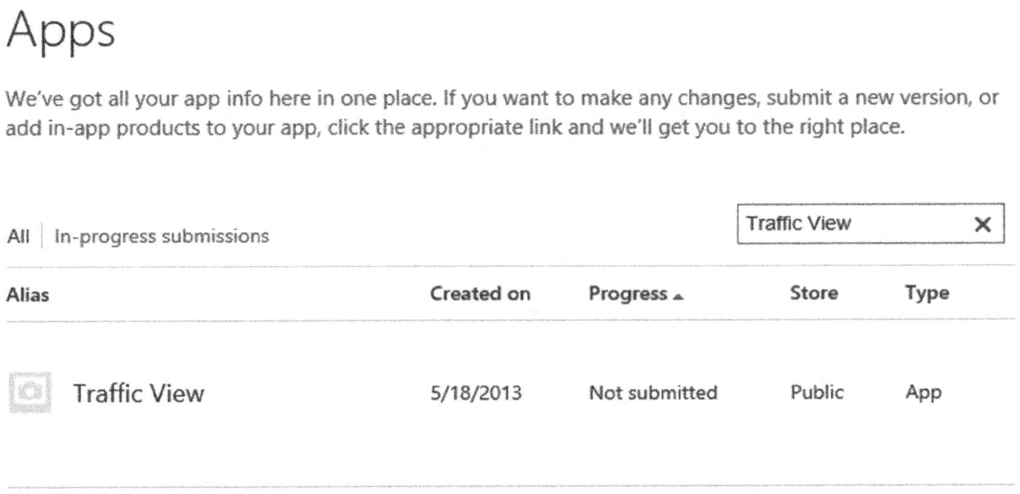

Apps

We've got all your app info here in one place. If you want to make any changes, submit a new version, or add in-app products to your app, click the appropriate link and we'll get you to the right place.

All | In-progress submissions

| | Traffic View | ✕ |

Alias	Created on	Progress ▲	Store	Type
▢ Traffic View	5/18/2013	Not submitted	Public	App

Figure 14-21. *View in-progress submissions from your Dashboard*

From your Dashboard, you can click on the Alias to go to the application information page in your Dashboard. Within this page, you can view more details about your application. When your application is submitted, you can view stats about daily and overall downloads, crash rates, user reviews, current pricing, application details, and in-app products, if relevant.

If your application submission has been initiated, but not completed, you will see a Current submission box at the top of the details page as shown in Figure 14-22.

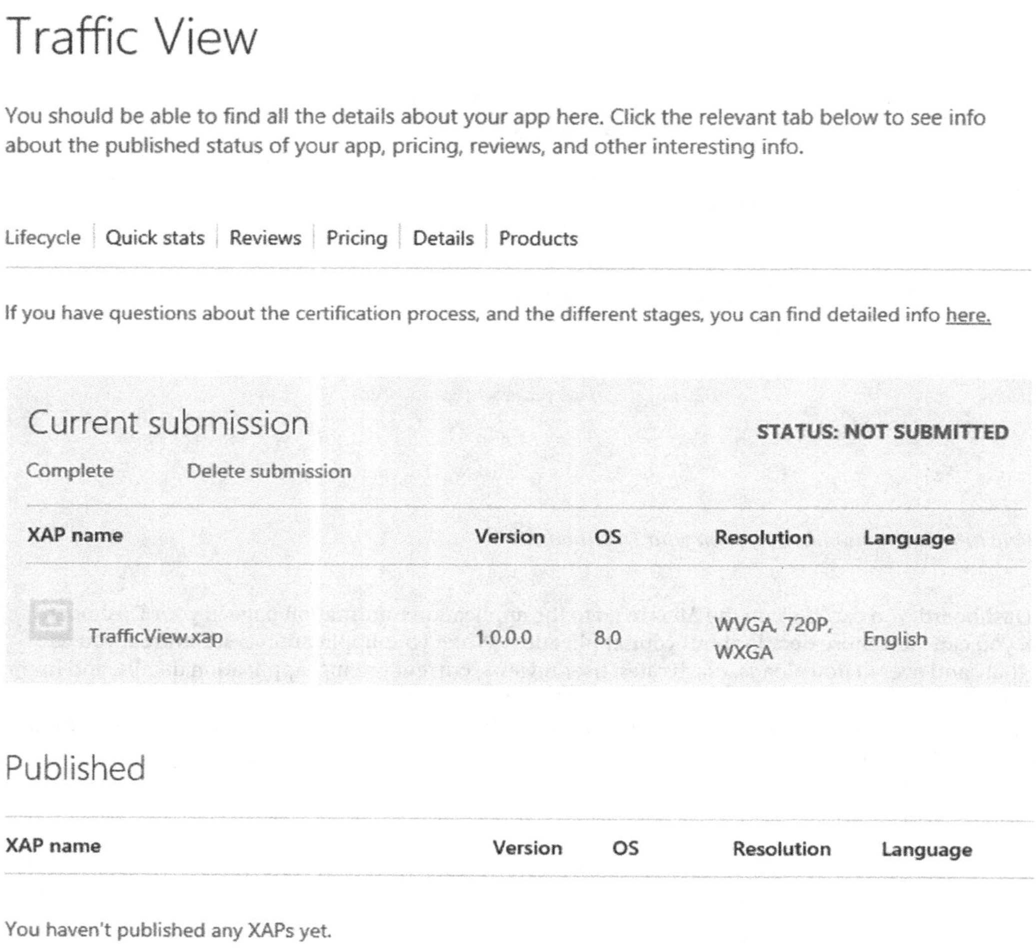

Traffic View

You should be able to find all the details about your app here. Click the relevant tab below to see info about the published status of your app, pricing, reviews, and other interesting info.

Lifecycle | Quick stats | Reviews | Pricing | Details | Products

If you have questions about the certification process, and the different stages, you can find detailed info here.

Current submission

STATUS: NOT SUBMITTED

Complete   Delete submission

XAP name	Version	OS	Resolution	Language
TrafficView.xap	1.0.0.0	8.0	WVGA, 720P, WXGA	English

Published

XAP name	Version	OS	Resolution	Language

You haven't published any XAPs yet.

Figure 14-22. *Application details page displaying an in-progress submission*

Click on the Complete Submission link in this page to load the Submit app page. At this point, you can modify any information you included in the app submission, or you can choose to submit your application. When you are satisfied with the application submission information, click the Review and Submit button on the Submit app page.

Congratulations! You have successfully published a Windows Phone 8 application! The testing and certification stage could take a week or two before you receive any indication on the state of your application. While your application is going through this process, take the time to relax and enjoy your accomplishments thus far. Or, you can start designing another Windows Phone app!

Index